THE INVESTIGATIVE BRIGADE

A BOOK IN THE SERIES LATIN AMERICA IN TRANSLATION /
EN TRADUCCIÓN / EM TRADUÇÃO

This book was sponsored by the Consortium in Latin American
and Caribbean Studies at the University of North Carolina
at Chapel Hill and Duke University.

THE
INVESTIGATIVE
BRIGADE

Hunting Human Rights Criminals
in Post-Pinochet Chile

Pascale Bonnefoy Miralles

TRANSLATED BY RUSS DAVIDSON

THE UNIVERSITY OF NORTH CAROLINA PRESS

CHAPEL HILL

Translation of the books in the series Latin America in Translation / en Traducción / em Tradução, a collaboration between the Consortium in Latin American and Caribbean Studies at the University of North Carolina at Chapel Hill and Duke University and the university presses of the University of North Carolina and Duke, is supported by a grant from the Andrew W. Mellon Foundation.

The University of North Carolina Press has been a member of the Green Press Initiative since 2003.

Originally published in Spanish with the title *Cazar al cazador: Detectives tras criminales de lesa humanidad*, © 2018 Pascale Bonnefoy Miralles and Penguin Random House Grupo Editorial, S.A., Santiago, Chile.

Cover illustration: Protest against torture and violation of human rights during Pinochet dictatorship, Santiago, Chile, 1985. Courtesy Julio Etchart / Alamy Stock Photo.

Complete Library of Congress Cataloging-in-Publication Data is available at https://lccn.loc.gov/2022015122.

ISBN 978-1-4696-7015-7 (cloth: alk. paper)
ISBN 978-1-4696-7016-4 (pbk.: alk. paper)
ISBN 978-1-4696-7017-1 (ebook)

CONTENTS

TRANSLATOR'S NOTE

THIS TRANSLATION OF Pascale Bonnefoy's book, shortened by her for its publication in English, arrives not long before a key event: the fiftieth anniversary of the September 11, 1973, military coup that toppled Chile's democratically elected government led by President Salvador Allende. Today, 9/11 is instant shorthand for the terrorist attacks carried out by al-Qaeda in the United States. But Chile had its own September 11. In the years since then, there has been no shortage of articles, essays, books, anthologies, blog posts, and more documenting and analyzing the causes of the coup, the seventeen years of dictatorship that followed, and their staggering human cost. The studies number in the hundreds if not the thousands. Yet for all the analysis and reportage, nothing quite like Bonnefoy's book has appeared until now. Her book reveals, for the first time, the work of a small, largely anonymous team of detectives who gathered the evidence needed to bring human rights violators to justice in post-Pinochet Chile. Their story is one of unswerving dedication and courage under fire.

A few words about the translation's style and language: Certain titles and ranks used in Chile's plainclothes police force have no exact equivalents in English. In such cases, I have either tried to find what corresponds most closely—deputy superintendent for *subcomisario*, for example—or, if it seems clearer, simply used the Chilean title in direct translation, as in "director general." The official name of the plainclothes police in Chile was (and remains) the Investigations Police, as distinct from the Carabineros—the militarized police responsible for public security and order. The names "plainclothes police" and "Investigations Police" are used interchangeably, though "Investigations Police" predominates in the text. And while the current acronym for the institution is the PDI (Policía de Investigaciones), I have used "PICH" (Policía de Investigaciones de Chile) because that is the abbreviation that was used during the period covered by the book.

Finally, my thanks to Pascale Bonnefoy, who cheerfully reviewed chapters as I finished them, clarifying for me the definitions and meanings of Chilean legal concepts and terminology. Her assistance at every step along the way was an invaluable aid.

PREFACE

WHEN DEMOCRACY WAS RESTORED in Chile in 1990 after the seventeen-year dictatorship of Augusto Pinochet, the investigation of human rights crimes committed during the military rule was entrusted to a unit specially created for this purpose within the Policía de Investigaciones de Chile, or Investigations Police (PICH). What has always surprised me about this unit is the pronounced youth of its detectives. These are men and women in their twenties and thirties, many born only shortly before the country began its transition back to democracy, with others at that point still learning to read. For them, investigating the tortures, executions, kidnappings, and disappearances committed during the darkest period Chile has known in its contemporary history is akin to unraveling "cold cases." For the relatives of victims and their descendants, the wounds from the past have still not healed, but for these detectives, investigating these crimes has meant digging up the past with threadbare, unreliable documentation and without fresh testimony or the ability to access the original scenes of the crimes. In many instances, both perpetrators and witnesses have already passed away.

I found it intriguing that these police officers hadn't lived through the time of the dictatorship, that they may have had victims or assassins within their own families or had perhaps only read something about those years in a book. Or maybe everything related to the military dictatorship was foreign to their lives. I wondered what they thought or felt when interviewing torturers and those who murdered human beings or made them disappear, those who continue to deny irrefutable historical facts, and those who—so many decades later—continue to look for their loved ones and to seek at least partial justice.

I wanted to interview the detectives who today comprise part of the Investigative Brigade for Crimes against Human Rights within the PICH—also known as the plainclothes police, to distinguish the force from Chile's Carabineros, the militarized police charged with preserving civic order and security. I pictured myself accompanying these young men and women on the ground to excavation sites with forensic experts in search of the remains of persons who were detained or abducted and never subsequently accounted for. I wanted to understand how they interacted with the past; how they related to the accused and to the relatives of victims; and how the wheels of justice involving police, judges, forensic experts, lawyers, and witnesses functioned.

I wanted to start at the beginning, and that is where I stayed, in the turbulent, postdictatorial 1990s transition, amid the detectives who—against all odds—made steady progress toward establishing the truth.

I began to understand the process the PICH went through after military rule and got to know the detectives who, from one day to the next, had to investigate a criminal past of which their institution formed a part. The PICH was seriously compromised in the political repression of Pinochet's dictatorship. This involvement meant that it had to investigate itself at a time when former security agents were still in its ranks and torture was still practiced in some of its precincts.

In that span of years, the PICH's Homicide Brigade designated three teams to investigate various high-profile assassinations. Due to the public commotion these cases produced, they were assigned to special judges from both an appeals court and the Supreme Court of Chile.

Less well known, however, is that in April 1991, one year after the restoration of democratic government, the new director of the PICH created a top-secret unit within Department V of Internal Affairs. The unit's mission was to investigate the remaining cases involving human rights violations. These cases, presided over by lower-court judges, had been opened or reopened thanks to new disclosures and information given to the courts by the Rettig Commission, an ad hoc group created in 1990 by President Patricio Aylwin (1990–94) to gather testimony and evidence and establish the truth about the executions and disappearances that occurred under the military dictatorship.

Initially, the unit had only two members. It slowly expanded, bringing on young male detectives, almost all of modest origins and from outside the country's capital city, Santiago. The great majority had enrolled in the PICH's police academy during the dictatorship, when the institution was directed by an army general and formed part of the state's machinery of repression.

This special unit was the seed for what today is known as the Investigative Brigade for Crimes against Human Rights of the Investigations Police, which now uses the acronym PDI.

The context at the time was fascinating. The detectives confronted numerous challenges: a towering wall of silence and active resistance from the military, a lack of trust on the part of survivors and victims' relatives, threats and surveillance from army intelligence, the total absence of cooperation by the armed forces and the Carabineros, a timorous government that nonetheless increased the PICH's resources, and a judicial system that—with few exceptions—did not rise to the occasion.

Yet despite major obstacles and meager resources, the detectives managed during the years of democratic transition to amass and piece together a huge body of information and evidence about the dictatorship's organs of repression and to identify their agents and establish specific accountabilities. What the PICH did not and could not accomplish in those years was to bring about effective justice, certainly not in the way that the magnitude of the crimes demanded.

While I consulted a variety of documentary sources in researching this book, the principal one was the archive of the PDI's own human rights brigade, opened up to a journalist for the first time. I conducted interviews with people from different organizations, institutions, and walks of life—but above all with the detectives who worked the cases. The great majority are now retired. I came to know and admire many of them along the way.

For various reasons, I was unable to meet and interview some of the detectives who served in the unit. They had either passed away, or their health did not permit it, or they simply could not be located. Two detectives declined to be interviewed. The majority of these police officers are unknown to the public. Their names and faces rarely appeared in the press, and for obvious reasons they maintained a low profile. They undertook no crusade, they insist, but instead merely fulfilled their institutional mission as members of an auxiliary branch of the justice system.

Nonetheless, virtually all of them professed that this experience changed their lives and that they had contributed to changing the country's course. They haven't sought public recognition but regret not having received it.

This book does not aspire to turn them into heroes, though clearly there was a dose of heroism and certainly of sacrifice and resolute commitment in their actions. Rather, my intention is to portray a period in Chile's recent past illuminated by its complexity and instability, when a model of transitional justice was continually tested and the shadow of military power still loomed. Moreover, I have constructed and written this history from the perspective of a police force that was undergoing its own internal transformations.

I am deeply beholden to all those detectives who offered me a window into their personal and professional lives so that I might tell this story, a story that is at once individual, institutional, and national in its scope.

I am especially grateful to the veteran detective Luis Henríquez, without whose help this book would in all likelihood not have been possible; to Nelson Mery, former director of the PICH, who welcomed me into his house to share long conversations; to another great detective, Nelson Jofré, for his constant assistance; to the successive national chiefs of the PDI's human rights brigade, Tomás Vivanco and Sergio Claramunt, who allowed me to consult the brigade's archive; and to Superintendent Braulio Abarca, who over many weeks willingly endured my presence in the brigade's offices while I combed through files and documents.

I am also indebted to my former journalism student Arak Herrera for her assistance in gathering press clips; to journalist María Olivia Mönckeberg, for her support; and to all my friends and close associates, who put up with me during the many months I bent their ears about the doings and ventures of the police.

I am also grateful to Melanie Jösch, editorial director of Penguin–Random House in Chile, and to the entire editorial team—particularly Aldo Perán, for his dedication and contagious enthusiasm.

Finally, I am grateful to two others: my friend Peter Kornbluh, both for his unstinting support and for the encouragement he gave me to propose a translation of my book; and Elaine Maisner, executive editor at the University of North Carolina Press, for the opportunity to publish in English this untold police story that offers a unique window from which to observe Chile's post-Pinochet political transition.

Santiago, December 2020

THE INVESTIGATIVE BRIGADE

1

LOST IN FRESIA

THE RAIN POURED DOWN in torrents, and wind whipped against the small Cessna plane suspended in the black of night in flight from Santiago to Puerto Montt. The four passengers on board bounced around like Ping-Pong balls, joking and squirming childishly to calm their nerves. Eduardo Giorgi, their pilot from the Investigations Police of Chile (PICH), scolded, "Quit clowning around!"[1]

The trip was short but filled with tension. Former detective Héctor Silva recalls that the aircraft, buffeted by gusts of wind on its approach, nearly plunged to the ground as it came in for a landing at Puerto Montt's Tepual airport.

"Mamo is haunting us," Silva thought. "He doesn't want us to get there."

It wasn't the stormy southern weather that was putting the detectives' nerves so on edge. They had a great deal at stake: their unpredictable mission was to find and detain retired general Manuel "Mamo" Contreras Sepúlveda, the former chief of the Directorate of National Intelligence (DINA), the military dictatorship's first arm of repression.

It was September 17, 1991, and the detectives—each trained in the investigation of homicides—were about to embark upon a daring venture.

Gen. Augusto Pinochet's words, pronounced at the end of 1989, months before he relinquished the presidency—but not power—still resonated.

"Lay a hand on one of my men, and the rule of law is over!" he warned any and all future civilian government leaders. Manuel Contreras, the object of the detectives' search, had been Pinochet's right-hand man, the one who gave a report to the general, and to the general only, every morning. Contreras was the one who with great efficiency directed the dirty work of the dictatorship's first years. And Contreras, no less than Pinochet, still retained an aura of untouchability.

Thinking back on the flight, now retired detective Nelson Jofré recalls, "I don't believe, at that moment, that we had sized up what it all meant. We knew the matter was delicate, and we went from being calm one moment to nervous the next. Between this and that joke, we just went with the flow. It was a kind of therapy."

They were traveling to Chile's southern region to arrest and detain the country's once second-most-powerful man, and no one knew how their journey would end. They hadn't taken anything special with them, only their badges and standard-issue handguns.

As for a plan, they didn't have one.

Against the Clock

Weeks earlier, the Supreme Court of Chile judge Adolfo Bañados had been designated to investigate the 1976 assassination of former Chilean foreign minister Orlando Letelier. The assassination, carried out on the DINA's orders, had occurred in Washington, D.C. In turn, Bañados asked the PICH's Metropolitan Homicide Brigade for two detectives to work on the case with him. Acting on the request, the head of the brigade, deputy prefect Osvaldo Carmona, appointed the deputy superintendent Rafael Castillo, and Castillo brought with him inspector Nelson Jofré.

The two men made a good pair. They first worked together in 1989, when Jofré joined the brigade. By then, Castillo had already spent almost a decade working homicides. From the outset they matched up well and soon formed a close friendship. Their investigations focused on common crimes until March 1991, when they were called upon to handle a politically motivated case: the killing of army major and military doctor Carlos Pérez and his wife, carried out by members of the Manuel Rodríguez Patriotic Front, a political-military faction created by the Communist Party in 1983 but which broke off from the party and became independent in 1987. At the onset of civilian rule (1990), the Front began a campaign to deliver justice by its own hand against human rights violators. Pérez had served as a physician-torturer for the National Center for Information (CNI), the successor agency to the DINA.[2] Aided by a lucky break, Castillo and Jofré quickly solved the case. They were hailed by the interior minister and became star detectives of the brigade. Carmona did not have the slightest doubt in naming them to work with Bañados.

The two PICH officers met every day with Judge Bañados to receive instructions from him and review intelligence and progress on the Letelier case. Carried out on the streets of the U.S. capital's diplomatic enclave, Letelier's assassination was the first act of international terrorism committed on U.S. soil, and it shook the foundations of what until then were amicable relations between the U.S. government and the Chilean military regime.

Before receiving this assignment, the thirty-three-year-old Jofré did not know who Orlando Letelier was, much less any of the details surrounding his death. During those first weeks, as he studied the file and listened to the testimonies of relatives and witnesses, Jofré began reading books about human rights and the country's recent history to understand the terrain that he was navigating. He came to know Letelier, both the man and his life, in the process learning names and places and bit by bit discovering the covert, undisclosed history of his country. It was a swift induction into the iron hand of the DINA and the grief of its victims.

Judge Bañados was working against the clock. The fifteen-year period prescribed by the law for bringing charges expired on September 21—the date on which the car bomb exploded that blew apart Letelier's body in the middle of Sheridan Circle and also killed Ronnie Moffitt, a U.S. colleague who was in the passenger seat.[3] There was clear evidence to charge both General Contreras and the DINA's second-in-command, Brig. Gen. Pedro Espinoza Bravo, with having masterminded the crime, but doing so rested on assuring their appearance in court. The imperative now was to bring them before the judge, who would take their statements and indict them. A judicial notice stipulating that they not leave their current abodes had been issued weeks before.

As a judge, Bañados was extremely discreet, well known for his thoroughness. After taking charge of the investigation, he saw it through to the very end. Since assuming responsibility for the Letelier case in August 1991, Bañados had interrogated some 100 civil and military figures tied to the DINA, and as the target of death threats he lived with a police guard on permanent duty in his home. A gaggle of journalists stood sentry outside his office, alert to any new development.

On that morning of September 17, with few preliminaries, the judge informed the detectives that he was handing over to them two arrest warrants that needed to be executed immediately: one for Contreras, the other for Espinoza. He said little else. Bañados was a man of few words.

The detectives looked on speechless at these documents ordering the arrest and detainment of the DINA's onetime top figures. After leaving the judge's office, they telephoned their superior, PICH director Gen. Horacio Toro. Informed that Toro was not at police headquarters but in the interior minister's office, they headed there right away.

Reaching the presidential palace, where the minister had his office, Castillo and Jofré asked to speak to General Toro.

"Director, we need to talk with you privately about a matter of utmost urgency," Castillo told him.

General Toro stepped forward.

"Sir, Judge Bañados has handed us a detention order for Manuel Contreras and Pedro Espinoza."

Toro maintained his composure. "Go to my office and wait for me there," he said.

Castillo and Jofré hurriedly walked the few blocks that separated La Moneda Palace and PICH headquarters in the city center.

Meanwhile, Toro relayed the information to the interior minister, Enrique Krauss, and Krauss passed it along to Chile's president, Patricio Aylwin.

"Do you know where Contreras and Espinoza are?" Toro asked the detectives after meeting them back at the PICH building.

"We know that Contreras lists his residence as being a rural estate in Fresia called El Viejo Roble and that Espinoza has a place in Osorno," Castillo replied.

Both army officers, like other former DINA agents, had purchased land in the South of Chile. Contreras had acquired his estate some years after retiring in September 1978, as a direct result of the Letelier case, and he managed the operations of his timber business, Imeteg, from there.

The network of agents living in the surrounding area and a local population that tended to be conservative afforded Contreras and Espinoza some measure of security. And happily enough for them, in January 1988 one of their own had assumed command of the general staff of the Fourth Army Division in Valdivia. Brig. Gen. Miguel Krassnoff, who had been a DINA leader, was now in charge of seven military regiments stretching from the city of Angol to Puerto Montt in the country's southern region.

Toro called Mario Mengozzi, the deputy operations director, into his office, and together they analyzed the steps that needed to be taken. Mengozzi was directed to coordinate, together with the head of the police's aerial brigade, the use of a PICH airplane for a flight to Puerto Montt.

"The two of you are going south," Toro declared.

Mengozzi immediately called the PICH police chief in Puerto Montt.

"A team from the Homicide Brigade," he explained, "is traveling to the city tonight. Kindly arrange for a good vehicle to be put at their disposal, since they will have to visit several places in the region." Mengozzi asked that the team be picked up at the airport, but he did not venture any clue as to the nature of the mission.

The chief of Homicide, Carmona, decided to add two other officers to the mission. Castillo thought of a detective from the Second Subprecinct, Héctor Silva. Castillo regarded him highly and knew him to be a good detective. Moreover, Silva had been good friends with Jofré since Investigations School, where they had gotten to know each other. Silva possessed other traits that could prove useful for this undertaking: he was restrained, had a pleasant manner, and—what is more—had served in the CNI during the last four years of the military dictatorship. Such experience could perhaps be useful to them. Castillo recommended him to Carmona.

"Sir, could you tell me what the mission is about?" Silva asked the head of the brigade when contacted.

"It's something very specific," Carmona replied and proceeded to explain the mission to him.

"I'm not really eager to go, Sir," Silva ventured. "It's that General Contreras has a son who is a bit off his rocker, and the likeliest thing is that he plans to do something."

"You have to go," Carmona told him.

Silva had no way out.

"I was worried, but at the same time, if they were calling on me for something as important as this, I had an equally good feeling about it. I thanked Castillo for the confidence they had in me," Silva notes.

The other person chosen to detain Contreras and Espinoza was a detective from the Homicide Brigade's Fourth Subprecinct, Bernabé Cortez.

They were given a couple of hours to go home, pack a bit of clothing, and say their good-byes. To their families they confided only that they were leaving the Santiago area and did not know when they would return. Everything happened in a blur. There was no chance to question the order or the situation itself, but a cloud of uncertainty hung in the air.

The four detectives met up at the Cerrillos Airport, in the southwestern part of the capital, where they were joined by the two aviation police pilots. Dusk was enveloping Santiago and the sky was gray. Before they boarded, Nelson Jofré asked someone to take his camera and snap a photograph of the group. He still has the photo of the six of them, smiling in front of the Cessna aircraft. They alone know its underlying story.

They made the trip that same night, and as they passed over Concepción, the storm set in.

"Friends of Manolo's"

When they arrived at Puerto Montt's main police station, they explained the reason for the trip to the head of the unit.

"It all but gave him colitis. I'll never forget that," says Jofré, laughing. "The station chief became really alarmed and was very upset, but even more agitated was the driver whom he assigned to us when he found out where we were going. Manuel Contreras and Pedro Espinoza were well known in the area, and everyone knew what lurked behind them."

The detectives asked for a driver who was familiar with the region and its back roads, and close to midnight, they set off along a dirt road in a van toward Fresia, situated some sixty-seven kilometers northeast of Puerto Montt. For the moment, the objective was to reconnoiter Contreras's property and somehow manage to find out if Contreras was there.

The driver already knew the location of the El Viejo Roble estate and right away warned the four detectives: "Coming into Fresia we're going to go by a Carabineros police post, and Manuel Contreras is going to instantly know that someone is heading to his place, because the Carabineros are in radio contact with his guards. We all know when Contreras is around because his security detail is activated."

Detective Silva recalls that there were sharpshooters in the area. "Contreras was well protected. The team debated how to deal with the situation without precipitating a confrontation," he says.

Around one in the morning the van pulled up to El Viejo Roble and came to a stop at the gate. There was a security hut and a man on guard duty. He was a soldier sporting a Spanish-style poncho, and he carried a rifle: a military man, then, in active service protecting the private property of a retired army officer.

"This is the place," the driver said nervously.

"Stay here. I'm getting out by myself," ordered Castillo, the group's leader.

Not much was visible in the darkness. The detective spoke to the guard self-assuredly, concocting a story for him.

"Listen, we're friends of Manolo's," Castillo told him, affecting the speech of country folk. "We're on our way somewhere else now, but we want to come by to see him tomorrow. Will he be here?"

"Yes, yes he's here."

That was all they needed to know.

"Rafael was very smart. He always wanted to be an actor and was very good at disguising things, like those old-time cops. When he wanted to discover something, he launched into a long story; he was adept at extracting information. Rafael was a man of the streets, someone who could draw you in, and good at soccer. That was his calling card," Jofré says.

Castillo backed away from the guard and returned to the van. They continued for a long way along the same interior road but got lost. They couldn't turn around and go back because that would have meant passing in front of Contreras's property again. They ended up going all over the place traversing country roads until finally coming across Puerto Montt at three in the morning. Still, the drive back found them in a calmer frame of mind.

As soon as they reached the main police station, they called Toro to fill him in on what they had found, namely that they had driven by the estate, acquainted themselves with it, and verified that the subject would be there, on the grounds.

"Very good," replied Toro. "Wait for instructions."

Toro contacted Castillo a short time later. "First thing tomorrow go to Osorno to check on whether Pedro Espinoza is there," he ordered.

That night they slept in the station.

Espinoza's Rural Estate

The next day broke with a gray sky but absent any rain. Osorno's PICH headquarters was a modest structure, and when the Santiago detectives arrived the guard was still sleeping. Their driver reluctantly accompanied them.

"He was scared to death. Everyone knew Espinoza's estate, and the driver knew who Espinoza was and easily located his place. When we explained to him why we were going there he let us know that he didn't want to go," said Jofré.

Espinoza's rural estate was east of Osorno. The entry gate was a very simple affair and easy to vault over. Climbing a hillside, one caught sight of a small house, probably the dwelling of a tenant farmer. Apart from that, there was nothing to be seen, just countryside. The detectives were unsure of what to do. They were authorized to gain entrance and to break in should it be necessary. They decided to enter farther into the estate. The driver stayed in the van, choosing not to get out even to stretch his legs.

The locals had told them that Espinoza owned some dogs that were as big as lions, so the detectives grabbed sticks to defend themselves if the beasts showed up.

"Barnabé and I glanced around at the trees to see which ones to climb into when the creatures made their appearance, but they turned out to be two very small dogs, quite inoffensive," Silva recalls.

The detectives went on, cracking jokes while proceeding farther into Pedro Espinoza's land, the attempts at humor helping to settle their nerves and relieve tension. They took to imagining how the scene looked from the point of view of the house's owner: four men with pistols, intruding without permission on the private property of a high-level army officer and, on top of that, brandishing sticks. They were not even wearing the PICH's distinctive parkas that would identify them.

Suddenly a man appeared, very surly in his manner.

"Who are you?" he yelled.

"We're policemen and we want to speak with Don Pedro," responded Castillo.

"He's not here; he hasn't come around. He's in Reñaca," the man told them, referring to a beach town on Chile's central coast, near Viña del Mar.

The back-and-forth in Santiago, the urgent calls between the ministers of the interior and defense and the head of the army, General Pinochet, had reverberated across the country's southern regions. Pinochet had already communicated with Contreras, and Espinoza learned about it immediately. He had left Osorno right away, taking refuge in the house of some relatives.

The detectives thanked the man and returned to Puerto Montt.

Once again, they got in touch with Toro to update him.

"OK. Now go back to Manuel Contreras's estate and proceed with the arrest and detention. If anything comes up, get word to me," Toro instructed them.

They had to move fast.

Pinochet's Reaction

The reopening of the Letelier case further strained the already tense relations between the government and the army during the initial years of the transition back to democratic rule, and the prosecution of Contreras and Espinoza was going to put Pinochet's reaction to the test. It was a unique case, the only human rights crime that remained exempt from Chile's Amnesty Law, which had been imposed by the military regime and covered the years 1973–78.

After the 1976 car bombing, the FBI conducted its own investigation and quickly confirmed the lead role that the DINA had played in what counted as the first act of international terrorism carried out on U.S. soil. In 1978 a group of Cubans residing in the United States were charged in federal court with the crime, along with Manuel Contreras, Pedro Espinoza, and another DINA agent, Capt. Armando Fernández.[4] Despite this, the Chilean Supreme Court denied the request for their extradition to stand trial in Washington.

On the other hand, the Chilean government did turn over former DINA agent Michael Townley to U.S. custody. Townley was an American citizen who had come to Chile as a teenager in 1957, when his father was appointed manager of the Ford Motor Company's operations in Chile. He would be sacrificed so that he might take full blame for the crime. Confessing his responsibility, Townley agreed to cooperate with the FBI and serve as a witness against the group of anti-Castro Cubans who took part in the double homicide (see below).

After several years of imprisonment, Townley entered the U.S. Federal Witness Protection Program. Supplied with a new identity, he has continued to live in the United States. Townley made his statement before American authorities in Washington on the very same day that the four Homicide Brigade detectives flew to Puerto Montt.

The car-bombing assassination brought about the retirement of General Contreras and the dissolution of the DINA, which was replaced by the CNI. It was against this backdrop, in 1978, that the military regime decreed, as a gift to itself, the Amnesty Law, which granted the regime immunity for the crimes it committed in its first five years in power. Nevertheless, due to pressure from the U.S. government, the law did not apply to the Letelier case.

In line with the FBI's investigation of the car bombing, the United States demanded that Chile conduct its own inquiry. The criminal proceedings that took place in Santiago were related to the use of false passports by the DINA operatives who took part in the affair (known as the "Passports case"). The proceedings, however, were under the control of the military justice system, which after essentially doing nothing, closed the case in 1986.

The American authorities, though, kept up the pressure. In December 1990, following President George H. W. Bush's visit to Chile, the U.S. Department of State publicly announced that President Aylwin had promised to shift the case from the military to the civil justice system and would seek to name a Supreme Court judge to investigate it. At the same time, the State Department announced that the Chilean government had fulfilled the requirements to allow the United States to resume providing the country with military assistance. Military aid to Chile had been cut off in 1976 in the aftermath of the Letelier and Moffitt murders.[5]

Yet as Department of Justice officials warned, if this time around Chile did not indict and try the instigators of the crime, the United States would again find itself obliged to request their extradition.[6] Chile's newly installed leader was thus in a tight spot.

At the urging of President Aylwin, whose request occurred while negotiations began over a free trade agreement between Chile and the United States, on August 1, 1991, the Supreme Court picked Judge Adolfo Bañados to investigate the assassination of Orlando Letelier. This move was possible because the so-called Cumplido Laws (named after justice minister Francisco Cumplido) had been approved in February 1991. The laws provided that, among other things, the Supreme Court would have jurisdiction over cases that could affect Chile's relations in the international sphere, a stipulation clearly designed with the Letelier case in mind.

"I believe that this concern went from the president of the republic on down; that is, everyone—the defense minister, the interior minister, the director himself—we were all waiting to see what was going to happen. From the conversation with Director Toro we understood there was concern about how General Pinochet was going to react. I remember perfectly that this was an issue, as well as how to prepare for whatever situation might arise," Jofré related.

Infantrymen Travel by Land

They found the same soldier as the night before stationed at El Viejo Roble's gate.

"We've come to see Manuel Contreras," Castillo informed him.

The guard looked at the vehicle, which did not have any emblems.

"Who are you?"

"We're from Investigations. Manuel knows me."

It was true. Castillo came to know Contreras personally three years earlier, in 1988. That year it fell to him to investigate the death of retired army major Joaquín Molina,[7] CNI's liaison to the ad hoc military prosecutor's office (*fiscalía militar*) directed by Gen. Fernando Torres. Molina was murdered by Manuel Contreras's son, also named Manuel Contreras, or Mamito, who in those days worked with Torres, the military prosecutor.

The younger Contreras was not one to apply himself with any consistency. He was briefly a cadet in the military academy and later studied law at Gabriela Mistral University but abandoned this effort, too. He and Molina's daughter were a couple. On October 30, 1988, during a family party at Molina's house, Mamito succumbed to a fit of jealousy when his girlfriend was saying good-bye to one of the guests, the son of a high-level CNI official. Mamito began to hit him, at which point Molina tried to intervene, and the former proceeded to fire twelve shots into Molina. In record time, the judge assigned to handle the case declared herself incompetent to hear it and transferred it to the military courts. Meanwhile, Mamito had fled, only to be discovered sometime later to have suddenly contracted a case of hepatitis, resulting in his admission to the army's military hospital in Santiago.

Chile's Supreme Court ruled that Mamito's case should in fact fall under the umbrella of the civil courts and designated Judge Bañados to carry out the investigation; only a few years later he would be performing the same role vis-à-vis Mamito's father. The junior Contreras claimed that he shot Molina in self-defense, and he was found not guilty. It was through this affair that PICH officer Rafael Castillo had made the acquaintance of Manuel Contreras and—for the same reasons—that detective Silva considered his son to be "a bit off his rocker."

From the estate's entrance only the security hut, a road, and the unpopulated hillside could be seen; there was nothing else around but forest.

They waited for the soldier to make radio contact with someone but didn't manage to overhear the conversation. A bit later a Land Cruiser showed up with an officer behind the wheel.

"Climb in," he ordered them.

"We'll go in our own vehicle," Castillo replied.

"No, climb into the jeep."

In the interest of avoiding a conflict, the detectives left the van with their driver and got into the jeep. They were escorted by soldiers armed with Kalashnikov rifles. "We were all but kidnapped while being driven up [the hill]," Silva recalls.

The driver was silent, saying nothing to them as they came up the road toward a modest house. It wasn't fancy; it seemed more like a cabin. To one side was a building with several doors. These opened into the rooms where Contreras's guards—who numbered close to ten—slept.

As they entered the house, they found Contreras seated in an armchair. Behind him was his son, armed with a pistol and dressed like a soldier, despite not being one. Contreras's guards milled about, on the alert.

"How are you, Manuel?" Castillo offered.

"What brings you around here?" Contreras asked sharply.

"Here we are, General. We've come on a mission that's not at all pleasant for you. We have orders to take you back under arrest to Santiago."

Contreras picked up a fax from a desk and showed it to him. "I've just received a fax from my general Pinochet, and *he's* instructing me to return to Santiago. He's offered me a helicopter," Contreras said.

The ex-dictator had maintained his position as commander in chief of the army, and Contreras was confident that Pinochet's dictum—that "no one lay a hand on any of his men"—applied especially to him. As recently as the previous week, in an interview with the newspaper *La Nación*, Contreras had stated that he felt "backed by my institution totally, absolutely, and by my general Pinochet as well." Furthermore, he went on to say, "I'm not at all worried because I've said it a million times: we had nothing to do with this. . . . Look for the assassins in the United States."[8]

"General," Castillo told him, "we have the agency's airplane at our disposal for you to make the trip with us."

"I'm not going to go with you. I'm going the way that I want. I'm an infantryman, and as an infantryman I feel safer [traveling] by land. I've already informed my general Pinochet that I'll set out from here tomorrow at 0800."

A hard-nosed interchange ensued between the two men. Castillo insisted that the arrest order meant that he should go with the detectives, but Contreras stayed on the defensive, defiant. Above all it was necessary to maintain a peaceful atmosphere and not get Contreras agitated. The goal was to get him back to Santiago. When and how to accomplish this was resolved in a tense tug-of-war.

"I can't question the word of a general if you say you are going to go," Castillo began, "but you should go with us."

"I'm going with my people, with my own security," Contreras insisted, unmovable.

"Fine, but one of our detail has to go with you. And I say to you again, our plane is here; it's a long trip," Castillo rejoined.

"There's no problem with one of your men going with us, but I always travel by land."

"Fine. We'll show up here early."

Contreras would make the trip to Santiago by land, in his vehicle and with his guards, and one of the detectives would accompany him. It was an agreement sealed by word.

"It was a tough, coarse conversation. Contreras was demonstrating that General Pinochet was superior to the Supreme Court and had total control over the situation. Our strategy, I believe, was sensible, because to have taken him by force was a ridiculous notion. I don't know what would have happened with the guards. We were four and they, counting all of them, something like fifteen," Jofré reflects.

They left and returned in the jeep to the entry gate, where their driver was waiting for them inside the van. On the journey back to the Puerto Montt police headquarters, Castillo announced his decision: "Jofré, you are going tomorrow with Contreras, and we'll return by plane to Santiago."

"It was the longest trip of my life," recalls the detective.

A Frustrated Marine Biologist

Jofré's life began in the country, in a quiet, peaceful town near the central coast. His father was a noncommissioned telecommunications officer in the Chilean Navy and his mother a housewife who took care of the family's four children.

He passed his time between the countryside, insects, plants, and the Guillermo Rivera school in Viña del Mar. Jofré took the train every day to get to his classes. Each Thursday, he sat down in front of the television to watch a show called *The Undersea World of Jacques Cousteau*, broadcast on the national station. He enjoyed it so much that he decided he wanted to study marine biology.

"That was my true passion," Jofré stresses.

He even wrote a letter to Cousteau, and the famous French scientist and ocean explorer answered him. He still has the letter. Cousteau eventually came to Chile, but by then Jofré had moved to the city of Copiapó, in Chile's northern desert area, where he was studying mining engineering at the state technical university. He had failed to earn high enough grades to pursue marine biology. He began the program at this university in 1977 but soon found that it held little appeal for him. In addition, although the university was free back then, there were still a number of expenses to cover, starting with living on his own in the city. It proved very hard on his parents. Jofré returned home and applied to the University of Chile, where he received a degree in mathematics. It turned out, however, that a career as a mathematician no more suited him than one as a mining engineer. Thus in 1979 he enrolled in the Investigations School, becoming a member of the same class as the man who became his lifelong friend, detective Héctor "Tito" Silva. He had always enjoyed investigating things. "I had a curious nature," relates Jofré, "and an obsession with looking for the truth." Perhaps the impulse ran in the family, because his brother Raúl was already a detective.

"I found out about the crimes of the dictatorship from my classmates in the Investigations School, after I came to Santiago to study. They were witnesses to those events, to the arrests of neighbors, to the bodies turning up in the Mapocho River. Where I lived in Quilpué [part of the Valparaíso Metropolitan Region], I never saw police raids take place or anything of that sort," says Jofré.

Jofré was fifteen when the military coup occurred and has little sense of what actually happened. His father was quartered that day on the ship *Latorre*, under the command of Capt. Carlos Fanta. The elder Jofré continued his naval career for another three years, retiring from the service in 1976. Only years later did he describe to his son what he had witnessed during those tumultuous days in 1973.

In 1981, shortly after finishing his training at the school, Jofré and another twenty-nine recent graduates were assigned to the intelligence-gathering unit of the plainclothes police. Not only had he not studied for this type of work, but he also quickly realized that he wasn't cut out for it. Jofré and his companions received orders to visit foreign embassies to identify the persons who had been given refuge in them. It was straight political espionage work, and Jofré wanted to investigate crimes. He lasted less than a year in this line before requesting a transfer, and in 1982 he was reassigned to the Eleventh Santiago Area Precinct of Las Condes.

Every Monday a bulletin was posted in the precinct asking for volunteers to join the CNI. Potential recruits were lured with the offer of a 19 percent salary increase and other benefits. All the same, they were warned even by their superior officers not to sign up. "They told us, 'Look, guys, don't be fools, after a while the tables will turn, don't get mixed up in it,'" Jofré recalls.

He and his comrades were afraid of the CNI agents. Jofré again: "CNI types were capable of anything. You had to be cautious with them. When we went out at night it scared us to drive near their stations because we used unmarked cars. . . . We shied away from contact with them."

In the 1980s Jofré circulated through several precincts, and while stationed in the central coastal town of Papudo he decided he wanted to continue his studies. Accordingly, he returned to Santiago and enrolled at the University of Chile to study auditing. He worked part-time in an administrative unit so he could attend classes in the afternoon but was forced to drop out of the program because of its cost. By then the regime's education reform had eliminated free public university, so school ate up a good part of his income—and now he was married with a child. Jofré abandoned his studies and focused on being a detective. Perhaps even more to the point, administrative work bored him. By now, being out on the streets had gotten into his blood and he wanted to do something more specialized. Once again, he requested a transfer, and in 1989, following the same path as his friend Tito Silva, Jofré joined the Homicide Brigade.

In this unit he met Rafael Castillo, the man who ordered him to travel alone to the capital with Manuel Contreras.

Eleven Hours on the Road to Santiago

Early the next day the group drove to El Viejo Roble to drop off Jofré. The same military jeep, with its driver and a companion, met them at the estate's entrance.

"Which of you is going with my general?" the detectives were asked.

Silva offered to accompany Jofré on the trip, but General Contreras would not allow it. Nelson Jofré got out of the van, bid his companions good-bye, and climbed into the jeep. The others returned to Puerto Montt to board the Cessna that would take them back to Santiago. Jofré had nothing with him but his badge and a .38-caliber revolver.

"I believe that what Nelson did was very risky. He was alone, and at that stage nobody knew what this man [Contreras] might do," Silva observes.

Manuel Contreras had arranged for four vehicles for "his people," and they were being wiped down. Very few words were exchanged. Contreras, the DINA's onetime director, got into a red Mercedes-Benz with his wife, Nélida Gutiérrez, and his son Mamito. They motioned to Jofré to get into a Ford that the detective describes as "one of those typical CNI cars." Up front was the driver, with an army officer riding shotgun, and seated in the back, by himself, Jofré.

The entire lot were military men in civilian attire. During the chaotic departure from the estate, two of the vehicles crashed into each other, and one of them was left behind because its bumper was stripped away.

The vehicles made their way, one after the other, with Jofré's car staying be-hind the Mercedes. The caravan, however, did not drive toward the main road that would take them to Route 5 and to the north along the Pan-American High-way. Instead, they left by an interior gravel road that snaked through the forest. Jofré grew fearful. He had no idea where they were headed and could see nothing but a forest.

Anything can occur around here, he thought. "If something's going to happen to me, I'll do something with my weapon. I stayed calm but prepared for any eventuality. I felt in some way as though I were a prisoner," Jofré recalls.

He had no way of communicating with his companions, the Puerto Montt police station, or PICH headquarters in Santiago. The detectives did have some simple walkie-talkies, but Jofré didn't have one with him. It would not have helped in any case, because there was no coverage in the countryside. Jofré did not even have the arrest warrant; Castillo had held on to it.

Inside the car, neither other occupant spoke to him. Jofré was nervous but watchful, all his senses on high alert. He tried to start a conversation with the soldier seated in front of him but got no response.

"What do you go by?" Jofré asked him.

"Major Flores," he replied sharply. Some hours later Jofré realized that Flores wasn't his real name.

At last, they came out from the tree-lined gravel track onto a paved interior road. Jofré was unable to get his bearings. They had been on this route for an hour, and he still had no idea where they were. Just before reaching a junction with Route 5, the vehicles came to a stop. Jofré was uneasy. Were they not going to head toward Santiago? He had his gun on him, but it was a poor defense against Manuel Contreras's armed guards. He didn't know what to expect.

"What's happening here?" he asked.

"We're waiting for a vehicle," "Major Flores" answered.

A car soon appeared on the scene. It drove up quickly and stopped near them. A man got out of the car and climbed into the Ford, sitting next to Jofré. When he greeted the officer in front, Jofré found out that "Major Flores" had a different name. They set off once again. For the detective, the trip was a trial of endurance, an eleven-hour ordeal.

"I've never forgotten my conversation with him. He said he was a navy officer from Talcahuano and a member of Contreras's security team. Straightaway he spoke to me about my father and said he knew him. But I think it was a lie; he wasn't old enough. This business, I thought, is pretty strange."

Jofré breathed more easily when the column of cars at last took off northbound along the Pan-American Highway. They only stopped once for gas and to drink some coffee. Jofré bought himself some crackers, but, pointedly, nobody said a word to him nor would the guards let him get near Contreras. On the hours-long drive to Santiago, he was comforted most by the fact that every time they passed an exit to some city, there was a police car on the highway with its lights flashing, relaying word about the progress of Manuel Contreras's caravan en route to PICH headquarters in the capital.

They reached Santiago around midnight on Thursday, September 19, and headed straight for the army's general garrison command in the city center. Awaiting them there was the chief of the Homicide Brigade, Osvaldo Carmona; Deputy Superintendent Rafael Castillo; and the garrison's commander, a military judge for the Santiago area, Brig. Gen. Guido Riquelme. Carmona and Castillo assumed charge of Contreras, now a detainee, and took him to the military hospital, then directed by Col. Atiliano Jara.[9] Contreras was confined to suite 530, one of six special rooms reserved for army officers holding the rank of general.

Pedro Espinoza had held out, defying authority for a period that could not last long. The game was over; it behooved him now to obey the order of his commander in chief. The DINA's onetime second-most-powerful man, still in active service, was placed in custody in the army's telecommunications command in Santiago, where he remained for three months, until December.

The following day, Friday, September 20, the Chilean Supreme Court rejected an appeal by Contreras's defense that sought to halt the investigation. That same day, without anyone knowing, Judge Bañados indicted Contreras and Espinoza for the murder of Orlando Letelier and for the use of false passports.[10] The press learned about it three days later, on Monday.

That is how inspector Nelson Jofré spent the country's Independence Day in September 1991.

A Titanic Task

Despite the public's mounting sense of anticipation regarding the Letelier case, little or nothing was actually known about the specifics of bringing Contreras and Espinoza before Judge Bañados. Even as Contreras resisted signing the judicial notice of his indictment and refused to be booked, the front-page headlines on September 20 applauded the "civic-military celebration" and the previous day's "brilliant military parade" held in O'Higgins Park, signaling a firm path toward national reconciliation. Yet in those timorous first years of the democratic transition, that artificial reconciliation was light years away.

The Letelier case stirred up the latent doubt over the question of just how far a judge could go in pursuing an investigation of persons inside the ex-dictator's most trusted circle. Much less attention was paid to whether detectives from the

PICH, an institution that still wasn't fully purged of Pinochet loyalists, would be able to carry out their work unhampered or assert authority over military officials who enjoyed the backing of their commander in chief—the person ultimately responsible, at the time, for the crimes that had been committed.

In exchange for leaving the presidency and allowing a peaceful transition to civilian rule, General Pinochet had his own demands. In August 1989, a few months before the general election that buried his dictatorship, Pinochet, still the master of the country, solidified his position, and by extension that of the army, on future efforts to exact justice for the human rights violations committed during his regime.

Commemorating the sixteen years since he was promoted to commander in chief of the Chilean Army by the same president whom only weeks later he would overthrow, Pinochet laid down the hard lines that the new government could not cross if it hoped to govern peacefully. In short: no meddling with the nation's current economic model—Pinochet's institutional legacy—or his men or his family. With regard to human rights, Pinochet established four imperatives: keep in force the Amnesty Law of 1978; respect the authority of the military justice system, which continued to claim jurisdiction over the investigations into human rights cases so as to close them down later or leave them in limbo indefinitely; "ensure Order, Public Security, and the prestige of the Armed Forces[;] and prevent any attempts at reprisal against its members for political reasons."[11]

According to the logic of the military and those who supported the military's reign, investigating crimes committed by agents of the state and imprisoning them was a politically motivated reprisal against patriots who risked their lives in 1973 to lift the country out of ruin and reestablish civic order because Chileans called for it. It was outrageous, dishonorable, and indeed no less than unjustified persecution that true heroes might have to appear in court when the fault lay in the lies propagated by international Marxism. A war had been fought to save the country, and with wars come losses. The incidental excesses of a mere handful of people could not be used to condemn an entire institution. They were the price to pay for civic peace and for the successful market economy that the armed forces, in tandem with a visionary entrepreneurial/business class, had bestowed on the country. The ungrateful were just that—a thankless lot.

President Patricio Aylwin's government was navigating turbulent waters, and its mission, especially during its first years, was to stabilize the ship. A series of critical questions dogged Aylwin: How could he reconcile the democratization of the country with the political, legal, and constitutional limitations left in place by the military regime and supported by an obstructive opposition on the right? How could he live with an illegitimate and authoritarian constitution that nevertheless allowed him to take office and he was committed to respect? How could he achieve the full subordination of military to civil authority and, at the same time, fulfill the desire for truth and justice? How could he satisfy the enormous and varied expectations and social demands and deal with groups exercising de facto power while simultaneously ensuring governability along with economic stability? It was a titanic task on multiple fronts, and the country was almost always in crisis over one of these issues.

The armed forces preserved spheres of power in the new system, which could not yet be called democratic, and they continued to play a political role, offering an opinion on and intervening in all manner of things.[12]

A government report in June 1990 called attention to the fact that "the Army is a key political actor in the process [of transition], like it or not."[13]

The military had not entirely returned to its barracks, and amid this "protected" democracy, or "supervised" democracy, the government ended up backing off every time Pinochet pounded the table. This much was already evident in December 1990 with the *ejercicio de enlace*, a special army readiness and coordination operation. A parliamentary commission was entering the final stage of its investigation into three payments, totaling the equivalent of US$6.5 million in today's currency, paid the year before by the army command to Augusto Pinochet Jr., the general's oldest son, for the purchase of Valmoval, a small military arms manufacturer. The investigation into the so-called Pinocheques cast a shadow over the commander in chief. The ex-dictator therefore decided to call his generals together and place the troops on high alert. It was an unmistakable warning to the civil authority that it should not stick its nose where it did not belong and a challenge to the powers of the Chilean Congress, newly convened in March after a forced recess of seventeen years.

Pinochet disguised the troop garrisoning, labeling it a mere "security, call-up, and coordination exercise" that "had no extra-institutional significance," a characterization the government relayed the following day in a press release. But the message was heard loud and clear, and for all that the army and government tried to play it down, it was the image of defense minister Patricio Rojas's chin trembling at the possibility of a military uprising that registered in the eyes of the public.

The parliamentary commission's report absolved Pinochet of all responsibility, just as he had demanded; the ex-dictator continued his command of the army, and the Pinocheques investigation was conveniently tucked away into a drawer. This was the pragmatic outcome of negotiations between Enrique Correa, the government's chief of communications and a principal political operative, and Gen. Jorge Ballerino, head of the Strategic Political Advisory Committee for the commander in chief.[14]

An analysis conducted by the president's ministerial advisory body reached the following conclusion about the government's relations with Pinochet, days after his tantrum:

> The recent garrisoning of the army doubtless constituted a trial response to a [perceived] situation of harassment, with a view toward establishing both the external and internal reactions to such an action. Put another way, every time we've entertained the belief that Pinochet is sufficiently weak to allow us to pursue matters in a certain direction, we have had to retreat, instead of advance, in our strategy. . . . The analysis of Pinochet's position cannot exclude, going forward, the hypothesis of some level of extraconstitutional mobilization. Beyond evaluating the absence of conditions for a successful putsch, we should focus on avoiding any situation that provides a motive for actions of this type, to whatever degree.[15]

Weeks later, in a public declaration, the army reiterated both its "unqualified loyalty" to Pinochet and the "indestructible institutional cohesion that surrounded him." The declaration was disseminated by the director of Chile's War Academy, Col. Juan Emilio Cheyre, who in 2002 would become commander in chief of the army. According to the army, the parliamentary commission's investigation was an "irresponsible and systematic form of aggression" that "posed a grave threat to national security."[16]

With the Lion at One's Side

Patricio Aylwin's term in office swung on a continuous pendulum of friction, run-ins, and negotiations, both formal and under the radar, over the new politicoconstitutional system, legal reforms, the influence and role of the military in a democracy, and the sensitive, barbed question of what to do about the crimes of the past.

The program put forward in 1989 by the Concertación de Partidos por la Democracia, a multiparty coalition formed in the late 1980s, included trying cases of human rights violations committed during the dictatorship, repealing or annulling the Amnesty Law, and reforming the system of military justice.[17] Nevertheless, there was never enough political courage or enough votes in Congress to implement it. Even today, although in practice the courts no longer enforce it, the Amnesty Law still hasn't been formally repealed.

The governing coalition also could not come to an internal agreement about how to handle the issue of justice: Take it on directly, by opening investigations and annulling the Amnesty Law? Uncover the truth and grant amnesty afterward, at least for crimes that took place before 1978? Offer incentives or degrees of impunity in exchange for information? Investigate and impose punishment for some violations, which in turn would serve as symbolic justice for all other cases? Or simply wash the government's hands of it and leave the issue to the courts?

But how were they to leave the fate of justice in the hands of the same deferential judges who turned down all of the earlier writs of protection filed on behalf of victims, who applied the Amnesty Law without even ordering investigations, and who funneled cases into the military justice system? The government never reached a single defined position on these matters.

The armed forces and police never acknowledged their own responsibility, either institutional or individual, in the crimes. Consequently, their collaboration was an empty vessel. They would perhaps tolerate the investigation of a small number of cases, the fruit of "overly zealous" individuals, but wanted to put an abrupt end to the "human rights issue." Put a full stop to it and make a fresh start for the sake of national unity and reconciliation and in the interest of recognizing the unselfish historical role of the armed forces.

The government coalition's Commission on Human Rights and Justice had settled the issue in December 1989. In a 10–2 vote, the commission agreed to recommend that uncovering and revealing the truth should take priority over seeking criminal prosecutions.[18]

This was "justice to the extent possible," as summarized by the president. "That phrase—of which I was the author—was criticized by some," Aylwin said in an interview conducted for the Audiovisual Documentation Center of Chile's Museum of Memory and Human Rights. "But it simply expressed the minimum realism that was necessary in order not to deceive people, [by] creating illusions that we, coming into power, were going to be able to bring about full, undiluted justice."[19]

Realizing "justice to the extent possible" meant giving priority to the search for truth over punishment for crimes. Obtaining truth and justice on the matter of human rights, the government admitted, was limited and conditioned on the one hand by the very political restrictions built into the agreed-upon process of transition and its relationship with the military and, on the other, by objective institutional constraints: the Amnesty Law still in force, the excessive powers of the military justice system, and a Supreme Court filled with judges appointed during the military dictatorship.

"It can be said," in the words of a report prepared for the president, "that the notion of 'possible justice' was not the response to a particular fear but a formula inspired by realism; it was the result not of a lack of moral courage but of an ethic of responsibility that forces us to consider the consequences and thus do only what is possible given the political and institutional reality in which the process of transition takes place. In this sense and on the judicial plane, 'possible justice' was enunciated not as a promise of punishment for those responsible for human rights violations but as an eventual and circumscribed achievement."[20] To respond to the public's demand for truth and justice and at the same time avoid flare-ups with the military, the way forward was to seek the truth, acknowledge responsibility, pay reparations, and grant pardons for the crimes. Reconciliation would naturally ensue. As for justice—it could occur only if it was possible and did not ruin the prospects of the above. There would be time one day to design a longer-range policy of justice and to think about revoking the Amnesty Law. Meanwhile, the focus was on reforming and revitalizing the power of the judiciary and on cleaning up its auxiliary arm, the PICH, to bring the training of its detectives in line with the requirements of democracy.

As Edgardo Boeninger, chief adviser to the president, declared in a 1991 interview with the *New York Times*, "Our feeling is that if we can avoid confrontational politics, we are better off. . . . We are in a time of transition to democracy. Not everything is possible."[21]

For the purpose of establishing an official account of what transpired in Chile between 1973 and 1990, Aylwin's government, in one of its first decisions, created a commission to take testimony from the families of the executed and the "disappeared." The commission's work would enable the country to acknowledge the victims of the dictatorship, create an official record of their identities, and—equally important—recommend policies for making reparations to their families.

Aylwin, as he later made clear in an interview, needed first to convince the two members of his cabinet closest to him, Edgardo Boeninger and Enrique Correa, who were opposed to the idea. "I was convinced it was the pathway to open doors," Aylwin averred.

> If I wanted the military to be open in solving this, I had to be candid but at the same time prudent; thus the phrase that I used, to seek "justice to the extent possible"—for which I've been amply criticized—corresponded to a minimum of prudence, because if justice was going to be nothing short of total, that would have meant prosecuting Pinochet and all of his people and touching off a civil war. "To the extent possible" was a viable path, because it would allow for some criminal investigations but not a wholesale defenestration or aggressive action against those who continued to have the power of arms.[22]

The Commission on Truth and Reconciliation, chaired by the jurist Raúl Rettig, delicately balanced political forces that included prominent participants in the coup, such as the lawyer Gonzalo Vial, one of the ideologues of the fictitious

"Plan Z," a fabricated plot that the military used to justify the coup and the savage repression that followed.[23] Starting on May 9, 1990, the commission began to meet with the relatives of victims and witnesses to the crimes and to compile background data on events from different organizations and institutions, both national and international.

Once the Rettig report was issued, the government tried to maintain a clear recourse to the law for families and other affected parties. Notably, however, it did not commit itself to securing justice. Rather, according to a government report from October 1990, not pursuing criminal prosecutions seemed to be the trade-off to gaining the votes in Congress from the right-wing opposition needed to reform the judiciary: "Faced with a scenario in which the reality of [leveling] criminal sanctions against those who violated human rights appears highly improbable, the government is in a position to demand a commitment from the Right on modernizing the judiciary," the report indicated.[24]

Meanwhile, "as the maximum of concessions with respect to its original program and to achieve the subordination of military to civil authority," the government "could accept the relative impunity represented in the 1978 Amnesty Law, given the recent Supreme Court rulings."[25]

Nelson Mery, a former director of the PICH whom President Aylwin appointed in 1992, understands the caution displayed by the government in those years, though not the excessive restraint exercised by later administrations. "What President Aylwin did does not deserve criticism of any sort," he maintains. "He was there with the lion at his side and did what he could."

Just Some Bad Apples

The excitement stemming from the transfer of power from Pinochet to Aylwin on March 11, 1990, had yet to abate when the first discoveries of the remains of disappeared persons were made in the nascent democracy. On March 21, the skeletons of three people who had been executed were unearthed on army grounds in Colina, a district north of Santiago, which the army had used as a shooting range.

It was round one in a series of grisly findings made throughout the year that caused the military's hair to stand on end. As the Commission on Truth and Reconciliation began its work, those who had personally witnessed atrocities as well as anonymous sources with information began to point toward secret sites where persons executed by the regime's henchmen were buried. More than a decade earlier, in 1978, the remains of a group of the detained and disappeared were discovered in an abandoned lime kiln in the town of Lonquén (located in

the Santiago Metropolitan Region). This event confirmed for the military regime that the disappeared could eventually "reappear," so the army gave orders,
a short time later, to carry out Operación Retiro de Televisores (or, in rough
translation, Operation Withdrawal of TV Sets). The operation entailed exhum-
ing the remains of disappeared persons and guaranteeing that they would never
be found, either by dumping them into the sea, dynamiting them into oblivion,
or using some other equally effective method. On many occasions, however,
evidence of the mass killings was left behind or there were witnesses to them.

Then, in June 1990, the corpses of nineteen people rounded up after the coup
were found at one end of the cemetery in the northern coastal town of Pisagua.
They had all been murdered in 1973 after being imprisoned in the internment
camp in this area. The exhumations in Pisagua sent even greater shock waves
through the country because—thanks to the dry desert climate of the North—
the bodies were preserved in a virtually mummified state. The expressions of
horror on their blindfolded faces and the signs of violence on their bodies graced
the front pages of the newspapers for many days.

In the government's judgment, the gruesome discovery in Pisagua had fueled
"a moral and emotional climate" that buttressed the coalition's stand that the
only basis for reconciliation lay in full disclosure of the truth. This realization in
turn demonstrated the timeliness of having created the Rettig Commission. At
the same time, the administration was also concerned with the effect the Pisagua
discovery would have on the reputation and position of the armed forces, and
particularly Pinochet's, having "eroded their prestige in society."

> Although this result is opportune for the government, there is a risk—as a
> government analysis pointed out—that by creating a permanent sense of
> indictment of the army, a hard-line attitude and position, of the "alone be-
> fore the world" type, would solidify within the army and could strengthen
> Pinochet's position, significantly hindering relations with the Commission
> on Truth and Reconciliation and accentuating the breach between both the
> government and the army and the army and society at large. It bears asking:
> How far is it appropriate to go in weakening the social reputation of the
> army? An army clearly alienated from society and democracy is undoubt-
> edly an impediment to the construction of a solid and normal civil-military
> relationship.[26]

The situation, however, continued to worsen. Skeletal remains were later found in
the commune of Futrono, located in the Los Ríos region of southern Chile. The
following month, a secret grave site was found in Calama, in the Atacama Desert, that contained minute traces of twenty-six individuals.[27] They were among

the victims of what became known as the Caravan of Death, a small military group commissioned by Pinochet and led by Gen. Sergio Arellano Stark that traveled in October 1973 through the country's northern and southern provinces, leaving in its wake more than seventy victims of its mass executions.

Moreover, in July 1990, the remains of four persons who had been executed were found thirty kilometers from Tocopilla (in the Antofagasta region), in the mine shaft of La Veleidosa, on the side of the Tres Puntas mountain. The mine had been dynamited with the intent, unsuccessful as it turned out, to remove any evidence of the executions. That same month, small bone fragments of seventeen campesinos who were massacred in 1973 were discovered in Chihuió, in southern Chile.[28]

In August, in the cemetery in Copiapó, the remains of thirteen persons were found, all victims of assassination by the Caravan of Death. This discovery was followed by one in Paine (in the Santiago Metropolitan Region), where between September and October the remains were found of seventeen persons from the area who had been detained and "disappeared."

All of these discoveries demanded a response from the government as well as from the courts and the armed forces. Military officials, their political allies, and their appointed representatives in the Senate justified the killings, ascribing them to the inevitable losses that occur in situations of "war." They increasingly fell back on the "excesses" of some individuals as an explanation.

Against this backdrop, its impact magnified by the inquiries directed at the ex-dictator in the Pinocheques case, the Communist Party and some members of the Socialist Party demanded Pinochet's resignation as commander in chief of the army. The calls for his resignation had been heard for many years and from all sides during the dictatorship, and they multiplied right before the advent of democracy. In his first meeting with the outgoing dictator, as he assumed his new office, President Aylwin requested the general's resignation. Pinochet's reply was "You are mistaken, President. No one is going to defend you better than I."[29]

The first director of the PICH appointed during the democratic transition, retired army general Horacio Toro, joined in these calls. During a televised June interview, he fired a strong message at Pinochet. In reference to the discovery of the bodies in Pisagua and Pinochet's responsibility in the case, Toro did not mince words: "There is a time-honored principle within the military that decrees that the commander, the man who leads, is responsible for what his unit does and for what it fails to do. So that, from the point of view of the military principle, General Pinochet, although he might not have known about these events, is morally responsible for them."[30] Therefore, he added, the commander in chief should resign his post.

The army, for its part, demanded Toro's resignation from the PICH and lodged a formal complaint against him for "insults [leveled at] the armed forces," deeming his words to be "grave, unfounded, and entirely out of bounds." He was expelled from the Association of Retired Generals and Admirals and subjected to a court of honor. To maintain the relationship between the government and the armed forces, General Toro found himself obliged to back down, declaring that it had not been his intention "to cast aspersions on the dignity of the High Command."[31]

The army had never liked Toro, who in less than a year would create a small unit within the plainclothes police to investigate the army's crimes.

All of this drama was happening in the midst of confidential negotiations taking place between the government and Gen. Jorge Ballerino to "shorten the time" that Pinochet would remain in command of the army. The two sides looked for a way for Pinochet to step down before 1998, as set down in the constitution, in exchange for letting certain subjects fade away, among them the notorious Pinocheques. After the "call-up exercise" of December 1990, however, these negotiations reached a dead end.

What is more, according to an internal government analysis, the calls for Pinochet to resign actually worked in his favor. Within the army, as a June 1990 report emphasized, they tended to create "the climate of a fortress under siege, which reinforces a psychology of confrontation among the military and, therefore, a leadership that instead of being conciliatory becomes more energized. This scenario causes a growing need on the part of the army to make itself heard, taking it to the brink of [resuming] a deliberative role, which the government should try to prevent and control."[32]

Furthermore, in demanding Pinochet's resignation, the accusations of responsibility for the crimes were shifted from the individual to the institution and the chain of command; this, the report added, "contradicted, in a way, the present governmental policy," that is, that the responsibility was borne by individuals only and was not institutional.[33] In other words, it was a matter of bad apples, not of crimes against humanity. More than a decade had to pass for this equation to be reversed.

As another analysis of government-military relations prepared by presidential staff in mid-1990 pointed out, the former dictator "continued displaying a defiant, generally nonconciliatory, and insubordinate attitude toward higher authority." Nonetheless, the report added, "there is agreement that any calls for the repeal of the Amnesty Law or requests for Pinochet's resignation are not politically viable, in addition to being irresponsible."[34]

Still, according to another presidential report, the fact that some military officials and their political allies acknowledged that isolated "atrocities" were committed during the dictatorship opened a window of opportunity.

"Insofar as such 'atrocities' have been acknowledged, it has been possible for the government to contend that in the political crisis of 1973 'we are all responsible,' as the interior minister put it. . . . In this way, a wide and growing consensus has emerged regarding the need to obtain all available information concerning those human rights violations [that are] yet unrevealed."[35]

The army promised to cooperate with the Rettig Commission as long as the laws and the constitution were respected, meaning the Amnesty Law and the statute of limitations for criminal prosecution, which to this point the judges had applied religiously, closing cases immediately after beginning to investigate them. But the army never supplied useful information or cooperated effectively. Theirs were empty words.

With Hands Tied

The remains of 124 bodies, all unidentified, were exhumed from Patio 29 of the Santiago General Cemetery shortly before the Homicide Brigade's detectives made their trip to the South in 1991 to arrest Manuel Contreras.[36] The Chilean Forensic Anthropology Group estimated at the time that identifying these remains could take up to three months. As of October 2021, seventy-six of the 124 exhumed bodies had been identified.[37]

In response to the fact that many of the victims in Patio 29 were buried two to a grave, Pinochet's mocking reaction was "But how efficient!" As expected, the former dictator, who had bragged that not a leaf stirred in Chile without his knowing about it, claimed that he had known nothing of this affair.

During this same period, the government was also wrestling with several other issues: A short while before, the Manuel Rodríguez Patriotic Front had kidnapped Cristián Edwards, whose father owned the country's principal newspaper, the conservative *El Mercurio*, thus creating a new crisis. As the government strove to coordinate a response to this event with the PICH, the Carabineros, and the Edwards family while keeping all developments around it secret, it also needed to conclude the annual process of ranking officers in the army, determining who would receive promotions and who would go into retirement. It was still trying to impose its authority over military officials who clearly needed to be either ousted from active service or, if the situation warranted it, incarcerated for insubordination, corruption, or criminal acts.

Numerous members of the armed forces involved in human rights violations continued to hold high-level military posts: Col. Jaime Lepe, who had participated in the 1976 assassination of former Spanish diplomat Carmelo Soria, was the secretary-general of the army;[38] Gen. Hugo Salas, part of the Army Intelligence Directorate (DINE) and later director of the CNI, was now head of the army general staff;[39] and Brig. Gen. Miguel Krassnoff was chief of the general staff of the IV Division in southern Chile.[40] Hundreds of DINA and CNI agents continued serving in military units across the country.

The CNI, the successor agency to the DINA, was dissolved by law in February 1990, and its assets, records, and the majority of its agents (totaling more than 1,200) transferred to the army, specifically to the DINE. The defense budget for 1991 even allocated 1.2 billion pesos (or nearly US$3.3 million) to maintain the contracts of 900 civilian employees of the CNI who were absorbed into the DINE.[41]

The government continued trying to purge the army of these agents and even floated the possibility of discharging them in exchange for granting them credits to pursue business ventures. The plan was that some 300 would accept retirement in 1992, leaving almost 700. In June 1992, the commander in chief presented a draft bill on severance pay for CNI agents, but it did not pass.

In exchange for Congress's approval of the annual budget, Aylwin promised that upon completing his term in March 1994, "no fewer than 1,000 former civilian CNI agents would give up their current positions in the army."[42]

"They will be out in the 1994 budget," indicated a 1991 end-of-year Defense Ministry report. "Those who leave normally find work as private security guards. . . . The army tries not to leave them footloose, and it keeps track of them. They have lots of information about past dealings."[43]

Despite the wish to see this policy through, by the end of 1993, 354 onetime CNI agents remained in the army. Some never moved on, continuing their employ in the DINE and in other army postings almost through the present day. President Aylwin summoned Pinochet to La Moneda Palace to talk about the definite dissolution of the CNI and the delivery of its records to the government, but the former dictator assured Aylwin that the agency did not have such records, asserting, moreover, that they had never existed.[44]

Today it is known that many of the CNI's records, including those that it inherited from the DINA and were microfilmed beginning in 1977, were stored between 1990 and 2000 in an underground vault in DINE headquarters. In early 2000, they were destroyed, incinerated in a furnace on the grounds of the army's School of Intelligence, located in Nos, a district in southern Santiago.[45]

In 1991 Aylwin was intent on removing Gen. Hernán Ramírez as director of the DINE. In the middle of that year, it came to light that DINE agents were spying on both the government and the director of the PICH, Horacio Toro. A CNI agent turned DINE employee revealed that the DINE was tapping Toro's telephone, surveilling his movements and his house, maintaining a watch on his secretary, and then giving all this information to Pinochet's advisory committee.[46]

But the government's hands were tied. The government lacked the power and authority to compel either Ramírez's retirement or that of any other military officer. On the brink of 1992, the government submitted a proposed law to Congress that would restore to the executive branch the authority to appoint and promote military staff as well as mandate their retirement.

The president got half of what he wanted. Pinochet sacked Ramírez from the intelligence directorate at the end of 1991 but promoted him to commander of the II Army Division, with jurisdiction over Santiago, a position that also made him a military judge for the Santiago region.[47]

It wasn't yet known, but during these months General Ramírez, in collaboration with the army's legal department, was directing a highly secret operation of vital importance to the army. He was orchestrating what many years later became known as Operación Control de Bajas (or, in rough translation, Operation Casualty Control): arranging departure from the country—to places far outside the reach of detectives and judges—for agents who had played an active role in the repression. This operation was accomplished with additional collaboration from intelligence officials in the Southern Cone, notably Paraguay, Argentina, and Uruguay. In the coming months, detectives would pursue many of these fugitive agents.

The PICH had still not freed itself from its repressive past, but it continued to be the auxiliary arm of justice tasked with fulfilling judicial orders. Its detectives were the ones charged with investigating the crimes of the dictatorship, even though this meant investigating themselves.

The mission was entrusted to a very small team created by PICH director Toro in April 1991 within Department V of Internal Affairs. Together with officials from the Homicide Brigade, this group of detectives was quietly amassing, with few resources, the body of evidence that many years later put dozens of human rights violators behind bars.

The detectives in Toro's specially created unit were carefully chosen based on trust, work ethic, and their discretion in carrying out investigations. Their lead man, the undisputed chief for many years, was a detective who had remained with President Salvador Allende to the very end, as the presidential palace went up in flames on September 11, 1973.

2

MAKING ENEMIES

LUIS HENRÍQUEZ SEGUEL was on the second floor of La Moneda Palace and getting ready to come down the stairs when the first rockets launched by the Chilean Air Force landed and destroyed the colonial-era building and buried President Salvador Allende's socialist experiment beneath the rubble.

The young detective from the Investigations Police (PICH) and his colleagues David Garrido, José Sotomayor, and Quintín Romero could not manage to get to the building's underground area to look for gas masks. The shock wave separated them and sent them flying. A fire immediately broke out, followed by more rockets, the explosion of munitions left behind by the Carabineros who abandoned the palace, and tear gas fired through the windows. The smoke and gases were suffocating them. Outside the building: the sound of incessant shooting.

Around fifty people, a cross-section of government personnel, had remained in La Moneda, among them two former directors of the PICH, Eduardo "Coco" Paredes Barrientos and Arsenio Poupin Oissel, along with advisers, physicians, members of the presidential security detachment (known informally as the Personal Friends Group), and seventeen detectives who formed part of a section of the PICH assigned to the office of the presidency.

"Apart from our personal leanings, we were individuals conscious of the responsibility that we accepted upon forming part of the presidential guard, which—abiding by the 1925 constitution governing us—obliged us to protect the country's head of state. We understood loyalty as faithfulness to a sworn institutional oath, to a republican code of laws, and to democracy as a political system," inspector Juan Seoane Miranda, the head of this group of presidential guards, wrote years later in his autobiographical book, *Los viejos robles mueren de pie*.[1]

The day before Allende took the reins of government in November 1970, outgoing president Eduardo Frei Montalva named retired army general Emilio Cheyre Toutin director of the PICH.[2] He was confirmed to the post by Allende, who installed Coco Paredes as deputy director. Cheyre, in turn, appointed inspector Sergio Alcaíno Duchens as head of the PICH's presidential guard.

On September 1, 1971, however, Alcaíno, along with two civilian pilots and a Carabineros lieutenant, died when the PICH's small aircraft in which they were flying disappeared between Bogotá and Guayaquil. No trace of the plane, acquired just a year and half earlier, or of its occupants was ever found. Alcaíno was on the last leg of an advance mission laying the groundwork for President Allende to visit Peru, Colombia, and Ecuador. The PICH had suffered another tragedy in the air two years earlier, when its veteran director Emilio Oelckers Hollstein and a PICH deputy inspector, Fernando Formas Ortiz, died when their plane crashed in the mountains near Curacautín, en route from Puerto Montt to Santiago.

With the death of Alcaíno, Juan Seoane—next highest in rank—was named head of the presidential guard. Months before, Allende had replaced Cheyre as the PICH's director with Coco Paredes, a physician only slightly older than thirty and a member of the central committee of the Socialist Party.

When he joined the guard, Luis Henríquez had already chalked up several years' experience helping protect important visitors to Chile, beginning with former U.S. vice president Richard Nixon in 1967 and Cuban president Fidel Castro in 1971. Like his fellow guards that day in La Moneda, he had moved to this select group from the PICH's Information and Intelligence Department (Depinfi), or, as it was more commonly called, the "Political Police."

The Depinfi interfaced with the intelligence departments of the armed forces and with the government, in particular the Ministries of Interior and Foreign Relations. It maintained a section that furnished daily bulletins to the government "[providing] information on labor conflicts, union activities, politics, etc., as well as a comprehensive archive that recorded information obtained both via open sources and through its own means, which centralized intelligence efforts."[3]

Henríquez came to this unit in 1971. His boss was David Garrido, who had seniority. The two eventually became great friends. Once in the Depinfi, it fell on Henríquez to watch the movements of the ultra-right-wing paramilitary group Frente Nacionalista Patria y Libertad. Surveilling and tracking this organization led him to detect a suspicious North American by the name of Michael Townley. Tailing the leaders of Patria y Libertad, Pablo Rodríguez and Roberto Thieme, on the highway going south toward the small city of Parral, Henríquez observed firsthand how the two went up a gravel road that led to the controversial German community called Colonia Dignidad, where the organization received paramilitary training. Those names and places proved very familiar to Henríquez decades later.

On September 11, 1973, together with other members of the guard, Luis Henríquez arrived at La Moneda before eight o'clock in the morning, convinced that on that day, at twenty-six years of age, he was going to die. The presidential guard's detectives who gathered that morning to fulfill their duty numbered eighteen in all. From the palace, and with the coup already under way, Inspector Seoane placed a call to then director general of the PICH, Alfredo Joignant Muñoz, a militant socialist and history professor.

"Director, I'm at my work post. As of right now, eighteen of the staff have arrived. I await instructions," he said to Joignant.

"Remain at the president's side. And protect him."[4]

After the military junta issued an ultimatum demanding the president's resignation, one of the members of the guard, a young detective, overcome with emotion, left the palace and did not return. Hours later, one of the PICH patrols found him seated on the edge of the sidewalk near the PICH's headquarters. He was sobbing.[5]

President Allende spoke alone with Seoane. He thanked him for his loyalty and released him and his men from their service. It never crossed Seoane's mind, however, to back out. He called his men together and, deeply affected, relayed the president's message to them. He told them that his own choice was to remain and freed them from responsibility should anyone wish to leave.

A tense quiet pervaded the atmosphere.

"We have already made a commitment to stay here; we've always said that, independent of what our duty might be," said José Sotomayor solemnly.[6]

"All of us understood that we were duty-bound and responsible, ethically and professionally, to remain in place, whatever the circumstances might be," relates Henríquez.[7]

These police officers did not necessarily have a political commitment to President Allende; rather, they were complying with their institutional mission. Each officer carried a Browning pistol and a Walther 9-millimeter submachine gun. Most were under thirty years old.

When it was clear that there would be no reversal of the coup d'état, Director General Joignant and Deputy Director Samuel Riquelme Cruz, who was also a member of the central committee of the Communist Party, abandoned the PICH's headquarters. Both ended up being detained, brutally tortured, and eventually sent into exile. The military junta appointed one of the PICH's highest-ranking officers, René Carrasco Montecinos, as interim director. The following day, the junta installed an army general, Ernesto Baeza Michelson, as head of the plainclothes police, forcing Carrasco into retirement. Baeza remained in the post until 1980 and was succeeded by another army general, Fernando Paredes Pizarro. An official of deeply anti-Communist persuasion, Paredes directed the plainclothes police until the last days of the military dictatorship.

In 1974, the PICH, then accountable to the Ministry of Interior, was—like the

Carabineros—placed under the jurisdiction of the Ministry of Defense. With this adjustment, the Carabineros returned to their military origins. With the creation of the new Ministry of Interior and Public Security in 2011, both police institutions officially came back under the wing of the Ministry of Interior, but from a practical standpoint, as far as operational matters were concerned, they had been answering to the Ministry of Interior with the return to civilian government in 1990.

The seventeen police guards held on in La Moneda on September 11, and when all was lost and the nation's leader lay dead on a couch in the Hall of Independence, those who had opted to stay and defend the constitutional government surrendered as a group.

Twenty-one years later, in 1994, a young detective named Abel Lizama would be put in charge of conducting a police investigation of what had taken place that morning in the presidential palace.

The more than forty people who resisted in La Moneda wound up detained in the army's Tacna regiment barracks in Santiago. In contrast to the rest of the La Moneda prisoners who suffered lengthy periods of detention, torture, and exile or were killed and buried in secret locations, however, the detectives were released the following day and, except for their chief, Juan Seoane, taken back to PICH headquarters.

They were received by the PICH's new director, General Baeza. Baeza proceeded to tell them that under other circumstances they would be deserving of a meritorious service medal for having faithfully performed their duty, but since the wind was blowing in another direction, the action they took—remaining in the presidential palace—was considered an act of resistance to the military junta.

"For this reason, he had the obligation to put us on notice that he would not tolerate any political vacillating and affirmed that transgressing against his orders would lead to immediate execution by firing squad to set an example for the rest of the personnel," Henríquez recalls.[8]

Inspector Seoane was held back an additional day for interrogation, after which he was suspended from the institution. He was officially dismissed a week later, on his forty-fourth birthday, September 18, after twenty years of service.[9]

The Son of an Old Socialist

After the 1973 coup d'état, the majority of the seventeen La Moneda detectives remained in the PICH, but they found themselves in limbo, the future of their work, their professional careers, and the trajectory of their lives still to be resolved.[10]

The new leadership of the PICH, subordinated to the Ministry of Defense, wanted to discharge them but could not find a persuasive administrative reason for doing so. They set up something like a council of war before a military tribunal, accusing the detectives of armed resistance. But the guards could not be accused of having failed to perform their duties, because that was precisely what they did on September 11.

So their weapons were taken from them, and they spent several weeks biding their time with nothing more to do than sign the attendance book.

One day, when Luis Henríquez and David Garrido sat down to have lunch in the mess hall, a group of detectives from the Homicide Brigade moved away from them, remarking—between guffaws—that the two "reeked of cadavers."[11]

In early October, the detectives who had been in the presidential palace were sent back to join their original units, so Henríquez and Garrido returned to their mobile patrol unit but without their standard-issue firearms. At night, patrolling the city, one of their jobs was to report to headquarters on the bullet-riddled bodies they encountered.

For having been part of Allende's presidential guard, having likewise helped safeguard Fidel Castro during his visit, and having remained inside La Moneda on September 11, Luis Henríquez was seen within the institution as a leftist. The truth is that he was not very politically inclined. His father, however, was a socialist old-timer who had worked on behalf of Allende's campaigns. Henríquez remembers:

> He was in business and didn't know much of political theory, but he did read the newspapers. He was a socialist, I suppose, because he had to be a socialist. In 1947 they detained him during the time of Gabriel González Videla, the president who rose to power with a coalition of radicals, liberals, and Communists and then turned against the Left and outlawed the Communist Party. I would not have been admitted into the Investigations [Police] had it not been that when I applied for Investigations School the record that documented his detention had for some reason been lost.

From his rural town of Melipilla, on the outskirts of Santiago, he enrolled in the Investigations School in the 1960s, during the presidency of Christian Democrat Eduardo Frei Montalva (1964–70), with a recommendation letter from the regional governor, Carlos Avilés. Henríquez was the oldest of five siblings, and his family was experiencing financial difficulties. His uncle Luis was an official in the PICH and captivated Henríquez with detective tales. All the same, his uncle advised him not to follow in his footsteps, as the work was very hard and paid little. For Henríquez, though, joining the PICH offered the possibility not only of contributing to the family budget but of taking up a career that fascinated him.

In the wake of the military coup, his father was detained and ended up at the local police station. Their house was raided and Carabineros "poked into something like 500 places, looking for weapons that didn't exist," Henríquez recounts.

"Pedro Carrasco, who hailed from Melipilla, came to the rescue. He was an assistant to the prefect Julio Rada, and when he found out that my old man was being detained, he called a mutual acquaintance, a major in the Carabineros, and told him that this was my father and that I was working in the PICH. And they let him go free. That was the entire extent of my ties to the Left," Henríquez explains.

Henríquez circulated through different units, always bearing the stigma of having been "a La Moneda detective." His superiors never gave him the responsibility of handling any sensitive operations. "In my case, everything was always more difficult, more complicated. Luckily, though, I was never going to be commissioned to serve in the DINA [Directorate of National Intelligence] or the CNI [National Center for Information]."

General Baeza soon dissolved the mobile patrol unit. As a result, Henríquez and Garrido were transferred to the unit of the PICH that was more removed from political affairs than any other: the sex crimes unit. Several other detectives who had been in La Moneda likewise ended up in the same unit.[12] Rumors circulated about the fate of the La Moneda prisoners, but any attempt to run these into the ground was futile.

"When we tried to find out about something, they told us, 'You, keep your trap shut,'" Henríquez relates. Years later they learned that two days after the military coup, twenty-one of the prisoners from La Moneda were taken to army grounds in Peldehue, on the outskirts of Santiago, to be executed and secretly buried.[13]

Nor were political crimes ever really investigated. "While the top brass did not issue any categorical instructions to us that a particular case was not to be investigated, they made it clear, implicitly, that we should not get mixed up in problems. You can't get ahead because you will find yourself up against a wall, they told us. And to me they always said, 'And you less than anyone. Don't forget that you are under observation,' any question will draw us into a conflict," Henríquez relates.

In 1977 Luis Henríquez was assigned to the Eighth Police Precinct of Ñuñoa, in the capital, where his work focused entirely on "cases involving the poor:

the person who had been robbed of a camp stove, a blanket, a black-and-white television"—cases, he says, that did not matter to anyone.

"I went on carving out my own space in that unit and my own reputation, not as a genius but as a hard-working detective, like a *guy* who works from morning till night," he notes.

Over a span of eight years, within the Eighth Precinct, Henríquez molded many new graduates of the Investigations School in his own image. "Those are the detectives I later brought over to Internal Affairs," he declares.

In 1983, a decade after the military coup, Luis Henríquez realized that he was no longer considered politically suspect inside the PICH. This struck him during the fiftieth-anniversary celebration of the plainclothes police. As part of the ceremony, he was honored with a prize for having performed the best police work in the metropolitan region, the award being a Seiko watch and—doubtless of greater value to him—the confidence of his colleagues and superiors.

In 1986, the then director of the PICH, General Paredes, sent him north to the beach town of La Serena, and not long after his relocation, he became head of police for the region of Coquimbo. He had attained the rank of deputy superintendent and accumulated twenty-one years of service when, in September 1990, during the first year of the country's restored civilian government, an old colleague with whom he had lived through the September 11 experience in La Moneda reached him by telephone.

"Luis, it's Douglas Gallegos here. I'm letting you know that you've been posted to Santiago," Gallegos told him.

"OK, fine," he replied. Henríquez assumed that this was the annual shuffle of assignments and that he would be transferred to Santiago in December. After four years in the North, he was keen on returning to the capital.

"You have to be here tomorrow. That's an order."

Horacio Toro, President Patricio Aylwin's new appointee as director of the PICH, had named Gallegos as inspector general, one of the positions in the institution that demanded the greatest trust, and another "La Moneda detective," José Sotomayor, as chief of Department V, the internal affairs division.

The immediate need that Gallegos and Toro faced was to form a team dedicated to addressing the problem of corruption and lax internal discipline within the institution. Henríquez was a good fit.

"After a search process and analysis of pertinent data took place, Luis Henríquez came in as part of a group of officers who were recommended for positions in Department V," affirms Jorge Morales, a lawyer and former adviser to Director Toro and his successor, Nelson Mery.

"Sotomayor and Henríquez were the two 'fixtures' in that new structure. Top leadership made that decision. Henríquez fit the profile of a professionally competent and trustworthy official, in line with the institutional vision that was being formulated," Morales adds.

Transferring to Santiago was supposed to happen "yesterday," so that same afternoon, after hanging up his call from Gallegos, Henríquez formally handed over direction of the Coquimbo police operation, tossed some clothes into a bag, and made the trip to the capital so he could show up at the internal affairs department first thing the next morning. His family stayed behind in La Serena. Toward the end of 1990, when Henríquez had finished investigating drug and bribery incidents and turned to matters involving human rights cases, his wife and children became the first target of threats.

Henríquez's wife—who like her husband worked in the PICH—called him one day from La Serena. She was in tears. The housekeeper had taken a call on the house's private line, passing along the false message that Henríquez had just died in a traffic accident in Santiago. The following month the house was pelted one night with rocks.

"That happened right after the former CNI agents in the Arica regiment got wind of the fact that I was investigating human rights cases, so we rushed the family's move to Santiago," Henríquez asserts.

These were the initial acts of intimidation in response to the incipient investigations of human rights cases in the 1990s. There would be many more, for years to come, against Henríquez and the select group of Department V and Homicide Brigade detectives dedicated to pursuing them.

From the Pinnacle to "Treason"

Retired army general Horacio Toro was a devout believer, a conservative Catholic, and a man wedded to ritual and closely aligned with the Christian Democratic Party. He had shown no reservations about supporting the *tacnazo*, an insurrection by the army's Tacna regiment led by Gen. Roberto Viaux in 1967, and a few years later, during the period of Allende's government, he publicly criticized the military's high command, then headed by Gen. Carlos Prats.[14] Toro was almost ousted, but the coup d'état got in the way. Pinochet declined to discharge him. At this historical crossroad, Horacio Toro aligned himself with those who took part in the coup.

Toro was deputy chief of the military junta's advisory committee between 1973 and 1976 and later spent a year as Chile's military attaché in France. He was both a privileged observer of and direct participant in the apparatus and inner workings of the dictatorship. Given his high position during the harshest years of political repression, he certainly knew of its crimes, and given also how close he was to the pinnacle of power, it could be said that he was complicit in them.

After the dictatorship ended, the former military general publicly maintained that its human rights violations had never sat well with him and that he had made his unease known to Pinochet.

"I brought up the problem [of human rights violations] before the advisory committee; we examined it, but it never gained greater traction. From that point on a serious problem of conscience set in. That was in 1975," Toro stated in an interview with the press some years later.[15]

Subsequently, in 1977, he committed the blunder of criticizing his commander's plan to hold on to power indefinitely. He was called upon to retire and treated like a traitor by his comrades-in-arms.

"They rid themselves of him in a way that bordered on the grotesque," recalls Enrique Krauss, interior minister during Aylwin's government. "They forbid him from going into all of the armed forces properties and grounds; they even drove off his horse. One day he found the animal grazing outside the regiment."

As the years went by, Toro's opposition to the dictatorship became less and less subtle. He served as secretary of the Command of Independents for Democracy, collaborated with the Committee for Free Elections, and called on citizens to vote no in the 1988 plebiscite, which Pinochet tried to use as the basis for remaining head of state for eight more years. For Toro, the system created by the military regime had a "neofascist" stamp.[16]

With respect to human rights violations, however, he seemed to be more concerned with granting forgiveness than with seeking justice. Following the victory of the "no" vote in 1988, General Toro feared a possible "spirit of vengeance" on the part of Chileans toward the army. "A process of reconciliation has to be based on forgiveness and on respect for the defeated," Toro said in an interview with the magazine *APSI*.[17]

He and President Aylwin seemed to be on the same wavelength regarding the political transition. The government received positive references on him as a "very studious, talented, and honest" man, notes Krauss. The Christian Democratic leader, Radomiro Tomic, was his professor at the Pontifical Catholic University, where Toro earned a degree in political science, and characterized him as one of his best students.

Furthermore, in the search for a new leader of the PICH, the government had few options. The 1979 Organic Law underpinning the PICH stipulated that the appointment of its director could go only to the deputy director, a police official holding the highest rank, or an officer of the armed forces. Only in 2005 was the law amended establishing that the position of PICH director would fall exclusively to someone within its ranks.[18]

"It wasn't possible for us at that time to appoint someone from the institution. To begin with, we had no detailed inside knowledge about it. All the information at our disposal indicated that it was a thoroughly corrupt institution. We had to resort to a military officer, and the list of trustworthy officers in the military was very slim," Krauss points out.

That the director of the PICH would not be someone from its own ranks was hardly a novelty. Its first director in 1933, Pedro Álvarez Salamanca, was a retired army major who had been an aide-de-camp to then president Arturo Alessandri. He lasted only a few months in the position. He was followed by a mixed bag of political appointees from different fields: Carabineros, physicians, lawyers, a history professor, and numerous army officials.

In fact, before the nomination of Nelson Mery in 1992—and discounting the prefect inspector René Carrasco, whose interim appointment on September 11 lasted less than twenty-four hours—only once in the history of the PICH was its director chosen from among the pool of career officers, that being Roberto Schmied Marambio, who was promoted into the position in March 1958. Schmied's tenure, as it turned out, was also brief—he was gone in eight months when a new president took office in November of that year. The appointment of the PICH director was a political privilege that resided with the government, quite apart from what the professional merits and competencies were of those appointed to the position. This feature was a constant, though it did not prevent friction and resentments among PICH staff.

Events demonstrated that placing an official openly opposed to the dictatorship in a position that sooner or later would come up against its criminal deeds carried a high cost. The political Right, an army that closed ranks around its commander, and the ties linking military intelligence officials, ex-agents of the CNI, and plainclothes police personnel ultimately made life impossible for Horacio Toro. In the eyes of the army, he never ceased being a traitor. And inside the PICH he stirred up resistance from the start.

An Agreement among Buddies

Although the two police forces—Investigations and the Carabineros—continued to be subordinated to the Ministry of Defense regarding administrative matters, the rest of their operations fell under the umbrella of the Ministry of Interior. This arrangement allowed for fending off both the lobby of the Right and the

Carabineros, who sought to keep the two police forces subordinated to the Defense Ministry and also proposed merging them. This latter idea was roundly rejected by the government, which kept working to bring the two forces back under the control of the Interior Ministry, as was traditionally the arrangement before the military dictatorship. This scheme would leave the PICH in charge of investigating crimes and the Carabineros the job of preventing them and maintaining public order.

The 1980 constitution imposed by Pinochet subordinated both police forces to the Ministry of Defense. Changing that condition required a constitutional reform that was impossible to achieve during the first months of civilian government. The way around this impediment was to settle on what former interior minister Enrique Krauss terms a "practical arrangement."

In addition to being fellow members of the Christian Democratic Party, Krauss and the defense minister, Patricio Rojas, had been fast friends for decades. They had worked jointly in Eduardo Frei Montalva's government, so coming to an agreement—with the consent of President Aylwin and of the Christian Democrats more broadly—cost nothing.

Krauss had family ties in both the army and the Carabineros, which made things easier. His brother Jaime Krauss was an army officer and his cousin Fernando Cordero an official in the Carabineros who, a few years later, rose to become its director general.[19]

As noted above, the two police forces came under the aegis of the Defense Ministry on administrative matters, as did their corresponding undersecretaries' offices. But again, on operational matters they answered to the Interior Ministry. This agreement was engineered and implemented by the government and conveyed to the Carabineros and to the PICH.

"At the outset there was some resistance on the part of the Carabineros, but between my insistence and the steadfast refusal that Rojas put up, in practice things functioned as we designed them to. The Carabineros wanted to engage with Rojas and would approach him, and he sent them to me," explains Enrique Krauss.

The PICH command had a formal relationship with Krauss's cabinet, including his cabinet chief, Jorge Burgos; the chief of the legal division, Rodrigo Asenjo; and the deputy chief of the division and former lawyer for the Vicariate of Solidarity, Luis Toro.[20] They were all Christian Democrats.

When situations arose in human rights investigations that the director believed could cause complications for the government because of their implications for the military, PICH leadership passed word to the interior minister.

Like Krauss, Asenjo also had family who served in the army. His father had been a cavalry officer, and at one point his service coincided with that of Horacio Toro. He knew Toro as a young man, when the future PICH director was a sublieutenant. Asenjo's younger brother, Gonzalo, likewise had a military career and worked in the CNI in the 1980s.[21]

Asenjo appealed directly to Krauss to link him up with the PICH. He had felt emotionally tied to it since the days of its former director, Emilio Cheyre. "Uncle Emilio" had toured him through all the institution's headquarters when he was director and Asenjo was a young law student.

A Destitute Police Force

Horacio Toro was an army general, not a police officer. He was ignorant of the trajectory of the PICH and knew nothing of its men and its internal culture. When he assumed the directorship of Investigations, he encountered an institution through whose ranks ran a decided Pinochet following. Some 300 of its personnel who had been assigned to the DINA, the CNI, or other agencies of repression continued to be deeply embedded in its units.

Abusive practices, torture, and physical, psychological, and verbal violence toward detainees and suspects had become standard practice, even before the advent of the dictatorship. The PICH had now operated for almost two decades free of democratic controls, and its high command remained loyal to the man Pinochet had appointed director, Gen. Fernando Paredes.

Toro perceived several major problems in the institution: at the top of the list a demoralized and politically resistant police force, a weak institutional infrastructure, a meager overall budget, and perennially low salaries. The PICH had always been the poor relative of the Carabineros and the armed forces. According to its own reporting, between 1982 and 1990 the PICH lost more than 1,000 slots in the Investigations School solely due to budgetary insufficiencies. The fiscal contribution to Investigations had consistently plummeted from 1984 on, until it reached its lowest level in 1990. By 1992 it had climbed back to its 1984 level.[22] The PICH's total budget increased sixfold between 1990 and 1998, without taking into account the injection of additional supplemental millions to finance infrastructure, equipment, vehicles, new quarters, salary increases, and new hires.

In 1990, however, PICH leadership complained bitterly that the Finance Ministry denied the funding that would permit the Investigations School to increase its annual quota of new cadets by 250, so that in four years it could recoup the

1,000 previously lost. On the other hand, the government awarded the Carabineros an increase of 4,400 slots for the next four years, "which equates to making proportional investments and expenditures in the Carabineros similar in magnitude to the entire current budgets allocated to the Investigations Police."[23]

The budgetary shortfalls Investigations experienced were drastic enough that its own staff needed to dip into their personal funds to cover work-related expenses, a practice that Toro ended immediately.[24]

"To drive about on our rounds, we had to put gasoline in the tank or else hoof it; we pooled money to buy bread and something to spread on the bread, something to drink, and we got around everywhere on foot. We used to buy our own paper to prepare the reports [we submitted] to the courts," recounts retired detective María Soledad Villanueva about those times.

Moreover, until the practice was abolished in 1990, a small portion of each staff member's monthly salary was subtracted and reallocated "to purchase paper, typewriter ribbons, and supplies to prepare reports and statements for the courts. . . . We also purchased desk and office items, cleaning supplies, and decorations for our offices. From our salary we also paid the salary of service staff. More than one detective had to reach into his or her own pocket to cover the expense of putting gasoline in the police car and pay the costs of legitimate assignments."[25]

On inaugurating events around the institution's anniversary on June 19, 1990, Toro underscored the spirit of sacrifice shown by its personnel, their "extremely modest salaries," and—despite the precarious state of the PICH's resources—its success in "realizing an efficiency [of operations], which if labeled as miraculous would be an understatement."

In front of hundreds of expectant officials, delivering his first anniversary address, Toro emphasized the core attributes and vital importance of personal and collective ethical conduct and set forth the principal objectives underlying his efforts: improve the image of the PICH, starting with its "renewed democratic spirit"; make it accessible to the citizenry; strengthen ties with state institutions to resolutely combat "narcotrafficking and the advocacy of political violence"; create an effective system of planning; regularize officials' professional career paths; and obtain the fiscal resources needed "for fulfilling, at least to a modest degree, the goals of the institution."[26]

Toro's new theme for the PICH was "the detective has a duty to the law and the law applies to the detective," a governing principle very far from that of his predecessor, Gen. Fernando Paredes: "When the criminal attacks us, we clamor to God and to the Detective. When the crime is solved, God is forgotten and the Detective indicted."[27] This was Paredes's farewell message in the last issue of *Revista institucional* produced under his command. And because the issue, published in March 1990, coincided with the arrival of the new director under a democratic government, Paredes added, "Note: In keeping with the independent character of the journal and convinced that it will not offend anyone in particular or in general, I have repeated this thought by virtue of considering it representative of the reality of policing."[28]

Off with Their Heads

As a stranger to the PICH, Horacio Toro came into its general directorate surrounded by a good many outside advisers ready to assist him in applying the drastic measures of purging and restructuring its ranks to adapt it to the new democratic playbook. He had more than a dozen advisers. The high command needed to be completely overhauled, the institution's bad actors rooted out, the technical-scientific training of its personnel strengthened, and the schooling of new detectives reformed to include a human rights component. The PICH needed to be at the service of the new state and quickly break away from its repressive past. Amid these actions, it also rehired certain employees who were expelled during the dictatorship.

"Toro was not seen as a very approachable person but, rather, as someone with leadership abilities, who was engaged and had the authority to command, someone committed to [the force] doing good police work," notes retired detective José Plaza. "However, he was not in the know about what the police did and how they did it and what, generally, their tasks were."

The inner core of his team of advisers included lawyers and journalists who came from the human rights community and the dictatorship's political opposition. Among them were Jorge Morales, a young Christian Democratic lawyer who worked with the Vicariate of Solidarity; Rodrigo De Arteagabeitía, who became Toro's press officer and was formerly the editor of the vicariate's journal, *Solidaridad*; Andrés Domínguez, the lawyer for the Chilean Human Rights Commission, who advised Toro on this same subject; and Felipe Pozo, former editor of the magazine *Análisis*, who advised on intelligence matters.

Toro immediately embarked on a massive project, in true military style, to weed people out: he swiftly got rid of them, starting with the high command.

"Almost without exception, I would say, the PICH high command was not trustworthy," his former adviser Jorge Morales notes. "That leadership was retained until mid-1990. There was a process to vet information during that period, and it culminated in a scheme, decided on by the director, for restructuring the command, as a result of which more than a dozen officials left. The hierarchy was shifted, moved about. This was Operation Carousel: some go up, some go down. Horacio Toro gave it that name."

When Toro made the decision to discharge members of the high command, he summoned the first officer to his office at 10:00 A.M. To show that Toro had the backing of the government, Rodrigo Asenjo, chief of the Interior Ministry's legal division, arrived an hour and a half earlier. He purposely showed up making considerable noise to register his presence and, by extension, the government's support.

"He had to summon up courage. Some of the high-ranking officers set to be discharged were, frankly, dangerous. Horacio was exceptionally nervous, very worried. He even kept weapons in his desk because these officials to whom he was going to give notice were dangerous types, involved in criminal activities. That high command group was to be feared," states Asenjo.

But no one resisted. At five in the afternoon, when Toro had finished notifying everyone who was going to be sent packing, he telephoned Asenjo. "Nothing happened," he let Asenjo know, sounding relieved.

The new high command altered to some extent the atmosphere in the institution and defined the following priorities:

- Selecting the leaders of police units
- Strictly supervising professional and ethical work standards
- Strengthening training in its moral dimension
- Optimizing human and material resources in the work environment
- Incentivizing the best detectives
- Maintaining a register of dishonest staff[29]

There was a serious problem with corruption and drugs in the police ranks, which started with ex-director Fernando Paredes and worked its way down. Asenjo was able personally to verify this during a trip he took to Europe in January 1991. He had accompanied Interior Minister Krauss to request help for the Chilean police forces.

In 1991, with confidence accrued from his years of excellent political relations with the then prime minister of Italy and leader of its Christian Democratic Party, Giulio Andreotti, Patricio Aylwin asked him to provide material resources for the two Chilean police forces, such as vehicles, communications and computing equipment, and armaments. Chile's president cited his country's inadequate resources for policing as well as the political need to strengthen the Carabineros and the PICH in order to rid their leadership of its right-wing members, who were on a permanent campaign to blame the government for a growing sense of "public insecurity."[30]

From Italy Asenjo traveled alone to Germany, while Krauss returned to Chile. Visiting Interpol's main national office in Wiesbaden, Asenjo was shown three metal filing cabinets, each with four boxes in it. They were fastened with locks and rods.

"Each of the three filing cabinets had a filing card on it that read 'Fernando Paredes Pizarro.' They had information about his participation in drug trafficking in the North of Chile," relates Asenjo.

The PICH's detectives were very susceptible to taking bribes and dealing drugs, given their meager salaries and the fact that they were constantly around narcos and criminals. Many on the staff ultimately gave in to using drugs themselves, even falling into addiction. They protected drug dealers; the police used traffickers to supply themselves, and some detectives went so far as to sell drugs right out of their own units. Everyone knew about it but turned a blind eye.

It was during Toro's time, recalls former PICH director Nelson Mery, that sacks of marijuana were discovered in the guardroom of the José María Caro Police Precinct. It was being sold by some of the unit's guards, who even maintained a ledger recording their sales. The inspector general's office of the PICH intervened, relieved the unit's chief of his command, and ordered that disciplinary action be taken. The chief claimed this activity was simply the currency in which they paid for the information traffickers gave them—a handy device for extracting intelligence.

"I would say that certain pockets of serious corruption existed," notes Morales. "At the top was the Assaults Investigation Brigade, which had ties to the CNI, and just below it was the Narcotics Brigade. And there were some extended practices as well, such as collecting payoffs as part of acting on orders to investigate a case. If somebody filed a complaint that required an investigation, the detectives charged for supposed 'expenses' before getting on the job. That qualified as light corruption. Nonlight corruption was when the accused paid up in order not to be incriminated."

Introducing a focus on human rights within the PICH was a gamble by President Aylwin, who agreed with General Toro that the course of study for police candidates in the Higher Institute (today called the Academia Superior de Estudios Policiales, or Higher Academy of Police Studies) should include a component on human rights.[31] The government needed to count on a depoliticized law enforcement institution that identified with democratic principles, which it could trust, especially if Pinochet continued controlling the army and maintaining influence over the other branches of the armed forces. The government could not place its trust in the Carabineros, because it never gained control over their directorate or high command. Indeed, through the present, no civilian government since the dictatorship ended has undertaken any process to restructure, or change in any significant way, the training and formation of the nation's militarized corps of Carabineros. Nor has it ever acted to purge and reconstitute the Carabineros' top leadership, as Aylwin and Toro did with the PICH.

Toro tasked his adviser Andrés Domínguez, coordinator of the Chilean Human Rights Commission, with introducing human rights courses. In confronting this challenge, states Domínguez, "one was up against the deplorable state of the institution, permeated by multiple corrupt practices, with a staff whose self-esteem was at the lowest level in its history, having to share ranks with officials who had taken active part in the worst human rights violations committed on people or in the trafficking of drugs, along with others who had tried to uphold a standard of professionalism in their work, which was not acknowledged by their superiors and ran up against huge difficulties owing to logistical insufficiencies, the woefully low salaries, and impoverished work conditions."[32]

Together with the massive purging and the restructuring of the high command, this new area of emphasis in the training of the plainclothes police introduced more potential conflict for Director Toro. The reception given to Domínguez wasn't a pleasant affair either. He took on the work convinced of his mission, but—as he relates in an article—"it also dealt an emotional blow to my family, to fellow [Human Rights] Commission members, to friends, and to police staff as well, who, imbued with an ideology of struggle between friends and enemies, did not find it easy to accept this interference."[33]

His initial attempt to approach PICH officers was greeted with hostility. And like Toro, Domínguez did not know the institution, either its history or its customs save that of torture—the latter because he himself was part of the human rights organizations that denounced the practice.

Nonetheless, with time he won over a cadre of officials "not insignificant in number and very important in professional capacity, which had been . . . scorned by the leadership, their work and their persons devalued, badly treated, yet firm in their commitment to their public duty. This group was decisive for getting a mutual dialogue and common understanding off the ground, for creating the first elements of trust."[34]

A cluster of these committed, professional-minded detectives worked in Department V of Internal Affairs.

Pockets of Resistance

Created in 1982, Department V was in charge of investigating possible irregularities or complaints and reports with respect to the actions or conduct of the
institution's personnel, either because they infringed on a law or regulation or
because they crossed the line into the unethical or dishonest.

Nobody liked to receive a summons from Department V. It could only mean
trouble. The department was and is an instrument of internal control, a kind of
policing of the police.[35] Its officials must therefore have the complete trust of the
director. Starting in 1990, they were assigned the task of detecting those who
merited dismissal.

An October 1990 report produced by the PICH's general directorate summarized the process that guided the removal of personnel in this period:

> The process is under way to send into retirement all those staff who violate
> the basic principles and/or legal norms and regulations that must inspire
> those to whom the Law and society have entrusted their security and pro-
> tection. In parallel . . . we have begun an intensive and delicate process of
> review of each and every one of the personnel folders of individuals in the
> Institution, particularly those comprising the Police Force, with the purpose
> of identifying those who may have earned disciplinary sanctions for having
> in the past engaged in conduct that goes against morality and good prac-
> tice, so as to adopt measures that correspond to each case, in all instances
> guarding the privacy of each investigation, as well as the rights to a defense
> which are owed to each employee whose actions are called into question.[36]

An outsized number of staff were let go during the first two years of Toro's tenure. The main precipitating factor was their link to drugs or corruption. Approximately 500 police officers were called upon to retire in this period, leaving
a depleted force that it took the institution some years to rebuild. The resistance
put up inside Investigations was fierce.

During the initial years of the political transition, Department V's resources—
both material and human—were boosted well above the average of other units
in the PICH. The number of officers in Department V more than doubled, going
from nine to nineteen, and where there were only four general service employees
in 1990, now there were fourteen. This trend was due to the burgeoning workload of Internal Affairs, whose private investigations involving members of the
plainclothes police rose from fifty-eight in 1990 to 236 in 1995. The most frequent
complaints against PICH's personnel involved irregular conduct (illegal raids,

abuse of authority, and arbitrary arrest), followed by cases in which citizens suffered unwarranted harassment or physical injury by police. The accusations in
this last category jumped from six to thirty-seven cases between 1990 and 1995.

Internal Affairs also undertook investigations in cases of extortion, drug use,
and—to a lesser extent—usurpation of duties, debts, love affairs, faulty application of judicial decrees, and threats.

In the case of female employees, the principal complaints dealt with improperly executing duties or not at all, losing government-supplied materials, becoming pregnant out of wedlock, and engaging in wrongful conduct. They were
also sanctioned for cohabitation with their partners without legal union and for
marrying without the approval of their superiors.

Between 38 and 55 percent of the complaints lodged went unresolved.[37]

The investigations or legal proceedings that Department V carried out against
PICH personnel did not always honor accepted standards of due process, such
as granting the right to self-defense or proving beyond a reasonable doubt that
a crime or breach of professional conduct had occurred. The speed at which
an investigation was conducted frequently swamped the deliberate gathering
of evidence. In addition, some detectives were accused of wrongful conduct
by their colleagues simply for political or personal reasons, not because they
transgressed.

"I often pressed on Toro that he was getting rid of people purely on the basis
of gossip," Mery recalls. "I told him, 'They fill your ear about someone, and you
send the person packing.' Some exploited [the situation] to tip the scales against
other people. But Toro said to me that we were at war against narcotrafficking
in the ranks, and so naturally some who had nothing to do with it could take
the fall."

The investigation of colleagues involved in corruption, drugs, abuses, and lawless action inside the institution meant that the new director confronted what
Mery calls "pockets of resistance" within the police. A good many disliked Toro's
policies, his operational style, and his large number of advisers.

Along the path he had chosen to take, Horacio Toro was making a lot of
enemies.

That Old Practice of Torture

During these first post-dictatorship years, the PICH's work focused on three
main initiatives: making an internal effort to purge the ranks and strengthen
the institution; investigating human rights violations; and, significantly, dismantling armed groups on the left that were continuing to operate and had come

to be viewed as "terrorist" organizations, including by some of their former sympathizers who now found themselves ensconced in the government.[38]

In this antisubversion campaign, as well as in the treatment of common criminals, the PICH could not jettison the old practice of using torture. It was a modus operandi that had become normalized and was embedded in the institution since its inception.

"The difference always existed between those who were in favor of beating a suspect in order to get to the truth in five minutes and others whose position was 'I can wait a month but I'm going to wind up with this person in jail, without committing an injustice.' Those in the institution who approve of those brutal methods are easy to identify," notes Luis Henríquez.

More than eighty years earlier, in 1938, the director general of the institution, Osvaldo Fuenzalida Correa, proposed putting an end to the use of violence during interrogations.

"The 'skilled interrogation techniques' that have become well known will be ended forever. There will be respect for the person as a human being. Any and all individuals in the institution who avail themselves of torture to investigate crimes will be gone after relentlessly," Fuenzalida announced upon taking up the job.[39]

Yet many decades went by before this change took place.

Indeed, because of their years of experience, the PICH's detectives were a valuable asset for the Pinochet regime's security apparatus. Not only could they share the background information they compiled on individuals and organizations; they also instructed the regime's agents in techniques of interrogation.

"Members of the military did not know how to interrogate. Hence, they called on the PICH to incorporate detectives into the DINA. The detectives provided instruction on how to apply certain forms of torture, primarily the use of electricity, without killing the person subjected to such treatment," explains detective Freddy Orellana, who investigated human rights crimes over a period of seventeen years.[40]

During the initial years of the democratic transition, beating, applying forms of psychological pressure, and inflicting torture continued as part of the police's repertoire of techniques for extracting information and confessions. And as had happened during the military dictatorship, complaints were registered, but few were ever penalized. The PICH's leadership denied it all outright.

The word "torture" was a source of discomfiture, and within the PICH there was unease about even pronouncing the word. Nevertheless, Judge Dobra Lusic, who was invited to give the presentation inaugurating the 1991 school year at the

Higher Academy of Police Studies, addressed the topic directly: "We reject all forms of torture, psychological and physical, as a means of obtaining information or confessions," she asserted before a surprised audience of police officials.[41] She herself had investigated cases of the disappeared.

That same year, six active members of the leftist organization Mapu-Lautaro denounced the torture they had suffered at the hands of the PICH. They had been arrested for the assassination, months earlier, of police prefect Héctor Sarmiento. Their accusations were made by relatives via a press conference.

Horacio Toro met with the archbishop of Concepción, Monsignor Antonio Moreno, and after the meeting disavowed the victims' story.

"We are entirely certain that there was no maltreatment," he declared to the press.[42]

The judge who investigated Sarmiento's murder ordered an inquiry into the matter, but nothing came of it.

When the political detainee Ana María Sepúlveda reported having been tortured by the PICH in March 1992, Judge Marta Carrasco went to the police station with personnel from the national Legal Medical Service to check personally on the state of Sepúlveda's health. Carrasco said nothing after leaving the station, but once again Toro denied there was any truth behind such allegations. Moreover, he put words in the judge's mouth, claiming that in her opinion Sepúlveda's complaints were not substantiated.

"The old recourse to the *parrilla* [the metal bed rack prisoners were put on to receive electric shocks] and the use of electricity is not practiced in this institution!" Toro exclaimed.[43]

Other persons under arrest, in this case from the political-military Manuel Rodríguez Patriotic Front, also claimed they were tortured after the PICH took them into custody in 1992. The four individuals leveling the charge—Ricardo Palma, Maritza Jara, María Cristina San Juan, and Rafael Escorza—had participated in the kidnapping of Cristián Edwards (the son of Agustín Edwards, owner of the influential conservative newspaper *El Mercurio*).

The testimonies of these political prisoners lined up in their details, namely that in the hands of both the Carabineros and the PICH they had been subjected to beatings, sham executions by firing squad, and electric shocks; had drugs forced into them; been deprived of sleep, food, and water for days on end; been burned with cigarettes; been kept blindfolded or naked and forced to stand for extended periods; and had their relatives physically threatened.

In a 1994 report, the international human rights organization Human Rights Watch grimly warned about the resurgence of these practices. In the organization's words, the number of torture cases that involved the PICH had "increased significantly" during the second half of 1992 and at the start of 1993, especially against the militant members of Mapu-Lautaro.

In 1993 alone, stated Human Rights Watch, the Chilean human rights organization Committee for the Defense of People's Rights brought some forty criminal complaints for torture against the Carabineros and the PICH, though it didn't make explicit how many of those corresponded to the two institutions.

The report further stated: "Although Justice and Interior Ministry officials privately acknowledge that instances of torture continue to take place, the government frequently has reacted with skepticism to these complaints before undertaking its own internal investigations to get to the bottom of them. What is more, police officials continue resorting to making threats against those who file complaints about [specific] cases of torture."[44]

For his part, the United Nations' special rapporteur for Chile, Nigel Rodley, informed the Chilean government that he had received forty-seven reports of torture between 1991 and 1993. In the main, the Carabineros bore the brunt of the charges, but in many cases the PICH was also involved. Not every complaint was brought before the courts.[45]

The U.S. State Department's annual report on human rights for 1993 included a chapter on Chile, in which it was stated that "the Chilean police [without identifying which branch, the Carabineros or the PICH] were responsible for certain extrajudicial assassinations." The report cited the January 1993 incident that took place in a PICH police station in the southern city of Constitución, where twenty-three-year-old Juan Acevedo Salazar died, exhibiting signs of having been tortured. Arrested for stealing money, he was found hanging from one of the bars in his cell, an article of his clothing twisted around his neck. An initial autopsy, ordered by the court, found signs of third-party violence; later autopsies questioned those findings.

The State Department report also described the use of torture—generally consisting of beatings and electric shock treatment—on at least seven leftist militants. The general directorate, then headed by Nelson Mery, ordered Department V to prepare a detailed report covering each of the cases mentioned. In April 1994, prefect Luis Henríquez responded to the accusations one by one, discrediting each of them.

As concerned the seven "subversive criminals," Henríquez pointed out that when they came before the court, arrestees of this type customarily denied their responsibility for the crimes in question, instead complaining that to extract confessions from them, the police had resorted to abusive practices.

"With the intent of getting to the bottom of these accusations, internal investigations were carried out, which have not succeeded, either due to the lack of cooperation by the accusers' lawyers or because they [the lawyers] are not willing to facilitate [our] access to witnesses," Department V stated in its report, adding that the police station's records on the health of these seven individuals had been incinerated.[46]

The accusations of torture pointed toward a new antiterrorist unit of the PICH: the Assaults Investigation Prefecture, which operated out of the national headquarters building, though it also pursued work from other police precincts. The detectives who had participated in joint operations with the DINA or the CNI during the dictatorship, through the now-defunct Assaults Investigation Brigade or its predecessor, the Special Anti-Assaults Brigade, were concentrated in this prefecture.

"Toro ought to have dissolved the Assaults Investigation Brigade," notes ex-director Mery. "We differed on that; I don't know why he didn't do it. He saw it as an aggressive operational unit, but only went as far as changing its name—to the [Assaults Investigation Prefecture]."

The arrest and torture of two paid government informants in 1992 marked the beginning of the end for the Assaults Investigation Prefecture. The prefecture was dismantled, and its officials relocated to four new Assaults Investigation Precincts. This move helped decentralize and disperse the old practice of mistreating suspects and detainees but did not end it completely.

Indeed, it produced one of the most media-driven cases of torture during the years of political transition, one that strained relations between the government and Brazil.

A Case of Deferential Treatment

In the last days of March 1993, a Brazilian citizen, Tania Cordeiro, was arrested in her house along with her teenage daughter by members of one of the new Assaults Investigation Precincts. She was held incommunicado for forty-eight hours, during which she claimed that she was, among other abuses, tortured with electricity, raped, and forced to eat her own excrement. The police accused her of maintaining ties with Mapu-Lautaro (the man with whom she lived was a member of the organization) and participating in the robbery of a telephone company office in the municipality of Graneros, south of the capital. Her daughter was placed with relatives and eventually repatriated to Brazil; Tania was hauled off to jail.

Diplomats from the Brazilian consulate who visited her there declared that she was in very poor physical condition and needed medical attention urgently.

Gynecological examinations that were administered found evidence suggestive of sexual torture. A communiqué from the Brazilian president advised that his representatives in Santiago could verify that Cordeiro had hematomas and wounds that were scarring over. On top of that, the police had created obstacles to allowing them access to her.[47]

In August 1993, Cordeiro, with her consulate's assistance, filed criminal charges before a court on the grounds of having been tortured. Both the government and the PICH immediately denied there was any truth to the accusation, even before an investigation was carried out. In a public communiqué, the PICH directorate maintained that it had always afforded Cordeiro "deferential and respectful treatment."[48]

Brazil's government demanded an exhaustive investigation, and its president issued a public statement emphasizing that it was following the situation "with great concern" and trusted that the Chilean authorities "will not spare any effort to quickly clear up the case," in light of the visit to Chile that the country's president, Itamar Franco, would be making in mid-September.[49]

To forestall even greater problems with the Brazilians, the Chilean government asked the country's Supreme Court to step in and appoint a special judge to conduct an independent investigation. The assignment fell to Judge Alejandro Solís. Three months later, Solís prosecuted the Assaults Investigation Precincts' chief, Zvonco Tocigl, and six other detectives on the charge of making an illegal arrest. One of the six, Saturnino Silva, was later arrested for trafficking cocaine. Tocigl was also charged with committing violence (by using Cordeiro's daughter as a way to pressure her) and with falsifying records.[50]

Still, the judge was not able to prove the sexual violence and torture charges, and his finding was greeted as a "victory" by the PICH. The latter even issued a warning that it could take legal action based on "false accusations" made by Cordeiro and her lawyer, Héctor Salazar.

Director Mery invariably denied that Tania Cordeiro was tortured, on one occasion pledging—in a lengthy interview with the newspaper *La Nación*—"If it is proved to the contrary, I will resign then and there."[51]

To this very day, Nelson Mery does not admit that the PICH might have tortured anyone arrested under its authority during the democratic transition, whether a common criminal or someone accused of subversion, save in the case of the government informants Marco Antonio Villanueva and Evaristo De la Cruz Godoy.

"As far as I know, there isn't a single proven case of torture, with convictions," Mery states.

He is correct in that statement, although the absence of a court sentence does not mean torture did not take place.

In a report submitted to the United Nations at the end of 1993, the Chilean government noted that fifty complaints of torture against members of both police forces—plainclothes and uniformed—had been made before the country's courts between March 1990 and October 1993.[52] Between 1995 and 1996, the Committee for the Defense of People's Rights received twenty-five criminal complaints against the PICH for having committed human rights violations.[53]

Remnants of the Past

Securing the removal of former CNI and DINA agents from inside the PICH unfolded more gradually. Some were let go during this initial stage not because of their participation in the political repression but, instead, because of their entanglement in drug or corruption cases. The process by which the PICH freed itself of detectives who had come through the security apparatus of the dictatorship lasted years. The topic—that is, devising a strategy to rid the PICH of this element—was discussed among the institution's top leaders on many occasions with the government, which was engaged in a similar battle to remove CNI agents from the army. As Director Mery explains, "It would not have been very smart, I think, to have booted them all out together, because they were numerous and could organize themselves, form paramilitary groups, execute kidnappings, etc., etc. It could have been worse. It was impossible to retrain these people. It was better to remove them incrementally. Besides, if they were tossed out purely and solely for having been in the DINA or the CNI, they would have recourse to protective measures and would get them." (That is, they could appeal or take the matter to court and would probably manage to overturn their dismissal by arguing that they had been assigned to the DINA or the CNI by the institution on official work, so were therefore just performing their duties.) In 1992, top staff in the PICH's personnel department compiled a list of the institution's staff who were assigned to the DINA or the CNI during the military dictatorship. The list revealed that sixty individuals continued in active service; only seven were dismissed under Toro.

Five officials whose service began in the CNI in the 1980s remained in the PICH until at least 2008. One was promoted by Toro himself, states Mery.[54] All five attained high leadership positions, one of whom was Héctor Silva—the same Héctor Silva who in September 1991 traveled to Fresia to place Manuel Contreras under arrest.[55]

Silva did not leave the PICH, Mery says, because "he wasn't mixed up in any-thing" and "he collaborated in setting the record straight on situations." Silva went into retirement in 2011, while serving as national chief of the Property Crimes Division.

Mery estimates that in March 1992, when he assumed the directorship, only 20 percent of the staff who came up through the DINA or the CNI had left the PICH, and the other 80 percent continued working in the PICH after the resto-ration of democracy.

THE CACI'S MEN

AFTER JOINING DEPARTMENT V, Luis Henríquez did not last long in his mission of weeding out the corrupt elements among the Investigations Police (PICH) ranks that director Horacio Toro wanted gone. He soon began to clash with some of his colleagues and ended by rebelling against his superior officer, José Sotomayor. Henríquez had similar qualms to those of Nelson Mery: "I was partial to the idea that things should get done according to the investigative method, but it was typical that shortcuts got taken, bypassing this approach," says Henríquez. "I began to fall out with Sotomayor because he wanted us to act in haste. But errors were committed, and innocent people wound up going into retirement."

It was not the business of Department V to take charge of human rights cases, but the different police precincts that were receiving orders to investigate them were failing miserably in this regard.

The cases involved the disappeared (*detenidos desaparecidos*), old cases in which it was not possible to examine the crime scene, collect physical evidence, or rely on fresh testimony. Therefore, to meet the legal bar for the truth about crimes that had taken place as many as eighteen years ago, it was necessary to adapt investigative methods to these circumstances. It was a struggle for the police to gain access to information, and the military offered no help at all. The halting investigations of 1990 got nowhere. In addition, the majority of the detectives who were expected to comply with these judicial orders made little effort to do so.

Consequently, at the end of 1990, when Department V received the first round of orders to investigate human rights cases, Deputy Prefect Sotomayor decided that Henríquez was the ideal person to carry them out.

"That way Sotomayor pulled me out of the daily confrontations that everyone was having with me," he relates.

And so, too, Luis Henríquez's career path in the PICH changed permanently.

Fewer than fifteen officials worked in Department V, all of them focused on matters that concerned "internal affairs." Henríquez was virtually alone in handling the human rights cases. Not long after, however, a colleague joined him: deputy superintendent José Miranda, who came over from the Police Intelligence Brigade (BIP).

Miranda had only been in the BIP a few months, transferred into it from the criminal records unit of the Technical Assistance Department, or Asetec. His family was from the city of Castro, on the island of Chiloé, in Chile's far South. Miranda's father was a merchant seaman, and his mother a housewife and supporter of the Christian Democrats. When he was still young, his family moved to the central part of the country, to the port city of Valparaíso, because his father had gotten a job with the South American Steamship Company. Thanks to his father's voyages abroad, they never lacked for anything at home, not even in the worst moments of the economic crisis of Allende's government.

At the time of the military coup, Miranda was a high school senior, with plans to study architecture. He gave them up, however, when he found out that classes in architecture involved a good deal of mathematics. Miranda had a natural curiosity and was an avid reader, more than likely because his house was always full of books and magazines. Two magazines that he read on a regular basis were *Vea* and *Life*; their police mysteries especially attracted him. The Investigations School seemed like an interesting option, and he enrolled in it as the military dictatorship took control. His first assignment was in Copiapó, followed in 1981 by an assignment to the Antinarcotics Brigade in Arica, in northern Chile, where he remained for eight years. From there he was posted to Asetec and then to the BIP.

"I was starting out in the BIP when they asked for people to transfer to Department V. The BIP did not want to part with its more experienced detectives, so—as I had just joined it—they sent me," he explains.

Now, in Internal Affairs, it fell to Miranda to investigate the first cases involving the army and the National Center for Information (CNI): "La Cutufa" and the murder of a restaurant owner, Aurelio Sichel.

A Premature Assessment

Before the Rettig Report was published, and before a team focusing on human rights was created in the PICH, Department V's detectives were already looking into the activities of CNI agents.

In July 1989, Aurelio Sichel—proprietor of the restaurant Rodizzio, in the capital—was assassinated, but the investigation into his death had not made any headway. Even though the judge who investigated the crime, José Miguel Varela, knew about the affair early on through the declarations of Sichel's widow, it was only in 1990 that one of the many secrets the army carefully kept broke into the open and became public knowledge: the operation of an illegal pyramid scheme called La Cutufa, set up in the 1980s by members of the army, in which Sichel and high-ranking military officials had invested large sums of money. At the top of La Cutufa were Capts. Gastón Ramos and Patricio Castro. Castro was an ex–CNI agent and Sichel's partner in the Rodizzio restaurant.

An internal review by the army concluded that four generals and another sixteen officers were involved in the scheme. All twenty were compelled to retire. An entire class in the War Academy—every member an investor in La Cutufa—was sanctioned.[1] Nearly 150 individuals, virtually all from the military, lost their savings in the fraud.

A parallel investigation focused on the fraudulent bankruptcy of the Santa Bárbara transport company, belonging to the ex–operations chief of the CNI, Álvaro Corbalán. The former agent had retired after participating in the June 1987 assassination of twelve members of the Manuel Rodríguez Patriotic Front, an incident known as Operation Albania, after which he founded the pro-Pinochet political party National Advance (Avanzada Nacional).

Corbalán became friends with Sichel, whom he recruited into his new party. And the restaurant owner, desperate to withdraw his money from La Cutufa, turned to Corbalán to help him get his money back. He threatened to reveal what he knew about the CNI operations he overheard discussed in Rodizzio, where its agents socialized. The restaurant was also the hub of operations for La Cutufa.

"Sichel had videos of some of the CNI's operations, because Corbalán brought him along to them," Miranda attests.

Sichel's assassination, the La Cutufa affair, and the Santa Bárbara bankruptcy were cases with high public visibility that involved the army and the CNI. The government gleefully rubbed its hands at the purely internal army shake-up, and the scandal influenced the restructuring of the army's high command, affected the morale of the institution, and undermined Pinochet's image.

"A picture began to take shape whereby a quick resolution of the human rights problem, in the root questions [that it raised], was anticipated . . . [and] to which the army and Pinochet increasingly exhibited the greatest weakness [they had] shown in years," notes a government report on the situation, prepared in November of that year.[2]

Before this unfolding scene, the government visualized a "resolution" under the following formula: "Truth (via the Rettig Report), partial justice (to an extent as yet undetermined, which would entail the release of political prisoners, relatively high procedural and penal guarantees for the armed forces command and high-ranking officers, particularly in the figure of Pinochet). With respect to the commander in chief of the army, the most likely outcome is his retirement."[3]

This optimistic assessment was premature.

Grazing the CNI

Director Toro referred the La Cutufa and Sichel assassination cases to Department V, despite the fact that they did not have anything to do, strictly speaking, with the "internal affairs" of the PICH. Police staff from different units came on board as reinforcements.

Patricio Castro was captured in Paraguay in November 1990 and expelled to Chile after being indicted as a principal suspect in Sichel's death. To secure his expulsion—and thereby avoid a lengthy and uncertain process of extradition— political, diplomatic, and law enforcement efforts were mounted, notes ex-adviser Jorge Morales. This action was possible thanks to the interventions of both governments at the highest level, as happened two years later with the expulsion, also from Paraguay, of a civilian agent, Miguel Estay Reyno, known as Fanta, whom the government sought to bring to justice for his involvement in human rights crimes.

When he received notice that the PICH was tasked with apprehending the fugitive Castro, Toro appointed a special group to travel to Asunción. It was composed of officials from both Interpol and Department V, including the latter's chief, José Sotomayor, and a female staff member who specialized in makeovers to see that Castro was taken off the plane without being recognized.

Deputy Superintendent Miranda had the job of going to the airport to pick him up.

"Given the political climate and circumstances of the time and the fact that he was a military official, security measures were put in place," explains Miranda.

Castro was disguised while still on the plane from Paraguay and once it landed was quickly put on board one of the PICH's small aircraft and flown to Santiago's Cerrillos aerodrome. From there he was taken by automobile to PICH headquarters.

He was interrogated at headquarters by detectives from Department V. Patricio Castro explained to them how he launched and organized La Cutufa, justifying the fraud on the grounds that he had a disabled son whose treatments were costly. Castro was indicted for bouncing checks and swindling and remained under arrest, but he never admitted to participating in the assassination of Sichel, his partner and friend. Although the upper court judge who investigated the murder indicted Castro, the Supreme Court's Third Chamber—of all the court's chambers, the group of magistrates most subservient toward the military—revoked the indictment.

"Getting Castro back was an important milestone because he was tied to the CNI and some of its shadiest dealings. His capture had clear symbolic value," says Morales.

In December 1990 the PICH, in simultaneous operations carried out at dawn, arrested in their respective homes three Chilean Army generals: Gustavo Abarzúa, director of army intelligence; Patricio Gualda; and Patricio Varela. All three had just gone into retirement because of their involvement in the La Cutufa scandal. The PICH detectives brought the three officers before the appeals court judge, Marcos Libedinsky.

The situation required deft handling, because the generals lived in buildings or condominiums with locked, secured entrances and doormen who notified residents whenever someone came to visit. So the first order of business for the detectives was explaining to the doormen why they were there and then making sure that the person they sought was not alerted to their presence.

As Miranda now tells it with respect to the general he was tasked with arresting, "Some verbal fireworks took place with these military men. He came out with a robe on and berated me angrily: 'Don't you realize I'm a general of the Republic,' he said to me. '[Well,] I'm a detective of the Republic and I'm bringing an order from a judge of the Republic,' I responded."

Miranda proceeded to spell it out for him in graphic terms: "If you don't cooperate I'm going to have to take you in by force, and that means there will have to be a physical encounter between the two of us, and if that gets dragged out my partner is going to call for help, reinforcements are going to arrive, they are going to come out with a megaphone to tell you to hand yourself over, and behind them will come the press."

All of this back-and-forth lasted almost half an hour. The military had still not absorbed the fact that the police could act against them by means of a judicial order. In recent months the detectives had been tasked with arresting or summoning a good many military officials, and they resisted. It occurred to José Miranda to speak with Dr. Elías Escaff, a psychologist who had worked in the PICH since 1971 and directed the Center for Assistance for Victims of Sexual Assaults, which he established in 1987.[4]

"Dr. Escaff told me that I should try to put myself in their shoes. He explained to me that they had been giving orders for forty years and that [suddenly] along comes a person who could be their son who is giving them orders. . . . [For them] it's upside down. So you had to treat them tactfully. We started asking them to accompany us, telling them that the faster we got onto it, the faster the judge would attend to him. After that, things became easier," Miranda relates.

In January 1991, Judge Mario Carroza issued a warrant for the arrest of Álvaro Corbalán. Detectives José Miranda and Jaime Olivares, who was recently transferred to Department V from the Assaults Investigation Brigade, got down to the task of verifying his whereabouts. They managed to confirm that Corbalán regularly came to a building on Martín Zamora Street, located in the upscale Las Condes district in Santiago, and that he arrived in either a blue or gray Volvo. Both vehicles had been registered to the CNI and then turned over to a provisioning unit of the army.

The intelligence they obtained was that Corbalán arrived at this address every night accompanied by two women. These two "ladies" were in fact members of the military but wore wigs to disguise themselves, says Miranda. They accompanied Corbalán to his apartment and later in the night went away. It appeared that they were bodyguards.

One day, early in the morning, Miranda and Olivares decided to go to his building to look for him. They spoke with the concierge to explain their purpose and make sure that he did not let Corbalán know they were there. The ex–CNI agent opened his door to them. He was alone.

"He was taken by surprise and very frightened. He thought that perhaps we were going to attack him. But when we showed him our badges and the arrest order he calmed down and accompanied us to the PICH building. It all went down very peacefully," says Miranda.

The Sichel, La Cutufa, and Santa Bárbara cases produced a shake-up in the army, but those responsible for the fraud and swindle received only small penalties, and the murder of Sichel went unpunished. Yet for the Department V detectives, this initial clash with the CNI marked a before and after.

"Beginning with bringing back Patricio Castro to Chile and the detention of Corbalán, now members of the military could be arrested," states Luis Henríquez. "Up to that moment it couldn't be done. No one in Department V had wanted to get involved. In addition, with the investigation a considerable amount of information was collected that was key for what came later."

And while the detectives were busy investigating these cases, the Rettig Commission was quietly sending the courts new evidence it was collecting on more than 200 human rights cases.

A Goal from Midfield

The Commission on Truth and Reconciliation, or Rettig Commission as it was popularly known, delivered its final report to President Patricio Aylwin in February 1991, and Aylwin took the heavy volumes with him to read on his summer vacation at Lake Llanquihue in southern Chile. The report identified and documented 2,115 persons who had been "disappeared" and executed. The commission was thus able to fully classify them as victims of human rights violations. For lack of conclusive evidence, 641 additional victims identified by the commission could not be placed in the same category.

On March 4, after returning to Santiago, the country's head of state appeared on national television to make the report known to Chileans and in the name of the nation apologized to the victims and their families. In this same address, Aylwin urged the armed forces and the Carabineros, as well as all who might have participated in the "excesses committed," to publicly "acknowledge the pain that was inflicted and contribute to lessening it."

The commission stated, Aylwin reported, that in the face of state-sponsored crimes, the country's judiciary "did not react with sufficient energy" by not granting protection to persons under arrest and offering agents of [the military's] repression a "growing certainty of impunity."

Although from both firsthand testimony and the declarations of witnesses, the Rettig Commission knew the names of many of the agents who had participated in the repression, it did not disclose their identities. Nevertheless, it did try to obtain them, at least in the case of those who were assigned to the Directorate of National Intelligence (DINA), by sending requests to different government departments but had little success in this regard.

At any rate, the government already possessed a list of nearly 1,300 DINA and CNI agents, including civilians, who had been members of the latter agency when it was dissolved in 1990. The list, which today forms part of Patricio Aylwin's presidential archive and is accessible to the public, specifies the full names of these agents and their units, ranks, and positions within the apparatus of repression. The list, however, was not made public at the time.

"Justice demands that the whereabouts of the disappeared be known and that the personal accountabilities [for them] be determined," President Aylwin stated. He later announced that the Rettig Commission had already sent the information collected on these cases to different courts.

"I expect that these will duly fulfill their function and investigate [the cases] exhaustively, to which—in my view—the Amnesty Law in force cannot serve as an obstacle," he stressed.

Internally, however, the government did not hold out much hope that justice would be done, as a January 1991 executive branch report indicated: "We fully realize that the matter of justice, in a strict and formal sense, eludes the government's possibilities. What is most likely, in this respect, is that once the CVR [i.e., the Rettig Commission] provides the courts with this evidence of criminal activity, they will decline to carry out a judicial investigation, as has already occurred."[5]

On that same day, President Aylwin sent a letter to the Supreme Court asking that it move on instructing the lower courts to activate "with all due speed" both the prosecutions of human rights cases that were pending and all new cases that warranted opening in light of the evidence provided by the Rettig Commission.

"I let them know," Aylwin said, "that in my opinion the amnesty currently in force, which the government respects, cannot be an obstacle to carrying out judicial investigations and determining accountabilities, especially in the cases of the disappeared."

In a letter to the president, the Association of Relatives of the Executed demanded that the government fulfill its international obligations to bring to trial those responsible for crimes against humanity and that it seek passage of a law that would annul the 1978 Amnesty Law, as it had proposed to do as part of its election platform.

For Aylwin, however, the current framework and approach formed part of a wise strategy.

As the former president emphasized in a 2009 interview, "To have created the Rettig Commission, furnished the courts with the evidence it collected, and begun the prosecutions—even as the ex-dictator continued as commander in chief of the army—is an experience unique not only to our country but universally. What we did was rational, intelligent, and effective."[6]

On March 27, 1991, Aylwin convoked a meeting of the National Security Council, an agency created under the 1980 Pinochet constitution that included all military chiefs.[7] The president wanted to consult council members about what they thought the fallout would be from the Rettig Commission's report. At four in the afternoon on that fall Wednesday, the National Security Council members met in La Moneda Palace's conference room. Present at the session were the commanders in chief of the armed forces, the director general of the Carabineros, the presidents of the Senate and the Supreme Court, the comptroller general, and the ministers of foreign relations, the interior, defense, economy, and finance.

After discussing whether their deliberations or what resulted from them were to be made public or kept under wraps, and following an all but childish exchange between the air force and navy commanders about the order in which the expositions would be heard, the four uniformed institutions presented their unflinching diagnoses. Admiral of the navy Jorge Martínez, air force general Fernando Matthei, Carabineros director Gen. Rodolfo Stange, and army general Augusto Pinochet justified the coup d'état, defended the actions of the judiciary, rejected the commission's recommendation to bring Chilean legislation in line with international treaties on human rights, likewise rejected its "offensive" recommendation that a culture of respect for human rights be inculcated in military and police personnel, and criticized what they called the report's bias.

As expected, Pinochet drained the report of any validity and offered a rigid defense of the work of the military regime. He was the most hard-nosed of all. The armed forces and the Carabineros, he explained to those present, "fulfilled their mission to the letter; defeated the attempt at installing totalitarianism; reconstructed and modernized the country's economy; reestablished social peace and democracy; restored civility to political affairs in a free, reconciled country whose inhabitants could live together in a climate of public and private security and peacefully exercise their democratic rights."

Chile's army, he continued, "certainly sees no reason whatsoever to apologize for taking part in this patriotic work." He added that the army "repudiates the campaign to make it look like it inflicted punishment on innocent people." Furthermore, Pinochet complained that the commission was giving more credit to what he called "extremist trash publications" than lawful procedures in mounting a campaign to disparage it.

"Chile's army solemnly declares," warned the ex-dictator, "that, having saved the liberty and sovereignty of the Fatherland at the insistent request of the civilian population, it will not accept being placed before the citizenry in the dock of the accused. Even less will it tolerate all of the preceding when, among those who try to raise themselves up in moral judgment of their fellow men are [found] the main people responsible for the tragedy [we have] lived through, in their capacity as the leading force driving the Popular Unity [Coalition]."[8]

Meanwhile, an indignant Supreme Court painstakingly drew up its reaction to the report, delivering it two months later, in May, to President Aylwin. In a twenty-six-page document, it accused the Rettig Commission of overstepping its authority and crafting "an intemperate, rash, and tendentious judgment against the courts, the product of an erratic investigation and of likely political bias."[9]

For Luis Henríquez, what Aylwin achieved with the Rettig Report had far-reaching implications. "The military believed that the commission was only going to extend benefits to the families; it had no idea of the quantity of information the commission had managed to assemble," he notes. "It was a goal [scored] from midfield. Here were the bits and pieces, and those bits and pieces had to be worked up into information, and that information into a means of proof, into something useful to a judicial investigation. That was our task."

How to Treat the Military

Two weeks after the presidential address, the inspector general's office of the PICH ordered the institution's chief legal staff to analyze the Rettig Report and determine what responsibility investigations police might have had for the human rights violations laid out in the report.

A committee was formed, headed by deputy prefect Óscar Garrido.

Garrido was assisted by two colleagues, deputy prefect Óscar Lagos and deputy superintendent Carlos Al-Konr. Because the Rettig Report did not include the names of state agents who were implicated in the crimes, the three could be guided only by the brief descriptions of the circumstances in which victims were arrested, killed, or disappeared.

They looked for references in the report citing the participation of PICH members. From that base, they compiled two lists: the first contained 156 cases in which PICH personnel "appear [to have been] implicated"; the second specified cases in which "there would possibly exist administrative and/or legal responsibility affecting staff" of the police force. These latter cases numbered forty. In all, based on what could be culled from the scanty background information included in the Rettig Report, PICH personnel were involved in the murder or disappearance of at least 196 political prisoners.

Garrido, Lagos, and Al-Konr noted, for example:

Page 108, column 3. Gastón Cortez Valdivia, 1 January 1974.
"Disappeared after having been tortured in the Antofagasta Investigations
     Precinct;"
Page 109, column 1. Bernadino Rodríguez Cortez, 6 March 1974.
"Disappeared from the Quillota quarters;"
Carlos Mascareña Díaz, 1 May 1974. "Died as the result of torture in the
     Puerto Montt Investigations precinct.[10]

The three-man committee delivered its report to the general directorate on April 5, 1991. In the meanwhile, at the request of the PICH's director, the top legal staff were systematizing the institution's own legal norms and regulations relative to the treatment of the military. They had already experienced difficulties while the La Cutufa and Sichel assassination cases were under investigation, and the manner for proceeding with other cases, going forward, had to be very clearly outlined.

On March 27, 1991, the head of the PICH's legal department, prefect inspector Roberto Libedinsky, brother of the appeals court judge who investigated the La Cutufa case, distributed a memorandum setting forth the legal framework for subpoenaing, detaining, and investigating members of the military and the police. With respect to subpoenas or summonses, he underscored the privileges that the Code of Criminal Procedure granted to officers with the rank of general, whether on active service or in retirement: they "will make their statement by means of a written record, indicating that they will render it under oath or as a promise to tell the truth."

In addition, they could do so from their homes, with prior notification and coordination of the day and time. If they were under arrest, it would be either in their military quarters or another place chosen by the armed forces or Carabineros.

Libedinsky put special emphasis on certain stipulations in the code as they concerned investigations conducted by the police: as an auxiliary arm of the justice system, the police could not question the basis, legality, or fairness of judicial orders. He also highlighted another point worth considering: police personnel who were untruthful in the reports they made to the courts would be sanctioned for false testimony and perjury.

He later spelled out some of the institution's own procedural rules, including one which pointed out that its staff "should treat members of the armed forces in a courteous manner, especially those who have attained the rank of General of the Republic."[11]

The army named its leading prosecutor, Gen. Fernando Torres, a staunch supporter of Pinochet, as the contact between itself, the courts, and the PICH with respect to all future judicial procedures pertaining to human rights cases.

An agreement was reached that if a member of the military had to be subpoenaed, his appearance in court would be requested through the office of the army's prosecutor general.

Moreover, and by order of General Pinochet, a new department—Department IV for Analysis and Planning—was created within the office of the prosecutor general for the purpose of monitoring judicial proceedings that involved army officials and of proposing lines of action to General Torres. Every official communication from the courts in which information was requested was to be answered by Torres's office, subject to prior review and approval from the chief of the general staff.

Among other things, the department had to maintain an ongoing system of coordination with actively serving and retired personnel who were implicated in judicial proceedings. The purpose was to make them aware that they enjoyed the army's support and to furnish them with legal advice, analyze the procedural situations faced by its officials "from the political, communications, and intelligence points of view," and propose courses of action. Monitoring judicial proceedings included tapping magistrates' telephones and illegally photocopying dossiers. The legal assistance was paid for with funds collected by the army's administrative support command via the monthly discounts applied to the army's salary payments. All these maneuvers and mechanisms, however, only came to light many years later.

The chief of Department IV was Col. Enrique Ibarra; the PICH's detectives had to go through and negotiate with him. During the dictatorship, between 1974 and 1976, Ibarra was part of a military court in Temuco. He was then appointed as undersecretary of war and, in 1981, to the Fourth Legislative Commission. Since the military junta had closed Congress at the onset of the dictatorship, and absent some sort of legislative power, a number of commissions oversaw legislation on different matters. Throughout the seventeen-year dictatorship, all laws were drafted by these legislative commissions and imposed on the population without discussion.

In court statements made many years later, Ibarra described his duties in Department IV as follows: "They had to do with the general information and publicly known facts that could be assembled about a proceeding for which information was required, to produce a computerized database, through which the concerns of personnel who had to appear in court could be cleared up, so that the person was knowledgeable and could order his thoughts on arriving to testify."[12]

After appearing before the police or judges who were investigating cases, these members of the military had to give a full accounting of what transpired to Department IV. Prosecutor general Fernando Torres periodically briefed Commander in Chief Pinochet about what he called the "judicial problems" of the army.

To establish the procedures to be followed, officials from the PICH's Department V met in the army's main building with lawyers from the prosecutor general's office. What the detectives did not yet know, however, was that Torres and Ibarra—at the same time as they offered assurances of wanting to collaborate by putting military forces at the disposal of the police and the courts—were also participating in the Army Intelligence Directorate's Operation Casualty Control, singling out which agents or members of the military had to be taken out of the country to avoid testifying in judicial proceedings.[13]

The PICH, the government, and the army were preparing themselves for what was to come.

In Absolute Secrecy

On April 8, 1991, Director Toro created the Analysis and Institutional Coordination Commission (CACI) within Department V of Internal Affairs. The CACI's mission was to centralize all information pertaining to human rights investigations at the national level and to receive, analyze, and process the information and evidence that the Rettig Commission had handed over to the courts.

Toro's new commission grew out of the need faced by the PICH's high command to develop "a general overview of investigative orders, or related matters, deriving from legal proceedings that emerged from the reports of the National Commission on Truth and Reconciliation."

"The CACI will likewise issue general and specific instructions to the units that find themselves investigating said events, establishing the coordination needed for the optimal development and conclusion of these investigations," notes the order establishing the commission.[14]

The following day, Toro named superintendent Luis Henríquez to head it.

"It could be for my having been in La Moneda, because I was sensitive to the issue [and] knew something about what everyone had denied," says Henríquez regarding his appointment as head of the CACI. "There were very few of us. The advisory team was bigger than the working team."

The Analysis Commission, as they called it, indeed had an ample group of advisers but very few personnel to carry out the investigative work itself. At the outset, they numbered but two: Luis Henríquez and José Miranda.

The advisers, however, were numerous: from the top echelon of the legal department, superintendent Carlos Lübbert; from the Homicide Brigade, deputy superintendent Sergio Riquelme; from the Financial Crimes Brigade, which had investigated the La Cutufa and Santa Bárbara company cases, inspector Víctor Pérez; from the personnel department, its informatics engineer, inspector Luis Fernández; and from the office supplying support staff, typist and deputy superintendent Eduardo Guzmán.

Superintendent José Sánchez served as the permanent contact between the Information and Intelligence Department (Depinfi, the former "Political Police") and the CACI.

All of these officials had to observe "the strictest confidentiality with respect to the work that was carried out by said commission," notes the order appointing its members.[15]

The commission worked out of the PICH's main building on General Mackenna Avenue. Two small rooms were fitted out for its use; the detectives worked in one of them, where they began to build up their first archive on human rights, and the advisory team met in the other room.

In ex-director Nelson Mery's words, "That a special group should be created to investigate human rights cases wasn't something that was heartily embraced."

Although the CACI was part of Department V, Luis Henríquez was accountable not to the head of the department but to the director general of the PICH, whose office was located on the second floor. Not even the chief of Department V, José Sotomayor, was told in detail about what the CACI detectives were doing. He felt uncomfortable having a group operating inside his own unit that answered solely to the director general.

Additionally, as Henríquez points out, Sotomayor never liked the fact that Internal Affairs had to take charge of human rights investigations.[16]

"This business of investigating human rights cases provoked resentment on the part of some purists in Internal Affairs, who said that the institutional mission of the department was to watch over internal discipline, not to investigate these cases. The objection at bottom was that we could remain exposed to some accusations," he states.

The element of secrecy was vital. The first thing they did was read and study the Rettig Report from beginning to end. This task would be the rite of initiation for all the detectives who came on board during that special unit's first phase.

They created a file card for each name included in the report and arranged them alphabetically. After that they cross-checked the background information and names with Depinfi's archives and information contributed by other state agencies and organizations.

Moving with alacrity, Toro entrusted this group with a report that dealt with the detectives who were involved in human rights violations. It was based on the study conducted by the PICH legal commission that had examined the Rettig Report to determine what responsibility the PICH had in those crimes.

Toro also convened a meeting of the high command, in which Henríquez participated, to analyze and debate their impressions of the Rettig Report. They covered its methodology, definitions, criteria, and conclusions. In their findings, laid out in a report, they zeroed in on the cases for which the PICH bore direct responsibility and in particular on the nine cases that occurred after 1978, which were not covered by the Amnesty Law.

Director Toro invited attendees to air their reactions.

"Apparently there are many cases in which the Investigations Police are mentioned but in which they play an advisory role, without decision-making authority," offered inspector general Douglas Gallegos, despite the clear indications that the PICH's personnel did in fact have direct responsibility in cases of murder.

For his part, Henríquez expressed his uneasiness over the lack of cooperation by the armed forces and Carabineros in complying with the legal proceedings that were already under way.

"They have even filed some complaints over the involvement of the PICH in these investigations," he added.[17]

This became an ongoing problem for the detectives in the years ahead.

The acronym "CACI" was very rarely used or invoked. On occasion, the team was referred to as the Analysis Commission, but many within the PICH were unaware of its existence. So real was this lack of awareness that the chief of police intelligence himself, prefect Guillermo Mora, still did not know its name almost a year later. In a January 1992 report to the general directorate, the CACI was called the "Rettig Report Coordinating Committee."

"It started out as something quite tiny, almost an object of contempt in the institution," recalls José Plaza, who was added to the CACI in late 1991. "It was a unit within Department V, but it set the foundation for believing there were detectives who could get the job done successfully, that it accomplished what had to be done, and that we were capable of taking on great challenges."

A Lax Police Attitude

While its operation was ongoing, the Rettig Commission sent a total of 210 criminal complaints to different criminal courts with reference primarily to cases of *detenidos desaparecidos*—the disappeared. This term encompassed individuals who were abducted by government agents and subsequently vanished. If, and only if, the families of the disappeared granted permission, the commission turned over to the courts photocopies of all related statements, testimonies, and documentation that might serve as evidence. The families of some victims were unwilling to grant such authorization.

In 1991 there were dozens of judicial cases that had been either stuck, dismissed, closed, or amnestied or had simply languished for years in the courts. The new evidence and data compiled and contributed by the Rettig Commission provided sufficient reasons for reopening or reactivating them, although judges, with few exceptions, continued to take the same stance they had during the dictatorship: conducting superficial investigations that amounted to taking statements from family members and witnesses, followed by applying the statute of limitations or the Amnesty Law, or by transferring cases to the military courts, where they suffered the same fate.

There were some legal cases on missing persons already in court that had been temporarily closed years earlier due to lack of new evidence. These court cases included the original writs of habeas corpus filed at the time of each victim's disappearance.

"This meant that a case from the 1970s, which was opened with such a motion [the writ of habeas corpus] and which had been afforded only a cursory investigation, could be reopened thanks to the new statements made before the Rettig Commission," explains Loreto Meza, a lawyer for the Chilean Human Rights Commission and member of the National Corporation for Reparations and Reconciliation (CNRR), which succeeded the Rettig Commission.

Court orders went to the different police precincts according to their jurisdiction, but some were sent directly to the general directorate of the PICH. In any case, however, the office of the PICH's director had necessarily to be informed about all investigative orders pertaining to human rights cases.

"In this way there was supervisory control exercised over the professional-institutional criteria for complying with those judicial orders. There had to be a particular methodology, quality parameters that would allow for a satisfactory degree of certainty that the substantive objectives of the courts were being fulfilled: to clear up crimes, and to determine the facts surrounding incidents and identify those who participated in these incidents," explains the PICH's legal adviser at the time, Jorge Morales.

The general directorate funneled most of the investigative orders to Department V, beginning a process through which the PICH developed a specialization in human rights that hadn't existed before. Some of the orders were handled by Department V and others by the Homicide Brigade teams, which worked directly with appeals court judges.

"Above anything else, confidentiality was the first priority, because we were not investigating the three little pigs but criminals who were deeply entrenched in the army, with capabilities and structures still in motion," indicates Morales.

As far as expediting the investigations, there was nothing the police could do about how the judges acted. Under the old judicial system they were practically omnipotent with respect to the cases they handled. On the other hand, the PICH *could* try to shake out of their lethargy those detectives who had the duty to comply with orders to investigate.

In February 1991, the PICH's general directorate furnished instructions to its personnel on how to proceed with the court orders, but cases frequently remained in limbo, victims—with a few notable exceptions—of the lax attitude displayed by judges and police officials.

In mid-April, with the CACI now in operation, Director Toro broadened these instructions, ordering that each brigade or police precinct appoint a "suitable, discreet, and competent" officer to comply with the judicial decrees. Those officials needed to get in touch with the members of the CACI to "channel and coordinate strict and effective fulfillment" of the judicial orders.

To that end, the CACI was at the disposition of police officials in Santiago every Tuesday and Thursday between four and six in the afternoon, and for those located outside the capital, contact would be via telephone. In "urgent cases," they could directly approach commission members as needed. The brigade and judicial police precinct chiefs were required to send the CACI copies of all the police reports already dispatched to the courts as well as those to be dispatched from now on, together with any additional information pertaining to human rights investigations. They also had to consult with the Analysis Commission if and when persons presumed responsible for crimes were issued detention orders or subpoenas.[18]

The CACI met twice a week to analyze the police reports that came in from different units across the country and evaluate the progress of investigations. Its members scrutinized the judicial decrees issued by the courts, and the CACI's legal adviser reviewed all of the actions and procedural measures that detectives were taking to see that they conformed to the law.

After one month had passed, it was clear that PICH detectives around the country were dragging their feet while their unit superiors were looking the other way.

Toro returned to the task at hand with renewed determination. In a letter sent to all police prefectures and district chiefs, written in a tone that conveyed his irritation, he lashed out at their inadequate efforts:

> From the review and analysis of some reports already dispatched to the requesting Courts, it has been verified that these contain minimal information, that they do not reflect the capabilities, suitability, and professionalism of the officer complying with those orders, being limited in some cases to interviewing the person reporting the crime, with at times incomplete data from the PICH ID Office, the Technical Assistance Department, and the International Police and the commonly used phrase "and other tasks that did not yield positive results," all of which, in the opinion of this General Directorate, demonstrates laxness and negligence in the performance of investigative duties.

In the letter, Toro insisted that the unit heads order and exercise control over their subordinates in the fulfillment of judicial decrees bearing on human rights cases. He demanded that police reports include the greatest amount of information available once all possible investigative work was exhausted. If police reports continued coming in that showed negligence and a lack of rigor, he warned, the measures to be taken would extend to the detective and the detective's superior.[19]

Toro reiterated these instructions after the creation, in February 1992, of the CNRR. The CNRR was the successor body to the Rettig Commission, and it was tasked with determining the whereabouts of the disappeared as well as of persons who had been executed but whose remains had not been handed over to their families and with continuing to investigate the 641 cases in which the Rettig Commission was unable to reach a definitive conclusion about the precise nature and extent of the violation of the victims' human rights. The corporation had one further vital mission: to provide legal counsel and social assistance to the families of victims recognized by the Rettig Commission.[20]

Director Toro was not through issuing orders. On March 12, 1992, he instructed all PICH unit heads to "offer all possible cooperation" with requests made by the CNRR, and to facilitate that, they were to maintain "constant and permanent contact with the Institutional Analysis and Coordinating Commission so as to furnish uniform and up-to-date information."[21]

And in August 1992, with Nelson Mery now at the command of the plainclothes police, the general directorate instructed all the district precinct chiefs to send information to the CACI on the disappeared persons in their region who had not appeared in the Rettig Report. Mery gave them two weeks to comply with his order.

Around this time the director sent two CACI detectives to speak personally with the Justice Ministry's regional authorities in different parts of the country, to ask for their assistance and update them on the work they were doing. They also capitalized on these visits to meet with the chiefs of local police units. José Plaza traveled to the South and José Luis Cabión, who was absorbed into the CACI midyear, ventured to the North.

"More than anything we went to encourage the detectives themselves, [emphasize] that special importance had to be assigned to this kind of investigation, that they not treat it as though it were just some ordinary thing, [but] must devote more time and urgency to it," states Plaza.

For the PICH's leaders, however, a practical problem also loomed: like the armed forces and the Carabineros, the PICH had destroyed a good part of its documentation bearing on the military dictatorship's machinery of repression. At the same time that Toro was pressing the officials under him to investigate more strenuously, he had to personally inform the courts about the lack of information housed in his own institution. The Ministry of Defense had ordered the general directorate to deliver whatever information it might have concerning the victims, but beyond the data held by the International Police and the Technical Assistance Department, it had little to contribute.

And as he had done with the detectives he criticized for their laxness, Toro again took up his pen and sent a letter to the courts, this time not to admonish but to excuse:

> At the time when the events took place, the Investigations Police complied with the orders issued by the military authority, in line with the powers granted to it by the state of siege under which the country was then living. Accordingly, it is possible that personnel from the institution might have collaborated in checking up on detainees' backgrounds, but owing to the fact that no pertinent documentation exists on the subject, as in accordance

with internal policy enacted during the period prior to this administration it was all incinerated, it becomes impossible to ascertain with any certainty the accuracy of the events referred to.[22]

Taking to the Streets

The investigations proceeded slowly, and resources were few. "We functioned under the most impoverished conditions but were used to that. They gave us the fourth-floor offices, but they had nothing in them—not even furniture. Whatever they tossed out, we picked up for our office," notes then deputy superintendent José Miranda. In a few months, however, with the assistance of the general directorate, Luis Henríquez managed to build up the CACI's infrastructure, add to its staff dedicated to human rights legal cases, and transition the commission to a stage of actual operation from one of mere analysis.

There was a treasure trove of information in the hands of human rights organizations, but the PICH did not have its own archive. During those first months, while the advisory team analyzed the progress being made by police complying with court orders, the detectives spent time collecting information, reviewing media reports, reading pertinent bibliographies, collating and checking facts, requesting information from public institutions and human rights groups, and putting together a Kardex containing everything they managed to compile—in the old-fashioned way: with filing cards and folders. They created a separate file for each criminal court that entertained human rights cases.

They had to start almost from scratch. They analyzed the Rettig Report inside and out to pinpoint and break down where the responsibility for crimes lay institutionally, at least those that were specified by deponents before the Rettig Commission, because in those cases, there was evidence or witness testimony that could document participation by government agents or the military. The Carabineros topped the list, with 577. They were followed by the army, with 527; the DINA, with 339; the CNI, with eighty-three; the air force, with seventy-seven; the PICH, with fifty; and the navy, with twenty-one. There were another 104 victims of combined police, military, and civilian responsibility. There were also other cases for which the responsibility was not clear.

In mid-1991, despite this total number of more than 1,775, there were only ninety-five open cases in the criminal courts at the national level, sixty-two of which belonged to the greater Santiago Metropolitan Region, with the remainder spread across nine other regions of the country.[23]

The CACI had scarcely anything it needed to get its work done: two typewriters "on loan," a four-drawer filing cabinet, 500 hanging folders, two staplers, a paper punch, and other assorted office materials.[24]

It likewise lacked a vehicle. On June 11, 1991, Henríquez asked the director to provide them a car and a driver. They needed these, he said, to speed up their work outside the office. Up to that point, their investigations had not produced the hoped-for results "because of the lack of continuity in them."[25]

In addition to the car and driver, he requested another filing cabinet, a shelf for folders, and a computer, together with a table to put it on, a lamp, and a sofa. Things arrived in a trickle. At the end of June, the first computer was delivered: an ACER 1100 SX, which was set up temporarily in the Police Operations Center. The detectives began to enter the data compiled from the copies of human rights case reports that the police from different units were sending to the courts. The next piece of equipment added to their inventory was a printer.

At the end of July 1991, Henríquez renewed his request for more resources to strengthen the team and inject new energy into the investigations then under way. They needed more furniture and accessories (a larger table for the computer, two armchairs, and two lamps) and additional staff.

The CACI's head man estimated that if they wanted to make progress at this stage, the team had to take on operational work. "The job of analysis requires an operational phase to verify or amplify the information that has been compiled, in order to computerize it," Henríquez emphasized to the director general.[26]

To take the work out onto the streets, more human and material resources were necessary. They could not count on the CACI's advisory contingent, because these officials shared their responsibilities on the commission with the duties they had in their own units. Deputy superintendent José Miranda, for example, was required to deal with situations in the Internal Affairs division; deputy superintendent Sergio Riquelme shared his time between the CACI and the Homicide Brigade; inspector Víctor Pérez was attached to the Financial Crimes Brigade; and inspector Luis Fernández, from the personnel management staff and the commission's go-to person on computer-related issues, was pursuing studies in human resource administration.

To deal successfully with the work ahead looked daunting; it seemed to be coming at them like a great wave that submerged the few resources at the CACI's disposal. Henríquez painted a picture of the situation for Toro. Nearly half a year ago, in February, he told the director, with the information contributed by the Rettig Commission—which was based in turn on an extensive statement by the ex-prisoner turned DINA collaborator Luz Arce—a legal case was opened against DINA agents, in Santiago's First Criminal Court, on the grounds of illegal arrest and unlawful treatment. In Luz Arce's fifty-six-page statement, she singled out six detention centers, eighty-three agents from various security organizations, and seventy-eight detainees.

"If what seemed on its face to be a simple job," Henríquez pointed out, "the complexity of it became evident once on the ground, since all the information had to be verified, numerous obstacles cropped up, including among the affected parties, who had to be approached very delicately to obtain their statements, since they were not normally inclined to be trusting [of the police]."[27]

By then—July 22, 1991—the CACI had met twenty-three times, its detectives had prepared and had on file more than 1,000 cards, and the courts had dispatched 107 investigative orders to a host of district precincts. In addition, the detectives had interviewed thirty-five individuals and identified forty alleged perpetrators of human rights violations.[28]

Ultimately, Henríquez argued, if Director Toro wanted, as he had requested, imminent delivery of the information about detectives involved in those crimes, he and his colleagues needed the resources they had asked for as soon as possible. Henríquez had yet to receive an answer from the CACI's legal office regarding his latest request: they needed a detailed list of human rights judicial cases in which the police were implicated, indicating the court in question, the case number, the officers involved, and the current state of the legal proceedings or sentence being handed down.[29]

In August 1991, the detectives were still getting around on foot. They kept asking every so often to borrow Internal Affairs' vehicle or the one belonging to the office of the inspector general, but these were not always available. Given the nature of the mission entrusted to them, Henríquez made clear to Toro that they couldn't use their own cars.[30]

By the end of the year, the CACI finally had its own vehicle—and the only one it would be given for a long time to come—a brown Chevrolet Monza. One of the institution's drivers, Luis Núñez, was assigned to them. Toro ordered that both the car and the computer were to be used exclusively by the CACI.

Henríquez continued trying to strengthen the team and build up its infrastructure. He requested that two additional members be assigned to the team: the assistant typist Miguel Reinoso and one police official selected from a list of three that he himself proposed. The list consisted of inspector José Plaza, who was detailed to the Las Condes police precinct; inspector Hugo Rebolledo, from downtown Santiago's precinct; and inspector José Gajardo, from the Assaults Investigation Brigade.

"The first team member, José Miranda, had been designated for me by the head of Internal Affairs. But I chose the next one, Hugo Rebolledo, because I had tutored him in the Eighth Precinct of Ñuñoa," relates Henríquez.[31] "I was bringing on detectives who had worked with me, because it was such a delicate business entailing such confidentiality."

Inspector Rebolledo was the first arrival; inspector José Plaza was added to the CACI staff a few months later. They were supplemented by three administrative staff: Patricio Barros, Miguel Reinoso, and Hugo Oteiza. Oteiza came from a police precinct, while Barros and Reinoso had been working in the police intelligence bureau. Barros had valuable experience in processing and archiving data, and Reinoso was a typist for Depinfi. He remained in Department V until his retirement in 2004.

The role of the administrative staff was limited for the most part to inputting data and organizing the CACI's police archive. However, as hands were always in short supply and—ideally—work out on the streets needed to be done in pairs, some staff, such as Reinoso, accompanied the detectives in taking statements and looking for witnesses.

The administrative staff were not police; they had not come through the Investigations School but instead had applied and were admitted directly to the PICH as civilian administrative personnel. Reinoso took this route in 1974 after leaving the Ford Motor Company, whose assembly plant in Casablanca, where he worked in the accounting division, was on the verge of being shut down.

Reinoso came from a working-class family in the San Miguel district in Santiago and graduated from a commercial high school. His father was a worker in the Ford plant, which is how Reinoso got his first job. His mother was a dressmaker but also knew the rudiments of providing first aid, which enabled her to supplement the family budget by going out at night to administer shots to people who needed vaccinations. Reinoso was looking for a more stable job and applied for an administrative position in the PICH. The institution in those days was deeply compromised by its involvement in the campaign of political persecution, but what struck Reinoso even more was its level of corruption.

"My image of the civilian police at that time was that a good many of its employees were taking bribes and kickbacks, and I confirmed that firsthand through a chance situation with my mother in the mid-1960s," says Reinoso.

His first posting was in Depinfi, where he stayed four years, until 1978. From there Reinoso moved to the public relations department, with an intervening year in the Las Condes police district, followed by one more year in the Investigations School. In 1986 he returned to Depinfi, until the CACI called on his services in 1991.

On the Analysis Commission, the three new administrative assistants had the job of entering all the data in the Rettig Report into the computer.

"We had to read the entire report. It was horrifying," says Reinoso.

A Leap of Faith

With this fund of information now computerized, the CACI's detectives had created the plainclothes police's first database on human rights. On the victims' side, it included names, telephone numbers, addresses, aliases, political affiliations, organizational memberships, and any related judicial case histories. On the opposite side—that of members of the military or government agents who participated in executing or "disappearing" people—the information was of a similar nature: personal data, the institution to which they belonged, the detention centers to which they brought people or in which they operated, and judicial proceedings in which they were involved. The detectives began to cross-check the information, map out the apparatus of repression, and connect agents to specific detention centers and the persons they had victimized.

After dozens of cases were reopened thanks to new information provided by the Rettig Commission and the ensuing legal actions brought by families, the CACI's detectives devoted a good part of 1991 to taking statements from witnesses, relatives of victims, and survivors of the military regime's secret detention centers. Dozens of ex–political prisoners—men and women—were invited to make statements.

"The stories they told brought me to tears," recalls Reinoso.

Reading about torture in a report is very different than hearing about it from the person who was subjected to it. I realized that we had lived in a bubble, that what the news showed were pure lies. I remember the case of a woman we interviewed who was from the Santiago district of Estación Central. She had four or five children. The Carabineros showed up at her house because someone ratted on her. They marched her husband onto the patio, tied him up to a tree, and shot him in front of his little ones. These things left me stunned.

To take the step of going to PICH headquarters, a place associated with repression and torture, both the relatives of victims and former political prisoners had to break through a barrier of mistrust. Who were these detectives who just now began to show concern for them? What was their past record? What would all this be good for? Although some placed their faith in a turn toward justice, many victims' relatives had no faith that the investigations would get somewhere. And still fewer trusted the police, who had formed part of the dictatorship's apparatus of repression.

Luis Henríquez had earned a reputation as a detective who had stayed behind in La Moneda on the day of the military coup, but that in itself wasn't enough, nor was he well known within the circle of relatives' groups and human rights organizations.

"A woman, the relative of a victim, once hit me with her handbag," recounts Henríquez. "Why, they reproached us, were we coming around now to investigate after so many years? It was very complicated at the beginning, and we had to turn to human rights lawyers such as Nelson Caucoto. They didn't trust us either at first. We began gaining their confidence later, as things progressed. It was a years-long process."

The police requested help from human rights organizations, such as the Vicariate of Solidarity, the Christian Churches Foundation for Social Assistance, the Committee for the Defense of People's Rights, and the Chilean Human Rights Commission, to help build a bridge to witnesses and survivors of prison and torture. Not many wanted to take this leap of faith. It was one thing to offer a statement and another to work openly and directly with the police. Nelson Caucoto, Sola Sierra—storied leader of the Association of Relatives of the Detained and Disappeared—and former political detainees Erika Hennings and Viviana Uribe were among the few to take this step.

"I wasn't mistrustful of the detectives," relates Hennings. "I felt that they truly wanted to get at the truth. They asked Viviana and me to find and speak with witnesses as a first step, because some felt extreme anger, were mistrusting, were fearful. At that point some treated us like traitors, but those were the consequences we had to endure. I was convinced that we were going to achieve justice."

Hennings had been a political prisoner and was the widow of the Movement of the Revolutionary Left activist and philosophy student Alfonso Chanfreau, who had been kidnapped by the DINA in July 1974. Both were detained in the Londres 38 torture center, and one of the tortures to which they were subjected was to be present as the other was being tortured. They had married very young, at the age of twenty-one or twenty-two, and had a daughter who was only a few months old. Alfonso Chanfreau was taken away and disappeared by DINA agents, and Erika Hennings was transferred to the Tres Álamos detention center. She remained there for three months before her expulsion to France in November 1974. In 1983 she began returning intermittently to Chile, and in 1989, Hennings settled back permanently in the country.

Through successive meetings with other former political prisoners returned from exile, they began to make sense of the experience they had lived through and search for a way of contributing to the cause of truth and justice. They created an informal group called the Witness Survivors Group, composed primarily of former DINA detainees, and organized it around detention centers: Londres 38,

Villa Grimaldi, La Venda Sexy, José Domingo Cañas, and the National Stadium. They shared their recollections, their experiences, and what they knew about other detainees who had not managed to survive. They compared notes, visited the sites, cross-checked information, and between everyone, made up a card for each victim about whom they had some knowledge. They turned over all of this, together with their own testimony, to the Rettig Commission.

These ventures brought Erika Hennings back in touch with Viviana Uribe, a comrade in political activism. They had gotten to know each other in 1974 while both were being held in the Tres Álamos detention center. Viviana was the sister of Bárbara Uribe, who was kidnapped and disappeared in 1974 together with her husband, Edwin Van Yurick. At just twenty years of age, the two were active in the Movement of the Revolutionary Left and had been married for only seven months. Their names appeared on a list of 119 disappeared persons, published in 1975 in Argentinian and Brazilian media outlets, who were supposedly killed because of internal partisan infighting—a scenario, known as Operation Colombo, that was concocted by the DINA to conceal their abduction and disappearance in Chile.

Unable to continue her studies in sociology after the military coup, Viviana Uribe, then a young Movement of the Revolutionary Left activist, was detained in September 1974 by members of the PICH, along with her uncle and one of her sisters. She was held in four detention and torture centers: Cuatro Álamos, José Domingo Cañas, Londres 38, and Tres Álamos. Expelled to Mexico in March 1975, she returned secretly to Chile at the end of 1983. In 1987, when she was able to formally legalize her presence in the country, she began to work with the Committee for the Defense of People's Rights and the Association of Relatives of the Detained and Disappeared.

Both women had seen and known many people who disappeared during their passage through different detention centers, and they wanted to do more than simply file a legal complaint. They firmly believed that it was necessary to go beyond this. It was imperative to speak for those who could not, amass and collate information from the survivors of the torture centers, examine judicial dossiers, investigate how the DINA had been structured, and go after those who bore responsibility for the crimes committed.

Erika Hennings had already gone to the PICH and made a formal statement to Luis Henríquez and José Miranda in the offices of Department V at the end of April 1991, just two weeks after the creation of the CACI. She was one of the first former detainees to do so.

Only a little later, however, both she and Viviana Uribe, as well as the former political prisoner Cecilia Jarpa, were summoned together to PICH headquarters. It was not to have them go through the process again of making a statement. The motive was very different: the police wanted to ask for their help. The meeting with Director Toro, CACI leader Luis Henríquez, and some other detectives and lawyers was purposely low-key, but its informality did not ease the tension.

The women showed up. They were in the grip of uncertainty, in the dark about what the group had in mind for them, and the mere fact of meeting with the PICH was itself a very strange prospect.

"They told us that a team had been set up that would be working in the human rights area and asked us to work with it to gather testimonies, because they knew we were beginning our efforts with the survivors group. Toro explained that the team enjoyed a lot of confidence on the part of the government. We immediately said yes; if it dealt with advancing judicial proceedings we were going to do everything possible to contact people, to convince them to go to the police and make a statement," recalls Uribe.

They divided up their tasks. Once they had left the meeting, the three women fell to talking about the surreal nature of the encounter. It was the first time they had been called to a meeting by people who represented the state, and the police on top of that. To get surviving prisoners to cooperate would not be easy. The element of mistrust persisted for many years.

"Both Viviana and Erika were extraordinarily inquisitive and in addition had an unreserved warmth and friendliness about them," Henríquez recalls. "They were unselfish. I think that they were on a mission to find out the truth about their family members but also about all the other cases, in particular victims from the Movement of the Revolutionary Left."

The cost was steep of laying themselves open, publicly, before the survivors group and, what is more, working with the police. They experienced threats, monitoring, and a lack of understanding on the part of their comrades. The owner of the house whose second floor Hennings rented asked her to leave, because she feared the possibility that "they would come for her." In her new quarters, Hennings regularly received threatening telephone calls, or the telephone rang in the early morning hours and the caller hung up. On one occasion her mother even received a call, with the voice on the line whispering, "You will die, you will die."

"Initially, in 1990, there were fifteen of us in the survivors group, but within a few years we had more than 100 members. We used to meet frequently, and the great leap we managed to make with this group was to get statements made before the courts, something which was considered almost impossible for torture victims or their relatives to do. Sworn testimony began to be an exercise in memory and to have a historical feel to it. Our testimony, the spoken word, narrated before a judge, became an act of enormous reparation. It was a pretty slow and difficult road," says Uribe.

It all started at the beginning of the year with Luz Arce.

4

LIFTING THE VEIL

DEPUTY SUPERINTENDENT José Miranda was continuing to investigate the Sichel and La Cutufa crimes, when in mid-February 1991 he was called on to investigate a complaint involving illegal detention and abusive treatment (*apremios ilegítimos*).[1]

Director Horacio Toro had yet to create the Analysis and Institutional Coordination Commission (CACI), and since the judicial order came into Internal Affairs and had to do with physical abuse—but said little else—he was inclined to think that some Investigations Police (PICH) detective "had gone too far" with a detainee.

What it reflected, however, was that the First Criminal Court had received the testimony that Luz Arce made to the Rettig Commission in October 1990, after which the case landed in the hands of Judge Mario Carroza. Carroza sent the investigative order to the PICH, and the head office referred it to Department V.

In the first days of March 1991, Miranda visited the judge's chambers to find out what this was about.

"This is a very special, very delicate case," the judge explained to him. "It has to do with the Rettig Commission. I'm going to pass on to you a witness's statement."

A court employee made photocopies of Luz Arce's fifty-six-page statement and handed them to Miranda.

"This cannot leak out," Carroza warned him.

The subject of the judge's investigation was the disappearance of three individuals: Edgardo Enríquez Espinoza, María Teresa Eltit Contreras, and María Cristina López. The judge immediately put a gag order on information being released to the media about Arce's testimony, but it got out just the same. Parts of her statement received prominent coverage in several magazines, including the weekly *Hoy*, which put Arce on the cover of its March 24, 1991, issue with the title "Confessions of an Informant."

The deputy superintendent went straight to the head of Department V, José Sotomayor, to let him in on this development, and the two went upstairs together to Toro's office to update the director.

Crossing the Line

Luz Arce was an exceptionally valuable source of information, the key that could open the Pandora's box of the Directorate of National Intelligence (DINA), so for that very reason she was vulnerable to reprisals, a witness with a bull's-eye on her back. In 1972, in the full flush of Allende's Popular Unity government, Arce—an athlete and university student with little notion of politics—began a meteoric rise in the military wing of the Socialist Party. She first worked as a secretary in La Moneda, then a short while later joined the Presidential Security Detachment. From that post she moved on to the party's Cadre School, to groom and instruct its up-and-coming leaders, and later she joined the Special Support Group of the party's central committee, a clandestine operations team.

Arce was detained for the first time in a Santiago soda fountain in March 1974, two weeks before her twenty-sixth birthday. After being seized by the DINA, she was initially taken to Londres 38, a building-cum–secret detention and torture site in the center of the capital that had belonged to the Socialist Party before the military coup. From there she was transferred to the Tejas Verdes prisoners camp, within the army's engineering school in San Antonio—a seaside town in the Valparaíso region. She was subsequently taken back to Londres 38 and after being shot in the foot, spent several months recovering from the wound in the army's military hospital, where she suffered repeated sexual abuse by a male nurse.[2]

Although Arce regained her freedom in July 1974, it lasted no more than a week. Seized a second time by the DINA, her living hell of torture at the hands of that agency included stays in three secret detention centers in the capital: Cuatro Álamos, José Domingo Cañas, and Villa Grimaldi.

It was in this last building that a severely tortured and psychologically broken Luz Arce crossed the line. Through a process of reversal that overtakes some victims of torture, she began to collaborate with her captors. Within a short time, she made the switch from prisoner to agent of repression, participating in the DINA's operations and interrogations, informing on comrades, and sinking into an intimate relationship with the DINA agent Rolf Wenderoth. She was officially hired as a DINA operative in May 1975 and continued working in the state's security agencies until 1980.

In October 1978, with the DINA now dissolved and the majority of its agents transferred into the National Center for Information (CNI), Arce tried to quit her job, but her superiors refused to accept her resignation. Instead, they offered her a second option: that she undertake and fulfill a three-year CNI mission in Argentina. This assignment, however, required her to first spend a year in Uruguay, the purpose of which was "to cut myself off from Chile and evade the actions of the Vicariate [of Solidarity]. In that country I had to secure an identity for myself, and [devise] an infrastructure that would allow me to complete the mission, which was called Operation Celeste."[3]

One of the DINA's agents, Manuel Provis, brought her to a cemetery to find the grave of some deceased woman so Arce could adopt her name and identity, but it didn't work out. Provis then told her to take the name of a housekeeper, Mariana del Carmen Burgos, and Luz Arce proceeded to travel to Uruguay under that name in February 1979. She boarded a LAN Chile flight carrying US$3,000 in her handbag and entered the country posing as a tourist. Arce settled down in Montevideo, obtained her temporary residence status, and opened a bank account in dollars, into which the CNI began to make monthly deposits of US$350. She stayed in Montevideo until October of that year, when she returned to Chile and again asked to resign from the state's clandestine security service. Her request was granted in March 1980.

Luz Arce spent a good many years fleeing from the police, the courts, and the Vicariate of Solidarity, which in the 1970s was already trying to locate her as part of its efforts to gather information. In May 1982, now out of the CNI and trying to lead a normal family life, Arce was notified by a state security agency official that the PICH was out looking for her to bring her to court. The CNI's official policy was to deny her existence.

Arce dove into a secret life. She was also escaping from herself. In the final years of the dictatorship, thanks to the help some people gave her and a recently discovered Christian faith, she began to face her past, to recognize the Luz Arce who ceased to exist in 1974 and plan a future for herself. And that meant revisiting and acknowledging everything, even the most humiliating, most horrifying parts of her life as a secret agent. She set out to write down all that she remembered and in October 1990 recounted it to the Rettig Commission. However, it wasn't of her own initiative. She was approached by one of the commission's lawyers, who managed to convince her to take this step. Her testimony lasted several days.

One of Arce's most valuable contributions was to present the commission with an organizational chart of the DINA and the full names of its top officials. She identified forty-seven agents who came from the army, seven from the Carabineros, four from the PICH—with last names only for the latter—and one from the navy. The great majority were still in active service.

In addition, Arce identified fourteen civilian agents. These included Osvaldo Romo—one of the DINA's most notorious torturers, whose brutality was described by numerous political prisoners—as well as two political detainees, Marcia "Skinny Alejandra" Merino and María Alicia "Carola" Uribe, who, like her, turned into DINA agents. Merino also testified before the commission.

Arce also provided the commission with the names of professionals who had collaborated with the DINA: five physicians—among them Patricio Silva—and six lawyers, including Miguel Ángel Poblete, who facilitated the transfer of properties to both the DINA and the CNI, and Guido Poli, who served as one of the army legal department's contacts with the PICH and the courts.[4]

Finally, Arce explained to the commission how the different detention centers operated and told them as much as she could about other detainees, both those who survived and those who had died or been disappeared.

Deputy Superintendent Miranda now faced a mountain of intersecting work. He needed to confirm the statements that Arce made to the commission, and he had to pursue the multiple trails and investigative angles that her testimony opened up. This required looking for the persons whom Arce had identified as political prisoners, looking for the relatives of victims and other witnesses and interviewing them, sorting out, bit by bit, the history of each torture center and each agent she had identified, and pulling together as much background information as possible about the dozens of documented victims or about those known to have been kept in the various detention centers. Although much of this information was in the hands of human rights organizations and contained in hundreds of habeas corpus appeals going back many years, Miranda now faced the task of cross-checking everything, then formalizing all this new evidence, and finally channeling it into the courts.

Accounting only for what Luz Arce had furnished the Rettig Commission, this work implied, as a start, isolating, locating, and interviewing at least 150 people.

"I knew already from seeing some of the names [mentioned] in her testimony just where I was going to be able to go with the investigation," Miranda recalls.

Before anything else, the PICH deputy superintendent needed to be acquainted with Luz Arce's complete, original statement to the commission, because the one delivered to the courts was a summary version.

And after that he had to meet her.

The detective decided to ask the Vicariate of Solidarity for its help. He wanted to find out who on the Rettig Commission took Luz Arce's statement. He was made to wait two hours, seated on a wooden bench in front of a large window. It was Miranda's first experience being inside the Vicariate, which was located at 444 Plaza de Armas, next to Santiago's main cathedral.

"And who are you?" Héctor Contreras, the lawyer from the Vicariate's legal department, asked him.

"I'm Deputy Superintendent Miranda from Investigations," the detective replied, showing Contreras his badge and investigative order. He explained to the lawyer what had brought him there.

"OK, I'm going to confirm it. Come back the day after tomorrow at three in the afternoon."

Miranda found out afterward that the Vicariate placed a call to the PICH's general directorate. It was hardly customary for a police official to pass through the corridors of the Vicariate. The PICH's legal adviser, Jorge Morales, acted as a liaison to the Vicariate, where he had recently worked for several years.

"I knew what could and could not be asked for and how to ask for it, within the protective boundaries that the Vicariate had to maintain around the information it held. From a detective's vantage point, this collaboration was insufficient at times, and access to certain things could not be gained because of the protection that the Vicariate maintained, but its collaboration was always good," Morales affirms.

Director Toro told them that Miranda was trustworthy and asked that they help him. A pattern was established: whenever a detective went to the Vicariate to request information, its lawyers checked with Toro.

"It was entirely justifiable and understandable and did not bother me in the least. To earn [their] confidence was a lengthy process, hard and difficult, and that's how it had to be," recalls Miranda.

When Miranda returned to the Vicariate, Héctor Contreras informed him that the person who had interviewed Arce and taken her statement was Jorge Correa, a lawyer from the Christian Democratic Party who worked in La Moneda. Correa, who served as secretary for the Rettig Commission, received him in the presidential palace right away. The verdict: Miranda could not have access to the original testimony.

"So where is Luz Arce now?" the deputy superintendent asked him.

"She's in Austria."

Miranda went back to Department V and updated his chief. They both understood that the road ahead would be an uphill struggle. They had no experience in this kind of case; there were few resources or personnel to call on, and they knew they would be given little help.

A Paper Album

In December 1990 Luz Arce was notified that she needed to appear and testify before Judge Gloria Olivares, who was investigating the disappearance of Alfonso Chanfreau. The Chanfreau case had been dismissed in 1980 and reopened in 1990. Although she knew she would be treated like a traitor, like a DINA agent, Arce nonetheless asked for help from the lawyer Carlos Fresno, a member of the Rettig Commission, appealing to him to put her in touch with Erika Hennings, Chanfreau's widow. She had seen the two in detention in Londres 38. Hennings agreed to Arce's overture.

"I hadn't seen her since I was a prisoner," says Hennings. "Luz wanted to speak with me to request a favor: that I go and speak with the judge to prevail on her to take [Luz's] testimony as discreetly as possible, so she wouldn't be exposed and could afterward leave the country."

They met by themselves while Viviana Uribe waited for her friend Erika in the latter's home. Hennings proposed to Arce that they continue the conversation where she lived. The stage was set for Luz Arce to begin working with former DINA political prisoners to investigate the agency. The two women—Hennings and Uribe—were spurred on by the urgent need to know the truth about their disappeared relatives.

"We were investigating, providing testimony, responding, and filling notebooks about everything she was telling us. It was a very powerful experience. I had seen her in detention in Londres 38, badly tortured. I had the expectation, the belief, the hope that she knew much more about the disappeared, that she was going to reveal a lot to us. There were people who got extremely upset with us because we spoke with Luz Arce," Hennings recalls.

After testifying before Judge Olivares on January 9, 1991, Arce decided to leave the country. Not only had she exposed herself to possible reprisals on the part of her former tormentors, but her life was now taking a new turn; she was confronting herself anew. Hennings and Uribe got the money together to pay for her tickets and also arranged contacts abroad so there were people to receive her.

"Their acceptance [of me] was like a freely granted pardon," Arce wrote in her memoirs about them. She was forever grateful.[5]

On January 15, 1991, Fresno, Hennings, and Uribe took her to the airport. On the road, while in the car, Arce affixed her signature to each sheet of her testimony before the Rettig Commission and authorized the document to be given to the courts. She boarded an Iberia Airlines flight to Europe with her two sons, aged twenty-one and seven. Arce settled down in Vienna, Austria.

Some weeks later Deputy Superintendent Miranda took to Santiago's streets in search of her relatives. The testimony that Arce gave Judge Carroza included an address in the northern Santiago district of Recoleta, where she had lived with her partner, Juan Manuel Espiñeira.

Miranda found him in his apartment.

"She took off and I don't have any contact with her," Espiñeira told him.

"None?"

"[That's right], none."

Before leaving, Miranda slapped him with a summons to come to Department V at the beginning of March 1991. He didn't put much stock in what Espiñeira told him. He *has* to know, Miranda thought. They must communicate in some way, especially if they have a young child in common. He was entirely correct. Time and physical distance had brought the couple even closer together. Espiñeira left Chile that same year to meet her in Austria, and they got married.

Miranda then went in search of her immediate family: her younger brother, Enrique Arce; her father, also named Enrique and retired from the state railway company; and her mother, Ada Sandoval. He also interviewed Rafael Riveros, a businessman who lived in the upscale Las Condes district, to whom Arce had been briefly married at the end of the 1960s.

Meanwhile, Miranda poured over the details of Luz Arce's testimony before the Rettig Commission. He tried to confirm who, exactly, had detained her, but the Carabineros responded to his inquiry by telling him that information about staff in police units in 1973 no longer existed.

Miranda had his doubts about Luz Arce—not about what she had lived through but about the slant to the information she gave the Rettig Commission.

In her account, Arce gave the impression that it was she who controlled the course of the interview. Miranda found her to be very shrewd. In his first police report to the court in July 1991, the deputy superintendent commented that it seemed to him that Luz Arce had manipulated the members of the commission to see things her own way, and that—for all their good intentions—they lacked experience conducting investigations.

In addition, he added, having been a DINA agent, Arce had to know who her captors were in 1974; Miranda found it suspicious that she might not be able to identify them.

"Any person in those circumstances, and with the relationship she had with the DINA's top leadership, could have found out the rest," Miranda wrote in his police report.[6]

The detective probably underestimated the long-lasting psychological and emotional effect of Arce's torture and submission and how each person reacts to such conditions differently. He may not have taken into account the subjugation and dependency to which Luz Arce was reduced with respect to her DINA captors. There was no way he could understand it; it was all still very new to him.

Miranda tracked down the former political prisoners whom Arce said she had seen in different detention centers. In parallel, he also compiled a list with the names of everyone—from all branches of the armed forces and the PICH, as well as civilian agents—whom she had mentioned as having participated in the torture of detainees. He checked and confirmed their identities in the ID database and searched for data on them in other institutional sources.

Miranda also secured photos of them and put together an album with loose sheets of paper. He pasted three photos on each sheet and drew a frame around each one with a black marker. Each photo had a number associated with that person's data. This was the PICH's first mug shot album of human rights violators.

Just Office Work

Miranda started by issuing summonses to those close at hand: officials from the PICH who had been on assignment with the DINA. Luz Arce had named four people in this category. One was untraceable because his last name, Brindizzi, did not turn up anywhere in the personnel records of the plainclothes police.

"Detective Bustamante" turned out to be deputy superintendent Juan Fernando Bustamante, chief of the Temuco police district. He provided a statement on March 13, 1991. In either 1974 or 1975, Bustamante declared, he had been detailed to the Executive National Secretariat of Prisoners, whose headquarters were in the closed National Congress building, to work in its archive. During the first half of 1976, the DINA's second-in-command, Pedro Espinoza, informed him that the Executive National Secretariat of Prisoners archive was being moved to the DINA's headquarters, so he had to move with it "in order to instruct those newly in charge of maintaining it."

Bustamante duly settled into the DINA's main offices, located at 11 Belgrano Street, to work in its confidential archive. During the following year, 1977, he took a six-month course in basic intelligence work at the National Intelligence School, which the DINA ran in Santiago's district of Maipú. A year later, he returned to the PICH's Homicide Brigade. Bustamante stated that he did nothing but "office work" and never participated in operational units.

"I have no knowledge of operational units and personnel, because due to [the policy of] compartmentalization nobody knew what could happen outside of his own office," Bustamante testified.[7]

Another detective in service to the DINA, with the surname Fieldhouse, could—as it happened—be one of two brothers, both police officials, Juan and

Eugenio Fieldhouse. At this time, Juan Fieldhouse, who had the rank of prefect, was chief of the metropolitan region's Third Police District and between March and August 1990 served as the liaison between the Ministry of Interior and the PICH. On March 19, 1991, he showed up for his appointment with Deputy Superintendent Miranda in the Internal Affairs office without causing problems of any kind. The matter at hand had nothing to do with him; he had never "been on assignment" with the DINA, but his brother, on the other hand, had.

The following day it was Eugenio Fieldhouse's turn to be interviewed. He admitted to being in the DINA from mid-1974 until 1978 but—like everyone else—only in the capacity of "fulfilling administrative duties in the offices of the chief of staff."

At first, he said, he worked in the DINA's archive and later for the agency's chief of staff in the Villa Grimaldi torture center. His work there fell under the orders of one of the principal leaders, Maj. Rolf Wenderoth, "whose functions," Fieldhouse stated, "were solely administrative, related in general to documentation."

With respect to Luz Arce, he added, "I knew of her collaborating with the DINA, specifically in the top staff's offices, where she looked at documents and dealt directly with Wenderoth."

Fieldhouse further stated that he had not participated in either detentions or operational missions, never saw the prisoners, did not know about abusive treatment, and worked typical office hours.[8]

A few days later "Jiménez," a police official already in retirement, made his appearance. The man in question was Nibaldo Jiménez, who in 1974 was assigned to the José Domingo Cañas torture center "to work in the archive and also serve in an advisory capacity on police-related matters," according to the statement he made to Deputy Superintendent Miranda. He never participated in operations or interrogations, and his work was solely office based, Jiménez stated. He knew Luz Arce and described her as "quite intelligent and having an abnormal personality, like a pathological liar, well-educated, bright, with a highly developed imagination."[9]

In keeping with the time-honored practice, they all swore they carried out nothing more than administrative tasks in the DINA's offices.

The army and the Carabineros declined to collaborate, taking the position that they would only hand over data and information directly to the courts, if requested.

"The army never collaborated on anything. They invariably sent official letters with a negative response," states Henríquez.

Via official letter the CACI contacted the military hospital to confirm whether the doctors Arce named in her testimony had worked in the facility. It also requested the report on the medical treatment she received there in 1974 for the gunshot wound in her foot.

The then director of the hospital, however, Atiliano Jara, said that any reply had to come from the army's general staff, which predictably did not comply with the request, at least not by the time Miranda delivered his first police report in July 1991. The medical report was also off-limits, unless requested directly by the court.

One of the doctors identified by Arce as the specialist who treated DINA agents for alcoholism, Roberto Lailhacar, did not obey the summons he received to appear at Department V, because he was too busy with his private practice and his classes at the university. A psychiatrist, Lailhacar served as deputy chief of the DINA's Department of Psychological Operations; there is testimony that he tried to hypnotize prisoners. At the end of the 1990s, he was president of the Chilean Society of Sexology and Sexual Education and maintained a private practice in one of the capital's wealthiest neighborhoods.[10]

The lawyers who were tied to the DINA refused to speak with the police.

A Religious Analyst

At this stage, Miranda's efforts to confirm the ranks and current circumstances of alleged perpetrators of torture were only minimally successful. Furthermore, out of the ten or so agents he did find, the number he managed to interview was even smaller. Among them was Ingrid Olderock, a retired major in the Carabineros and former DINA agent.

Simply locating her was an all-consuming job because her addresses in the civil registry corresponded to military units. He finally verified that she lived at 347 Coventry Street, in a house in the capital's Ñuñoa district.

On April 17, 1991, the deputy superintendent rang her doorbell. A woman of stout bearing and curt manners opened it, and several dachshunds came running out. She let him into the house.

Ingrid Olderock was a sadistic DINA agent of German origin who had used dogs to torture and rape prisoners, both men and women. She lived alone. The two seated themselves on armchairs and began to converse about her past and Luz Arce's testimony about her.

"Luz Arce: Was she or was she not a DINA agent?" Miranda asked her.

"Yes, she was. Incidentally, I have a notebook with a list of women who applied to be DINA agents," she told him.

"I'm going to serve you a summons to Investigations Police quarters so that you'll come in on your own and bring the notebook. How about tomorrow morning?"

"Agreed."

Olderock showed up at Department V first thing in the morning on April 18, 1991. She carried the notebook with her and handed it to the detectives so they could photocopy it.

"She told me that she was in the first graduating class of the Carabineros' School for Women, that she spent time around Colonia Dignidad; she ranged over several topics. She told me about the 1981 attempt on her life,[11] convinced that General Mendoza had ordered her killed.[12] And per the usual, as happened with all the agents I interviewed—every last one—she claimed she did only office work. I knew of the cruelty she inflicted by using dogs; I already knew that she was evil," Miranda recalls.

They spent almost the entire day at PICH headquarters. Olderock told Miranda that she had been assigned to the DINA in October 1973, when the organization was just taking shape in the offices of the army's War Academy. Then Col. Manuel Contreras had ordered her to bring a group of women together, in the exclusive Rocas de Santo Domingo seaside resort, to take a course in intelligence work. She chose sixty names from a list of applicants who had been rejected by the Carabineros' school and recruited them for the DINA.

"Their relatives later came to me and told me that these women had had children out of wedlock, were violent, and had changed completely," Olderock added in her statement.[13] Almost all of them were around twenty years of age.

In 1975 she became attached to the DINA's Purén Brigade in Villa Grimaldi where—according to her—she analyzed religious documentation: books, pamphlets, magazines, and letters that were removed, she said, "in a completely illegal way" by the DINA from the offices of the Chilean postal service. Dark-colored sacks, full of letters and packages, arrived in Villa Grimaldi with the logo of the Chilean post office stamped on them. There the agents distributed the material according to its subject matter; they analyzed the contents and prepared reports on the opinions and information expressed or passed along by those who had mailed the items. Olderock worked a regular office schedule, 8:30 A.M. to 5:30 P.M., using the alias Miriam Ayala, she said. Her boss was the army major Raúl Iturriaga.

She witnessed the physical torture of women, men, and children, she claimed, "involuntarily." She described in detail for Miranda how the agent Marcelo Moren tortured a man of some forty years of age, how she heard the screams of women who were beaten and tortured with electrical current, and how the DINA kept three or four children, who were no more than ten or eleven years old and whose eyes had been covered with adhesive tape, in a darkened room.

The children "were beaten by hand and with chains, sticks, or whatever there was, so that their parents could hear them crying and [consequently] would blab," Olderock said. "I couldn't do anything about it, so I just went home."[14]

One day, Olderock related, the Carabineros lieutenant Ricardo Lawrence came in spitting curses because he had poured boiling oil into a prisoner's mouth and the man was dying on him. Lawrence was enraged because he couldn't keep interrogating him and threatened an army doctor with death in order to force him to revive the prisoner. When he had the chance, the doctor, out of fear, jumped over the Villa Grimaldi's wall to escape, Olderock added.

According to the ex-torturer, Luz Arce was a DINA collaborator-agent, put in charge of interrogating detainees in the right wing of the detention center with Moren. Both tried to administer hypnosis on prisoners, she said. She also assured Miranda that she wasn't present at the death of any detainees and did not know the fate of any of the disappeared. As for the twenty-three prisoners named by Luz Arce who were in Villa Grimaldi, Olderock claimed not to know anything about them, neither who they were nor where they might be found.

Olderock remained with the DINA until 1976, engaged solely in administrative or analytical work, she stated. She did admit, however, to having traveled—on every occasion for the DINA—to Peru, France, Italy, and Spain. The purpose of those trips, she explained, was to pin down the location of Chilean "activists" whom the DINA "had to assassinate."

In 1978 she was assigned to the Air Force Intelligence Directorate (DIFA) and later to the Carabineros Communications Directorate until her retirement in 1981, after the attempt on her life.

By then, Olderock wanted to desert and travel to Germany and toward that end was in conversation with a German nun, with whom she had been put in touch through the psychologist who was treating her.[15]

She steadfastly denied interrogating or torturing a single person in any of the three organizations in which she served: the DINA, the DIFA, and the Carabineros Communications Directorate. Her work was always administrative, never operational, she claimed.

Ingrid Olderock forgot to mention the tour of duty she carried out, in 1974, in La Venda Sexy, a secret detention center located in Ñuñoa where the principal method of torture was sexual violence, hence its name. She was known in this place for torturing prisoners in its basement with a dog named Volodia, whom she had trained to sexually assault people.

According to Miranda, despite not conceding that she bore any responsibility of her own for these criminal actions, Olderock was the only person who gave him useful information, information that allowed him to widen his search for the agents of state repression. She identified certain agents, implicating them in acts of torture; described the techniques of torture they used; and spoke about how the DINA maintained a toehold, including its own interrogation quarters, in Colonia Dignidad.

Olderock had mentioned another DINA agent, Irma Guareschi, with whom she traveled abroad. Miranda confirmed that Olderock took trips to Spain, Peru, Panama, and France between 1974 and 1975 and that Guareschi traveled, on DINA and CNI missions, to Peru, Brazil, Argentina, and Ecuador between 1974 and 1990. They also took trips as tourists. Olderock gave the detective a black-and-white photo of the two women, taken in 1975 by another DINA agent, as they visited some ruins in Italy. This was the same year in which the exiled Chilean Christian Democratic leader, Bernardo Leighton, was targeted for assassination (and seriously wounded) in Rome by the DINA.

Miranda paid a visit to Guareschi's house in the Las Condes neighborhood but did not find her at home. He left a summons for her to appear in Department V. Although she failed to show up on the appointed day, an army lawyer, Rodrigo González, did—sent, he said, by the commander of the army prosecutor's office. He wanted to know why they were calling in Guareschi, who—it turned out—was an active service captain in the army and former member of the DINA's counterintelligence unit. Miranda posed a simple question, asking the lawyer to confirm whether she had been a DINA agent, as Olderock had testified.

The army never supplied an answer.

Ingrid Olderock returned to the PICH in November 1991 to make further statements, and she repeated this formality many times in connection with different human rights cases up to her death in 2001. Her DINA colleagues and superiors were also compelled to testify before the PICH starting in 1992, but none claimed to have the slightest knowledge about anything.

"I Have Another Life"

It took the plainclothes police considerable time to locate and approach the relatives of the victims Luz Arce had identified. They paid visits to the old addresses but, in some cases, family members no longer lived there. Instead, there were new owners or renters who knew nothing about the past occupants; in other cases, the address was incorrect or did not exist; in still others, people were unwilling or reluctant to talk. In those days, a detective knocking on the door to ask questions about a disappeared loved one was something to be feared, or at least it raised suspicions.

Miranda managed to track down certain families, and in some instances he requested third parties to intercede and help him by inviting relatives to come to the PICH building to offer testimony. By the time he delivered his report to Judge Mario Carroza on July 1, 1991, after asking for two postponements, very few witnesses or relatives of the victims had provided testimony.

Those who did amounted to no more than a handful. In the meantime, Erika Hennings and Viviana Uribe had written a letter to Skinny Alejandra and left a telephone number where she could call them. Quite a bit of time went by, but she finally answered Erika, who had signed the letter. The two women got together.

"It was difficult. She didn't admit to much. I think she was very frightened. That was the first go-around; later it would be before the courts," Hennings recalls.

Hennings and Uribe had decided to approach people such as Luz Arce and Skinny Alejandra, bearing up under the criticisms and hostility of other former prisoners and their relatives. But it was a window of opportunity that pointed toward the DINA, a way of getting a hold of fragments of the truth.

"The survivors and the human rights organizations all but pronounced judgment on us as if it were the Nuremberg trials," Uribe remembers. "They indicted us for going to the extreme of having spoken with these collaborators, these 'traitors.' But we felt that it was what lay within our power to do."

Miranda also managed to find Marcia Merino Vega, known as Skinny Alejandra, and who also—like Luz Arce—went from being a victim of torture to informer to DINA agent.

Skinny Alejandra became politically active in the Movement of the Revolutionary Left (MIR) while a student at the University of Concepción at the end of the 1960s. In May 1974 she was detained in Santiago and in due course imprisoned in Londres 38, where she got to know Luz Arce. Later, she was taken to the Cuatro Álamos and José Domingo Cañas torture centers and then, finally, to Villa Grimaldi. She began early on to turn over information, collaborating not only by informing on her comrades but—under duress—by accompanying her captors on operations to detain them.

Broken as they were both physically and psychologically, Marcia Merino, Luz Arce, and María Alicia Uribe—whom Merino delivered into the hands of the DINA—lost little time in living a day-to-day life as part of the state's machinery of repression. At first, they occupied a small cabin on the grounds of Villa

Grimaldi, separated from the rest of the prisoners. In time they shared an apartment rented by the DINA in downtown Santiago. By 1976 they were working in the DINA's main quarters on Belgrano Street.

Three years later, when Skinny Alejandra's superiors told her that the MIR was planning to execute her, the CNI paid for her to have plastic surgery in Santiago's Santa María Clinic. The agency then sent her to Arica, in the far North, to hide out. It maintained her in Arica, placing her under the charge of one of its agents. As 1978 came to a close, Merino returned to Santiago, to her mother's house, and—in her words—cut herself off completely from the CNI.

Miranda checked first with her mother about her whereabouts, but her mother shrank from offering any help. He continued making inquiries and learned that Merino had a partner from Easter Island and that they lived on Republic Street, in Santiago. After some effort, he found the residence.

It was three in the afternoon on a day in early April when the deputy superintendent knocked on her door. Marcia Merino opened it and Miranda told her who he was. Skinny Alejandra broke into tears.

"How did you find me?" she asked him.

"Look, I need to interview you," Miranda explained. "Sooner or later, you are going to have to do this."

"It's [just] that I have another life now."

The detective convinced her to come to the PICH's main building the following day. So on April 3, 1991, Skinny Alejandra showed up to testify at length in an office of Department V. She was accompanied by her partner, who seemed upset. They spent the entire day in the building and had lunch at the desk.

"I want to get this over with soon," said Merino, once she had signed the seventeen sheets of her statement to the police.

Miranda was not able to interview María Alicia Uribe, also known as Carola. She was still working for the Army Intelligence Directorate and was protected by the institution. Carola never expressed any regrets or attempted at any time to abandon the ranks. Whenever the CACI's detectives went to the army's legal department offices to summon her to testify, they were told that the court needed to request her appearance directly from the chief of the army's general staff. Uribe retired as a civilian employee in 2000, not once having contributed toward establishing the truth or securing justice for the atrocities that occurred in Chile.

The detectives were still getting around on foot, or in cars borrowed from other PICH units, or by taxi and hopping buses. It was during this period that the CACI's chief began making requests for a computer. The information they accumulated could no longer be handled purely with cards and a filing cabinet.

The computer, in fact, was set up in the CACI's offices just days after Miranda delivered his police report to Judge Carroza. Delivery of their vehicle was delayed a few more months.

In the main, Chileans were quite removed from these affairs. A July 1991 survey conducted by the company CEP-Adimark indicated that only 11.16 percent of the population was concerned with the government's efforts in the area of human rights. Out of twelve issues of public interest included in the study, human rights came in next to last. The principal problem on which the respondents wanted to see the government focus more attention was, by far, crime—which registered at 61.2 percent.

For months, through the press, the opposition on the Right had been stirring up a false sense of insecurity in the country, making out criminal behavior to be worse than it was and accusing the government of being soft on acts of political violence or "terrorism." This push notwithstanding, beginning in 1990 the PICH's own reports recorded a strong drop in incidents of arson and assaults using explosives and in armed attacks and confrontations carried out by leftist paramilitary organizations.

Confessing All

To this point, the detectives had managed to identify and interview former political prisoners who remembered seeing Luz Arce in torture centers. They had also managed to identify the majority of the people imprisoned by the DINA whom she had mentioned. In addition, they had identified a significant number of the DINA's agents from different military and civilian institutions and confirmed that Luz Arce employed at least five false names while a member of the DINA. They knew a great deal about her life story and her DINA and CNI experiences, but a critical piece was missing: they had yet to make contact with Arce herself.

José Miranda decided to speak again with the Ministry of Justice lawyer, Jorge Correa Sutil. He needed to take a firsthand statement from Luz Arce and asked Correa to help him. Eventually, through intermediaries, Arce requested that they send her a list of questions. Miranda composed approximately twenty-five questions about her political activities and her experience in the DINA.

The police, government authorities, former political prisoners, and human rights lawyers collaborated to have Luz Arce return to Chile to provide testimony and contribute to the PICH's investigations. Arce proposed a meeting in Vienna, where she lived with her two sons, but this idea was quickly rejected. The plainclothes police had few resources to finance assignments abroad, though just a year later policy changed, and such work became more customary. Another idea was to have each party travel to Mendoza, Argentina, where the detectives would meet Arce and interview her. In the end, she agreed to make the trip to Chile on two conditions: that no one (outside of the tight inner circle) learn of her decision and that she receive maximum security protection. In January 1992 Miranda went to the airport to pick her up.

"The only thing she wanted was that nobody find out," Miranda stresses. "She did not want to run into anyone from the CNI or the DINA who might get their hands on her. With help from the head of the International Police at the airport, they allowed me to take a van onto the tarmac—jetways for airplanes were still not in use—and I waited for her at the foot of the plane."

"Señora Luz Arce, how are you? I'm deputy superintendent José Miranda."

He showed her his badge and quickly swept her away from the airport, without leaving any record of her arrival.

"She knew that if military intelligence learned that she had come back to Chile they would kill her," states former CACI chief Luis Henríquez.

There was an outstanding order to detain Arce, so arrangements were made with a judge to enable the police to admit her into the country without having to oblige the law and arrest her upon arrival, notes Henríquez.

For security reasons, Miranda took her to a PICH guesthouse in the district of Ñuñoa, where they housed visitors or police personnel who came from outlying regions. Arce was alone there. She had come to Chile with her younger son, whom she left in her father's care while she remained for approximately ten days under the protection of the PICH. They visited her on a regular basis in the guesthouse.

Every day, first thing in the morning, the detectives would show up to bring her to PICH headquarters. On Luz Arce's initial encounter with Superintendent Henríquez, she said to him, "I know you."

Initially, he had no memory of her but later realized they had seen each other in the presidential palace during the time of Allende's government and in Allende's private residence on Tomás Moro Avenue. Henríquez had been serving as the PICH's security detachment, and she had belonged to the president's personal security detail known informally as the Personal Friends Group.

The sessions with Luz Arce—reviewing her testimony line by line, stripping information down to its exact details, and probing more deeply into different aspects of her case—were exhausting. They spent entire days in the building, working until nightfall. Before the sessions were over, the detectives had used numerous cassette tapes to record them, and Arce had drawn an organizational chart of the DINA.

"She [opened up and] spoke about everything. The good, the bad. All that happened to her. The torture. How she was made to snitch on people. Everything," Henríquez underscores.

Her contact with the plainclothes police "has come as a pleasant surprise for me," Arce wrote two years later in her book, *El infierno*. "After years of fleeing from the police, today I can appreciate the officers I've come to know, and I believe that their contribution will be decisive in some day establishing the truth of what took place," she added.[16]

After her sessions with the police concluded, Luz Arce emerged publicly by going to court. Her first sworn testimony occurred in February 1992 before Judge Mario Carroza and lasted five hours. She recounted everything for the press as well, not even omitting her love affair with Wenderoth. She no longer had anything to lose.

"I'm not leaving. I'm going to tell everything that I have to," she said to a dozen journalists who were waiting for her outside Carroza's chambers.[17] Arce acknowledged that though it brought her a great deal of sorrow and pain, "everything" she knew did not include the location of the disappeared.

On the following day, Saturday, she spent another two hours testifying. On Monday, three more, and on Wednesday, as many again. She moved about with police protection.

Over the days and weeks to come, Arce testified time and again before different judges who were investigating cases that involved people who had been detained by the DINA and then disappeared, including—again—the Chanfreau case. She also provided testimony concerning the DINA's role in the murder of Orlando Letelier. At times she made an appearance in one office and later entered another in the space of a single day.

The CACI began to issue summonses for the DINA agents she identified, but few of them showed up. For the most part, they refused to speak with the police. They would only do so—if at all—in front of a judge. The DINA's former leaders put off their appointments, invented reasons to excuse themselves, and when no other way out remained, simply lied.

The appearances that Luz Arce and Marcia Merino made to offer testimony, both in the PICH's Department V and before different criminal courts, regarding victims of human rights abuses were spread over not just months but years. Moreover, they were forced to come face to face multiple times with their DINA handlers and the agents who had tortured them.

In Luz Arce's case, the encounter she had in October 1992 with Miguel Krassnoff, one of her principal torturers, was perhaps one of the most intense. Krassnoff was insolent toward her and courteous with the judge, Gloria Olivares, who was investigating the kidnapping of Alfonso Chanfreau. Arce's body doubled over, automatically, in the same way it had after he tortured her.

"Without my realizing it, the mere presence of that man made me bend down into a quasi-fetal position, inclined forward, looking for a bit of warmth to ease the physical and mental pain," Arce wrote.[18]

In 1992 alone, Arce relates in her book, she participated in sixty-three judicial proceedings in connection with different cases.

"The two [Luz Arce and Marcia Merino] provided testimony in almost 1,500 proceedings," says Viviana Uribe. "Luz herself gave me this figure. I asked her once, 'How can that number be possible?' She told me: 'If you add it up, it's three years, and between the two of us we were providing testimony almost every day.'" Even as they collaborated with the PICH, they also appeared in one court or another day in and day out.

Both former DINA members had to undergo prolonged psychiatric treatments. There were several years when they declined to participate in some judicial proceedings on medical grounds. Dr. Paz Rojas, who had built a distinguished career in attending to victims of human rights abuses, and Dr. Luis Peebles, himself a survivor of atrocious torture in Colonia Dignidad, treated them unselfishly, nonjudgmentally, looking past their treason to deal with its consequences.

"The starting point was here, with Luz Arce," Miranda says. "For eight months, I worked from seven in the morning until one the [next] morning. I went door to door, issuing summonses to everyone mentioned in Luz Arce's testimony. It was exhausting, but I kept thinking about the victims and their families who were waiting for answers. I bought every newspaper every day. I made a copy of everything, so that no one could later say that this didn't happen."

"White Fang" Is Taken to the PICH

On a day that Deputy Superintendent Miranda had summoned a retired army colonel to appear in the offices of Department V, he detected that military officials were recording all his interviews. Every few minutes, as the officer asked Miranda to repeat his questions, he would adopt an odd physical posture and carefully emphasize and go back over certain points.

Miranda decided not to confront him with his suspicions, but he made it difficult for future agents. He moved the interviews to a room in the basement that had an extractor fan that was on all the time and made a dreadful racket.

"They always tried to hurry things up because the cassettes they had were thirty or forty-five minutes per side," Miranda relates. "So, I chatted with them about the weather, soccer, how their day had gone, anything to stretch it out. I took something like thirty minutes with this small talk and then started to take their statement: Name? Place of birth? Ah, such a pretty place, I remarked to them, and continued prolonging it."

A colleague of Miranda's later confirmed that military officials recorded these sessions so that afterward they could analyze the testimony with the army's legal department, coordinate their responses and answers, and prepare themselves for the next summons.

The situation with civilian agents was different. They were less shielded, lacked the discipline that came with the military's strict hierarchy and a career in the service, and necessarily dragged up the rear as the weakest link in the chain. The first agent the CACI detectives brought into headquarters under arrest was a civilian employee in the air force, Otto Trujillo. He was very much on his own, and he opened up.

Trujillo's interactions with the CACI began to unfold one day near the end of 1991, when a detective climbed aboard a Santiago bus, showed up at his house, and rang the bell.

Over the course of that year multiple human rights cases were reactivated or reopened, whether based on information contributed by the Rettig Commission or through new legal actions brought by victims' families. The CACI received investigative orders pertaining to dozens of the disappeared, including victims of the Joint Command (Comando Conjunto), a secret organization created in 1975 under the aegis of the DIFA. The Command brought together agents from the air force, navy, and Carabineros intelligence services, plus detectives, doctors, and civilians. It focused mainly on striking against the Communist Party and the MIR and operated until the beginning of 1977.

In June 1974 the PICH's general directorate detailed at least four officials to the Joint Command. Their own colleagues would have to investigate them almost twenty years later.

Trujillo, known as Colmillo Blanco, or "White Fang," was recruited to serve in the Joint Command. He was a civilian who developed ties with pro-coup military officials in his work for a state organization in Punta Arenas, in the country's far South, during Allende's government, and he had participated in the repression in that city that began on September 11, 1973. In 1974 he was transferred to Santiago and began to carry out assignments under the orders of the DIFA.

In 1991, the families of three Communist Party members filed separate criminal lawsuits against agents of the Joint Command who had detained their relatives, tortured them, and caused their disappearance.

The complaints were based on statements gathered by the Rettig Commission, especially those offered by onetime Joint Command member Andrés Valenzuela, who used the alias "Papudo," in reference to his place of birth. Valenzuela, formerly a soldier in the air force, submitted his testimony to the commission in November 1990 from his self-imposed exile in Paris.

Papudo had entered the air force in 1974 and that same year, together with fifty-nine fellow conscripts, was tasked by the Air Force Intelligence Service to watch over more than sixty political prisoners—the majority from the MIR—who were being held in eight or so classrooms located in the basement of the air force's War Academy. He also took part in as many as 150 raids and detention operations.

When the DIFA was created in March 1975, Valenzuela was taken on to serve in it. He moved to its offices at 6 Juan Antonio Ríos Street, in downtown Santiago, offices also known by the shorthand "JAR 6." Sometime later, one of the DIFA's sections called Special Operations began to work in conjunction with members from other branches of the armed forces. Valenzuela was added to the teams that operated Joint Command torture centers located in four neighborhoods in the Santiago Metropolitan Region.

The teams that worked in these places were composed of civilians from Patria y Libertad (Fatherland and Liberty, a right-wing paramilitary group created to sabotage the Allende government); intelligence agents from the Carabineros and, in time, the navy; and political prisoners who had become agents of the state, such as Carol Flores, René Basoa, and Miguel Estay Reyno. All three had been members of the Communist Party and ended up cooperating with the air force. When the Joint Command was dissolved in 1977, Valenzuela returned to the DIFA and, before deserting in August 1984, collaborated with the Carabineros Communications Directorate and the CNI and participated in staging fake confrontations in September 1983, which resulted in the deaths of five leaders of the MIR.

Valenzuela deserted in 1984. Before fleeing the country with the help of the Vicariate of Solidarity, however, he made a series of confessions: to Mónica González, a journalist at the opposition magazine *Cauce*; to lawyers with the Vicariate; and—on two occasions—to a notary public in Santiago. The Vicariate handed over Valenzuela's statements and information to the judiciary and asked that a superior court judge be appointed to investigate them, but its request was rejected.

In extensive declarations taking up nearly thirty sheets of paper, Valenzuela related in detail how the Command functioned; listed thirty-four of its agents and leaders; provided the names of persons who were detained in its different sites, explaining how they were tortured; described the Command's vehicles and infrastructure; and accounted for what happened to some of the political prisoners.

He decided to desert, he stated, because "that system, in addition to destroying the victims, [also] destroys the one who victimizes them, in his emotional life, it kills his feelings and turns him into an animal."[19]

Andrés Valenzuela's testimony wound up incorporated into another case. In 1985, appeals court judge Carlos Cerda began an inquiry of the Joint Command as part of his investigation into the late 1976 disappearance of thirteen people: eleven top-level Communists and two MIR activists. In January 1986, Valenzuela sent Judge Cerda his testimony from France.

At that time, the leaders and agents of the Command, including Otto Trujillo, had been identified by their victims and had to testify in court. Despite pressure brought by the Supreme Court to close the investigation quickly, Judge Cerda firmly carried on, interrogating and confronting dozens of military, police, and civilian agents. All of them resorted to lying. When Trujillo's turn came around in September 1985, however, the man cracked. He told the judge that he knew they would kill him.[20]

Nearly a year later, the judge indicted some forty individuals for organizing and participating in the disappearance of the thirteen militants. They included air force general Gustavo Leigh, who was a former member of the military junta, and the hard core of the Joint Command—civilians and detectives—among them Dr. Alejandro Forero, who collaborated in the torture of prisoners.

Such a judicial blow was inconceivable during the years of the dictatorship. Nonetheless, in October 1986, the Supreme Court nullified the indictments, ordering Judge Cerda to close the legal proceedings and apply the Amnesty Law. Because the judge paid no heed, the court suspended him, removed him from the case, and replaced him with another judge who wasted no time in dismissing the case.[21] In June 1987 the Supreme Court confirmed the case's definitive closure.

After this charade, the Carabineros reabsorbed all the offenders back into the institution, and Trujillo returned to his civilian life.

The CACI continued as a tiny, bare-bones unit, with few staff and resources, when the order came in to bring before the court, upon penalty of their arrest, a dozen members of the Joint Command, including Otto Trujillo. By this point, inspector Hugo Rebolledo had been added to the team.[22]

The young detective managed to locate White Fang's address and set off alone for his house, skipping the usual, commonsense practice of always going in pairs, especially if it meant detaining someone. Apparently, he hadn't expected to find him at home.

"Rebolledo told me that he went to check out the residence by himself, but discovering that Trujillo was there, decided [on the spot] to bring him into head-quarters," says Miranda. "We had planned to go together early the next morning, but he went ahead on his own."

Detective Rebolledo had gone by bus, and he came back the same way with Trujillo now in tow.

"Hugo came in quite pleased, saying to me, 'Chief, look who I've just brought in.' I had to let the director know right away, and when I did, he all but fainted. He was the first agent we had placed under arrest," recalls Henríquez.

The first thing they did was call in the medical examiner to run a check on him. The detectives questioned Trujillo in the CACI offices. White Fang had a lot to say and passed along valuable information about the structure of the Joint Command.

"Trujillo was calm, at ease. The agents weren't particularly worried as yet," states Miranda.

Director Toro, however, had good cause to be. By all reason, the minister of the interior should have been informed about a legal move of this kind in advance, especially in those first months of the democratic transition when the army, the government, and the police were groping their way, each assessing how far they could go.

"This shook the ground under us because of its implications," states Henríquez. "The government didn't expect it. There was never any limit placed openly on our operations, but the message came through loud and clear: take it easy, slow down."

After the commotion in PICH headquarters died down, the CACI's detectives arranged for Trujillo to appear in court.

A Twenty-Four-Page Report

As 1991 drew to a close, and with several cases related to the Joint Command ongoing, the courts acted. They ordered the PICH to find out if the Command had in effect existed and gather all related information. The job was assigned to inspector José Plaza.

Because of his family's economic constraints, Plaza had enrolled in the Investigations School in 1976, while the Joint Command was busy stalking its victims. As yet, however, he had no notion of any of that. Plaza was in his second year studying electrical engineering at the State Technical University when the military coup took place. As fate would have it, he slept in that day, saving himself from the nightmare experienced by hundreds of teachers, staff, and students who were rounded up on campus by the military and hauled off to the National Stadium, which was turned into a prison camp.

Plaza lived with his family in the capital's Renca district. His father was a metallurgical worker for a company called Socometal, and his mother a traditional housewife. While the atmosphere at home was devoid of politics, Plaza says, and no one in his family was politically active, "we agreed with the principles of Allende's government and knew that he was well intentioned. But we lived detached from what was happening. We suffered through the shortages of goods and the long lines, but we didn't take a stand on who was responsible for them. Politics wasn't our thing, we simply lived through it."

Plaza tried to go on with his studies as best he could, but the family's finances made it impossible, so he looked for options to help boost their income. The Investigations School had opened new candidate slots, offering the possibility of a stable career in the police. Here, Plaza figured, was the opportunity to obtain work and a solid profession. Once admitted, though, he experienced an immediate emotional shock.

"Mentally, I felt bad. It was another environment altogether, another way of life, but I toughed it out, because it was the only opportunity I had. I came from a pretty humble home and my possibilities of getting ahead were few," he recalls. "On one occasion they took us to the Investigations main building to give [us our] first [direct] contact with criminals, but the way they were treated, the cells, the odor, I found it distasteful. I said to myself, 'This isn't for me.' But I kept on with it."

When Plaza graduated from the Investigations School, he was assigned to the Eighth Police Precinct in Ñuñoa, to work at the side of detective Luis Henríquez. He remembers Henríquez as a meticulous investigator, a stickler for details who asked himself the reason for everything. Plaza acquired these qualities and learned his investigative techniques from Henríquez.

This is where he had his first brush with the CNI, as he watched how some colleagues changed after being assigned to this intelligence agency. "For them it was a reward to join the CNI, because they enjoyed autonomy, they felt they had attained a higher status in the police. They visited us sometimes and came in 'full of themselves,'" he recalls.

Plaza spent seven years in the Ñuñoa precinct. In the mid-1980s, he was detailed to the airport, to work with the International Police and stayed in that assignment until 1991. He hadn't been in his latest posting even a year in the Las Condes precinct when his old tutor, Luis Henríquez, offered him the chance to join the CACI. Plaza didn't learn its mission until he was on the inside.

"We need someone for a work group, on a special assignment to Department V. Would you join me?" Henríquez asked him.

"I'd love to!" Plaza responded.

When Plaza joined the CACI, José Miranda and Hugo Rebolledo were already on board, in addition to Henríquez, three administrative assistants—Patricio Barros, Miguel Reinoso, and Hugo Oteiza—and the driver, Luis Núñez. That was the team. Plaza's addition was due to another imminent move: Department V's chief, José Sotomayor, was about to become the director of antinarcotics and was taking Miranda and Rebolledo along with him.[23] Within a few weeks, Plaza would be left virtually alone on the commission, apart from the administrative assistants.

The first thing he did, just like the others in this initial period, was to read the Rettig Report. Meanwhile, Luis Henríquez initiated him into the world of human rights, introducing him to the lawyers at the Vicariate of Solidarity, the leaders of the family associations, and the former political prisoners who were collaborating with the police.

"There was a lack of trust on their part that was noticeable, but they didn't openly express it," Plaza points out. "It's understandable. Barriers existed that had to get lifted, but it was a gradual process. That kind of confidence was [only] built up by doing things, when they saw that we acted responsibly. But with Luz Arce, who was also cooperating with us, I always had my doubts, and even more so with Marcia Merino. I always wondered whether they still had connections with the CNI. I was afraid they might be telling the Army Intelligence Directorate what we were up to, [what we were] inquiring into, and where we were headed," notes Plaza.

After the detective had come up to speed, Henríquez asked him to carry out a "sweep," that is, compile all the information about the Joint Command available from different sources. Plaza carefully scrubbed Andrés Valenzuela's testimony and the statements made by witnesses and the Command's agents. He read word for word and line by line the recently (1989) published book on the Joint Command coauthored by the journalist Mónica González and the lawyer Héctor Contreras, combed through articles in the press, examined the wealth of information compiled by the Vicariate and other human rights organizations, and verified, processed, and cross-checked everything.

Plaza put together an organizational chart of the Command and tracked down information on its agents through different public sources, such as the civil registry, which also enabled him to get full names, national identification numbers, addresses, photos, and fingerprints of the Command's principal agents.

Through his superiors at the CACI, he asked the Border Control Department for travel records on thirty-three agents. The great majority were from the Joint Command and others from the DINA. The lion's share of trips was made to Southern Cone countries, especially Argentina, although some agents traveled to the United States, Spain, and Sweden.

Plaza's painstaking research resulted in a twenty-four-page report, plus attachments, replete with background information and analysis. He had fully identified twenty-seven members of the Joint Command and another fourteen by their aliases.

The report was submitted for review to the CACI's advisory team before it was sent to the courts, as was done with all police reports during those initial two years. Later, the pace and scope of police investigations in human rights cases made it impossible to maintain this routine.

"That meeting with the advisory team was crucial, since it demonstrated that we were operating in a very serious, rigorous, and objective way. When the advisers were satisfied [the report] was sent to the judiciary and right away various courts began to ask for it," states Plaza.

The detective delivered his report in mid-1992, when the CACI team was already fully on the hunt for the torturer Osvaldo Romo in Brazil, and police from the Homicide Brigade were tracking down agent Miguel Estay Reyno, alias "Fanta," in Paraguay.

Plaza's report, titled *The Joint Command and Its Activities: Analysis and Compilation of Background Data*, swelled the contents of the CACI's filing cabinet and its ever-expanding database of information. Year after year, colleagues and judges requested copies of the report.

The Fourth Criminal Court in the district of San Miguel soon broadened its earlier investigative order concerning the Joint Command. In September 1992 it asked the plainclothes police to confirm whether PICH detectives Jorge Barraza and Manuel Salvatierra had belonged to the organization. It fell to Inspector Plaza to take their out-of-court statements. They both denied they once belonged to the Joint Command or had known either its agents or any of the victims whose deaths the court was investigating.

Nevertheless, they admitted they were sent on assignment to the air force's legal department in 1974 with two other colleagues: Marcos Cortés and Werther Contreras. Plaza set out to look for them as well. His search did not yield much. Cortés's statement was similar to that of Barraza, and Salvatierra and Contreras, already in retirement, eluded him.

Plaza, however, was undaunted. He obtained Barraza's full CV and prepared a detailed analysis of his career. He showed how Barraza's assignments and the operations for which he was congratulated by his superiors correlated with the dates and places on which and where leftist militants had been assassinated. He gave the information to the court along with the background data compiled on the Joint Command and issued summonses for Salvatierra and Barraza to appear in court.

5

A CAREER OFFICER
AS DIRECTOR

WHILE ON A TRIP TO CANADA, Horacio Toro saw how his days at the helm of the plainclothes police were coming to an end, and he was powerless to do anything about it. The political Right was calling for his head; the army was complaining about him to the government; and President Aylwin was demanding that he return to the country immediately.

His troubles stemmed from a batch of secret Investigations Police (PICH) documents that had been leaked by an unknown police intelligence official in Limache, a small city some eighty miles northeast of the capital.

When he became head of the PICH, Toro stipulated that its own intelligence service, the Jefatura de Inteligencia Policial, or Jipol, should have an official serving as a liaison in every police district in the country. In January 1992, one of them—the Jipol contact in Limache, Juan Manuel Arias—leaked copies of a series of confidential instructions. These came from the top of the institution and detailed surveillance operations targeting professional associations and political, Catholic Church, syndical, labor union, and military figures. The documents were dubbed the "Planes Halcón," or "Falcon Plans."

Arias delivered the documents to Sergio Díaz, head of the Army Intelligence Directorate's (DINE's) Information Center. In turn, Díaz shared them with two members of Chile's Chamber of Deputies, Andrés Chadwick and Pablo Longueira. The two legislators represented the ultraright party, the Independent Democratic Union. When Chadwick and Longueira went on television on March 17, 1992, and made the documents publicly known, Toro was in Ottawa on official business at the invitation of the Canadian Mounted Police.

Falcon Plan I was designed on the fly, as a way to maintain close watch over the military's movements, adopted in quick reaction to the army's December 1990 "call-up and coordination exercise." Accordingly, Director Toro ordered the head of police intelligence, prefect Guillermo Mora, to devise a plan for monitoring the military to determine the full reach of its actions.

Falcon Plan II was the subsequent response to the lack of preparation demonstrated in the face of the call-up and coordination exercise. On the night of December 19, 1990, as the military movement was under way, Toro verbally ordered the head of police intelligence to prepare a formal plan aimed at preventing similar episodes in the future.

The Falcon Plan II documents were distributed to the PICH's six administrative zones and sought to detect movements inside the armed forces aimed at subverting public order, pressuring the government, or putting the nation's stability at risk. Months later, before a Chamber of Deputies investigative committee, Toro gave assurances that the plan was meant to be implemented only in the face of exceptional events.

The eight Falcon Plan documents went into considerable detail: "When going to military barracks for investigations or other purposes, make the most of your presence there by getting to know people, their ins and outs, where they are posted, and the types of vehicles they use as well as civilian personnel such as gardeners, plumbers, or waiters who work there. Do everything possible to identify them, locate their residences, verify background information, and determine in what way they can eventually be turned into our informants."[1]

Meanwhile, other documents contained in the Plan de Búsqueda de Información (Information Search Plan), likewise leaked by Arias, went much further:

1. Monitor the activities of the governing coalition and the Socialist and Christian Democratic Parties, their public and secret alliances, and project the likely results for the two in the June [1992] municipal elections. With respect to the DC [Christian Democrats], they should take notice of any possible breaking away of the "younger generations."

2. Conduct surveillance on the activities of the [Independent Democratic Union], the sources of its election financing, and the public or private support of the armed forces for its candidates.

3. Conduct surveillance on the private life of some labor leaders, especially in relation to possible "legal scandals."

4. Take the pulse, again, of the religious camp, bringing information up to date on the activities of priests in the Iglesia Popular [People's Church] and check on the conduct of socialist-leaning bishops. Read the pronouncements of some bishops to see if they contradicted the conservative line of the new secretary of the Bishops' Conference.

5. Verify the inclinations of higher court judges named during the dictatorship or of those who might have attended exclusive meetings with
   military officials.

6. Monitor the activities of economic groups linked to the dictatorship's
   leaders and to businessmen with ties to Sofofa [the country's principal
   industrial association].

7. Keep watch over all high-ranking members of the military who leave or
   come into the country.[2]

Jipol's Information Search Plan encompassed four main areas: domestic, foreign, economic, and military.[3] In other words, it encompassed virtually everything, including the private lives of individuals.

"The general idea was to know what members of the military were doing, if they were siding with democracy or not. The mistake was in how it was done. Those plans explicitly stated the methods [to be used] for monitoring and also included the principal religious activities. Being a freemason myself, I said to Toro: meddling in the Church is a colossal mistake. At that time the Catholic Church had much more power than now," says Nelson Mery.

The Independent Democratic Union—setting aside its own behavior during the dictatorship—condemned the fact that the PICH had a virtual "political police" operating within it. In fact, that operation had always existed. It was part of their work.

The Right leapt into action. In a meeting with interior minister Enrique Krauss, Chadwick and Longueira asked for Toro's resignation, promising to go further and pursue higher authorities.[4] In addition, they announced that they would submit a writ of protection to the courts, seeking the confiscation of "all personal and political information found in the PICH's archives dealing with our party and its leaders."[5]

The Right applied pressure to have a criminal investigation opened over the invasion of personal privacy. The army made its displeasure officially known to the government.

Krauss placed an urgent call to Toro, who was still in Canada, and on President Aylwin's instructions, the director quickly came back to the country. Krauss publicly disavowed him and ordered the acting director, prefect Nelson Mery, to withdraw the plans from circulation.

Toro was not eager to move up his return to Chile, but he had to do so on March 20. His fate was sealed at 8:40 A.M. that day, before he even stepped onto solid ground. Mery went to the airport to pick him up. Toro had a long meeting that morning with the PICH's Senior Advisory Council and the unit chiefs. From there, he went to La Moneda and that same day presented his irrevocable resignation to the president.

Jipol's chief, Guillermo Mora, also handed in his resignation. Deputy Commissioner Arias was subjected to disciplinary action by the PICH and investigated by the judiciary for leaking documents.

In a written response to Toro's formal resignation, President Aylwin pointed out that the contents of some of the documents were "unacceptable for my government."

Those circulars, he added, "seem inspired by security schemes common to authoritarian systems—from which our country suffered under the previous regime—and do not accord with the respect for rights and freedoms that democratic principles and our own political constitution guarantee to people."

On accepting Toro's resignation, Aylwin concluded, "I do it with deep regret, because I greatly value the loyalty, selflessness, courage, enthusiasm, and efficiency with which you have performed the difficult functions I entrusted to you."[6]

The Cost of Doing Things

The existence of Falcon Plans I and II and the Information Search Plan set off a political earthquake. Minister Krauss announced the revamping of all intelligence-gathering rules and regulations then in force.

Within a few days, the Chamber of Deputies created a special commission on intelligence services. The commission's objective was to examine the services' functioning as of March 1990, clarify irregularities that might have occurred, and analyze existing legislation respecting security and intelligence, the regulations governing the different services, the procedures they followed, and the use they made of the information collected. The commission was also charged with recommending legal changes that would upgrade intelligence work.

The concern went beyond the Falcon Plans. The commission inquired into a series of complaints that involved both the DINE and the PICH from 1990 on: army vehicles tracking leftist militants, efforts by DINE agents to acquire information about Socialist Party contacts in the Interior and Transport Ministries, DINE agents watching Director Toro's house and tapping his telephone, and surveillance on the commanders in chief of the army and navy and the president of the Supreme Court.

And just when the special commission thought it was completing its mission, the Piñeragate scandal blew up. On August 23, 1992, the owner of Chile's television station Megavisión, Ricardo Claro, interrupted a program with a portable Kyoto radio and pressed the play button. What viewers heard was the then senator and pre-candidate for the presidency, Sebastián Piñera, conspiring with his friend Pedro Pablo Díaz to ruin the electoral prospects of congresswoman Evelyn Matthei, Piñera's friend and also a presidential pre-candidate of the same party, Renovación Nacional.

The special commission's deadline was extended to include this latest development, which was eventually traced back to a DINE office on García Reyes Street, where the telephone conversations of government, Carabineros, and PICH authorities, among others, were intercepted and recorded. This time, apparently, the call was caught and recorded on request.

The commission concluded that the Falcon Plans infringed constitutional guarantees and constituted an abuse of the PICH's authority and powers. Toro and Mora were alone held responsible for developing the plans, and Arias wound up being prosecuted in Limache.

Mery assured the commission that Falcon Plan II was never actually implemented. It was meant to be activated only in the case of a new "call-up and coordination exercise" or similar situation.

Nonetheless, according to ex-adviser Jorge Morales, "It was a blunder, a mistake that cost dearly."

"It was a very simple thing, very normal, but it was ineptly worded and carelessly distributed, and in addition they gave it a pompous name. It was a very difficult moment, because very strong measures were being pushed inside the institution and we were going through a rather tense situation, but we all assumed that that was the cost of doing things," states Morales.

A Huge Blunder?

During Horacio Toro's two years as director general of the plainclothes police, the institution's budget increased by 50 percent and its fleet of vehicles by 30 percent. There were also significant capital and infrastructure improvements: ten new antinarcotic units established; four outposts created along the northern border; two new judicial police precincts added in the Santiago Metropolitan Region; and twelve headquarters buildings rebuilt or remodeled.[7]

The additional funds awarded by the government outside the PICH's regular budget were key to outfitting the police with highly specialized technologies "to upgrade the work of the police from the scientific, technical, and crime-fighting perspectives."[8]

Furthermore, in an effort to adapt the PICH to the requirements of a democratic society, the police academy's program of studies was reformed, and the foundation was laid for the major human rights investigations to come.

"I have the personal satisfaction," said Toro on publicly announcing his retirement, "of having fulfilled what amounted to our initial project, making Chile's Investigations Police into a force that shall be worthy of the democratic process that we are living through in the country."[9]

Despite howls of protest by the Right, and even as the Chamber of Deputies investigative commission continued its inquiry into the supposed espionage plan, the newly resigned director was hired on a paid contract basis at the beginning of May by the Interior Ministry to advise on security matters. His contract ran until the end of the year.[10]

Toro also spoke publicly about an intelligence operation designed to remove him from his post. The reason, he said, "ties in with the development of Investigations' capabilities to help resolve the crimes, disappearances, and human rights violations that occurred before 1990, in the spirit of the government's effort to arrive at the truth in order to achieve forgiveness and reconciliation."[11]

Nevertheless, what Toro and some of his close associates characterized as a plan to get him out, or at least as a communications blitz that seized on circumstances to achieve the same end, was—for ex–interior minister Enrique Krauss—the outcome of a huge blunder by the director himself.

"The intelligence operation [to obtain his resignation] was an excuse that Horacio cited on leaving, but the truth is he committed numerous mistakes. He was in a hurry, a little disingenuous, at times he lacked judgment. It was Toro's own stumbling, not an operation to get rid of him. Nonetheless, he really cleaned up an institution whose prestige had suffered greatly," states Krauss.

The Aylwin administration analyzed the possible motives behind the leaking of the documents. They concluded that the operation sought the following objectives:

a. Double-down on the campaign against the government for its supposed negligence on the issue of public safety.
b. Help to draw together the sectors of the political and economic Right with respect to the army to discredit constitutional reform initiatives aimed at the armed forces.
c. Insist on the advisability of the armed forces' participation in the work of domestic intelligence.[12]
d. Win over the business establishment, which was beginning to sympathize with the government and believe in its credibility due to the seriousness of its economic policy and abidance to the law.

e. Forge ahead with efforts aimed at ending General Toro's command (ex-Investigations and [National Center for Information] chiefs are involved in narcotrafficking, especially Gordon and Paredes).

f. Bring down the defense minister, whose presence is "irritating" to Pinochet and his men, who perceive his administration as constantly infringing on the army's autonomy and professional capabilities.[13]

When Toro stepped down from the directorship, Nelson Mery took his place on an interim basis. He was then in the second line of command, focused especially on reforming the plan of studies in the police academy, including eliminating courses such as geopolitics and national security.

"I said that if they put a military official over me as director, I would resign. It meant going backward in everything," states Mery.

The concerns of the Association of Relatives of the Detained and Disappeared were focused elsewhere. The leaders of the organization were alarmed at the possibility that Mery might assume the directorship, due to his brief stint in the army's artillery academy in Linares in 1973. Following the military coup, the artillery school in Linares served as one of the main detention centers in the Maule region in southern Chile.

Sola Sierra, Mireya García, and Viviana Díaz requested an audience with justice minister Francisco Cumplido and asked him not to confirm Mery as PICH director.

"We handed Cumplido detailed information on everything we had and requested that [Mery] not be appointed, but . . . he was named all the same," Mireya García, the ex-leader of the Association of Relatives of the Detained and Disappeared, told the newspaper El Mercurio.[14]

PICH's future director general then told Minister Krauss what the episode was about that caused their objection.

"He informed us that he received orders to transfer detainees from Santiago to Linares, and that he even offered them food, but was not involved in any crime," states Krauss.

For the government, this explanation was sufficient. It supported the new director blindly.

Judas Nelson Lenin

Born in Santiago in 1941, Judas Nelson Lenin Mery Figueroa moved with his family to the city of Los Andes, in the central Valparaíso region, when he was just a child.

His parents named him Judas for Saint Jude Thaddeus, the patron saint of lost causes, to whom they had made an offering. Not only was Gastón Mery unemployed, but the young couple had gotten married without permission after Rebeca Figueroa became pregnant. As a result, she was turned out of her house. They asked three things from Saint Jude: for the father, a job; for the mother, a safe delivery and a healthy child. They were granted all three. Gastón Mery began to work for the prison service in 1941, the year in which his first child was born.

One afternoon, when Nelson Mery was fourteen, he informed his mother—after coming home from his school, the Instituto Chacabuco run by the Marist Brothers—that he wanted to be a priest. She greeted the news with joy.

That same night he announced his decision to his father, who at the time was warden of the Los Andes jail. Without uttering a single word, his father placed him in a secular, public high school the very next day. What is more, Gastón Mery insisted that the school assign him to a coeducational class.

From the very first, Mery's name caused him problems. In the Marist school, his classmates taunted him with the epithet "traitor," since they all thought he bore the name of Judas Iscariot, the apostle who betrayed Jesus. His parents named him Nelson in honor of Horatio Nelson, vice admiral of the British Royal Navy, famed for his exploits during the Napoleonic Wars. They added Lenin to his name because his father, a Socialist Party sympathizer, wanted to.

When Nelson was about sixteen, his father was appointed warden of the Linares jail, so the family—now with five children—moved again. In Linares the teenage Mery was associated with a small leftist group whose activities basically amounted to going around and scrawling slogans on walls. Although he never latched on to any party or organization, Mery—by his own lights—was radicalized during his adolescence through seeing injustice, the arrogance of landowners, and the submission and abuse inflicted on peasants. Almost everyone in his family was a follower of Allende, and since Linares was a small town, everyone knew it.

He wanted to study biology but ultimately opted for physical education. After spending a year and a half in the University of Chile's Institute of Physical Education, Mery decided to strike out on his own. He no longer wanted his father to continue paying for his education, so in 1960 he enrolled in the Investigations School.

In 1963, his father was promoted to lieutenant colonel and named director of the Santiago penitentiary. By then, Mery had graduated from the school and was attached to the second judicial precinct in Santiago. Because his father had to move to the capital, he asked his eldest son to return to Linares to be near his mother and siblings.

A decade later, in 1973, the military coup took him by surprise in the Linares police precinct. Mery was thirty-one and a detective in Depinfi, Investigations' former "Political Police."

The Convoy to Linares

The episode that would forever haunt Mery began when the chief of the PICH in Linares, superintendent Ricardo Hernández, appointed him as liaison between the plainclothes police and the army's artillery school. On the very day of the coup, September 11, 1973, Hernández received new instructions. The officer in charge of the zone under the state of siege ordered him to designate two detectives to liaise with the Linares army regiment. Hernández selected Nelson Mery and inspector Héctor Torres.

"According to the unit chief's version of the story, Mery struck him as the right person to serve in this capacity. He tapped him because he dressed well, was clean-cut, and made an excellent impression on people. Mery was someone who took the trouble to educate himself, to read," explains Luis Henríquez, who years later investigated Mery's time in Linares.

The police precinct of San Javier sent four of its own detectives: Luis Espinoza, Manuel Vejar, Carlos Neves, and Nelson Volta. It was Torres, however, who remained the longest in the Linares regiment—until mid-1974—and the one whom testimony singled out as the most brutal in his treatment of prisoners.

"The first thing I did," Mery explained in a 2006 interview with the online news outlet *Crónica Digital*, "was to present myself to Colonel Gabriel del Río [director of the school], and he assigned me to Department II of Military Intelligence, so I presented myself to Major Jorge Zincke Quiroz.[15] Since so many detainees began to flood in, Intelligence ordered me to check their personal records in the PICH's Information Office in both Linares and Santiago. [And] as the number of detainees kept growing, they assigned me the function of taking their statements. I worked alone, because I was in charge of looking into the information Investigations had on the political background of detainees."[16]

Mery maintains that he never mistreated any detainee and, to the contrary, that prisoners described to him having been tortured by other agents. He further asserts that he always passed this information on to the regiment's chief of military intelligence, Major Zincke.

In November 1973 Capt. Claudio Lecaros was designated chief of military intelligence for the artillery school. The following month, on December 18, Lecaros ordered Mery to travel to Santiago to detain and bring back Patricia Contreras, who was accused of hiding weapons in Linares. Mery knew her; she was a friend of his brother.

Mery traveled that day, with the mission of detaining Contreras, to the capital in one of the regiment's jeeps. He was accompanied by a sergeant from the artillery school's intelligence department, Antonio Aguilar, and by Detective Volta. In Santiago, they stopped at the Military Institute's command operating out of the army's military school, where more military vehicles joined up with their own. No fewer than twenty men, under the command of Capt. Humberto Julio, departed toward the old section of downtown Santiago. Julio had arrived two months earlier from Linares, where he served as an assistant in the artillery school's directorship.

According to Mery, all those additional troops to detain a woman in Santiago came as a surprise. But according to Julio, Mery oversaw the operation and had asked for reinforcements. They arrived at a building located on Cienfuegos Street. A Movement of the Revolutionary Left militant, María Isabel Beltrán—accused of infiltrating the armed forces—lived on the third floor. Patricia Contreras was staying with her at the time. The apartment was raided and the two women placed under arrest.

Beltrán was a student of music education at the University of Chile. Her partner, Javier Pacheco, an active member of the Movement of the Revolutionary Left, had been arrested and executed two months earlier, leaving behind the now-widowed twenty-one-year-old Beltrán and a young daughter.[17]

Both the women and their captors spent the night in the army's military school. In a convoy the next morning, they drove back to the artillery school in Linares. In judicial statements provided many years later, Humberto Julio said he returned to Linares and to his previous duties in the artillery school two days after the convoy departed Santiago.[18]

Two weeks after her capture, during which she was interrogated and tortured, Patricia Contreras was transferred to a local jail. She was freed in mid-1974 and went into exile. The last time Mery saw Beltrán, he said, was in a hallway of the artillery school's intelligence department, just before he completed his liaison assignment and returned to his police unit at the end of December 1973.[19] Beltrán's mother, as well as conscripts and other prisoners, said they saw her in January 1974 in very bad physical condition as the result of torture. Sometime that month, Beltrán disappeared.

Investigating the Boss

In the mid-1990s, the National Corporation for Reparations and Reconciliation filed a complaint in the criminal court of Linares over the area's disappeared prisoners, among them María Isabel Beltrán. This action meant that several detectives in Department V would have to investigate the participation of the PICH's director general in a kidnapping case.

The situation sparked friction between Director Mery and Luis Henríquez, who at the time was chief of Department V. Henríquez points out:

It was terrible to [have to] investigate our own director. The judge in charge of the case asked me to interview Bishop Carlos Camus and the governor of Linares, with instructions not to let Mery know about it. But within five minutes he learned of it and asked me what I was up to in Linares. I told him, and he was put out because I hadn't informed him. I fell out of favor with Mery over that because he believed that I was investigating him in order to cause him trouble, but it wasn't like that. I was investigating to seek the truth.

As part of the wider investigation, detectives Freddy Orellana, René Sandoval, and José Luis Cabión took statements from former political prisoners, witnesses, ex-conscripts, military officials, and PICH police officers, including Ricardo Hernández, who by then was retired.

They did not personally question their chief, Nelson Mery. Instead, to avoid any suspicion, Mery appeared directly before the court to make his statement.

"They had full freedom to investigate and obtained some damning statements. But I never asked them to alter anything, nothing," assures the PICH's former director.

Lorenzo Antich, who in those days was a conscript in the artillery school, told detectives René Sandoval and Freddy Orellana that the interrogations were carried out in the offices of the school's academic registrar, which were occupied solely by the Military Intelligence Service. Antich described the treatment of the detainees as "very inhumane, they were constantly beaten and tortured, some more than others."[20]

Between December 1973 and January 1974, Antich was able to see and speak several times with María Isabel Beltrán and a second detainee, Héctor Contreras. Contreras had also been seized in Santiago and transferred to Linares. He and Beltrán were kept in a different room from the rest of the prisoners. They told the conscript they were tortured by Sgt. Antonio Aguilar and PICH inspector Héctor Torres.

At the close of January 1974, Antich saw Beltrán and Contreras being bundled into a vehicle; their heads were covered with canvas hoods, and they were driven off to parts unknown. They never returned. Another soldier witnessed, on various occasions, military trucks driving up at night to the school's shooting range about ten kilometers away, where they executed and buried prisoners. Soldiers then shot and buried that night's victims.

One of the detectives added to the regiment, Carlos Neves, stated that the fate of each detainee depended on the chief of military intelligence, Capt. Claudio Lecaros, and the artillery school's high command. Interviewed by Department V's detectives, Lecaros insisted he had no information. He assured them that he never had contact with the prisoners and knew nothing about María Isabel Beltrán or the other disappeared detainees.

Testimonies gathered by the police in the mid-1990s agree that torture was inflicted by Detectives Torres, Neves, and Volta, as well as by army and Carabineros personnel, but not by Nelson Mery, who worked alone. Antich portrayed him in the following way: "Nelson Mery distinguished himself by being a very gentlemanly person and different from those who worked in the school. He helped the prisoners and was very humane toward all of them."[21]

"I interviewed the provincial governor in Parral and he spoke very well of the director," notes Luis Henríquez. "He indicates that thanks to Mery he came away alive. Everyone we interviewed said that Mery was a very correct person and that the rest were savages. I believe that Nelson Mery is a decent man in that he did not participate in torture. As for the others, I can't put my hand in the fire."

A former political prisoner and bank employee in Linares who knew Mery, Gerardo Villagra, related that Mery twice released him from torture, shared his sandwich with him, and—from what he saw—never delivered a blow to anyone. Nonetheless, he stated that Mery participated together with Torres and Aguilar in staging mock executions on the shooting range.

"To investigate your director general was not easy. Likewise, there was an element of fear. But I didn't receive any pressure or suggestion from Mery with respect to the investigation in Linares," says René Sandoval.

The former PICH director mounted his defense, arguing that his mission was to detain solely Patricia Contreras and not María Isabel Beltrán. He admits responsibility for Contreras—who years later testified in his favor—but not for Beltrán. Julio was responsible for her, and she was a target of the military unit in Santiago, maintains Mery.

All the same, even if he did not resort to violence or take part in firing squads, the fact that he participated in the detention of the two women as well as other people in Linares, witnessed torture taking place in the school, and interrogated prisoners has raised questions around Mery.

The lawyer Loreto Meza, a plaintiff representing the National Corporation for Reparations and Reconciliation in the Linares case, traveled on many occasions to the area with her colleague Piedad Karelovic to interview relatives and witnesses. She also requested a meeting with Director Mery, who received the two in his office at PICH headquarters.

Meza relates how, during that time, congressman Jaime Naranjo, a socialist representing the district, called to demand an explanation as to why the director of the plainclothes police was being investigated. Years later, Meza was going to advocate for Mery's indictment in the Linares case, but a colleague convinced her it was futile. The PICH director enjoyed the government's unequivocal support, a close relationship with the Socialist Party, contacts among the judiciary's judges, and solid connections within Chile's freemason community, to which he belonged.

"We had a bead on who Nelson Mery was and that he was an untouchable person because he was the director general of Investigations and had access to information on everyone. I consider that it was a huge mistake. Mery formed part of the torturers' team, he was torture's 'good cop,' the one who offers cigarettes, sandwiches, the one who recommends that you cooperate so nothing really bad happens to you. Being a part of the artillery school [prisoner operations] turns him into a perpetrator," states Meza.

Detectives Abel Lizama and Sandro Gaete continued pursuing the police investigation of Linares's disappeared prisoners starting in 2000, when its supervision was handed first to Judge Juan Guzmán and then to Judge Alejandro Solís. They again interviewed members of the military and detectives and gained access to the testimony of old as well as new witnesses. The widow of Luis Tapia, one of the disappeared prisoners, told them that Mery participated in her husband's arrest. The former political prisoner Osvaldo Salazar assured them that Mery was among the group that detained him.[22]

"Mery never inhibited the investigation. The only thing he asked was that he be kept informed. There were people in Linares who in their statements said very bad things about Mery. I saw his horrified look when he read the statements, because he read all the statements. But he never said anything. He never raised any objection or made a comment to me. I simply saw his horrified look," states Gaete.

Nelson Mery was never indicted for the disappearance of María Isabel Beltrán.[23]

When he returned to his unit from the artillery school at the end of 1973, Mery remained in the immigration section of the Linares police precinct. In 1975 he was sent to the town of San Javier (in the Linares province). Two years later he moved on to the northern city of Iquique, where he took classes in English and public relations at the regional branch of the University of Chile. In 1982 Mery entered the PICH's Higher Academy. After completing its program in 1984, he was assigned to the International Police, stationed in the Santiago airport, for two years. In 1986 he became vice director of the Investigations School and held a tenured professorship teaching police tactics and operations, security in police quarters, institutional organization and regulation, and police ethics.

"At the end of the 1980s, when I was the school's deputy director, one of my cousins read my horoscope and told me that I would be the director general of the PICH. I didn't believe him," Mery confesses.

You and I Are the Same

Nelson Mery's appointment as director general of the PICH was confirmed on June 4, 1992. He was fifty years old at the time, with more than thirty years of service in the plainclothes police.

According to ex-adviser Jorge Morales, arranging Nelson Mery's ascent to the PICH's top post required two operations to clear away its high command, one that took place in 1990 and another in 1991. These left an open path to the general directorship. Mery was always part of the plan.

"We settled on Mery after a lengthy process of vetting information, in which it fell to me to participate very directly, lending a hand to the director. Changes were made with him in mind, definitely. He had the profile we were looking for: a solidly honest background, very firm intellectual preparation, and leadership qualities," states Morales.

Even though the PICH would now have a career police official as director, many of Nelson Mery's colleagues criticized him for having reached the top without scuffing his shoes on the streets. He was a desk officer, and for that they viewed him with disdain.

Mery's retort: "They've always criticized me because 'I've never done anything,' I've never kicked in doors, interrogated [suspects], that I'm an office man. I accept that. But to them I say, Why didn't you complain about Toro, Paredes, and all the other director generals we've had who hadn't so much as passed by the front of an Investigations headquarters before being appointed?"

It was indisputable that Mery had the great advantage of knowing the institution from within. For detective Nelson Jofré, then in the Homicide Brigade, Mery possessed a special quality: "He knew how to exploit people's positive aspects. He knew all of us quite well and knew how much each of us was worth. And he was a straight shooter whenever he had something to say."

Mery's rise in the hierarchy of the plainclothes police was swift. As of 1990 he was a deputy prefect and deputy director of the Investigations School but left the position after being appointed to take a one-year course at the National Academy of Political and Strategic Studies (Anepe). By April 1990 he was already at the rank of prefect.

On June 19, 1990, during a cocktail reception held to celebrate the fifty-seventh anniversary of the institution, Mery spotted Horacio Toro crossing the room, walking straight toward him. The two men were not personally acquainted, but Toro indeed knew a lot about Nelson Mery. He asked Mery how his studies at Anepe were going and then sought his opinion about people being let go from the PICH.

"I told him that I agreed with what he was doing but not how he was doing it," recalls Mery. Two months later, Toro called him into his office. On that day—August 30, 1990—many officials were receiving their notice of retirement. Operation Carousel was moving full steam ahead.

"Nelson, you are taking charge of instruction," Toro informed him.

That same day Mery rose to become inspector prefect. He had to leave Anepe without managing to complete the thesis he was preparing with a colleague. It was titled "The Importance of the Elite in Chile."

Mery oversaw the entire educational program of the plainclothes police: the Investigations School, the Center for Professional Training, and the Higher Academy of Police Studies. Toro entrusted to him the task of restructuring the curriculum of the Investigations School and the Higher Academy.

Months later, Toro informed him that in November the two of them would travel to Paris, at the invitation of France's interior minister, to attend a meeting of police officials.

"You will have asked yourself why the two of us are traveling by ourselves," Toro put to Mery on board the Air France flight.

"Yes, to take in new experiences."

"Nelson, I know who you are. I know where you've studied, what you've done, where you've been, the stances you've taken, the problems you've had with your bosses. Look, you and I are the same."

"Excuse me, my general?"

"Don't 'my general' me!"

"On Your Knees"

On a December day, near the end of 1991, Toro called Mery into his office.

"Mery, down on your knees," he ordered him.

"Sorry?" the startled head of instruction replied.

It sounded like a preamble to prayer, and Nelson Mery wasn't Catholic; he was a mason. But Toro repeated the command, in military style.

"On your knees, there," as he pointed to the spot.

Mery knelt in front of a large coffee table. The director moved to the spot and did the same. Then he took out a huge roll of paper and unfurled it on top of the table, facing Mery.

"What do you think?" Toro asked him.

It was a new organizational chart for the plainclothes police, which, starting in January 1992 and in line with Toro's plans, would be reorganized from the top down. Nelson Mery would become the second-in-command of the institution and preside over the new Executive Advisory Committee.

"You are going to be my number two," Toro informed him.

In 1991, as the new year rang in, operations deputy director Mario Mengozzi suggested to Mery that he extend best wishes to Toro, who was celebrating his birthday on January 2.

"Mengozzi still had no idea that he would no longer be the deputy head," notes Mery.

They agreed to stop by Toro's office at eight the next morning to offer birthday greetings, and Mery showed up at that hour.

"You're late," the chief of staff told him. "Mengozzi came in an hour ago and left fuming. Don't you know? You've risen to number two."

That same day Toro issued General Order No. 1042, creating the Executive Advisory Committee and putting in place a new institutional high command "in agreement with the requirements imposed by significant historical changes."[24]

Beginning in 1992, with Toro's new organizational chart, twenty-one high-level PICH officials went into retirement, including operations deputy director Mengozzi, administrative deputy director Juan Lizama, and inspector general Douglas Gallegos, the "La Moneda detective" who had brought Luis Henríquez into the Internal Affairs Department.

"It was the same structure that the military used, the structure that he was familiar with. That lasted until I took over and we went back to the old system, which was more dynamic," notes Mery.

Five days after assuming the interim directorship, Mery rescinded the general orders Toro had issued in December 1991 and February 1992 affecting the organization and functions of the Department of Police Intelligence. General Order No. 1042 was canceled in August 1992.

Austerity

Nelson Mery became interim director amid the institutional crisis triggered by Toro's sudden departure and the public questioning about what the work of the plainclothes police ought to be. A widespread perception still existed of a corrupt police force, one complicit in the military dictatorship. At the same time, relations with the Carabineros were, in Mery's words, "deeply damaged." In addition, the PICH lacked adequate means and resources.

All those circumstances, he states, "undermined motivation inside the institution and lowered staff morale. To this were added cases of corruption, of police abuse, and the continued presence of around 300 active employees who had belonged to the [Directorate of National Intelligence] and the [National Center for Information], who hatched pockets of resistance to change. The Investigations Police appeared delegitimized, discredited, and diminished relative to the rest of the state's agencies."

When he was confirmed in the position, Mery publicly announced that he would continue on Toro's path to return the institution to its technical-scientific mission and create a police force accordant with the new times.

For his part, interior minister Enrique Krauss told the press that a timetable was already in place that would enable the PICH to enjoy a full workforce by 1993, filling the vacancies left by Toro's massive purge of the ranks.[25]

Ten days into his directorship, Mery met with the sizable team of civilian advisers Toro left in his wake. He spoke to them about his own institution, the one he had served since 1961.

"I've listened to all of you attentively," he told them. "Everything you've said to me I consider excellent for any director who comes from the outside. But I'm from right here, inside, and have more than thirty years of service. What I want from you are solutions to the problems, because the problems—I am already familiar with them."

While the advisers were holding forth, huge sandwiches were brought in. Mery, drinking his usual herbal tea, shot a look of extreme displeasure.

"This is over! Crackers at most!" he ordered.

The lion's share of Toro's advisers was gone within a month. Remaining on board, among others, were the lawyers Jorge Morales and Andrés Domínguez, the journalists Felipe Pozo and Rodrigo De Arteagabeitía, and the sociologist Ramón Silva. Pozo left a little while later; Morales stayed on until the end of 1996; and others, such as De Arteagabeitía and Domínguez, continued advising Mery throughout virtually his entire tenure.

Mery's routine, many say, was "nocturnal"; he worked deep into the night. Detectives had to accustom themselves to long shifts and late-night calls.

"His work schedule was complicated. We frequently worked until three in the morning, and we had to take shifts in case he needed something, if he asked for some information. Someone had to be there," reports Freddy Orellana, who joined Department V two years later.

At the end of his first year as head of the plainclothes police, after the annual officer review process, Mery retired seventy-seven officials. Five others, all inspector prefects, retired voluntarily.

Nelson Mery directed the PICH for eleven years. His time as its chief is the longest on record.

6

ON THE HUNT FOR
FATSO ROMO

"SEÑOR OSVALDO, the Chilean police are here. Do you want to go to Chile or some other country?" was the question Achilles José Larena asked Osvaldo Romo Mena. Larena was one of Interpol's officials in Brazil.

Larena's question flabbergasted the Chilean detectives who accompanied him, since they were ready to board the airplane to bring the ex–Directorate of National Intelligence (DINA) agent back to Chile to face justice. But this was not out of the ordinary: Chile's most notorious torturer from the time of the military dictatorship was being expelled from Brazil. As such, he had the right to choose his destination.

Still, inspector José Plaza was dumbfounded. After months of leads, diplomatic and political efforts at the highest level, and countless conversations with Romo to convince him that expulsion to Chile was his best option, had it really come down to this? Just when Brazil's federal police were at the point of handing over the prisoner into their custody? By this time, he thought, surely they and the Brazilians were on friendly terms.

"No, I'm going with the Chilean police," Romo replied meekly.

Romo stepped into the Varig airline's plane, and the relieved Chilean officials took hold of him. He wasn't handcuffed. Though only fifty-four years old, Romo was a sick man, and his body was worn out. He was obese, had extreme hypertension, cardiac insufficiency, and diabetes, and required insulin. He had also suffered a brain hemorrhage and a blood clot that affected his movement on the right side of his body. He could no longer see out of his left eye. Romo's chances of escaping were completely nil.

Before boarding the plane, superintendent Luis Henríquez, who led the group of Chilean detectives that had tracked down the ex-agent's whereabouts in Brazil, issued a warning to his team.

"He told us we had to be careful, that we had to be secretive and on the alert because 'they can remove a screw from the airplane, and we'll go down.' He wasn't being literal, but we were very nervous," Plaza recalls.

It was eleven fifteen on the morning of November 16, 1992, when Romo left Brazil and surrendered his freedom forever. In Chile, seven arrest warrants awaited him.

He took off for Santiago with detectives from both Interpol and the Analysis and Institutional Coordination Commission (CACI). There was only one journalist on board: Pablo Honorato from Channel 13. A longtime court reporter known for his easy access to the higher-ups in the Chilean military dictatorship and its intelligence services, Honorato was the only journalist who got word in time that the ex-agent was being expelled from Brazil, on board Varig flight 920. Like many of his colleagues, he spent months traveling to and from Brazil once Romo's July 1992 capture was revealed. Now he was covering Romo's return to Chile. But only Honorato managed to sit next to Romo on the plane, and he seized on that opportunity to interview him.

"The police did not want us to film him for TV, but we did it anyway. I didn't know him. He was a bit of a loudmouth, talked an awful lot and in *portuñol* [a mixture of Spanish and Portuguese]. He seemed to come across as normal, though very cold," Honorato related in a press interview.[1]

Romo conversed in a mixture of Spanish and Portuguese, fruit of the seventeen years that he stayed hidden with his family in Brazil. He complained of pains in his legs but didn't appear particularly worried. He put his faith in what the Chilean detectives had assured him of time and again: that they needed his valuable cooperation to clear up certain past events but that nothing would happen to him. The crimes, they insisted, fell under the statute of limitations, and he would be compensated for the incriminating information. They told him that the courts would unquestionably apply the Amnesty Law, as they always did.

In October Chile's Congress passed the controversial *ley de arrepentimiento eficaz* (analogous in some respects to the policy of turning state's evidence), which reduced a possible sentence significantly if the accused provided information or helped break up the criminal terrorist organization to which this person belonged. The law would be in effect for four years.

Romo was an ideal candidate to put the law into practice. He would no longer have to continue hiding abroad and could soon turn his life around. He would cease being Andrés Henríquez, a Chilean family man who lived on a disability pension in a poor neighborhood of São Paulo. At last, he could go back to being Osvaldo Romo Mena, "Fatso Romo."

From Provocateur to Torturer

Osvaldo Romo was a small-time crook who had never finished high school and passed himself off as a local-level leftist leader at the end of the 1960s and during the Allende years. He was married to Raquel González Chandía. They had five children, a son and four daughters. The youngest daughter was born a few months before the military coup. His wife was semiliterate and confined herself to domestic work and the care of her children.

After the coup, Romo turned snitch, informing on left-wing coworkers. He was recruited by the DINA in 1974. He joined the Falcon group, a unit in charge of hunting down members of the Movement of the Revolutionary Left (MIR), and began to torture prisoners in the secret Londres 38 detention center and later in Villa Grimaldi. He participated in the abduction, torture, rape, and disappearance of dozens of MIR militants, turning himself into one of DINA's most sadistic agents.

Romo had no firm convictions. His educational, political, and even military preparation was a void. He was a crude man, of few ideas, a thug with a criminal background, prone to blundering. He divulged too much and bragged about what he did. He liked his victims to know who he was. He left his face uncovered and blurted out his real name. He went back to the homes of persons he had arrested, under the pretense of asking for money or clothes to take back to the detainees. Needless to say, these offerings never got there. Frequently enough, the detainees were already "disappeared," but Romo continued telling their families that he would do what he could to help them.

Many people identified him long before his arrest in Brazil. They knew that one of the DINA's agents, among those who had carried off their loved ones, was Fatso Romo—the same person who had been featured in the press two years earlier as a neighborhood leader, hurling insults at President Allende. His name turned up in dozens of legal reports associated with MIR militants because he participated in their arrests. He was listed in writs of protection, in testimonies before the Vicariate of Solidarity, and in the internal documentation of left-wing parties. Everyone knew his name and could describe him. They remembered him as a disheveled man, obese, smelly, sweaty, and singularly cruel.

Fatso Romo became a problem for the DINA. He was undisciplined and left too many trails behind him. He was of no use to them anymore. In addition, Romo tended to inflate his importance and even boasted about the crimes he committed. He was unable to control himself and could not keep quiet and maintain the discretion and secrecy DINA operations required. Pulled from the civilian ranks, he was simply an informer, a lowly specimen of brute force. The risk that he might reveal more than he should was too great. Sooner or later, the authorities would come looking for Romo to make him face justice.

That day arrived in 1975, when a police sergeant showed up at his house with a court summons. The court was investigating the disappearance of Jorge Herrera, a high school student and MIR militant who was abducted in December 1974. Romo refused to receive the notice, indicating to the police officer that any summons had to come through the Military Intelligence Service.

Months later, in December 1975, another court subpoenaed Romo in connection with the abduction of Mauricio Jorquera, a nineteen-year-old University of Chile sociology student and MIR militant. He had been detained by the DINA in August 1974 and subsequently disappeared.

The court sent official letters to the DINA requesting Romo's appearance. When it failed to get any reply, it asked the Investigations Police (PICH) to find him. PICH detectives followed up by going to the DINA's Terranova post in Villa Grimaldi. They interviewed DINA officer Hugo Morales. Morales admitted that Romo had belonged to the DINA but stated he had been let go in mid-1975. It was not a lie.

Judge Tomás Dahm was also searching for Romo and requested that the DINA turn over its torturer. The DINA's director, Manuel Contreras, had already made complaints about this judge. In a letter to interior minister Gen. César Benevides, Contreras objected that Dahm was being very meddlesome. He asked the minister to impose "the most severe measures and sanctions against Judge Tomás Dahm."[2]

Judge Dahm, however, was not put off. On January 6, 1976, he issued a warrant for the arrest of Osvaldo Romo, but it was not attended to. It was the first of various arrest warrants and judicial subpoenas directed at Romo in the years to follow.

By then four criminal complaints had already been filed against him in different courts; he had been named as a criminal agent in more than 100 writs of protection filed with the court of appeals, and dozens of former political prisoners identified him as their torturer. Such was his notoriety that an ad hoc United Nations committee on human rights in Chile classified him, in a 1975 report, as "the most expert torturer in Chile" and requested he be brought to justice.

But Romo had slipped away.

Señor Andrés

It was June 1975, and DINA agent Gerardo Urrich had just come back to work as a torturer in Villa Grimaldi after a lengthy medical leave.

"You must get out of the country," he told Romo.

It wasn't safe to stay in Chile. The DINA allowed him to select a country in which to drop out of circulation: El Salvador, South Africa, or Brazil. Things were complicated for Romo. His wife and children didn't know what the head of household was really doing for work. They thought he was employed in a factory.

Romo chose Brazil because it was a big country where he could feel safer. In addition, it was closer to Chile. Days before their trip, the entire family was brought to a shop to have photos taken for their new passports and identity cards, with false names and real fingerprints. Romo offered no explanation to his wife for the sudden trip, assuring her that they would soon come back. He was equally silent about the false names on their new documents. As she dismantled her home and filled suitcases and baby bottles, Raquel González thought none of this made any sense but was powerless to do anything.

Led by Carabineros official Tulio Pereira, DINA agents showed up at the Romo residence on the morning of October 16, 1975. They drove off in several vehicles to take the family to Santiago's Pudahuel airport. On the tarmac, just before boarding the plane, the family was handed tickets, passports, their family documents, and US$8,000.

The passports on which Romo and his wife traveled to Brazil bore the names Osvaldo Andrés Henríquez and Raquel Rojas Chandía. Both entered as tourists. The five children, who traveled under the false names assumed by their parents, ranged in age from two to thirteen. None of them had any idea about their father's past.

With the cooperation of airport employees, the family's departure went unrecorded. Following the instructions in the envelope he was given at the airport, Romo had to be the last person to exit the plane after it landed in Rio de Janeiro. Once on the tarmac, he was to look up and exclaim, "It's really hot!" Someone would then appear at his side, whom he needed to follow. Romo did as instructed. The stranger took the passports from the family, gathered their luggage with the help of a customs employee—without passing through the International Police controls—and brought them to the Riviera Hotel on Rio's Flamengo Beach. Several days later, the DINA rented an apartment for Romo in São Paulo and continued furnishing him money. In mid-1977 Chile's consul in Brasilia, Pedro Uriarte, presented the Henríquez-Rojas family with new passports. Armed with this documentation, Romo was "recycled" in Brazil into a new profession: he was now an "industrial safety engineer." Despite lacking any such training or preparation, he was given a job as head of industrial safety at ADAP, a plant that manufactured metallic furniture. It was located a couple of hours from São Paulo, in the municipality of Mogi-Mirim. Romo moved there with his family and, in addition, began to teach classes in industrial safety at the government's National Service for Industrial Training (Senai).

"Shielded by the industrialists who aided Brazil's military dictatorship, Romo secured various positions using false documents provided by the DINA. These represented him as being an expert in industrial safety or an engineer. He obtained a pension under his false identity," explains Luis Henríquez.

The following year, in July 1978, the family's passports were renewed. Two years later Romo got a job in Mogi-Guaçú, a small municipality of no more than 100,00 inhabitants in the state of São Paulo. The DINA gradually began to cut itself off from maintaining its ex-torturer.

"While we were in Brazil we lived entirely on Osvaldo's earnings from his work. Nobody offered us any help when he was ill and had two brain hemorrhages and a blood clot in his right leg. Afterward came his heart problem, diabetes, and high blood pressure. No one helped us, neither Chileans nor Brazilians," said Romo's wife when appearing before a Chilean court in 1993.[3]

At home in Mogi-Guaçú, "Andrés Henríquez" passed himself off as a leftist, cozying up to people tied to left-wing parties in Brazil. According to police reports, citing leftist political leaders in Brazil, Romo invited Chilean exiles to his house every year to commemorate the death of President Allende. They sang the national hymn while facing a Chilean flag.

In 1986, when the Brazilian military dictatorship was replaced by a civilian government, Osvaldo Romo obtained an identity card for foreign residents of Brazil, lying about his and his parents' names, his date of birth, and his occupation. With this identity card he secured employment as an adviser and cabinet official for the recently elected leftist mayor of Mogi-Guaçú, Carlos Nelson Bueno.

By then, in Chile, Romo's participation in at least sixty abductions of disappeared persons had been confirmed, and dozens of political prisoners—men and women—had submitted criminal complaints denouncing him as their torturer.

When captured in July 1992, "Andrés Henríquez" was subsisting on a disability pension granted four months earlier. In Brazil, he had converted himself not only into an engineer without any academic preparation but also into a soccer coach. His team even won a local championship. Romo kept the press clippings as a memento.

A Lone Civilian

Throughout 1991 criminal charges and arrest orders accumulated against Romo for the abduction of various victims. The DINA leaders involved in these crimes were already identified. Nonetheless, the CACI's team concluded that Romo could crack open this state security agency even more. His cooperation would complement the trove of information already offered by the two former MIR militants turned DINA collaborators, Luz Arce and Marcia Merino.

"Romo was a civilian and on his own. When our interest turned to him, we already knew that he figured in at least fifty cases and had participated in detentions and torture. We discovered that he was a key player, an accessible player, because he didn't have institutional backing," states Plaza.

They decided to start from scratch. They made a sweep of testimonies, court statements, legal complaints, writs of protection, arrest orders—every jot of information related to Osvaldo Romo.

They scrutinized newspaper and magazine articles, studied the police reports of previous investigations conducted during the dictatorship, and went back over everything that the police and the judicial system had done, or not done, or done badly.

They sought him out in a house in the Santiago neighborhood of Ñuñoa, where, according to police records, he appeared to be living, but the house had been demolished. They also checked a home in the Santiago-area municipality of Peñalolén, where he had previously lived, but now it was owned by another family.

They exhausted all leads bearing on Romo's presence in Chile. The likeliest prospect, the detectives judged, was that he was living under a false identity, perhaps outside the country.

Initially, Romo was suspected of being in Spain, due to a story published in 1980 in the newspaper *Las Últimas Noticias*. The newspaper piece stated—without citing sources—that in 1978 Romo had plastic surgery in Brazil, then left to live in Spain. "He enters Chile periodically with his wife and two children under a false name to prevent reprisals against him, owing to the fact that he finds himself under a death sentence [pronounced] by international Marxism," the paper stated, again without citing sources or a shred of evidence.[4]

Spain was quickly dismissed.

The attempt by the CACI's detectives to run down his location was already under way when the arrest order issued by Judge Gloria Olivares reached them on March 25, 1992. Coincidentally, or perhaps not, General Pinochet was in São Paulo at this time. Judge Olivares sought Romo for the disappearance of the MIR militant and philosophy student Alfonso Chanfreau. Both he and his young wife, Erika Hennings, had been tortured by Romo.

During one of these torture sessions, Romo took off Hennings's blindfold and made her look at him. She never forgot his face and figure. "When I think about him fear comes over me," Hennings told the magazine *Análisis* in 1986. "But I need to find him to confront him, without the naïveté of that time. I've been looking for him all these years, on the streets, everywhere. He knows a lot and has to provide answers."[5]

Six years later, Erika Hennings did confront him in the PICH's headquarters.

When they received the order to detain Romo, the detectives were already investigating the whereabouts of his wife. They requested information from the Border Control Department about Romo's and his wife's possible movements, trying various combinations of names and surnames, but nothing turned up.

The search for him had to start on his own turf. The detectives went looking for his relatives, theorizing that if he was living out of the country, he at some point would have contacted someone in the family for a birthday or to address some need or merely to say hello. Romo was careless, which worked to the advantage of the detectives. At last, they hit on his father-in-law, Raquel González's stepfather, Roberto Sanhueza, a peanut street vendor. They asked Judge Olivares to issue a summons so they could question him.

"We didn't get much out of the father-in-law, but we told him he had to cooperate because he was covering up a very important investigation and we had to subpoena his son-in-law," Plaza recalls. "He told us that he knew Romo 'had been in the military government' but didn't know more than that and didn't want to furnish more information." Nevertheless, he admitted to having gone to Brazil to visit him in 1978, during the celebration of Carnival.

For her part, Judge Olivares subpoenaed Romo's brother-in-law, Luis González. He also said he had visited Romo and noted that he worked at a company called ADAP. A short while later, he went back to the court and handed the judge a letter bearing a return address in Brazil: a post office box in Mogi-Mirim. The letter was sent by "C. Rojas." The true sender was Raquel González, his sister.

The police then asked the Santiago Interpol office to communicate with its counterpart in São Paulo to check whether there was an Osvaldo Romo living in Mogi-Mirim. They came up empty. There wasn't anyone with that name residing in Brazil.

From Parral, Just the Right Man

By early 1992, the CACI team was effectively down to two men, inspector José Plaza—who had come on board in late 1991—and Luis Henríquez. In February 1992, the members of the original team were detailed to other missions: Department V's chief, José Sotomayor, was appointed head of the Antinarcotics Brigade and took with him José Miranda and Hugo Rebolledo. Sotomayor was replaced by deputy superintendent Miguel Jara Sáez, whose tenure in the post lasted only a little more than a year.

So the CACI's staff was reduced to five individuals: its chief, Luis Henríquez; Plaza; and three administrative employees. It was further reduced in March 1992, when Henríquez began a term in the Higher Academy of Police Studies, which required him to divide his time between Department V and the academy.

During the first months of 1992, the CACI team continued studying and analyzing information and reviewing the police reports that arrived from around the country. The detectives also interviewed victims' relatives and former political prisoners and complied with some orders sent by the courts. The pace was slow, but that was going to change abruptly. The inquiries aimed at locating Romo began to take off.

Although institutional regulations dictated that Henríquez dedicate himself exclusively to the academy, he never cut his ties with the CACI. He continued functioning as its chief, with the consent of interim director Nelson Mery. Plaza reported daily on progress to Henríquez, and Henríquez, in turn, gave an account to Mery.

"How was I going to ditch the commission's work? There was never an order that might relieve me of that responsibility, that might set aside General Toro's order. I had to study, and I was immersed in both things. I went from the academy to the office to work until one or two in the morning," he notes.

In one of those meetings with Henríquez, Inspector Plaza raised a problem that he considered urgent: if they proposed to find Romo or make progress on any other investigation, the team needed reinforcements. With the few resources and employees then available, it was a constant juggling act.

"Look for somebody you judge capable of serving. Bring me a candidate," Henríquez proposed.

It was no easy task. There were many competent detectives, but this operation was different. It involved vile crimes committed by agents of the state, and their own institution wasn't purged of all the elements tied to the repressive machinery of the military dictatorship. The great majority of police reports sent to the CACI by different units were as before: scanty reports a few pages long that basically confirmed the crime and reproduced the legal complaints and testimony of relatives and witnesses. Rarely did they contain anything more than that.

Plaza, though, recalled a fifty-nine-page report, dated July 23, 1991, that came in from the southern city of Parral. It was from inspector José Luis Cabión. His police report on disappeared detainees in that zone reflected an investigation that was, for those years, bold and rigorous.

"The CACI team got together in the mornings, and we read those reports. Everyone liked Cabión's. He had done good work. It was what we needed," says Plaza.

Cabión became the deputy chief of the Parral police district in February 1991, after transferring from Calama, in the desert North. He was thirty-six years old, personable, a man from the countryside. Cabión grew up in a working-class family, in the city of Melipilla, near Santiago. His mother was a housewife and he had four sisters. Cabión graduated from a politically active high school but did not take part in any student protests or agitations. In fact, the order imposed by the nascent dictatorship was more to his liking. After leaving school he worked some months for Melipilla's social security service and then spent two years as a poultry salesman for the company Ariztía. But the country's economic outlook was not good, so in 1977—as the regime waged its covert political repression—Cabión enrolled in the Investigations School.

"I liked the system, I liked [the fact] that the country was stabilized, because of the inflation that existed, but I didn't know that crimes were being committed. The issue of repression was covered up," states Cabión, "and the media published whatever."

He was in the school in 1978 when the first remains of disappeared detainees were discovered in the Lonquén lime kiln, just forty kilometers from his hometown. But Cabión never learned about it. Information barely penetrated the school, and the subject didn't come up in any conversation with his fellow recruits, he says.

When Cabión graduated in 1979 his first posting was to the police district of La Reina. He knew that the National Center for Information was detaining and interrogating people, but he didn't question the official line. "Perhaps I was too naïve, but I didn't even know that Villa Grimaldi existed, and it was located nearby. We were told a story about extremists, and both the military and top officials of the police convinced us those people had to be confronted," affirms Cabión.

After a year in La Reina, he was sent in 1980 to the airport, to work in immigration control. Cabión spent three years in the old airport building, observing how people were sent into exile. National Center for Information agents asked police in the terminal for the lists of passengers traveling abroad in order to check their luggage and see what was making its way into the world outside.

"They even had a device they swept over [people's luggage] that spoiled tape recordings. Once they found a mountain of *arpilleras* [brightly colored hand-stitched burlap quilts that often depicted the horrors of the dictatorship] in a suitcase and confiscated all of them," relates Cabión.

In 1983 he moved on to the police command in his hometown of Melipilla. By then Cabión was married. Shortly after Chile's March 1985 earthquake, he was sent to Calama, where he was tasked with infiltrating the miners unions.

When Cabión settled in Parral, the Rettig Commission had just submitted a legal complaint in the local court over the 1973 disappearance of a dozen detainees in that area. Both the Carabineros and military from the Linares Artillery School were implicated in the crimes. The court had sent the investigative order to the PICH in Parral, but the detectives hadn't done anything with it. It was a "hot potato" that no one wanted to touch. On his first day on the job, Cabión was handed the order by the chief of police, deputy superintendent Roberto González. Detective Cabión interviewed relatives and witnesses, requested records of all the public services in the area, reconstructed the events, identified the abductors and other responsible parties, and subpoenaed them to testify—something unusual for the time.

José Luis Cabión was the right man for the job.

Fifteen years later he became chief of the PICH's Human Rights Brigade. He arrived in Santiago at the end of May 1992, when José Plaza was completing his report on the Joint Command. He joined the CACI's team as it entered the home stretch in its quest to capture Osvaldo Romo.

Precious Little

Two months had gone by since the inquiries to locate Romo began. Based on the information gathered thus far, the next step had to be a trip to Brazil. Up until then, the budget for special assignments abroad was very restricted and went mainly to trips to Interpol conferences or for some course in policing. Increasingly, though, it was also being allocated to fund human rights investigations.

Inspector Plaza decided one day to approach Director Mery as he was walking toward his office. "I observed that he had little faith in us. Perhaps he believed that we wouldn't get anywhere, but whatever the case, Mery reacted well. We explained to him why Romo was important, the position that he had inside the DINA, that he was a civilian agent, that reaching him was easy, and that we were closing in," says Plaza.

Plaza left for the academy, where he found Superintendent Henríquez, and told him about the conversation with Mery. Henríquez then pitched the importance of the trip to the director.

The CACI's detectives prepared a memorandum summarizing the background data dug up on Romo, who—they presumed—was living under a fictitious name. They sketched out his legal situation and the maneuvers they could make in Brazil. The first, they noted, was to secure the cooperation of that country's federal police.

Mery consulted with interior minister Enrique Krauss, who authorized a small group of detectives to leave for a week on special assignment to São Paulo.

On June 8, 1992, Henríquez and Plaza left for Brazil, breaking journey for a few days in Argentina. Their presence in Brazil went completely unnoticed—the Chilean press was more intent on covering the activities of President Aylwin who, around this time, was traveling to Brazil to participate with other world leaders in the UN's Earth Summit in Rio de Janeiro.

The first thing the detectives did was to speak with Romeu Tuma Jr., the head of Interpol in São Paulo. He, in turn, spoke with his father, also named Romeu Tuma, who was then director general of Brazil's federal police and headquartered in Brasilia. Despite the elder Tuma's questionable past in one of the Brazilian military dictatorship's main agencies of repression, both men promised to help the Chileans.[6]

"We worked out a very good relationship with the federal police. There were several officials who were exceptional, very out-front, true heroes of the story, among them Achilles José Larena and José Luiz Boanova. We communicated with each other in *portuñol*," recalls Henríquez.

The Brazilian federal police assigned a pair of officers as liaisons to the Chileans, and they began to make inquiries to locate Romo. They used an undercover agent to look for a Chilean who fit Romo's description and presumably lived in Mogi-Mirim. Henríquez and Plaza tried everything but came up empty.

"We even went into every telephone booth and went through the guides, searching page by page for Romo. It was foolish, perhaps, but we didn't have much of a choice. We got precious little out of that trip," recounts Plaza.

They met and spoke with Chile's consul in São Paulo, Fernando Pardo, who allowed them to go over consular records. They also spoke with the lawyer Belisario Dos Santos, who sat on the governing board of the Brazilian Bar Association and, in addition, was a member of the national Human Rights Commission. Dos Santos oriented them to the possible alternatives of expulsion versus extradition, should Romo be captured.

Once back in Chile, they leaned on the father-in-law, Roberto Sanhueza: What name did Romo really go by in Brazil?

"He's Andrés Henríquez," Sanhueza admitted.

In mid-June, Interpol's office in São Paulo confirmed that for at least the past ten years, the Chilean Andrés Henríquez had been living in Mogi-Mirim. There was only one problem; he was no longer there.

"A Certain Tina"

José Plaza knew that Chilean citizens living abroad had to go at set intervals to the consulate to renew their documents. They asked Judge Olivares to request the cooperation and facilities of the Foreign Affairs Ministry so they could review its consular archive. Armed with the judge's order, the CACI's full team—i.e., Plaza, Cabión, and the administrative employees, because Henríquez was away at the academy—set off on June 22 for the foreign ministry's Consular Historical Archive. They spent hours going through oversized books, alert to possible consular records of "Andrés Henríquez" and his family in Brazil.

Each person separately went through book after book, year by year. Suddenly, Plaza got up from the table and hugged Cabión.

"We've got it!" he exclaimed.

Plaza showed him a document: In an attachment to record number 832/503, dated August 23, 1978, and registered in Chile's general consulate in São Paulo, appeared the names of Romo, his wife, and their five children—under their false identities. The month before, they had renewed their passports. The team dug a little deeper and discovered another consular record that revealed that passports were granted to the Henríquez-Rojas family in Brasilia in 1977.

Romo's father-in-law had told Judge Olivares about a Chilean who lived in Brazil and knew Romo. The man had returned to Chile after falling ill with cancer. He remembered this person's name but not that of his wife. He said she was called "Tina." Accordingly, Judge Olivares furnished them with a very succinct investigative order, requesting that the man and "a certain Tina" be located.

"We looked for this man in Chile, but he had already passed away," says Cabión. "We went to the civil registry and the wife appeared in it as the person who had registered his death. We asked for personal details on this woman and located her residence, but no one was there. We went back several times. The neighbors we spoke to told us she worked in the Barros Luco Hospital. We left for the hospital and found her. At first, she denied knowing Romo, denied it aggressively."

This "certain Tina" turned out to be the medical assistant Cristina Saavedra. She was a friend of Romo and his wife in Brazil. Inspectors Cabión and Plaza summoned her for an interview on June 30 in the Department V office. They had put together a dossier on Romo and showed it to her, requesting her cooperation "under the conditions she would want," recalls Plaza.

She displayed the same reluctance to acknowledge her acquaintance with Romo before Judge Olivares, until the judge interposed that she was on the point of being detained for obstructing justice. That got her to talk.

Cristina Saavedra told them that her husband had gone to live in Mogi-Mirim in 1977 for work. One day, after he was there, he telephoned a fellow Chilean citizen, Andrés Henríquez. He had learned that Henríquez was a Chilean, recently arrived, and invited him to tea at his house. They became friends, and Saavedra's husband took up living in Romo's house. In April 1978 she and her children also moved to Mogi-Mirim, staying in Romo's house for a couple of days. They quickly rented their own house, but the two families continued fraternizing and spending Chile's Independence Day together. Romo told them that he had fled Chile for political reasons, because he was on the left.

The last time she saw him, she told the police, was in January of that year (1992), when she visited Henríquez in his house. He lived at 144 Rua Cambara, Jardim Ypê II, in Mogi-Guacú.

They showed her a photo.

"Is this Osvaldo Romo?"

"I don't know," Saavedra replied. "But I do know him as Andrés Henríquez."

The next day, via Interpol, the CACI's detectives asked their counterparts in São Paulo to check whether in fact the Chilean Andrés Henríquez was living at that address with his family, adding the following details: his son Simón (who went by the false name Antonio) had a karate school, and his daughter Rosa was married to a Brazilian.

Superintendent Henríquez was worried that Saavedra would alert Romo that the police were on his trail. In a memo to Director Mery, he emphasized that it would be well advised to speed up procedures, and he asked that two actions be taken: a request to Interpol for the detention and expulsion of Romo and a request to the Chilean government to officially inform the Brazilian government of the background to the case, followed by the latter taking the necessary steps.[7]

On July 2, a fax came in from Romeu Tuma Jr., Interpol's chief in São Paulo: The Chilean citizen Osvaldo Romo Mena had been located. His address was confirmed, as was his status as a permanent resident of Brazil. He was living in a public housing unit that he owned. Now they really had him.

That same day, Director Mery asked the Civil Registry Service to send over as quickly as possible the record of Osvaldo Romo's fingerprints, photographs of him, details on his personal history, and other background information. They had to go to Brazil to bring him back.

It was then that CACI officials summoned Erika Hennings, the widow of Alfonso Chanfreau, to appear at Department V. "We mentioned to her, to her alone and in strict confidence, that we were going after Romo, and that now we were sure about where he was. She thanked us and put us in contact with her lawyer, who responded very well to us," says Plaza.

The lawyer was Fernando Oyarce Chanfreau, Alfonso's nephew. Hennings had requested that the case be reopened with him in May 1990. Oyarce purchased a ticket and left for Brazil on his own. He reconnected there with the detectives.

I'm Osvaldo Romo

On July 27, superintendent Luis Henríquez and inspector José Plaza traveled again on assignment to Brazil. They were accompanied by the deputy superintendent of Interpol's Santiago office, Patricio Faúndez. They carried a thick dossier with them on Romo, along with a letter from Director Mery to Brazil's federal police, requesting the police's collaboration in the capture of the ex-DINA agent. Mery emphasized that Osvaldo Romo "is of vital importance for clearing up numerous crimes of homicide and kidnapping."[8]

Mery authorized the two officers to travel on assignment from July 27 to 31. Their stay, however, lasted much longer and became more complicated than expected. A short time later, the team in Brazil was bolstered by Cabión, who remained in São Paulo for more than a month.

"We had used up our travel allowance to pay the hotel, but Luis Fernando del Valle—then the representative in São Paulo of the Chilean airline LADECO, came to our aid. He provided the needed resources and put out the welcome mat for us," says Henríquez.

Before leaving Santiago, Henríquez spelled out the different scenarios for Director Mery.

One plan was to send a team of police officials to negotiate Romo's voluntary return, assuring him that his wife and children were free to stay in Brazil. If Romo's return to Chile could not be worked out, because Brazil's federal police intended to hand him over to the local courts for using false documentation, they would request authorization to interview him. To prepare for this eventuality, the team brought a questionnaire "with the maximum [number] of necessary questions to establish his participation and that of other persons in crimes involving human rights violations."[9]

There was a real possibility that the Brazilian courts would not hand over Romo but instead would sentence him to prison for violating the laws applying to foreigners living in Brazil. Henríquez told Mery that Belisario Dos Santos, the Brazilian lawyer, thought that the process of extraditing Romo had "very few chances of succeeding."[10]

First thing in the morning on July 29, 1992, the São Paulo Interpol officials, Achilles José Larena and Paulo Guilherme de Mello Dias, arrived at Romo's house and placed him under arrest. The ex-torturer was watching a soccer game on television. He offered no resistance. They told him they were there to check his papers, in light of the information furnished by Interpol Chile that he was living in Brazil under a false name.

Plaza stayed behind in the federal police office, waiting impatiently, while Henríquez and Faúndez followed the Brazilian police.

"We were driving on our own, because the federal police had to carry out the operation. We looked on from a distance. But on the way back to São Paulo those guys headed off with Romo, doing something like 180 kilometers per hour on the highway with their warning lights flashing. We got back about two hours later," said Henríquez.

As soon as they got to the federal police's immigration department in São Paulo, the police compared Romo's fingerprints and confirmed his true identity. A little later they brought him before the Chilean officials.

"They are Chilean police officials and say that you, Mr. Andrés Henríquez, have another name. What is your true name?" they asked him.

Romo looked at Plaza and Henríquez.

"Osvaldo Romo Mena," he calmly told them. And offered to shake hands.

"I didn't extend my hand to him, because he revolted me," Plaza remembers. "Shaking hands is a friendly gesture, and I couldn't stomach it. We had to speak with him, deal with him, but it was hard for me to approach him. I was always repulsed by him. He was a really dreadful person."

Romo admitted he was living under a false identity with phony documentation. He was instantly arrested. In front of a representative of the Chilean consulate, they informed him of his right to remain silent, but he didn't want to. He told them that he would respond to whatever he might be asked and that he intended to go to Chile to testify regarding the indictments that involved him.

Romo was placed at the disposition of São Paulo's First Criminal Court, his case assigned to Judge Toru Yamamoto. Yamamoto had to resolve Romo's legal situation. For bearing false documentation, Romo was charged with infringing three articles of the Brazilian penal code, which merited his expulsion from the country. He remained under arrest in a lockup of São Paulo's federal police department where other foreign detainees were being held.

Romeu Tuma Jr., the head of Interpol in São Paulo, told Henríquez that the best way to get Romo out of Brazil and back to Chile was by guaranteeing him that the crimes fell under the statute of limitations. "Romo is going to think that he'll travel to Chile and turn around and come back right away. That is the argument [to use]," Tuma told him.

Tuma spoke with Romo in Portuguese, explaining to him the advisability of going to Chile. Luis Henríquez nodded his head in agreement.

Nothing to Lose

Luis Henríquez asked Judge Yamamoto for permission to question Romo, and he was able to do so several days later. He brought a questionnaire with 108 typed questions, filling in the answers by hand and recording the conversation on a sixty-minute cassette tape. Romo wove back and forth between the delusional and the real. He told the detective that days before the coup he spoke with President Allende about his government and the armed forces and that the president helped him financially because he wanted to go to Europe to study. On the other hand, he got into details about Chanfreau's arrest, the leaders of MIR, and the DINA's agents and infrastructure. On a sheet of paper, Romo drew a partial organizational chart illustrating how the DINA was structured and, on the reverse, a general organizational chart of MIR's structure.

"Are you aware that current Chilean legislation entails an amnesty law and provides compensation for collaborating with information?" Henríquez asked him.

"No."

"Under the protection of this legislation, would you agree to answer to the Chilean courts?"

"Not because that law exists," Romo replied. "I've told you that I ought to go. I'm going because I think it's an obligation."

The only thing he asked for was the guarantee of safety in Brazil for his family and himself.

"I have nothing to lose, and I have things to gain," said Romo. "I have to protect [the welfare of] my family. I'm out of the DINA. . . . They threw me out and I haven't a thing in my house."

"Did you believe that the Chilean police would be able to sometime locate you?" Henríquez asked him.

"Yes."

"Do you believe that the Chilean police know your history as a DINA agent?"

"I think they know 50 percent of it," he said.[11]

"Romo was a bit submissive, and perhaps eager to spill everything he knew, but he was confused in his mind and had to be led. All of a sudden, he was checking himself or lapsing into the grotesque and saying that 'with some bastards you had to grab a razor blade and start to cut their testicles.' That was Romo," Plaza recalls.

On July 30, Director Mery informed interior minister Enrique Krauss about the steps his officials had taken in Brazil and Romo's willingness to return to Chile to testify. To accomplish that, Mery noted, they were counting on the favorable inclinations of the Brazilian federal police, the courts, and the lawyer Belisario Dos Santos, who was advising them on "legal options for [Romo's] expulsion."[12]

By now, Romo was tied to sixteen judicial cases; there were six warrants out for his arrest, and he was mentioned in dozens of other cases.

The following day, President Aylwin called his Brazilian counterpart to express the Chilean government's "keen interest" in Romo's expulsion. Brazil's president, Fernando Collor de Mello, promised to act accordingly.[13]

Immediately afterward, Chile's undersecretary for foreign affairs sent a secret telex to the embassy in Brazil. On the president's instructions, he requested that the embassy take "urgent measures with the competent authorities in order to secure Romo's expulsion to Chile."

The very next day, August 1, 1992, Chile's ambassador to Brazil, Carlos Martínez, met in his residence with the chief of protocol for the Brazilian presidency to ask for an expedited resolution to Chile's request. Two days later he reiterated his request. Beginning that same week of August, the Chilean ambassador and other members of the diplomatic mission met with the Brazilian president's chief legal counsel. They presented him with the full case background and also held four sessions with Brazil's justice minister, Celio Borja. They pressed on him that Romo had yet to be indicted in Chile, for which reason his extradition wasn't pursued. Extradition was a lengthy and tedious process they sought to avoid at all costs. His immediate expulsion was the better course.

The Chilean foreign affairs ministry held a confidential coordinating meeting on August 17 in Santiago to consider the steps to take to achieve Romo's expulsion. Ambassador Carlos Martínez, who was present at the meeting, suggested a plan of action that began with keeping superintendent Luis Henríquez in São Paulo, and that's what was done. He made two other suggestions as well: that they contract with a Brazilian lawyer to "collaborate [with them] discreetly," which they did with Belisario Dos Santos, and that they extend some type of financial assistance to Romo's family, as the consul Fernando Pardo had requested.

The initiatives taken by the Chilean government toward its counterparts in Brazil did not cease in the months ahead. But things did not proceed as expected.

Constant Tension

While the Chilean government began to mount political and diplomatic efforts, and lawyers and relatives of victims of the repression in Chile traveled to Brazil to press for Romo's speedy expulsion, the police were busy earning his confidence, to convince him that the best thing he could do was return to his own country.

The detectives went to see him with their hands full: they brought him toiletries, paper, food, and medicine. "We had to build up a relationship with him, get a dialogue started. At first, he reacted with a natural, understandable mistrust, but over time he began bragging about his feats," says Henríquez.

They went every day to chat with Romo. They asked him simple questions, nothing that could directly incriminate him, because the objective was to have him decide to go back to Chile voluntarily.

"The relationship we had with him was basically to reassure him, get him to trust us. We had to keep up his diet and occasionally make some nice gesture toward him. I told him, Look, Fatso, you won't be a prisoner here for more than six months," says Cabión.

Luis Henríquez maintained his optimism that the expulsion decree on Romo would be issued at any moment, so at the beginning of August he informed Director Mery that—barring some unforeseen development—the police would be in a position to bring Romo back to Chile during the week of August 10.

"In accordance with the negotiations taking place, it would be risky right now for the media to learn about these dealings," Henríquez indicated.[14]

Romo's detention continued to be a confidential matter. Furthermore, to facilitate negotiations, the intent was to keep it off the front pages of the newspapers. That didn't last long, as Superintendent Henríquez also informed his boss that he had spotted a journalist from the newspaper *La Época* interviewing the Chilean consul and employees of Brazil's Department of Immigration. Moreover, he added, reporters from the paper *La Tercera* were in the city but evidently hadn't gotten wind of any developments, as they were covering the activities of a private company.[15]

The leak came on the part of the Brazilians, obliging the Chilean government to react quickly. On August 8, the newspaper *O Estado de São Paulo* ran the headline "Ex–Pinochet agent is detained in São Paulo." That same day Ambassador Martínez announced to the press that Romo was, as reported, in police custody in that city. He also admitted there were Chilean detectives in the country to "be informed directly of the matter."[16]

In Santiago, Belisario Velasco, undersecretary of the Interior Ministry, informed the country that Romo's arrest came about when the Brazilian federal police surprised him carrying a false identity card. The Brazilians then informed Interpol, who in turn passed the information on to the PICH.[17] Such, initially, was the official version of events.

Local reporters ran down the hotel where the Chilean detectives were staying, São Paulo's Hotel Bristol, and from then on the journalistic siege was unending. Some reporters sent over from Chile also stayed in the Bristol. The CACI's officials lost their anonymity, putting the Chilean embassy and Brazilian authorities in an awkward position. One lived in "a constant [state of] of tension," as Henríquez described it to Director Mery.[18]

They Don't Remember, They Weren't There

Meanwhile in Santiago, the Palace of Justice was a beehive of activity. During much of 1992, Judge Gloria Olivares took statements from victims, relatives of victims, and witnesses. She also began to set up face-to-face encounters between former leaders of the DINA and their victims in connection with the disappearance of Alfonso Chanfreau and other cases that involved them. The judge continued insisting to the army that Miguel Krassnoff appear in court. Krassnoff was still in active service, head of the general staff of the Fourth Army Division in Valdivia. At the same time, new criminal complaints involving disappeared detainees kept piling up.

The army was furious. The parade of military officials through the courts had begun and constituted an unacceptable affront. The judge of the Second Military Court and ex-director of the Army Intelligence Directorate, Gen. Hernán Ramírez, asked Judge Olivares to transfer the Chanfreau case to the military justice system.

Judge Olivares refused to turn over the case to the military court, which threw the dispute over jurisdiction into the Supreme Court's lap. The country's highest court, like the military court, had made a practice of closing human rights cases by invoking the statute of limitations or the 1978 Amnesty Law. Grant amnesty without investigating—that was the motto. In fact, in January of that year (1992) alone, the military court granted amnesty in seventy cases involving disappeared detainees, as part of an indictment against former DINA director Manuel Contreras.

Now, because of the spotlight on Romo, the Amnesty Law was again monopolizing the public agenda. If he were brought back to Chile, would he be amnestied? Would the crimes be investigated before that? Would the case remain in the civil courts, or would it be shifted to the military justice system? And what will Romo actually say? Will he imitate his partners in torture, denying everything, or will he toss them all to the wolves? Might Romo's case mark a before and after in the judicial investigations?

The lawyers and relatives of victims kept on, as ever, pushing for the annulment of the Amnesty Law; short of that, the civilian courts at least needed to investigate. By mid-1992 an active citizens campaign was launched to collect signatures for the law's annulment.

The government was worried, because with members from its coalition of parties participating in the campaign, combined with the unending and widely disseminated revelations of the dictatorship's crimes, it feared that a "climate of confrontation" would balloon.

"The government's effort to shoehorn investigations of these events into a strictly judicial framework can be hampered by the demands made by human rights groups that ask for a greater governmental involvement in them, which would imply rolling things back to the state [of affairs] prior to the Rettig Report," noted an August 1992 government analysis report.

Amid all that, President Aylwin invited Erika Hennings to La Moneda to discuss her case. "He told me that I could say that he was not of the opinion that the case should pass over to the military justice system. He couldn't say it, but I could. He made sure there was wide press coverage of our meeting. It was his way of sending that message," recalls Hennings.

Judge Olivares kept moving ahead, and over a period of months took statements from victims, witnesses, and perpetrators, while indicting some agents. The DINA's agents did not always honor subpoenas or show up for face-to-face encounters in court. And, predictably, they never acknowledged anything. They claimed they remembered nothing, knew nothing, were never there, it wasn't them. They only shuffled papers.

In lengthy sessions in court, the agents were face-to-face with dozens of their victims. It was an exceptionally trying process. Erika Hennings had to confront her own captors in a court chamber and, together with some of those agents, reconstruct her detention as it had played out in her house almost twenty years earlier. When Krassnoff finally turned up in court in September, after ignoring six subpoenas, he did so in military uniform and surrounded by army officers. He was brought face-to-face with a dozen witnesses.

"He offered to shake my hand, but I didn't give it to him," recalls Hennings. "It was difficult, but at the same time healing in a way, because it was an opportunity to tell him to his face what happened."

Krassnoff told the judge that he had carried out only administrative functions in the DINA as an "information analyst."[19]

That same month, the National Corporation for Reparations and Reconciliation furnished Judge Olivares with information on seventy-three disappeared detainees in whose cases Romo was implicated.

Meanwhile, thanks to the reopening of numerous cases based on information supplied by the Rettig Commission or through new legal complaints submitted by victims' relatives, several criminal courts also began to subpoena DINA agents and bring them face-to-face with their victims. Predictably, they didn't always show up; they stonewalled by simply refusing to appear in court.

An Unexpected Maneuver

The Chilean police spoke with Romo again on August 12, after he was brought before Judge Yamamoto. Romo repeated that he wanted to help obtain justice in Chile but asked for special protection because he feared for his life. Furthermore, in return for his cooperation and after testifying before the court in Santiago, he asked that Chilean authorities help him return to Brazil to resume his life there. Two days later, Ambassador Martínez met with Brazil's justice minister to find out where the presidential expulsion decree stood. The minister told him it would be ready in fifteen to ninety days; it was awaiting completion on the current court calendar.

Everything seemed to be going well, although slowly, but in mid-August the situation took a new turn. During an interview with local reporters, Romo said he was afraid to return to Chile because he could be assassinated by the MIR. In addition, he warned, "If my life is threatened in Chile, I will talk, and I'll expose lots of people. Many people are going to tremble in their boots when I get there."[20]

"PEIN [person of interest], as is obvious, is not a trustworthy person," Henríquez wrote in his almost daily memo to Director Mery. "One assumes, with good reason, that now that he has been given some help, he's going to try any tactic that postpones his leaving the country. We've in fact proceeded very prudently to try to give him guarantees for his personal safety, and he's agreed to them, but afterward says the opposite to the press."[21]

A potentially greater roadblock, however, was that the lawyer Carlos Camacho, a leftist Brazilian militant who was a political refugee in Chile between 1964 and 1974, began to torpedo the negotiations on behalf of Romo's expulsion. A manager of hotels and restaurants and active member of Brazil's Green Party, Camacho announced to the press that Romo was responsible for the death of six Brazilians following Chile's military coup. Antonio Fernando Pinheiro, a member of São Paulo's Bar Association, said he would ask the public prosecutor's office to open an investigation into the matter. In that case, Romo would be detained in Brazil while the investigation went on and the question of his indictment was resolved.

It was a heavy blow to the plans under way. Henríquez was exasperated and let Mery know it. The Chilean embassy shared his frustration. Consul Fernando Pardo asked the detectives to start meeting with him daily in São Paulo's Interpol offices as of August 20 to coordinate efforts. Pardo calculated that if there were no presidential expulsion decree and the normal judicial process was followed, Romo could be on his way out of Brazil by early September.

"Consul Pardo informed the ambassador in Brasilia, and the ambassador informed President Aylwin, that we were between a rock and a hard place. The ambassador then made a trip to São Paulo and notified me that from that moment on I was to be attached to the Chilean consulate in Brazil to keep things moving until Romo's expulsion," relates Henríquez.

The CACI's chief had made at least half a dozen trips in this span of time, back and forth between São Paulo and Santiago, since there were certain things he could talk about only in person. He ended up spending almost three months in Brazil.

"The Investigations Police's administrative deputy director was annoyed with us because we were spending all the money he had on these assignments. They asked us to bring Romo back, but there weren't any more resources. But if they wanted Romo they had to invest more in it," Henríquez recalls.

The finance minister allocated supplementary funds to the PICH to cover the costs of assignments abroad so that Operation Romo and some others taking place simultaneously in Paraguay, Uruguay, Argentina, Mexico, and the United States could be completed. All these missions pertained to human rights.

Romo's case quickly ceased being a hot media item for Brazilians. Out on the streets, hundreds of thousands of people were demanding that President Collor de Mello resign. Brazil's president had found himself under fire since May of that year, when news broke about his participation in corrupt activities. Collor de Mello, the only person who could decree Romo's expulsion, was in a precarious position.

Nevertheless, things could get even worse.

Forgiveness

Lawyers from the Vicariate of Solidarity, victims' relatives, and leaders of human rights organizations started to arrive in Chile. Before flying to Brazil on August 16, Sola Sierra, the president of the Association of Relatives of the Detained and Disappeared, told the press that "we will leave no stone unturned in endeavoring to get to the truth, and if right now the truth is the information that Osvaldo Romo can provide the Chilean courts, we are going to find a way for him to be brought to Chile."[22]

With the assistance of the lawyer Dos Santos, they all worked with the Brazilian Bar Association, Judge Yamamoto, the justice minister, and other political authorities to speed up Romo's expulsion and discredit the case for his participation in the death of the six Brazilians. Carlos Camacho's move could have set back the entire process.

"It was necessary to lobby in Brazil, to maneuver politically. We went with

Viviana to talk to lawyers and politicians to [get them] to help us with the expulsion. Lucho [i.e., Luis] Henríquez was there, and we got together with him. We already had a bond of trust with him around the mutual objective of moving the investigation along," says Hennings.

That bond had been forged the year before, when the two women helped build bridges between former political prisoners and the police. And whenever Viviana Uribe chatted with Henríquez she told him, "We have unfinished business."

It was a very painful thing for her, impossible to overlook each time she walked past police headquarters on General Mackenna Street. It was PICH officials who had detained her, her sister Bárbara, and one of her uncles in 1974. They had been held in cells overnight, when the police handed them over to the DINA, severely tortured.[23]

As with so many other human rights cases, the abduction of Bárbara Uribe and her husband Edwin Van Yurick—detained hours earlier—was shut down in 1975, but the family filed a new criminal complaint that year (1992) in the Eighth Criminal Court.[24]

There, in Brazil, relates Uribe, "we performed a kind of act of contrition, he [Luis Henríquez] more than I." It happened on the first trip they made to that country after Romo's detention. Henríquez went to dine with the two women in the hotel where they were staying. Midway through their meal, Viviana again recalled for him that it was his institution that detained her and her family members, subjecting them to humiliating treatment and handing them over to the DINA. Uribe recalls:

> Luis told me that whenever he remembered that fact he was ashamed of his institution, that it caused him a great deal of pain to know that people such as I should have had to endure that treatment. At that instant, in all seriousness, with emotion and depth of feeling, he said that he, in the name of that institution, was asking me for forgiveness. It was a moment in which feelings and emotions were transfixing. And a moment, also, of silence, because he was a representative of the institution. I felt him to be a man of courage, dignified, sensitive, and respectful. His words had great significance for me, and with that a time of anger that I had gone through came to an end.

Henríquez, in Hiding

Beginning in September 1992, the political and diplomatic maneuvering seemed to have borne fruit. On September 9, Brazil's justice minister confirmed that the presidential expulsion decree would be signed that day and published the following week. In addition, Romo said that he did not plan to appeal the decision, because he wanted to cooperate with the Chilean courts. The Chilean police even assigned a code name to mark the initial phase of the expulsion operation: "Change of Hotel." Meanwhile, the National Corporation for Reparations and Reconciliation sought a lawyer to handle Romo's defense when he got back to Chile. The way was cleared. Everything seemed to be going smoothly.

But two days later, on September 11, Carlos Camacho went back on the attack. This time he worked a different angle. The accusation that Romo had participated in the murder of the Brazilians was disproven, because several of them had been executed in the National Stadium or on public roads after the military coup in 1973, when the DINA still didn't exist and Romo had yet to be recruited into the agency. So Camacho chose to file a writ of protection to block Romo's expulsion. After that, he asked the attorney general's office to investigate the CACI detectives still in Brazil for their "interference" in Romo's detention.

According to Camacho, the Chilean detectives "are disguised as tourists here, and with 'investigative' intentions, which harm national sovereignty." In his submission to the attorney general's office, Camacho underscored that the Chilean police officials should be "curbed in their mission via strict punishment and subjected to the corresponding legal processes."

Nearly two weeks later, he submitted another complaint, accusing the detectives of surveilling and following the leaders of the Green Party and further insinuating that persons calling their offices, voicing threats, spoke with a "typically unmistakable Chilean accent."

The actions of the Chilean police, Camacho argued, violated the constitution, the penal code, electoral law, and dozens of other Brazilian legal regulations, not to mention had a psychological impact on the Green Party's politically active members.[25]

On September 25, the attorney general's office recommended opening an investigation into the detectives' activities.

Consequently, as suggested by Brazil's own federal police, Superintendent Henríquez "went into hiding" to avoid being notified of the judicial action. He checked out of the Hotel Bristol and went to stay in the apartment of Alicia Valle, a Chilean who lived in one of the city's residential neighborhoods. José Plaza moved into an apartment-style hotel. Their travel allowance was already used up, so Valle's husband helped them out with money. Not even the Brazilian police knew where they were; Henríquez called them from public telephones.

"There I was, in effect, secretly awaiting instructions. I didn't go anywhere. I was shut up in the apartment. On Sunday my friend went to Mass, and I went with her. And to the market. One day she told me that she had to go the hair salon. And I went into the salon with her, mixed in among all the ladies, so as not to be shut in," Henríquez remembers.

Everything Goes Wrong

Within a few days, Brazil's domestic situation took a radical turn. On September 29, the country's Chamber of Deputies opened impeachment hearings against President Collor de Mello, resulting in his removal from office on October 2 and the departure of his cabinet officials involved in the negotiations concerning Romo. The Chilean government immediately restarted negotiations with the new slate of authorities, both in Brazil and with the Brazilian diplomatic mission in Santiago. To the Chileans' surprise, the interim president, Itamar Franco, signed the expulsion decree less than a week later.

Judge Gloria Olivares then met for two hours with Director Mery to tackle the question of arranging Romo's transfer and personal safety.

The onetime torturer, however, had changed his mind again. Now he no longer wanted to travel to Chile. According to his wife, per an interview with the newspaper *La Nación*, Romo was "despondent, in low spirits, crying a lot."[26]

That week, Flavio Augusto Marx—one of the most expensive lawyers in Brazil—took charge of Romo's defense. He filed a writ of protection seeking to render the expulsion null and void, alleging "political persecution."[27] It was never revealed who paid the lawyer's fees, although in an interview with the Chilean newspaper *El Mercurio* Marx insisted he was providing this service free of charge, out of "legal interest" and because he had come to an agreement with Romo to write his memoir. Marx laid claim to vast international experience for having successfully defended Gustav Franz Wagner, a Nazi fugitive in Brazil sought by the governments of Germany, Austria, Poland, and Israel. He also managed to prevent the extradition of the Italian mafia boss Tomasso Buchietta and was currently the defense lawyer for the widow of the infamous Nazi physician Joseph Mengele, who died in Brazil. Mengele's widow was charged with having buried him under a false name.[28]

The Supreme Court suspended the decree while it deliberated the appeal.

Carlos Camacho intervened on his own account, similarly appealing to the Supreme Court to step in and prevent the expulsion and again requesting Romo's indictment in Brazil over the disappearance of the six Brazilians in Chile.

While these events were playing out, Viviana Uribe and Erika Hennings made another trip to Brazil. Turbulence during the flight was so intense that things tumbled out of the bins. The passengers were gripped with fear.

"To think that we're going to die chasing after this miserable criminal," Viviana remarked to Erika.

In an analysis of the situation that Henríquez sent to Director Mery—a memorandum without any indication of the sender or recipient, dated in Santiago, because he was still in hiding—the CACI chief raised the possibility that Brazil's Supreme Court would rule in favor of Romo's expulsion but to Paraguay, not Chile. The judge leading the proceedings, he added, was a "thoroughly difficult man, mistrustful of everyone."

Furthermore, after Collar de Mello's removal, the position of Romeo Tuma the elder, the head of the federal police, was quite weakened, because several police chiefs and the institution's union requested his departure. And if he were to go, his son—the head of Interpol in Brazil—would also leave his position in solidarity, Henríquez noted.

The Chilean police officials remained in the sights of both Camacho, whom Henríquez considered a "front man," and the local and Chilean media. The Channel 13 reporter Pablo Honorato, Henríquez pointed out, maintained a "suspicious attitude," declaring his support for Romo's continued detention in Brazil.

"And beyond that, he tried to inquire into possible work-related activities that we might have carried out. Not getting answers, he began to look into the police-to-police agreement, what it entailed, what were the obligations that Interpol-affiliated countries had, etc. One gets the impression that it was to pass information to Romo's lawyer," Henríquez indicated.

"The situation," he added, "forces police officials coming here to use another hotel and [do so] as discreetly as possible (because of our media, who are the ones who create the most damage for us with their comments, since not having anything to report, they start to try to justify themselves, by speculating)."[29]

In fact, to Henríquez's point, Honorato had interviewed Romo a few days before through the bars of his cell in the federal police's São Paulo safehouse. As Honorato's taped interview indicated, Romo had written to the reporter the previous day.

By mid-October, the question of Romo's future was still unsettled, and the prospects for justice were dim. To persuade Romo to change his outlook, the detectives proposed extending him additional incentives. One possibility was to dangle financial assistance before the family, with whom the detectives had formed a good relationship.

"Luis Henríquez was very skilled in convincing Romo. He planted the idea in his head that the country's political situation was different [now], with a democratic regime in which human rights were respected, and the courts were eager to hear testimony in order to apply a corresponding amnesty; they needed his collaboration to provide the information that would allow cases to be closed. So his invitation was cast in the spirit of cooperation, whereby Romo would be a great contributor to [securing] justice," recalls Plaza.

Henríquez's ploy was successful, as far as it could go. On October 21, Osvaldo

Romo relinquished the writ of protection, but other appeals and actions were still pending. The Chilean embassy did not let up the pressure, day after day making its case to Brazil's judicial, ministerial, and police authorities.

In Santiago, one disaster continued to follow another. On October 23, the Supreme Court's Third Chamber, on which sat Fernando Torres, the army's attorney general, decided to transfer the Chanfreau case to the military justice system. It was precisely the investigation into this case that had jump-started the search for and capture of Romo.

When Romo's expulsion finally moved ahead on November 16, officials from Brazil's federal police notified Inspector Plaza, and Plaza passed the news on to Henríquez. Only Plaza knew where his boss was staying. Henríquez told the federal police where to find him. They brought him to a spot close to the airport and kept him there, waiting for the moment that Romo boarded the flight. Only then, just minutes before the plane's doors were closed, did the police get Henríquez on board.

"Our greatest fear in transporting Romo was that they would try to assassinate him," says Henríquez.

The Chilean government congratulated itself, and the Chilean embassy in Brazil celebrated the successful conclusion to the work it had done over the past 100 days.

Starting with President Aylwin's instructions on August 1, noted Ambassador Martínez in a report sent to foreign minister Enrique Silva, the diplomatic mission deployed "innumerable efforts that involved actions, contacts, reports, and interviews with different local authorities, from the foreign relations minister through the justice minister, the president of the Supreme Court, judges of that high court, the assistant attorney general . . . in addition to another set of high- and medium-level employees of these state and institutional authorities."

All of this was accomplished even as Brazil was living "through the deepest, most serious political crisis in its history," Martínez added.[30]

The Orión Safety Directive

Several hours later they landed at the Santiago airport. The first to come down the steps from the plane was José Plaza. Romo, wearing a short-sleeved sky-blue guayabera, managed it with difficulty. He needed assistance from Aldo Villanueva, a Santiago Interpol official who had traveled to Brazil to coordinate Romo's handover to the Chilean police with his Brazilian counterparts. Behind them was Superintendent Henríquez. Police were spread out on the landing strip and several police vans waited in the wings, in what the newspaper La Nación characterized as a reception "operation of gigantic proportions."[31]

"Mr. Romo, you are now officially detained," was how inspector José Luis Cabión greeted him. They had gotten to know each other in Brazil, but Cabión had returned to Chile earlier. They had chatted a good many times during Cabión's time in São Paulo.

Cabión read out the arrest warrant for Romo and read him his rights. He was being detained by order of Judge Olivares, of the Third Criminal Court, for the abduction of Alfonso Chanfreau. The order had been issued in March of that year. In addition, he was linked to thirteen kidnapping cases and two cases of homicide and was wanted on six other arrest warrants.

"Don't worry," Romo answered him. "I'm OK."

The group got into different vehicles, and Romo climbed into one with Inspector Plaza. Cabión had devised a maneuver to distract the media. Plaza would set off with Romo toward the air force's Group 10 base, situated nearby, at this same airport. From there they would put Romo on a small plane belonging to the PICH and fly him to the small airport of Cerrillos, in the western part of the capital. From Cerrillos he would be put into a vehicle and brought to police headquarters. In the meantime, another vehicle would set off, driving along the highway toward the center of Santiago with someone disguised to look like Romo.

"We wanted to avoid being harassed by the media, but beyond that, we wanted to keep Romo alive, for what he had to tell us. We'd laid out all the possible scenarios and one [of them] was that they could make an attempt on his life," explains Cabión.

As Cabión moved to get into one of the vehicles, he was surrounded by reporters. The Channel 13 cameraman who accompanied Honorato tried to snatch the folder containing the detention order and other papers.

"He tugged at the folder to try and get it from me," states Cabión. "Later I had to explain, in the police report, why the decree was totally crumpled, with parts of it torn. It was really fierce. I've had a lot of contact with reporters but never seen anything like that."

With Romo's arrival on Chilean soil, the PICH deployed resources and personnel to guarantee his safety. The day before, the PICH had cranked up the "Orión Safety Directive," ordained by Director Mery. It entailed a group specially designed for "watching over, attending to, and [ensuring the] safety of the detainee starting with his reception at headquarters until his handover to the justice system is provided for."[32]

The document that detailed this team's mission was confidential and had been distributed by the director's office three weeks earlier, on October 28, to ten departments of the PICH's staff.

The Orión Temporary Safety Group, at the command of Superintendent Henríquez, was composed of twenty detectives from a half dozen units that were added temporarily to the inspector general's office twenty-four hours before Romo's trip to Santiago. It included Inspectors Cabión and Plaza and detective Abel Lizama. Lizama, from the Seventeenth Police District of Buin, had been brought on to the CACI a few months earlier. He remained a part of it through 1993 and returned to Department V in 2000 to join the team of human rights investigators.

Romo's interrogation was conducted exclusively by CACI personnel. Henríquez was provided with a cellular phone—the first and for a long time only mobile device that the commission possessed. It was one of those huge, heavy cell phones that didn't fit in pockets and whose antenna could be unscrewed and taken off.

Romo was put in a separate basement cell. The police checked the conditions in the cell, disinfecting it from top to bottom and repairing the commode. They changed the cylinders on the locks of the office fitted out for the judges and for the CACI officials slated to take Romo's statement. They also installed emergency electric lighting and, to reinforce Romo's safety, purchased latches and padlocks to lock up the two entrances to the floor where Romo was located.

The watch on the prisoner was split up into three permanent visual shifts. In addition, whenever Romo was moved about inside or outside headquarters, the security measures were beefed up, especially if he had to appear in court or be taken to a health clinic.

Upon his arrival in the PICH building, Romo was subjected to a medical checkup, and a physician, nutritionist, and two medical assistants were on permanent call to attend to his care and needs. The police also put one of their ambulances, with a driver, at the disposition of the PICH in case Romo had a medical emergency. He was given a medical checkup every day.

The ex–DINA torturer spent ten days holed up in PICH headquarters, watched over day and night.

"Romo was useless to us dead," explains Cabión.

A Thick Skin

After Romo was brought to headquarters, the streets outside the building filled with former political prisoners and relatives of human rights victims holding placards demanding justice, as well as photographers, reporters, and cameramen. Erika Hennings and Viviana Uribe had returned to Brazil hours earlier and were inside, waiting for him. The two knew him from the torture centers. Uribe still remembered his foul smell when, in the José Domingo Cañas detention center, Romo came up close to her face and removed her blindfold.

"Do you know me?" he had asked her.

Romo told her his name and that he knew her entire family, that he had been in her house on many occasions.[33]

The two women wanted to confront him right away but had to wait. They felt certain that he knew what had happened to their disappeared loved ones, Alfonso Chanfreau, Bárbara Uribe, and Edwin Van Yurick.

On day two they asked to speak with Romo. Hennings, Uribe, and Cecilia Jarpa—another political prisoner—waited for him in the basement, where the cells were. They suddenly sensed a heavy footfall, chains clanging noisily. Romo's figure loomed from the end of the corridor. Uribe relates: "We see this enormous creature come into view, ugly, coarse in appearance, gross. We move to one side because he's surrounded by police, and when he was passing by us, he turns and says something to each of us. He said to Cecilia Jarpa: 'Jarpinha, I thought you were dead.' He said something about Alfonso to Erika, and to me: 'Viviana, I know what you are up to, looking for your sister and your brother-in-law.' These words were really overwhelming for us, because I felt that even as a prisoner, he continued being the perpetrator."

When at last they could enter his cell to talk to him, the women asked about their relatives. Romo told them he was tired and promised to tell them everything, that he was going to help them, that he had lots of information, but he was simply babbling nonsense.

"All the same it was shocking. Here is a man I didn't know, who is telling [you] your story, speaking of your comrades who are disappeared, and talking as though they were very close to him," adds Uribe. He gave them tidbits of information, but it was never clear how much was true.

Judge Gloria Olivares lost the Chanfreau case after it was transferred to the military justice system, but other judges also filed complaints against Romo. One of these was Lientur Escobar, who had handled the case of the MIR militant Álvaro Vallejos, detained and disappeared in 1974. Another was Judge Dobra Lusic, who had investigated almost a dozen crimes committed against MIR militants, including the murder of Lumi Videla and the disappearances of Sergio Pérez and Mónica Llanca. All three were captured in 1974. The CACI decided to have Romo appear before Judge Lusic, because she was investigating the largest number of cases that involved him and because PICH headquarters fell within her jurisdiction.

On day three, the military prosecutor Luis Berger turned up at PICH headquarters, demanding that Romo be handed over, because responsibility for the Chanfreau case was now vested in his office. Judge Lusic rejected his demand. The detainee continued under her remand and was held incommunicado.

"This is my detainee," the judge told him without yielding. She conversed with Romo every day.

At that point the detectives began to hold marathon sessions at PICH headquarters.

"When word got out that Romo was there lots of people showed up to provide testimony. They showed up in droves; he was really despised. Romo was a clown. When he found out there were numerous reporters outside, he was beside himself. He wanted to show off for them; he fancied himself a star," recalls one of the CACI's administrative employees, Miguel Reinoso.

The corridors overflowed with victims' relatives, survivors, and witnesses, waiting their turn to offer testimony against Romo, the DINA, and its torture centers. Word spread and dozens of people turned up spontaneously at the building to make statements on different cases. Many of them had been detained together and already knew one another. Whether or not their statements had to do with the cases Judge Lusic was investigating didn't matter. It was all useful; everything was interconnected. It was necessary to speak out, and this was the opportunity. One of the military dictatorship's most notorious torturers was now a prisoner. With Romo a small window was opened to learn the truth and, it was hoped, obtain justice as well. For the detectives, it meant taking a step toward recovering citizens' trust in the plainclothes police.

The detectives took statements throughout the day. They came in at eight in the morning and got off around midnight. They interviewed witnesses, wrote reports, analyzed statements, and questioned Romo.

"I went on learning about the cruelty, the way torture was performed, the grief of these people. To this day I ask myself how people with so much grief could have the capacity to talk about it and live day to day. It was difficult, more for them to open up in front of us and let on to us, and to me, [just] a kid. At the time I didn't catch on, but later I realized that telling the story was part of the healing process," reflects Abel Lizama.

Romo had the memory of an elephant. He drew organizational charts of the MIR's structures. He knew the responsibilities, aliases, and individual traits of its leaders. He offered detailed descriptions of his victims, their personal histories, backgrounds, habits, friends, what the house was like where he detained them, what sorts of clothes they were wearing, what they said.

He even compiled a list of the people in whose detention he had taken part but always maintained that there were two structures within the DINA: one in charge of detaining, torturing, and extracting information and another for doing away with victims. Romo insisted he knew nothing about the second one. They witnessed him crying on one occasion and one occasion only: when he spoke of Lumi Videla and said he had fallen in love with her. Romo asserted that the young MIR militant was smothered to death with a pillow. He never admitted it, but it was clear to the detectives that Romo was the one who had killed her.

"If I, as an investigator, want to get as much as I can out of him for the good of the investigation, I can't begin to argue with him or take the attitude of re-buffing him. What you have to do is create empathy and also have a thick skin in order to detach yourself from the things he's saying," says Lizama.

Various former political prisoners spoke with Romo at PICH headquarters over the course of those ten days. Hennings and Uribe did so several times. On one occasion the three sat on a bench in the basement corridor. Romo was in the middle, between the two women, and put his hands on their legs, greeted them, and asked how they were.

"Then he turns and says to me, 'You see? They don't hate me, I even touched their legs.' I saw that myself. He was very sly," says Cabión.

"Romo furnished us with information, though nothing very substantial. He wasn't a fool but rather a manipulative type, perverse, egomaniacal, a psychopath. The entire process was something really overpowering. My emotions showed themselves physically. I lived with [episodes of] nausea and dizziness through that whole period of face-to-face meetings, statements, the [presence of] the media," recalls Hennings.

Erika Hennings and Viviana Uribe continued visiting Romo for months in the penitentiary, with the constant hope that he might drop a sliver of information. Because they couldn't make a recording, they brought notebooks to jot down everything he said. At night they transcribed and filled out what they'd noted down.

"It was always exactly the same thing as at first. He always repeated the same thing, but the information he gave the police wasn't useful, at least not as concerned the ultimate fate of the disappeared. Who was discovered through him? Who was identified through him? What finding is owed to him? None. I was always left sickened and nauseous after meeting with him. It was extremely intense, but the need to know was even stronger. But it didn't work out, it was useless," says Uribe.

It wasn't worth it for Hennings, either. Looking back, she wouldn't go through it again. "People didn't understand it, we came out with nothing regarding the fate of the disappeared, we wore ourselves down, and the emotional toll was great. When I left there, it was really terrible. My life was deeply affected by it," she stresses.

The public exposure ricocheted onto the family. The former political prisoners were interviewed by the media, participated in demonstrations, and gave press conferences. All that backfired on Uribe. In those days she was living with her two daughters, trying to put her life back together. The girls were accustomed to the commotion stirred up by their brushes with the world of human rights but not to hearing on television how their mother had been tortured.

"I don't regret having done all that I did, except for an interview that I gave to National Television—[that], yes, I do. My daughters saw it and learned about things that I would never have liked them to learn about. I decided then to never again give public testimony. These things are too personal," says Uribe.

Eventually, both women decided to keep their distance from Romo.

Baptism by Fire

Following five days of intense questioning, Osvaldo Romo again testified before Judge Lusic. After three hours, his interrogation was suspended on instruction by the PICH's doctor, subprefect Juan Ritz. That morning, Dr. Ritz had delivered a medical report on Romo's condition. After enumerating his different pathologies, Ritz commented, "His age in years is fifty-four, but his physical-physiological age could correspond to a person of seventy." He recommended medical checkups at least twice daily and that the interrogations not exceed three hours.

Ten days after Romo's arrival in Chile, in a confidential memorandum to Director Mery, Luis Henríquez summed up the results as follows: "His testimony confirmed his participation in and responsibility for the detention of numerous people still unaccounted for who were active in or linked to the MIR. His version with respect to these events substantiates the existence of a group specially dedicated to the elimination of those detainees, who after being interrogated were not to be seen or returned to their families, either for strategic reasons or because their physical condition was shocking."[34]

For Henríquez, Romo was one of the most brutal criminals he knew over the course of his life.

On November 26, 1992, Judge Dobra Lusic indicted him for his role in five abductions.

Romo's capture was a baptism by fire for the CACI regarding its operational capacity and forever changed its initial function as a commission confined to mere "analysis and coordination." His capture vaulted Department V into the public arena. This success marked its debut in society.

"It was one of the key milestones. An array of efforts was deployed in his capture: diplomatic, law enforcement, judicial, [contributions by] a great many people, leading to a positive outcome. It highlighted the seriousness of what we were doing. Our credibility and firmness of purpose were solidified," states Jorge Morales, then legal adviser for the PICH director.

Osvaldo Romo was taken to the Colina jail, a facility on the outskirts of Santiago housing common criminals. He was treated as a special prisoner but a prisoner all the same.

In the meantime, in late 1992, ten parliamentarians from the Concertación (the governing coalition) introduced an impeachment motion against three magistrates and the army's chief legal counsel, Fernando Torres Silva, alleging breach of duty for their votes in favor of transferring the Chanfreau case to the military justice system. In January 1993, Chile's Senate voted to remove one of the magistrates, Hernán Cereceda, from his post but found the others innocent of the charge.

Six months later, in June 1993, Raúl Rozas, the judge for the Sixth Military Prosecutor's Office, where the Chanfreau case rested, closed it down. Rozas concluded that the investigation had reached an end, that nothing of substance existed in the record that might point to anyone, not even to the confessed captor, Osvaldo Romo. Rozas proceeded to revoke his indictment.

The drama continued to play out. On December 20, 1994, after effectively freezing the investigation into the abduction of Alfonso Chanfreau, the military court decided to apply the Amnesty Law and close the case. There was no operable sentence handed down in his case until 2015.[35]

In the next five years, the military court and the Supreme Court invoked the Amnesty Law and closed a dozen cases for which Romo had been indicted. He was sentenced, however, for other crimes after some judges and even the court of appeals revoked amnesty. Romo lived out the rest of his days in prison.

"He knew that he would have to remain in Chile, but he never imagined that he would die in jail," notes Cabión.

No Tears

Romo's family stayed in Brazil. Their lives were carved out there. Four of his children were married, and the grandchildren inherited the false names under which their fathers had departed Chile when they were children. From time to time his wife and children visited him while he was imprisoned in Chile, but the relationship was frayed and grew cold.

After his arrest in 1992, Romo cycled through three different jails. From the few people who ventured to visit him—including the detectives who maintained their conversations with him as part of their investigations into the DINA—he asked for pencils and notebooks, assuring them that he wanted to write his memoirs.

Romo, the one who bragged of torturing women as naturally as he ate a slice of bread, wrote with a scribbled hand, eagerly, making spelling mistakes. Although he lacked much education, he had a formidable memory. He requested the 100-sheet notebooks used in school math classes and wrote lengthy, chaotic accounts about the MIR's internal structure and its militants, aliases, and division of organizational responsibilities as well as about detentions and torture sessions, in all this reflecting a perverse admiration for his own victims. On the first sheet of one of these notebooks he jotted down, *They were Romantics and Idealistic Adventurers to their Death.* On the 100 pages that followed, he went into great detail about the activist lives of dozens of MIR members and the circumstances surrounding their detentions.

Romo didn't do this to relieve his conscience or to find absolution. He had no regrets. Today, many of his feverish writings are digitized, various copies of them shared among detectives, judges, and journalists. The detective Sandro Gaete donated some to Chile's Museum of Memory. They were virtually Romo's only material possessions.

Osvaldo Romo died from cardiopulmonary arrest on July 4, 2007, at sixty-nine years of age, while serving out his sentence in the Punta Peuco jail for the disappearance of seven MIR militants. During his stay in the hospital almost no one came to see him other than a nun who did so out of pity. He went entire years without anyone visiting him.

No one attended his funeral. It rained that day, and a gravedigger and priest were the only witnesses to the burial. There was no one who would solemnize his life with a single word. A week later two of Romo's grandchildren came from Brazil, and a gravedigger showed them his grave. They didn't bring flowers or say anything.

Nor did they shed a tear.[36]

7

FUGITIVE IN PARAGUAY

IT WAS THE FIRST TIME that Homicide Brigade superintendent Robinson Muñoz had flown on an airplane, and he had purchased a new suit for the occasion. The plane was a wide-bodied jet, three seats to a row. Muñoz's seat was in the plane's front section, next to his colleague and friend William Contreras. They were en route to Buenos Aires.

Muñoz's fellow officers in the plainclothes police were accustomed to calling him "Perlina," the name of an old, popular laundry detergent in Chile, because the Columbo-style raincoat he always wore had turned grayish with so much use. Muñoz carried it with him onto the plane that day in June 1992, as fall was about to turn into winter. Luis Henríquez added a bit more dash to the moniker, calling him Monsieur Perliné.

"With just one look, you could see that that raincoat had been through a lot," Henríquez laughs. "But Perlina was a remarkable detective."[1]

Two other detectives from the Homicide Brigade, Rafael Castillo and Nelson Jofré, were seated toward the rear of the plane, as was Interpol Santiago's chief, Patricio Faúndez. And José Plaza and Luis Henríquez, from the Analysis and Institutional Coordination Commission, were somewhere in the middle.

Suddenly Perlina came up to Castillo's seat.

"Hey, how much does lunch cost on the plane—is it very expensive?" he asked Castillo in a hushed voice.

The flight attendant had just passed by with the menu, with its two options. Castillo, not missing the chance to play a prank, proposed a deal.

"Yes, it's pretty costly. But buddy, don't worry. Let's do this: I'll pay for your lunch on the plane and when we get to Argentina, you buy me lunch."

Castillo spoke to the attendant to make sure Perlina's meal was brought to him. Then he took it to his friend's seat.

"OK, it's all set. Go ahead and eat," Castillo told him.

The detectives got to their hotel in Buenos Aires; they took photos in the Plaza de Mayo and went off to dine. So Perlina returned the favor, and Castillo tucked into a sirloin steak.

A couple of days later they split up into three groups of two and left on their respective missions. Castillo and Jofré stayed in the capital for several days to meet with Judge María Servini de Cubría about a case involving Gen. Carlos Prats (discussed below) and later continued on to Uruguay in search of the fugitive Directorate of National Intelligence chemist Eugenio Berríos.

Henríquez and Plaza flew to Brazil in pursuit of Osvaldo Romo. And Muñoz and Contreras consulted with Interpol Argentina about the comings and goings of the wife of communist turned agent Miguel Estay Reyno, or "Fanta" as he was known. A week later they traveled to Paraguay in search of him.

Each pair knew the others were going to be dealing with human rights cases, but they didn't broach the subject. Nobody wanted anything to leak. Their targets formed part of the weakest link in the dictatorship's intelligence apparatus: civilian agents.

"The detention of Otto Trujillo enabled us to deduce that this was the system's vulnerable point, because they lacked the discipline that members of the armed forces and the Carabineros have. Military officials did not let on, but civilians could be detained and made to open up. So we set our sights on targets who were vulnerable, who should have information and could disclose things. Miguel Estay Reyno and Osvaldo Romo were in that category," Henríquez explains.

The June 8, 1992, trip was a plan devised by Nelson Mery who, only a few days earlier had been confirmed in his position as director general of the Investigations Police of Chile (PICH).

The just-appointed director had spoken with interior minister Enrique Krauss, to explain that the government needed to authorize a special assignment. They needed to hunt down some fugitives from justice who were living outside the country. Mery required resources.

"The police used their own reserve funds for those assignments, but on occasion we supplemented them, paying for the cost of tickets, for example," states Krauss.

The government backed both this trip by the investigators and successive assignments in coming years to different countries in Latin America, Europe, and North America to locate secret agents or witnesses.

Mery had the detectives start their operation in Buenos Aires to prevent them from leaving traces in Chile of their departures to the other countries. PICH headquarters had already detected that Army Intelligence Directorate agents were following its officers, both to monitor their movements and to harass them.

Through their contacts inside the PICH, they even requested travel records on police officials, right up to the director himself.

The Fifth Subprecinct

To the great regret of families of the disappeared and executed, the government seemed willing to commit to its efforts in only a handful of cases, specifically those in which the State Defense Council had taken part. These were cases that the media characterized as "emblematic," an offensive distinction that set apart high-profile victims, whose cases achieved public notoriety, from all the rest.

Former minister Krauss asserts that the Aylwin government was equally interested in all cases and places responsibility on the courts for the fact that some might have obtained greater justice or more attention.

"A democratic government doesn't investigate; rather, the police do it and the justice system invigorates it. It's the justice system that has to get cases moving. The ministry's lawyers could ask for legal proceedings, but the courts displayed a passive attitude," says Krauss.

Those cases were investigated by upper-court judges from the court of appeals, not by regular criminal case judges like the others. Orlando Letelier's assassination was one of those "emblematic" cases. Others were the 1985 triple throat slashing of Communist militants Santiago Nattino, José Manuel Parada, and Manuel Guerrero; the 1982 murder of the labor union leader Tucapel Jiménez and the subsequent death of the carpenter Juan Alegría to cover up Jiménez's assassination; the fatal 1974 attack on ex–army commander in chief Carlos Prats and his wife Sofia Cuthbert in Argentina; and the 1976 assassination of the Spanish Chilean international employee Carmelo Soria. All of these were reopened or reactivated upon the resumption of civilian government.

In response to the judges' request that the PICH designate detectives to work on these cases exclusively, PICH director Horacio Toro created the Fifth Subprecinct for "special cases" within the Homicide Brigade. The Fifth Subprecinct operated independently from the other four subprecincts in the Santiago Metropolitan Region, and its teams answered to the PICH's general directorate and to the judge empowered to investigate a particular case.

The men of the Fifth Subprecinct were very diverse in experience, but they had all specialized in the criminal investigation of murders. Rafael Castillo and Nelson Jofré formed the team dedicated to the Orlando Letelier, Carmelo Soria, and Carlos Prats cases. The group led by Robinson Muñoz, filled out by William Contreras, Héctor Silva, and Horacio Piccardo, was in charge of the "Slit-Throats Case." Superintendent José Barrera headed up the largest team, the one that investigated the assassinations of Tucapel Jiménez and Juan Alegría. It included detectives Luis Garay, Héctor Moraga, Osmán Arellano, Rodrigo Díaz, and Alvaro Morales.[2]

"We had a good group in the BH [Homicide Brigade]; there was a good organizational climate, a strong team spirit, and we shared a lot," says Jofré. "We lived more in the headquarters building than in our own homes. Sometimes we closed up headquarters; we'd go off at midnight, at two in the morning, and the next day had to be in at eight thirty in the morning."

Even though all these cases had been partially investigated during the dictatorship, the Homicide Brigade's chief at the time, Osvaldo Carmona, thought it was better to start from scratch.

"It was necessary in each case to rehash the entire investigation because we couldn't start now, in this government [Aylwin's], investigating based on case files from the previous government. This was because we didn't know if people, witnesses, made statements freely or if they made them under pressure," he said in a press interview.[3]

Carmona had spent almost thirty years in the PICH and around one year in the Homicide Brigade. He had rotated through various judicial precincts across five regions: Tocopilla, Curicó, San Fernando, Arica, and Santiago.

Publicly, Prefect Carmona cultivated the image of a small-town detective, a man distant from the crimes of the dictatorship, despite having been a member of the Assaults Investigation Brigade, about which he said nothing. Only a few years ago, however, he was indicted for murders and kidnappings in Tocopilla and Santiago. Nevertheless, Carmona was committed to the human rights investigations carried out by his officers, although—except for certain situations—he didn't participate directly in this work.

The homicide teams worked in parallel with the Analysis and Institutional Coordination Commission detectives, and both zealously guarded their own investigations. They linked up to coordinate and share certain information but honored a policy of strict compartmentalization. The interchange was not always free flowing.

The Scene of the Crime

Inspector William Contreras was assigned to the Slit-Throats Case for a perfectly simple reason: he had been there at the outset.

On March 30, 1985, after two farmworkers reported the discovery of three cadavers lying on the side of the road to the airport in the Santiago district of Quilicura, Contreras was one of the first officers to arrive on the scene. Coincidentally, one day before, he had been taking statements from witnesses and residents in the area around the Colegio Latinoamericano de Integración, where two of the victims had been kidnapped days earlier: the school's director and leader of the Chilean Association of Teachers (AGECH), Manuel Guerrero; and José Manuel Parada, head of the analysis department in the Vicariate of Solidarity, whose children attended the school.

William Contreras was on guard duty with four fellow officers when he received the call from the Quilicura district Carabineros reporting three bodies yet to be identified.

"Their throats were slashed," the Carabineros warned.

The bodies were those of Guerrero, Parada, and Santiago Nattino, a graphic designer and also one of the leaders of AGECH. The three, all members of the Communist Party, were kidnapped on March 28. That night, armed men dressed in civilian clothes raided AGECH's main office on Londres Street, in the center of Santiago, carrying off four educators. The captors turned out to be agents from the Carabineros Communications Directorate (DICOMCAR).

Contreras called the PICH's radio patrol car to confirm the information, advised both the brigade's chief and PICH's director, and assembled a team to go to Quilicura.

A month earlier, the Homicide Brigade had purchased its first video equipment to film crime scenes, and Contreras was part of the group that had been trained to do it. The shift chief that day asked if he knew how to operate the equipment.

"Yes, [I do]."

"In that case you are in charge of doing the filming."

Then twenty-seven, Contreras was a six-year veteran in the PICH. He was born and raised in the northern desert city of Copiapó. After studying for two years at the State Technical University to become a surveyor, he left Copiapó in 1976 to enroll in the Investigations School. Without any military service under his belt, he admits that he found the disciplined routine of the school somewhat traumatic. Nevertheless, he stuck it out. He felt that it was right for him.

His father had been an employee of the Chilean Postal Service but was let go right after the military coup took place.

"We were left without anything," Contreras recalls.

By March 1985 William Contreras had served in the Homicide Brigade for three years, but nothing from that experience prepared him for what he saw in Quilicura.

"Seeing those bodies put me in a state of shock. The scene was so grotesque, so terrible. I tried to film but I forgot how to do it; I froze," relates Contreras.

Journalists, members of the Vicariate, judicial authorities, and Carabineros had already arrived on the scene. The police cordoned it off.

"Start filming," his chief ordered.

Contreras, still in a daze, pressed buttons until he connected with one that got the filming under way. They stayed there until nightfall, recording and documenting the crime scene.

On April 1, due to the public consternation caused by the triple homicide, the Supreme Court designated appellate court judge José Cánovas to investigate it. Cánovas quickly moved to separate the Carabineros from this process. As expected, the Carabineros offered no cooperation to help clarify the chain of events; instead, their officials lied, omitted information, distorted the facts, and destroyed evidence.

"At that time, they denied us lists of Carabineros personnel or sent us the wrong lists, false information. Judge Cánovas asked for the lists of those who formed their [respective] units and they sent us [different] ones," Contreras relates.

It was the National Center for Information (CNI), which wanted to monopolize the repression and separate itself from being tied in any way to this crime, that informed on those who carried out the throat slashing. The CNI sent a report to Judge Cánovas detailing the DICOMCAR operation, linking its agents to the Joint Command.

Within a few months and working under enormous pressure, Judge Cánovas traced the responsibility for the crime to DICOMCAR. Many of the names of the Joint Command's own leaders and agents overlapped with DICOMCAR, which had begun to appear on the radar of human rights organizations following the confession of the agent Andrés Valenzuela the year before.

Manuel Guerrero, a survivor of the Joint Command's predations, and José Manuel Parada, from the Vicariate of Solidarity, were investigating those tie-ins when Miguel "Fanta" Estay Reyno loaned his curved knife to slit their throats.

"It was Fanta, in a meeting, who explained that the best option was to kill them in this way because there was a curfew, and the sound of gunshots meant that patrol cars would show up. Slitting throats would be noiseless," says Contreras.

Ultimately, Fanta was able to flee the country and escape justice in 1987, assisted by the intelligence services of Chile, Argentina, and Paraguay. Executing him would have been another option. He was a civilian and a traitor. But he was also a valuable asset to the state's security agencies because of his great experience in the field of intelligence. And he knew a great deal.

Fantômas

Miguel Estay Reyno came from a well-off and, by tradition, loyal Communist family. Both his father and his younger brother Jaime were active in the party. He joined the Communist Youth organization in the late 1960s while in high school. He used the nickname "Fanta," derived from Fantômas, the archvillain-protagonist of a series of French detective novels. Jaime Estay adopted the sobriquet "Specter," Fantômas's brother and aide.

Estay advanced rapidly in his work for the party. He began by joining the Ramona Parra Muralist Brigade, then moved on to lead Communist Youth self-defense teams. He took a course in intelligence work during a three-month stay in the Soviet Union in 1971 and upon returning to Chile went undercover as a leader of the party's intelligence arm.

He was astute, capable, disciplined, and absolutely committed to the party. He enjoyed the full trust of its leadership and was one of a small number who guarded its most sensitive secrets.

Estay was captured by the Joint Command in the La Florida district on December 22, 1975, as part of a series of detentions carried out by that group, whose existence was still unknown to Chileans. He was hiding out in the house of a party companion, Mauricio Lagunas, who was arrested along with him. His captors were accompanied by Estay's chief on the party's intelligence team, René Basoa. Basoa had fallen into the Command's hands three days before. They were taken to the Joint Command's central facility. Lagunas was let go six days later.

According to the story told by journalist Nancy Guzmán in her book *El Fanta: Historia de una traición*, Estay began to cooperate on the very day of his arrest, even before reaching the Command's headquarters. He gave up the fight as lost before taking it on. He even helped, Guzmán notes, to mount the January 1976 operation to detain another party comrade, Víctor Vega, who remains unaccounted for, and Isabel Stange, his brother Jaime's girlfriend. Fanta hadn't reckoned that Jaime would also come on the scene at the same time and likewise be arrested.

Estay recounts the story differently: In his telling, he began to cooperate after being tortured and when his captors threatened to kill his brother and Stange. He won their freedom in exchange for detailed information on the Communist Youth and the party's intelligence apparatus as well as information about all the militants he had known.[4] Jaime Estay and Isabel Stange were freed within a month and sent into exile in Mexico, where the brothers' father was living, psychiatrist José Miguel Estay. The elder Estay had chosen to go into exile after the military coup.

The dilemma, according to Fanta, was either to cooperate or to be "disappeared."

"All of the people with similar characteristics and from my generation, who didn't establish some form of collaboration, today constitute part of the disappeared," claimed Estay in a 2007 interview.[5]

The truth was that Fanta followed in the footsteps of his party superior, René Basoa. When Estay went free in May 1976 he was already switching from informer to Joint Command operations agent, just like Basoa had. And he continued plunging into ever deeper waters, cultivating a close working and personal relationship with his new chief in the Joint Command, Roberto "Wally" Fuentes, who was a "tremendous friend" of his.[6]

Fanta delivered information, hideouts, and militants from the party to the Joint Command, planned and joined operations to detain his comrades, and participated in torture and interrogation sessions, including that of fellow Communist Youth member Manuel Guerrero.

In 1984 Wally recruited Miguel Estay—in the capacity of civilian employee— to become part of a special intelligence group, DICOMCAR, which had been created one year earlier. In those years of betrayal, Fanta explained in an interview, he was "coming across other people, with other ideas, and I began to adopt them. Just like growing numbers of Chileans, I believed in the stamp the military managed to impose, fundamentally in economic terms. And since, in addition, I possessed a certain degree of specialization in the area of intelligence, it made for a relatively natural tie with people in [those] services."[7]

Rage

Judge Milton Juica took over the investigation of the Slit-Throats Case when Judge Cánovas opted to retire from the bench, by which time Fanta had already spent two years outside the country.

When the case was reactivated, Juica asked that the detectives who had handled it before resume their work. Among them were Robinson "Perlina" Muñoz and William Contreras. The judge also placed a blanket prohibition on releasing information to the media.

In June 1992, when the detectives' group traveled to Buenos Aires, the Carabineros got wind of a plan to carry out an attempt on the judge's life. It was his third death threat. He had been given permanent police protection after the first one. Two detectives came by to fetch him every morning and accompanied him throughout the day. At night a detachment of Carabineros guarded the exterior of his home.

The institution most angered with Judge Juica was none other than the Carabineros. In March 1992, Juica took up the path forged by Cánovas. He indicted sixteen police officials, three of whom were active duty, and a civilian, Miguel Estay, for the triple crime and a second one associated with it—the kidnapping of the AGECH members. He indicted the former director of the Carabineros, the resigned general César Mendoza, as an accessory to a criminal organization. The Supreme Court revoked the indictment eight months later.

Judge Juica wanted to indict the current director of the Carabineros, Gen. Rodolfo Stange, but didn't do so. He was upset with him for what, at the very least, could qualify as a cover-up. Besides not pursuing his own investigation, the Carabineros' top leader negated or put off the appearance of the suspects before the court, concealed documents, destroyed physical evidence—even infrastructure—and deliberately allowed vehicles to go missing. There was even talk of a secret meeting at which Stange guaranteed support to those responsible for the crime and urged them not to furnish information to the judge.[8]

"The Carabineros caused trouble when the institution [PICH] had to present a subpoena to an official," affirms Mery. "In their opinion, they had to be given prior notification about anything that needed to be coordinated with them. When there was an arrest order, they always claimed that a huge group was going to [be party to] the detention. I wish the Investigations Police might have had that logistical capacity and all those vehicles. It was hard to assert authority over them."

In May Judge Juica indicted the six who had devised the throat-slitting crime, including Fanta in absentia and the man who had directed the operation, the retired Carabineros colonel Guillermo González, operations chief for the Internal and External Affairs Department of DICOMCAR. They called him "Bototo."

Some lower-level Carabineros officials attached to DICOMCAR had by now come completely clean, availing themselves of the *ley de arrepentimiento eficaz*, which afforded them reduced penalties in return for providing information. The first to cooperate was Santiago San Martín, detained in mid-May 1992. Judge Juica interrogated him at police headquarters. San Martín tied DICOMCAR to the crimes. He admitted that Parada, Nattino, and Guerrero had been imprisoned in DICOMCAR's main building, identified who brought them to that place, and how and by whom they were taken out to be killed, and he told the police that after the assassinations those involved went back to their unit to shower.

"San Martín was in the custody of the Homicide Brigade for something like a month. He supplied the names of everyone who had participated: the ones who went along in the vehicles, the one who gave orders. I think that when the full picture began to emerge, each one wanted to talk about what pertained to him and no more than that," recalls William Contreras.

Judge Juica told the chief of the Homicide Brigade to keep a careful eye on San Martín, to assure that nothing happened to him, and that he should not have contact with any of the persons indicted. Moreover, he ordered that San Martín receive a medical checkup every twenty-four hours.[9]

San Martín was brought face-to-face with several of those indicted, who—to a man—denied everything. The noncommissioned officer held firm, and days later another Carabinero, Luis Canto, joined ranks with him. Canto wanted, he said, to make a statement of his own free will "for his personal peace of mind." José Fuentes also opened up. He asked to make a statement before the judge "because," he said, "for seven years I've lived confused in my heart in the face of this situation."[10] He explained that he hadn't come forward before out of fear.

This wedge was the beginning of the downfall for the ex–DICOMCAR agents. And as the momentum continued to build, the detectives were increasingly aware of how they were being monitored and subjected to acts of intimidation.

"William and I detected that there were vehicles that followed us," relates Héctor Silva, who was also part of the team investigating the Slit-Throats Case. "Outside my house there were always different vehicles parked with men inside. Sometimes they were couples trying to pass for sweethearts or two guys in a pickup truck. More than doing anything to us, they wanted to know what we were up to."

At dawn on the day they went to detain Guillermo González, Detectives Contreras and Silva planted themselves in separate spots to keep tabs on him and watch for any movements. Silva parked his car near the house, and Contreras positioned himself a little farther away. Using a walkie-talkie, Silva relayed everything that went on to Contreras.

At 5:00 A.M. lights in the house came on and two hours later, Silva realized that Carabineros were now on the scene and that a police van was parked in front of the house. In a flash, police officers surrounded his car.

It turns out that someone had called the Carabineros to report a suspicious car parked near the house. Before they forced him out of his car, Silva managed to let Contreras know, through the walkie-talkie, what had just occurred.

They took his badge and gun, bundled him into the van, and began beating him and hitting him with the butt of a rifle. They wanted to arrest and take him away, even though he identified himself as a PICH officer.

"They interrogated me in the van, and I heard William, who had just come up, speaking with them so they would let me go," says Silva.

Contreras called the group's leader, Robinson Muñoz. Muñoz notified Judge Juica who, in turn, got in touch with General Stange about the situation.

The order to release the "suspect" eventually came through, but the plan devised by the police to detain González had been spoiled.

Silva was bruised all over and wound up in the emergency room having his injuries attended to. Bototo González appeared before the judge of his own accord.

Be a Man

Héctor Silva enrolled in the Investigations School at the age of eighteen, in 1979, when the CNI was at the height of its power. He was assigned to downtown Santiago's First Judicial Precinct and in time specialized in fingerprint work. In the mid-1980s he was sent to the Information and Intelligence Department, Depinfi, and from there was assigned to the CNI.

"I didn't want to go," states Silva. "They assigned me because I had problems with a police officer when I was in the First Precinct. I didn't agree with his treatment of the detainees, and that officer said that I was a wimp. One day I made it known to the unit chief and told him that I believed we had to investigate before beating people up. I made the mistake of telling the police officer, and he told the chief, 'Hey, send him to Intelligence so he becomes a man.'"

Silva appealed to the head of personnel. It made no sense, he said, for them to send him to the CNI, as he had good qualifications and was one of the best officers in the unit. It went without saying that those sent to the CNI were the unwanted; no unit chief wanted to part with good officers.

"You are going all the same, and if you say no, there's going to be a problem," the personnel chief responded.

"I told the head of Depinfi what had happened, that I didn't want to be sent off to the CNI, and he assigned me to a technical unit specializing in fingerprints," states Silva.

In the end, Silva spent four years in the CNI, from 1985 until 1989. He knew that afterward they would send him back to his original unit, the site of the problem with his fellow officer, and that was something he wanted to avoid at all costs. What he really wanted was to belong to the Homicide Brigade, so in 1989 he took a course in legal medicine, paid for by the PICH. It was a six-month-long evening class, part of an arrangement between the University of Chile and the National Legal Medical Service.

Around this time, he requested an interview with the chief of Homicide, prefect José Barra, and showed Barra his certificate in legal medicine. Within a week he was added to the unit. He met up again in the brigade with his friend Nelson Jofré, who had recommended him for the Letelier investigation.

Although he was asked to assist in the September 1991 detention of Manuel Contreras in Fresia, Silva was still not part of a team dedicated to human rights cases. When Osvaldo Carmona explained to him that the Fifth Subprecinct was requesting more detectives to work the Slit-Throats Case, he was welcomed by

Robinson "Perlina" Muñoz, whom he came to esteem highly. Perlina introduced him to Director Mery and Judge Milton Juica. The judge let him have two weeks to study the case record.

"I had been a guard for Judge José Cánovas when he was investigating the case [in the 1980s]. I was part of a security detail that accompanied him everywhere. It was a nice coincidence that after so many years they put me on the same case as the [one being investigated by] the judge I watched over," says Silva.

Stange's Complaint

After the detention of DICOMCAR colonel Julio Michea in April 1992, the Carabineros complained to the government about how the detectives were treating their men.

Colonel Michea was detained by PICH detectives on April 1, in his house, located in one of the capital's middle-class neighborhoods. Two PICH deputy superintendents arrived at his house during the lunch hour and rang the bell on the gate. A housemaid peeked out from the door and told them that her boss had traveled south. They knew it was a lie.

"We want to speak with your employer," they told the woman.

She went back inside. Michea sent a message through her telling them to go away. His son then drove up in a car, made some crude remarks to them, and huddled with his father in the house. The detectives asked for reinforcements.

When they finally managed to take Michea off to the Homicide Brigade facility, the police faced a dilemma regarding the customary booking procedure (fingerprinting and photographing him). As with any other arrestee, it was necessary to create an official record on him, but Michea was a high-level Carabineros official, and Carmona was worried.

"There's going to be a problem here because the pressure is huge. Let's ask about it first," the Homicide chief said. He went up to the second floor to call on his superior.

Meanwhile, a police officer arrived from the Technical Assistance Department to take Michea's fingerprints. He was a very tall sort and came into the brigade's main room, where Michea was being held, with an air of confidence.

"Where's the detainee? The 'piano has to be played' with fingers flying. Dry those hands of yours, Colonel, because I have to ink them up," he declared.

Michea shot him a withering look. Carmona came back down in the middle of this scene.

"[We need to] get on with it," he reported.

Rodolfo Stange had become head of the Carabineros following the August

1985 resignation of director general César Mendoza, and he found himself compelled by circumstances to dissolve DIMCOMCAR.

By now, tension and friction between the Carabineros, the former CNI, and the PICH had reached a point of physical violence, and PICH officers were taking things too far. Stange sent a memorandum to interior minister Enrique Krauss complaining about the methods used in detaining his officers who, he said, "suffered unnecessarily, and without distinction as to rank or position, all sorts of ill treatment and humiliation on the part of the Investigations Police."

Stange went on to describe these in detail:

Temporary detention of family members and illegal pressure exerted on them to get information on detainees themselves and obtain the names of superiors and officials;

Apprehension by deceptive means, claiming alleged subpoenas;

Home searches [conducted] without producing an order from a competent authority; confiscation of photos of social functions, appointment books, and irrelevant material of a private nature;

Disproportionate and unnecessary vehicular deployment; intimidation by using firearms and handcuffs;

Lack of consideration and poor judgment during questioning; holding the affected parties in inappropriate places, given that they are Carabineros; not providing food over considerably long periods of time; and, what is more serious, booking them by taking photographs of the affected parties, without a proper order.[11]

The following day, Krauss sent a copy of the memorandum to Mery, asking for his "opinion" on the matter as soon as possible. Mery, in turn, directed it to the head of the brigade, Osvaldo Carmona.

Judge Juica acted a little more cautiously from this point on. With ensuing arrest warrants that involved active-duty Carabineros, he instructed detectives to bypass police headquarters and put the officers immediately at the disposition of the courts.

By mid-1992, those responsible for the triple homicide had been identified and indicted.

Prefect Carmona was pleased with the outcome.

Why, he was asked in a June 1992 press interview, had it been possible now to make progress toward learning the truth but not before?

"The police understood what their function was," he responded. "[Previously], professionalism was dormant and wasn't accompanied by the necessary incentives. Now the police have bounced back and been revitalized, because—apart from reeducation—they've been furnished with other means in tune with technological advances."[12]

Now they only needed to catch the civilian Fanta.

The Godfather

In March 1992, while DICOMCAR agents were being indicted, Judge Juica ordered the PICH to locate and arrest Miguel Estay Reyno. He also entrusted Interpol with the mission of finding Estay, because he knew that Fanta had left the country via Argentina. The records of the International Police in Chile had been requested by the Homicide Brigade, and they appeared to show that Miguel Estay traveled to Argentina in August 1988 and came back to Chile in June 1989 under his real name. Five days later, also using his real name, he again made the trip by land to Argentina. There was no indication after this of a subsequent return to Chile.

The truth is that Estay had actually left the country two years earlier, in 1987, as had his wife, Verónica Koch, who flew to Uruguay in January 1987 without returning to Chile.

Fanta was secreted out of the country bearing a false passport with the name Camilo Concha Burgos. He passed through Argentina, where he was supplied with contacts and logistical support, so he could move on and set himself up in Paraguay, with assistance from officials of that country's police and military. A month later his wife and daughter arrived from Argentina to join him.

Judge Juica surmised that he was in Paraguay but didn't let it be known. At the end of March he authorized, for a ten-day period, the interception of telephone calls made by a dozen of the indictees as well as the private lines of both Fanta's mother and mother-in-law.

By June, the obvious next move was to shift the police's inquiries outside of Chile. Director Mery requested government support to help underwrite an assignment, so that Homicide Brigade detectives could travel to Paraguay in search of Fanta. That was when Perlina bought his new suit.

During the time that Robinson Muñoz and William Contreras remained in Buenos Aires, they managed to establish that Verónica Koch had traveled to Paraguay with her then-eight-year-old daughter. There was no record of a Miguel Estay Reyno having departed Argentina. They consulted with Interpol Paraguay, which provided an address for Koch in Asunción: 219 Lt. Col. Mauricio Escobar Street, in the Jara neighborhood. The two detectives asked their Paraguayan counterparts to verify the information. The Paraguayans reported that a year ago an Argentine couple was living in the house but had moved to the United States.

Now, with an address in hand, Muñoz and Contreras moved on from Buenos Aires to Asunción. After a meeting with Interpol officials, they went to the Jara neighborhood, a middle-class area near the capital's central district where Fanta and his family had lived. They confirmed that the house in question had not been previously occupied by Argentinians who left for the United States, as the police had told them, but rather by a Chilean married couple and their two children. The family had moved the year before to another part of the country.

When they later passed on this news to the Paraguayan police, "they blamed their own forces" for the faulty information they had supplied, states Contreras.

The neighbors told the detectives that the Chilean pair were Verónica and Camilo. In addition, they knew that the wife, Verónica, had a job as a social worker in a military compound, the Victoria Base, caring for veterans of the Chaco War (1932–35). The compound was located in the Reducto neighborhood in San Lorenzo, a city situated thirteen kilometers from the capital.

The PICH officials set off for San Lorenzo. Perhaps being too up front regarding their motives, they talked with the commander of the military unit, Lt. Col. Alfredo Troche. Troche confirmed that Verónica Koch worked with them and lived near the base.

Then they asked about her husband.

"What's going on with the my child's godfather?" Troche asked.

In addition, the commander was godfather to Miguel Estay's second child, born in Paraguay. Later they learned that the couple's third child was the godson of Commander Troche's daughter. The baptisms took place inside this same compound.

"It's been two months since I've known anything of him, and I don't know where he would be," Troche assured them.

He authorized the detectives to meet with Koch in an office but first spoke with her in Guaraní, to ensure they could not understand what was said. Koch declined to make a statement before the Chilean officers. She resorted to using the argument offered her by Commander Troche: that by virtue of working on a military base she was shielded by military law and, furthermore, was under no obligation to make a statement because the detectives had not come armed with a judicial order validated in Paraguay. On the other hand, she did tell them that she found work in the compound through a recommendation from Paraguay's defense minister, to whom her husband was "a friend."

Verónica Koch was no help at all and, parroting Troche, told the detectives her husband left home two months ago and that she had no idea of his current whereabouts. She went back into her office area in a nervous state, while Commander Troche pointed them toward the house where Fanta's wife lived, in the base's Victoria Village. It was some fifty meters from the main entrance to the military compound.

Perlina and Contreras confirmed that the house was owned by a former police superintendent, Alejo Zárate, who was then serving as Paraguayan consul in the Argentine city of Formosa, located in the Chaco region along the border with Paraguay. He rented the house for $100 per month.

They spoke with a farmworker who lived in front of Zárate's house. The man, unwilling to give them his name, knew "Camilo," because they had done some kind of business together. More than twenty days had gone by since he had seen him, he told the detectives.

"Apparently Fanta liked to lend a hand to people in the fields, in planting, and people said he was a good sort, who didn't have problems with anyone. But rather than work on his own they sent him money from Chile, and he focused on taking care of himself," says Contreras.

With no assistance from either Estay Reyno's wife or the army commander and godfather to Estay's child, Muñoz and Contreras moved on a week later and went to Mexico. They spoke with the country's attorney general and filled him in on information regarding Estay Reyno, because his father and siblings had continued living in Mexico from the time they went into exile. Fanta might try at some point to get in touch with them.

When they got back to Chile, they developed the photos they had taken of Fanta's house in Asunción, the other house in San Lorenzo, the entrance to the Victoria Village, the house of the farmworker they had interviewed, and the store where the Estay family bought its groceries on credit. They strongly suspected that Fanta was still in Paraguay.

The former agent was alerted right away. His neighbors, in fact, caught sight of him just a few days after Muñoz and Contreras's visit.

A Friendly Country

On June 10, 1992, while the six detectives were still in Buenos Aires before setting off on their different missions, President Aylwin began a three-day state visit to Paraguay—the first by a Chilean president to that country since both nations had emerged from their respective military dictatorships. Along with members of Congress, cabinet officials, and a large delegation of businessmen, the Chilean government's objective was to consolidate political ties but even more to foment business deals and establish connections with Paraguayan industry leaders.

Chile's government appeared to view Paraguay through sympathetic, if slightly paternalistic, eyes. Both countries were endeavoring to consolidate their postdictatorial political transitions, do battle with the residual power of the armed forces, and launch a new era of openness and civil liberties.

In contrast to the situation in Chile, the February 1989 toppling of Gen. Alfredo Stroessner, in power since 1954, was the result of a coup. It was led by a wealthy army general, Andrés Rodríguez, father-in-law of Stroessner's son and right-hand man to the dictator. Rodríguez became the country's provisional president and some months later was chosen to fill the post by the Colorado Party. He sent Stroessner, his daughter's father-in-law, into a golden exile in Brazil, where Stroessner lived peacefully until his death in 2006.

As Mario Sharpe, Chile's ambassador to Paraguay at the time of the delegation's visit, described him, President Rodríguez "has always been authoritarian, far removed from democratic practices and culture." He headed up the 1989 coup "for the simple reason of survival, not out of any conviction in democracy. He saw that his permanence in the Army was endangered and along with that the possibility of continuing to enjoy the official perks that come with it. . . . Nevertheless, he has firmly pushed the process of democratization," Sharpe reported to the Foreign Relations Ministry.

In Sharpe's opinion, Rodríguez was a person without affectation, "more of a country man," who spoke Guaraní better than Spanish and had good rapport with the peasants and poor of the country's interior.[13]

The military dictatorships of Pinochet and Stroessner had cultivated a close relationship, and their intelligence services had worked collaboratively. The Paraguayans had taken part in several grievous episodes linked to Chile. The country was strongly allied with the Chilean coup plotters even before 1973. It took in the fugitive assassins of Chilean general René Schneider, murdered by a rightist commando group in October 1970 as part of a plot to try and block ratification of Allende's electoral victory.

After the military coup in Chile, Paraguay was one of the founding countries of Operation Condor, the network of Southern Cone intelligence services created in 1975 at the behest of the Directorate of National Intelligence director Manuel Contreras. In 1976, at the express request of General Pinochet, the Paraguayan government issued passports bearing false names to Directorate of National Intelligence agents Michael Townley and Armando Fernández. The two men later traveled to Washington, D.C., to carry out the assassination of Orlando Letelier.

It was all but natural that Chile's intelligence services would seek to protect Fanta by hiding him in Paraguay. Even the resident Chilean colony favored it. The minister counselor of the Chilean embassy in Asunción, Francisco Ossa, characterized this community as formed in great measure by "exiles . . . of high social standing who have been supporters of the past military government."[14]

Although the thirty-five years of Stroessner's dictatorship had ended, neither Chile nor Paraguay—by 1992—had fully purged its armed forces or intelligence services, and neither country had brought to justice those responsible for human rights crimes. Chile was trying to take some action in this direction "to the extent possible," but Paraguay did not even bother trying. In fact, it did not establish a Truth and Justice Commission until 2003.

By June 1992, when Aylwin arrived in Asunción and the PICH was going after Fanta, Paraguay was experiencing economic difficulties and finalizing the process of writing a new constitution. Its National Constitutional Convention was installed at the beginning of the year. The new constitution was to be promulgated in June itself, designed to replace the illegitimate and authoritarian charter that Stroessner had forced on the country in 1967. The new constitution curtailed the possibility that Rodríguez might serve another term as president. The ex-strongman from the Stroessner era was not pleased with that prospect.

Far afield of the political agitation then rippling through the country, Aylwin's official agenda in Paraguay focused on achieving economic agreements; deepening Mercosur, the regional integration pact; fomenting "economic development with equity"; and consolidating the process of political transition. In addition, one of the issues that mattered most to Aylwin was getting Paraguay to support Chile's candidate for director general of the UN's Food and Agricultural Organization. The new director general would not be chosen until November 1993, during the organization's conference in Rome. The Chilean government, however, began 1992 with a strong campaign to corral regional support for its candidate, the Christian Democrat Rafael Moreno.[15] President Aylwin made the pitch to Rodríguez during the state visit.

Aylwin was awarded the Mariscal Francisco Solano López medal and conferred Chile's Order of Merit medal on his host. They were on friendly terms, and Aylwin invited his Paraguayan counterpart to visit Chile, which occurred four months later, in October.

Chile's Foreign Relations Ministry saluted itself. Aylwin's visit, it judged, had had a "positive influence" on Paraguay's transition out of the Stroessner dictatorship. It also proved effective six months later when Aylwin personally asked Rodríguez to expel Fanta from the country.

On the other hand, not a single word was said during the state visit about the military, human rights, or fugitives from justice. Or, if the subjects came up, it wasn't reported. The Chilean government was strangely silent on these matters, some plaintiffs complained, despite the substantial progress made in judicial investigations.

The Leak

The possibility that Fanta was hiding out in Paraguay broke in the Chilean media on July 6. For Judge Juica, and the confidential work of the Homicide Brigade detectives, the disclosure was disastrous.

Under the headline "Investigations [Police] Located 'Fanta' in Paraguay," the newspaper *La Nación* reported that according to "police and judicial sources consulted in both countries," Estay was living in a bungalow in a residential section of Asunción and working for an agency of the Paraguayan armed forces. Two Chilean detectives, the paper continued, had found him. He lived with his wife and a housemaid, it added.

The judge was dismayed by the paper's report, fearing that it would hinder the investigation. Now he had to make it known to the media that for some weeks the PICH had hypothesized that Fanta was residing in Paraguay, under a false identity and protected by military officials who had been allied with the Chilean dictatorship.

"Regrettably, that process which was well under way is [now] thwarted," the annoyed judge stated.[16]

As a result of the leak, the Chilean embassy in Asunción learned that Chilean police officers had been in Paraguay searching for Fanta. The detectives had not taken any steps to alert the Chilean diplomatic mission of their activities in the country.

"The embassy was not informed because we didn't know if those staffing it were from the past regime. So we went about our work with lips sealed," explains Mery.

Accordingly, Chile's ambassador in Asunción, Mario Sharpe, consulted with Interpol Paraguay and reported back to his superiors in the office of the undersecretary of foreign relations: "They've indicated they have no information with respect to the presence in this country of the person in question."[17]

That same afternoon, Sharpe had to file another report after the Paraguayan evening newspaper *Última Hora* featured a headline announcing that the Paraguayan government had expelled Estay Reyno as an "undesirable foreigner." The paper failed to cite any source, only noting that it "found out unofficially" about the expulsion that had supposedly occurred weeks earlier.

According to an unidentified source quoted by *Última Hora*, Estay Reyno was working for different companies in Asunción but was let go because of "activities [he engaged in] that bordered on the criminal." Due to the submission of a complaint, the police intervened and expelled him, or so the newspaper assured its readers, without providing any evidence.[18]

The Paraguayan police denied it. "We don't know where he is or if he's living in Paraguay, since he doesn't appear in the Registry of Foreign Residents. Perhaps he entered the country secretly and lives under an assumed name," stated the spokesman for the Asunción police force, superintendent Pedro Villar.[19]

Sharpe contacted the country's interior and justice ministers and its security agencies without achieving "positive results due very likely [to the] local authorities wanting to avoid [the] subject since it ends up somewhat compromising for them." Sharpe, however, was able to speak with the Paraguayan undersecretary of foreign relations, Marcos Martínez, who left it that he would undertake "urgent inquiries" and report back to Sharpe as soon as possible. Sharpe apologized for how little had come of his efforts, explaining that the "peculiar schedule [followed by] the state and government administration (they don't work in the afternoon) has made it difficult to obtain precise information."[20]

The following day, Paraguay's ambassador to Chile, Héctor Nogués, met with Óscar Fuentes, director of bilateral policy in Chile's Foreign Relations Ministry, in Fuentes's office. Nogués assured him that there was nothing to it beyond speculation cropping up in the newspapers of both countries and that no information existed that might confirm Estay's presence in Paraguay.

The Paraguayan ambassador said that his country would offer "the highest degree of collaboration" with the Chileans but also noted that if what the Chilean press published was correct, in referring to Chilean detectives investigating the whereabouts of Fanta in Paraguay, "they must have been here as tourists," since they were never in contact with the Paraguayan police. There hadn't been "any approach of any kind between Chilean police authorities or Interpol Chile with their Paraguayan counterparts," the diplomat maintained.[21]

Meanwhile, that same morning in Asunción, Ambassador Sharpe sent a diplomatic note to the Paraguayan foreign relations minister, Alexis Frutos, officially requesting efforts to locate Estay.

By this time, María Maluenda, a member of the Chilean Chamber of Deputies and the mother of José Manuel Parada, had traveled to Asunción with the lawyer Humberto Lagos to try and speed up the capture of Fanta. They met with government authorities, members of the Paraguayan Congress, and political leaders. According to Maluenda, Paraguay's interior minister assured them that Fanta was not being protected by the Paraguayan government or armed forces but, instead, by Chile's military, which sent him money to live on.[22]

On the day that the leak came to light, Director Mery summoned the chief of the Homicide Brigade, Osvaldo Carmona, and the chief and assistant chief of Interpol Chile, Patricio Faúndez and Eduardo Riquelme, respectively. The PICH's director also met with Judge Juica. Some hours later the two Interpol officials went to the judge's office.

Mery had decided to send a team to Paraguay for the second time.

On July 8, officers Robinson Muñoz, William Contreras, Héctor Silva, and Horacio Piccardo—all from the Homicide Brigade—left on a direct flight to Asunción, accompanied by Interpol superintendent Riquelme.

They were on an official mission and were received in the capital by the director of the Paraguayan police. Their hosts offered to put them up in the police's guesthouse.

"They told us, in the house where we were [staying], that there were Chilean newspaper and radio reporters who wanted to speak with the head of the group, with Robinson. Then and there we realized that this [mission] had failed," notes Silva.

The Escape

The Paraguayan police detailed three of their men to help the Chilean detectives in their efforts and movements. Héctor Silva was partnered with a former Investigations School classmate, Antonio Benítez, who had gone to Chile to study.

"For obtaining some information he was essential," says Silva.

The detectives went back to the Estay-Kochs' old house in the Jara neighborhood. The family no longer lived at 219 Lt. Col. Mauricio Escobar Street, but they showed a photo of the couple to a neighbor.

"Ah, yes, Camilo, I know him. He's a very good neighbor, well educated," the man told them. " "You know who can give you more information? The lady living in the front, who worked for Camilo."

The detectives found the woman. She had been his housekeeper in 1987, during his first year in Asunción, before the family moved to a small farm in Capiatá, a city some twenty kilometers from the capital. Because the woman had traveled on several occasions to visit them there, they asked her to show them where, exactly, the property was. They went together as a group. The house was locked up, unoccupied, but the detectives were later able to identify its owner, a physician with the last name Insaurralde, and speak with him.

"That was where Fanta made a mistake, because he signed a rental agreement using his alias: Camilo Concha Burgos. That was his undoing," relates Contreras.

Later, the detectives met the real Camilo Concha Burgos in Chile. He was a high school classmate of Fanta's.

The Paraguayan authorities had no official record of Estay Reyno's entry into their country even under this false name.

The PICH officers took other measures. They contacted a Paraguayan woman who had purchased a vehicle previously registered in the name of Camilo Concha, and they spoke with authorities in the headquarters of the Paraguayan Postal Service, trying to run down correspondence with the names Estay, Concha, or Koch.

They spoke with another neighbor, Hermelinda Mendoza, who over a three-year period worked for the couple on the Capiatá farm. She told them that the Chilean couple had moved in April 1991 to the Reducto neighborhood in San Lorenzo, site of the military compound where Verónica Koch worked. She also told them that as a rule her employer, Camilo Concha, went to the Capiatá office of the telecommunications company Antelco to make calls to Chile.

Armed with this bit of information, the detectives followed up by visiting the international call center. Furthermore, they asked the Paraguayan police to accompany them so they could gain access to the center's call record. On those lists they spotted a certain Camilo Concha Burgos making calls to four telephone numbers—all in downtown Santiago—beginning in 1988 and continuing through mid-1991. They were restricted numbers, not listed in Chile's telephone guides. A call had also been made to Puebla, Mexico, in February 1991.

"He called a retired air force intelligence general at an office in the center of Santiago that had the look on the outside of an ordinary company," relates Contreras.

The officer in question was Gen. Vicente Rodríguez. He oversaw the operation to protect Fanta. General Rodríguez had created the Office of Legal Assistance in mid-1985, when he was head of personnel for the Chilean Air Force and while Judges Cerda and Cánovas were investigating the Joint Command and the Slit-Throats Case, respectively. Rodríguez's function was to offer help to agents compromised over human rights violations. From this office, located at 251 Teatinos Street, a block from the presidential palace, $800 was sent every month to Fanta for his maintenance in Paraguay.

In April 1992, by order of General Rodríguez and shortly after Judge Juica indicted him over the Slit-Throats Case, Miguel Estay had undertaken to flee his agreeable life in Paraguay. That month, Rodríguez dispatched a lower-level air force official, José Uribe, to Paraguay with $500 to relay the message to Estay that he needed to go to Brazil by land. It was Uribe's wife who sometime later furnished this detail to the court.

A housekeeper of the Estay-Kochs told detectives that in May of that same year, a workmate of Koch's traveled to the town of Ciudad del Este, near the triple border with Brazil and Argentina. This woman met Estay and returned to San Lorenzo with new clothes for his wife and children, a development that the detectives managed to confirm later in the year.

For all his preparation in intelligence and counterintelligence work, Fanta committed a fundamental mistake. "He was never able to keep away from his family. He had an autistic child and never kept away from them," says Contreras.

The child, in fact, was cared for in a clinic in Asunción, and Estay served as president of the Association of Parents of Autistic Children in Paraguay. At the outset of that same year—1992—Fanta was even interviewed on the subject by that country's press.

Meanwhile, the media continued to follow the detectives' movements and featured speculative accounts about Fanta's whereabouts. Chile's La Nación reported that he was in the locality of Hernandarias, on the Brazilian border, as Capiatá's chief of police apparently informed the paper. Or Estay went there to look for work, because he ran into "problems with his boss," as the Paraguayan police apparently had it. A police official told the reporters that for a considerable time Estay did construction work for the owner of an electrical appliances store in Capiatá.[23]

Paraguay's justice minister, meanwhile, told the press that Estay had probably slipped out of the country to Brazil or Argentina.

In mid-July, Judge Juica issued an order, applicable internationally, for the capture of Miguel Arturo Estay Reyno, and the Chilean government made an official request to Paraguay that it apprehend and extradite him. In line with these initiatives, the Santiago Court of Appeals sent memorandums to the Interior and Defense Ministries as well as to the Carabineros and the PICH prohibiting them from releasing information concerning the judicial measures just taken. Judge Juica had criticized information leaks about Fanta, claiming that it had frustrated his capture in Paraguay.

Around that same time, the detectives from Homicide were reporting via telex to their superiors in Santiago on their efforts to locate Estay. They predicted that, on a scale of one to seven, the chances of locating Estay were at a six if they were allowed more time. They asked for two additional weeks. The request was denied, so four days later the detectives were on their way back to Chile.

At the very end of September, two months after Chile had asked the Paraguayan government to find Fanta, the request was acknowledged by Paraguay's foreign relations vice minister, Marcos Martínez. Martínez also offered the first pieces of concrete information: The Chilean citizen Miguel Estay Reyno did not appear under that name in their police records, as had been well known for months. But others with the name Estay, possibly relatives, did show up. One was French and another six were Chilean, including Fanta's wife, Verónica Koch Catalán, and his daughter.[24]

"This mission estimates that, according to information obtained on an unofficial basis, Mr. Estay Reyno would have fled the country in order to evade possible capture, leaving his family members in Paraguay," predicted Ambassador Sharpe in a report to his superiors in Santiago.[25]

The Tourists

After their return to Santiago, the detectives spent several months in the capital. The request by the Chilean government that Paraguayan authorities locate and arrest Estay meant that the responsibility to do so fell on Paraguay's police force. Nevertheless, after holding meetings with Judge Juica, Director Mery decided that two detectives from Investigations should return to Paraguay in December. The assignment was given to William Contreras and Héctor Silva.

The objective was to make inquiries into the grounds for the information collected during the earlier trip and get closer to Fanta's whereabouts. Robinson "Perlina" Muñoz remained in Santiago, staying on the track of the Office of Legal Assistance, located on Teatinos Street and directed by Gen. Vicente Rodríguez. The plan was that the two detectives would be ready in Asunción when the PICH raided the office on Teatinos.

"But you can't meet up with your police officer friend," Mery ordered Silva. "Go about it the smart way."

They went incognito, posing as tourists. They traveled by land, because Antonio Benítez—Silva's former classmate in the police school—was assigned to the airport and would be aware of their arrival.

Their first stop was in Buenos Aires. There they boarded a launch to continue on to Montevideo, across the Río de la Plata. They stayed two days in the Uruguayan capital and then took a bus to the Paraguayan city of Itá, a small municipality located some thirty kilometers southeast of Asunción.

"William tried to talk like an Argentinian, but at times forgot to do it. The Argentinians don't say compadrito [a belittling form of slang for compadre, or pal, used by Chileans]. We really cracked up over that one," recalls Silva.

After two days they continued traveling north, into the Department of Concepción, in the center of the country, and along the banks of the Paraguay River.

Benítez had mentioned to them that Fanta might have contacts with farmers in that area. Contreras and Silva settled for three days in a house near the one that Fanta supposedly visited. But nothing happened; they drew a blank, so they turned around and headed southward, to the Paraguayan capital.

"We wound our way very cautiously so that no one should spot us, because some police officers now knew who we were," Silva remembers.

They picked up new information from the telephone records they obtained on the first trip, confirmed facts, and checked up on other leads. They were doing this work when Mery ordered Silva to return immediately to Santiago.

Contreras stayed behind alone in Paraguay, under strict orders from Mery to await instructions and, in the meantime, to have no communication with anyone.

Héctor Silva returned to Chile by bus because he couldn't allow himself to be seen in the Asunción airport. He kept enough money for the return trip and left the rest with Contreras. Contreras had to hang on a while longer in Asunción, and the travel allowance they were given was rapidly dwindling. The shortage of funds to maintain the two officers on foreign assignment was one of the reasons dictating Silva's return. Since they were traveling incognito, they couldn't be sent more money.

"When Tito [Héctor] left, I switched from the three-star hotel we were in to a couples motel. I was in that motel for about two weeks. It was the cheapest one," says Contreras.

Silva took a bus from Asunción to Buenos Aires and from there got on another bus to Santiago. He spent a full day, twenty-four hours, on the road.

When he reached Santiago, Perlina and his colleague Horacio Piccardo were waiting for him at the bus terminal. They brought him directly to Mery's office, and he filled in the director on all the information they had sought to verify in Paraguay.

To watch for movements in and out of the Office of Legal Assistance, the Chilean police rented an office next to it, on Teatinos. Informed on by his wife, José Uribe was arrested on December 9. Uribe, who had traveled to Paraguay to deliver money to Fanta with instructions to disappear off the face of the earth, confessed everything, telling the police, first, who within the armed forces and Carabineros coordinated responses to human rights investigations and protected certain agents who had been lifted out of the country and, second, how they went about doing it.[26] Other high-level officials Uribe identified were also brought in, but their time in detention was brief.

When the detectives raided the Teatinos office, they found the false passport, bearing the name Camilo Concha, that Estay had used to leave the country.

General Rodríguez remained temporarily under arrest at the Air War Academy.

While these events were occurring, Fanta was hiding out in a small hotel in Foz de Iguazú, on the Brazilian side of the border with Paraguay, and realizing that the setup that protected him was collapsing.

Jorge Balmaceda, an attorney for the air force at the time and known defender of human rights violators, convinced Estay to turn himself in voluntarily, because by doing so he could reduce any eventual prison sentence. Either Fanta decided to come in on his own or he was ordered to do it.

"I believe that the general [Vicente Rodríguez] saw that all was lost, he made some calls, and Fanta handed himself in. I've often wondered what they offered Fanta to get him to turn himself in," muses Contreras.

Mery decided that Silva should stay in Santiago and that Muñoz, Piccardo, and Interpol's assistant chief, Enrique Riquelme, should travel to Asunción. The head of the Homicide Brigade, Osvaldo Carmona, would go with them.

At long last, Contreras received the call he was waiting for. At the other end of the line was the voice of the investigative team's leader, his friend Robinson "Perlina" Muñoz.

"William, just stay where you are. We're on our way. Fanta is turning himself in," Muñoz told him.

A Voluntary Handover

Shortly before lunch on Friday, December 18, 1992, the head of the Homicide Brigade rang the bell at the Chilean embassy in Asunción. He brought important news: That afternoon the fugitive Miguel Estay Reyno would show up at the embassy with his lawyer to hand himself over voluntarily to the courts. He needed to be transferred into the custody of Chilean plainclothes police officers, who were already in Asunción, lodging in the Hotel Guaraní.

The lawyer Balmaceda coordinated the handover with Osvaldo Carmona. The Chilean police were not authorized to detain Estay on Paraguayan territory but legally had the right to do so inside the diplomatic mission.

Ambassador Sharpe immediately placed a call to the Foreign Relations Ministry in Santiago, requesting instructions on how to proceed. Responding via an urgent, secret telex, the foreign relations minister, Enrique Silva, authorized Sharpe to sign a document confirming the handover, issue Fanta a valid passport, and arrange—with the Paraguayan authorities—his prompt departure from the country.

Interior Minister Krauss was already aware of these developments, having learned about them firsthand from Director Mery. As soon as President Aylwin emerged from a luncheon, Krauss looped him in on the situation.[27]

Meanwhile, Sharpe telephoned Asunción's police chief, Gen. Germán Franco, to present the Chilean government's position: namely that the preventive arrest order which had hung over Estay since July, for purposes of extraditing him, needed to be canceled. There were abundant reasons to take this action: It turned out that the fugitive was hiding on the other side of the border, in Brazilian territory, and was about to surrender voluntarily to the Chilean police at the Chilean embassy. Consequently, it wasn't necessary that he appear before a Paraguayan court. Wasn't it preferable to avoid a lengthy and needless extradition process?

It didn't seem that way to General Franco, who said he preferred to go on with the extradition proceedings. He told Sharpe that he could not do otherwise unless expressly authorized by President Rodríguez.

Ambassador Sharpe was waiting for Fanta to show up at 5:00 P.M. that afternoon, but he only appeared several hours later, at 9:00 P.M. An hour after that they called the detectives, who were in the hotel, and asked them to come to the embassy.

Estay, Balmaceda, and Carmona signed a document confirming the handover of the criminal fugitive to the chief of the PICH's Homicide Brigade. The Chilean consul issued him a regular passport, valid for three months. Miguel Estay would never use it again.

"He was calm but affected the attitude of a prisoner of war and said nothing beyond 'My name is Miguel Estay Reyno, my identity card is such and such, I'm Chilean.' We didn't get a single word out of him," recalls Contreras.

First thing the next day, President Rodríguez's private secretary, Luis Boetner, showed up at the embassy at the request of the embassy's minister counselor, Francisco Ossa. Ossa explained the need to expel Estay without delay, because it was no longer necessary to go through the extradition process. He told him that the Chilean government would ask Paraguay's foreign relations minister to suspend the arrest order, leading to eventual extradition, in order to allow Fanta to leave the country. The request, however, was not well received. The Paraguayans continued to be upset by the investigations that the Chilean police had carried out on their territory behind their backs.

Nonetheless, Boetner told Ossa that he would deliver the message to the Paraguayan president.

"But a direct call from Chile's president could facilitate matters," Boetner added.

That same afternoon, the Chilean government dictated a note to the Paraguayan foreign relations ministry, with the intention that it cancel the arrest order on Estay and facilitate his departure from the country under custody of the Chilean police. They formulated the note in such a way as to "preserve the dignity of the Paraguayan police" by creating the impression that Paraguay's police were in charge of capturing the Chilean fugitive, when, of course, they had been completely left out.[28]

They never got to the point of sending it. The obstacles were cleared a few hours later that same Saturday, following a conversation between the two presidents.

An Untimely Telephone Call

At this juncture, according to Ambassador Sharpe, diplomatic and commercial relations between Chile and Paraguay were "the best they had been in many years."[29] The Paraguayan president had concluded a two-day visit to Chile during the third week of October. Aylwin gave a dinner in his honor in the presidential palace, at which top-level government and armed forces officials and the business elite were present. In addition, foreign relations minister Enrique Silva organized a luncheon in the president's honor at the Undurraga Vineyard.

The Chilean government rated the visit a success, particularly on the business level.

Within Paraguay, however, the image and credibility of President Andrés Rodríguez had seriously eroded since Aylwin's June visit. The army's high command had withdrawn to the barracks between September 17 and 19 because of corruption accusations. The charges were leveled by an army colonel, and they tied high-level officers to a scheme to traffic stolen vehicles into Bolivia.

The explosive revelations of corruption, in which top officers who led the 1989 coup against Stroessner were implicated, also touched President Rodríguez and his family. Several generals were indicted, including the army's commander in chief. There was talk about "the trial of the century."

In a report to the Chilean foreign ministry, Ambassador Sharpe indicated that while a negotiated solution was being sought that would avoid a break in the process of democratization, "the possibility of a 'military uprising,' leading to an eventual armed confrontation, could not be discounted."[30]

Paraguay's political transition was experiencing its most trying moments, and the country's president was nowhere to be found that Saturday afternoon. He wasn't at home, and only a handful of guards knew where he was. There was no way for Aylwin to call him.

During the exploratory assignments in June and July, as Mery pointed out, the idea of bribing Paraguayan officials to obtain information about Fanta was toyed with, given the apparent level of corruption in Paraguay, even among the elite unit that guarded the president. The time had come to put the idea into practice.

Director Mery had furnished Homicide Brigade chief Osvaldo Carmona with money from special reserves and authorized him to use it to buy information.

The Chilean detectives in Asunción activated their contacts and managed to obtain a telephone number to call General Rodríguez. It turned out that the mystery of his whereabouts had nothing to do with politics.

"I called President Aylwin and gave him the telephone number. I told him that he was in a house but didn't explain whose house it was. One of Rodríguez's guards gave out the number. The cost: $100. Rodríguez was taking a nap at his mistress's house when Aylwin placed the call to him," states Mery.

After the untimely call, President Rodríguez agreed to expel Fanta immediately. He ordered General Franco to take all measures so that Prefect Carmona and the four PICH detectives could leave Asunción with Estay.

The Paraguayan police made a double VIP suite in the airport available to the group and to embassy personnel traveling with them. They were offered drinks, coffee, and—later on—food.

"The Paraguayan police in the airport shot us dirty looks. We had left them flat-footed and besides, they didn't even know we were in Paraguay," says Contreras.

At midnight on Saturday, December 19, they boarded Ladeco airline's regularly scheduled Flight 115 to Santiago and arrived in the capital at dawn.

The drama, however, was not quite over. In the early morning of December 24, the Chilean embassy in Asunción received an anonymous bomb threat in reprisal for the arrest of Miguel Estay.[31]

Twice an Informer

Miguel Estay was brought to the Homicide Brigade's headquarters on Condell Street, in the Santiago neighborhood of Providencia. Four guards were assigned to watch over him.

"Fanta came across as very meek, with a shrewdly affected humility. He wanted to be treated well and was very amiable to the police. To have arrested a man so sought after was such a huge deal that every officer wanted to know up close who he was. They all wanted to lay eyes on him," relates Silva.

Only some more senior detectives, however, were let through, but they couldn't strike up a conversation with the arrestee.

Fanta ended up confessing virtually everything, under the shield of the law that allowed for reducing penalties in exchange for collaboration. He faced indictments for the kidnapping of the AGECH teachers, the February 1985 kidnapping of the architect Ramón Arriagada, identity theft, and the kidnapping and murder of Nattino, Guerrero, and Parada.

The police brought him before Judge Juica on Tuesday, December 22. It marked exactly seventeen years since his initial arrest in 1975, when he began his conversion from disciplined Communist militant to proficient agent of the repression.

In Paraguay, Miguel Estay, or Camilo Concha, had already become a historical footnote, replaced by other shocking news that jolted the political landscape and the human rights community. On that same December 22 day, the Paraguayan lawyer Martín Almada led a spectacular discovery in a police office in the municipality of Lambaré, some ten kilometers from the Estay-Koch home in San Lorenzo. Lying loosely about were heaps of folders and files—the so-called Archives of Terror—tons of documents chronicling the repression and the crimes of the Stroessner era, among which was the participation of Paraguay and Chile in Operation Condor.

That day, for security reasons, Fanta was moved from the Homicide Brigade to the Investigations School at the other end of the city to face interrogation by Judge Juica. A taxi with two men in it had been spotted driving around near the brigade's building.

The following day, the judge returned to questioning the prisoner in the brigade's offices. Once again, a suspicious vehicle drove past and around the place. In addition, a group of teachers from AGECH gathered in front of the building and protested noisily.

As with the operation to capture Osvaldo Romo, the hunt for Fanta, and his handover, was—in all its complexity—one of the first great breakthroughs in human rights cases.

"It was important to [capture] and bring Fanta back because he was a Communist traitor who could commit treason again. He was arrogant, boasted about his skills at analysis, and [in truth] was a keen analyst," states Mery.

Estay was kept in isolation for many months by PICH. Christmas and New Year's came and went, and he remained confined all through the spring and summer of 1993. Initially, Judge Juica interrogated him in the office of the Homicide Brigade, but for security reasons they started bringing him for interrogation sessions to the intelligence unit at the Investigations School.

At the outset, the prisoner was not very forthcoming, but Judge Juica explained that if he cooperated, he would benefit from a lighter sentence. Not long thereafter, Estay was rounding out information that the PICH and the judge already possessed; then he began to confirm other facts and, over time, wound up telling them everything, accompanied by a wealth of details, relates Silva. It was a replay of his 1975–76 performance.

"I never saw any signs that he felt remorse or anguished," states Silva. "His verbosity and control over information were enormous. He had it all put together very effectively, he knew what he had to tell and what not. It was really exhausting. We spent hours upon hours and wound up completely wiped out. But he was just fine."

No one besides his mother came to visit him, and she brought clothes and food. The rest of the family was too grieved about the turn he had taken.

"The fact of having achieved results with Romo, plus what Perlina did with Fanta and what Rafael Castillo accomplished with Michael Townley, all in the same year, bolstered the PICH director and brought him around to trust our work," notes former Analysis and Institutional Coordination Commission detective José Plaza.[32] "It further consolidated the reputation of the police as a serious organization that people could trust. And the courts realized that they had a force with which they could work to push ahead with the investigations."

Fanta's confession did not prevent him from receiving a life sentence. In September 1994 the court of appeals increased the sentences for Miguel Estay Reyno and two other agents to life in prison. He shared a cell in the Punta Peuco prison for twelve years with Osvaldo Romo. They grew quite close.

Of the five who were sentenced to life for the triple homicide, only Estay was not released. Between 2015 and 2016 Alejandro Sáez, José Fuentes, Guillermo González, and Claudio Salazar were paroled.

In January 2017, the Supreme Court denied parole for Fanta. Perhaps that was the price to pay for continuing to be the weak link.

8

MOVING THE BOUNDARIES

AS 1993 GOT UNDER WAY, the air pollution in Santiago was so bad that people out on the streets could barely breathe. The topic dominated the news outlets and people's conversations at home and at work. Residents of the capital suffered from irritated eyes; children were deprived of physical education classes; and government officials wracked their brains wondering what to do and how to place controls on industries, buses that belched out smoke like chimneys, and the explosive growth in car sales and traffic. That was the year that saw the introduction of catalytic converters.

Nevertheless, a fresh breeze was blowing through the majestic building housing the country's highest courts. Things were changing, if only a little.

Osvaldo Romo and Miguel "Fanta" Estay were under arrest and confessing. The collaboration of Luz Arce and Marcia Merino allowed multiple human rights cases to go forward, and the investigation into the assassination of Orlando Letelier was moving ahead on solid ground, opening several new lines of inquiry. In October 1992 Judge Adolfo Bañados wrapped up the investigation and charged Miguel Contreras and Pedro Espinoza, the latter still in active service, with the crime.

The threat of impeachment against the Supreme Court judges who voted in favor of transferring the Chanfreau case to the military courts demonstrated to judges that granting impunity did not come without cost. Still shaken by the removal of one of their own for "serious dereliction of duty," one chamber of the Supreme Court ventured onto new legal ground. By three votes to two, in a December 1992 ruling, it adopted the principle that the disappearance of people constituted an open-ended abduction, as long as the victim in such cases did not surface. As an ongoing crime, it would not be covered by the 1978 Amnesty Law. Furthermore, because the crime was unsolved, the statute of limitations was similarly inapplicable.

As part of that same ruling, the First Chamber's judges adopted the "Aylwin doctrine": amnesty was not an obstacle to carrying out investigations.

This decision was a bitter blow for the military and the lawyers who defended it. They viewed the Supreme Court as their salvation—a trustworthy bulwark of protection against what, to them, was unjustified harassment on the part of some judges, the plainclothes police, and human rights organizations—all with the blessings of the government.

The Supreme Court's ruling revealed the first fissures in what, to that point, was taken to be a monolithic, antiquated body loyal to the military regime. Additionally, when President Patricio Aylwin named the deposed Judge Hernán Cereceda's replacement, six of the seventeen judges on the Supreme Court were now appointees of Chile's democratic government. Aylwin's gambit was to change the balance of forces on the country's Supreme Court and at the same time push forward a far-reaching judicial reform.

The National Corporation for Reparation and Reconciliation (CNRR) sparked a new round of complaints to the courts, adding to those already contributed by its predecessor, the Truth and Reconciliation Commission, or Rettig Commission, as it was popularly known. The task of the CNRR was to resolve old cases in which the Rettig Commission could not reach a conclusion due to lack of information as well as new cases brought to it between July and October 1992. (This period was later extended for sixty days, to cover April through June 1993.) The new cases considered by the CNRR numbered close to 1,000.[1]

The responsibility for investigating this full mix of cases was given to the Institutional Analysis and Coordination Commission (CACI) of the Investigations Police (PICH). Furthermore, the caseload now included information received by the CNRR about the possible location of human remains that could be those of disappeared persons in two more districts.

"We were looked on very unfavorably within the institution itself. They talked about us as if we were Communists; it was as though we had leprosy. Ours was an official assignment, but the thinking inside the PICH was that this was not a job for us to take on. Even Department V colleagues who investigated internal affairs, not human rights matters, told us, 'Listen, let the military be, just get to work.' Time and time again there were comments made in favor of the military," relates Abel Lizama.

Throughout that year, the CACI stepped up, adapting to an ever-increasing range of tasks. Between March 1992 and February 1993, it acted on 256 investigative orders issued by the courts, sent off almost 2,000 memorandums, and prepared more than 400 police reports. During this period, the CACI's administrative employees entered information on 870 agents of the repression. As the database grew, the records became more and more conclusive. By the end of 1994, the CACI's detectives had responded to more than 1,000 judicial orders and interviewed almost 2,000 witnesses.

The CACI staff, augmented by the addition of José Luis Cabión and Abel Lizama, was now able to occupy three offices attached to Department V in the basement of the PICH's headquarters building. Their material resources were slowly increasing as well. At the end of 1992, they had two mobile phones, one secure telephone line, and three vehicles (a Chevy Monza and two Fiat Tipos) and maintained subscriptions to the newspapers *La Nación* and *La Tercera* and the magazine *Análisis*.

While they still had only one computer, they now had five typewriters, more furniture, and—reflecting the growing operational role of the CACI—a FAMAE-brand submachine gun manufactured in Chile.[2] They were hunting members of the military and civilian secret agents involved in past state-sanctioned crimes.

Shifting Ground

By mid-1993, the number of reactivated cases came to 184, and some fifty officials still in active service had been required to make an appearance in court. The number of cases temporarily closed, but subject to being reopened at any time, numbered close to 600.[3] The "parade" of military officers through the courts continued taking place, frequently amid protests and shouting by persons who stationed themselves in the streets and hallways to rebuke the officers as they arrived for or left from an interrogation. The media, predictably, blanketed these events. For the armed forces and the Carabineros, it all constituted an unacceptable spectacle.

Starting that year, the appeals court began to revoke amnesty for certain cases, based on international treaties on human rights ratified by Chile, as the constitutional and legal standing of such treaties gave them higher juridical standing than national law. In its rulings, the appeals court referred to the Geneva Conventions on the treatment of prisoners of war and to the principle that the disappearance of people was an ongoing crime.[4]

This interpretation—which evolved years later to deem the forced disappearance of people a crime against humanity, one not subject to any amnesty or statute of limitations, under any circumstance—gave victims' families a window of hope that justice could be attained.

The strategy of "justice to the extent possible" operated on shifting ground, during times when the government tried to achieve legal reforms or changes to limit the scope of military justice. It sought to devolve onto the presidency the authority to remove commanders in chief and professionalize the armed forces, confining them to their proper sphere and role: subordinated to civil power, nondeliberative, and focused on the country's defense and external security.

The issue described by historian Steve J. Stern as a "struggle to define and shift the boundaries of the possible" was still being contested as autumn began in March 1993.

"For Pinochet and his closest allies, the struggle had taken an ominous turn. The reliability of the Supreme Court as guardian of impunity was slowly softening," Stern writes.[5]

Buffeted by these new winds of justice, the government feared that tensions with the army would continue building should the military think that the government's real intention was "total justice," not justice "to the extent possible." At the same time, it also foresaw that the greater demand for justice would end in "rising expectations," putting pressure on the government to be more proactive.[6]

Given these new circumstances, the office of the president warned in early 1993, "it's reasonable to expect a strong reaction on the part of the Armed Forces in the event that the solution to the human rights problem takes a direction that is intolerable for them."[7]

And it did, in the last days of May 1993, as a former Directorate of National Intelligence (DINA) conscript packed his bags to return to Chile to tell everything he knew.

Pure Lies

Samuel Fuenzalida was a draftee in Calama when the coup d'état took place. He was in Toconao around this time, doing hard labor, cutting up volcanic rock as a form of punishment. The punishment was for abusing a two-day leave. He had used it to travel to his family's home in the Santiago district of Quilicura. But Fuenzalida didn't want to return to Calama, so he settled in, planning to stay in Quilicura. His family convinced him to return to his regiment. He brought sweets and food with him because the conscripts were always hungry.

It was August 1973. Fuenzalida was roughed up, had his hair cut, and was made to wash the courtyard with a spoon. Then he was sent under arrest to the Toconao quarries, where other soldiers under punishment were laboring away.

"As part of the arrest they gave us a kilo of lentils, beans, and told us: now cook. What did we know of cooking? So we slipped out to hunt and rob the train. Trucks from Argentina loaded with meat came by from time to time and we stole meat," relates Fuenzalida.

Along with his fellow soldiers he found out about the bombing of La Moneda from a military radio broadcast. A few days later, they returned from Toconao to the regiment.

At nineteen years of age, Fuenzalida—born in the northern Chilean town of La Higuera, near Coquimbo—took part in raids and detentions in Calama. He witnessed the Caravan of Death as it passed through the city, helped plant explosives near access points to the Chacabuco concentration camp, and—when the "war prisoners" began to arrive—served for some weeks as a camp guard.

At the end of November 1973, Fuenzalida and other soldiers were summoned to the regiment's command post. There, an army captain informed them that they had been chosen to spend some vacation time at the beach. They were required to sign a document.

It was a simple form titled "Brief Communiqué," with the imprint of the "National Rehabilitation Department, DINAR," on which was written:

> On the premise that our personnel are our most valuable resource, we examined your health records and in view of the physical and mental strain placed on you, plus the valuable services you've rendered toward National Reconstruction, the top authority has decided to reward you, [by] sending you to the National Rehabilitation Center, the purpose being to grant you a deserved obligatory rest on the coast, in the countryside, and in the mountains so that in the near future you can again take up productive work with renewed spirits and energy. You will continue enjoying all the benefits and guarantees you have had up to this time in the Armed Forces and Carabineros, for as long as your period of rest and recuperation lasts, free of service, family, and domestic problems.

The document bears the date November 30, 1973, and is signed by Roberto Echaurren, the director general of the Committee for the Preservation of Useful Human Resources, a completely fictitious body.

The bottom left of the form, where as a rule the distribution list of a document was specified, simply contained the initials "P.M.N.C.N."

The young conscript, dreaming of a frolic on the beach, was put on a plane with other soldiers. After landing at Santiago's Cerrillos Airport, they were bused down to the Tejas Verdes regiment and wound up in some army cabanas in the exclusive seaside resort of Rocas de Santo Domingo. The following morning, after they fell into line, the installation's commander, Col. Manuel Contreras, appeared before them dressed in combat fatigues.

He told them they had been chosen to become members of the newly formed

National Intelligence Directorate, or DINA. It was Contreras who explained that the letters P.M.N.C.N., on the form they signed, stood for (in Spanish initials) "Pure Lies Don't Say Anything."

"Contreras told us we belonged to the DINA now, and he delivered a rousing patriotic speech. He presented the DINA as savior of the homeland. I was of the Left, always had been. Other conscripts [were] too, but everyone was afraid, and no one trusted anyone else," says Fuenzalida.

Starting then, everything they did was secret. Fuenzalida was one of the first participants in the National Intelligence School, which the DINA set up. Its instructors included Miguel Krassnoff, the notorious torturer who belonged to the DINA's top leadership, and Cristián Labbé, who later, under the democratic government, spent sixteen years as mayor of an upscale district in Santiago.

Fuenzalida was one of 600 who graduated from that class. In January 1974 he was sent to the headquarters of the Metropolitan Intelligence Brigade, located for six months in an area in the west end of the capital called Rinconada de Maipú, on land which the Ministry of Education had ceded to the army after the coup.[8]

Fuenzalida lived in Rinconada and worked as a DINA employee in the Londres 38 torture center, where he formed part of the Caupolicán Unit. His tasks included working as a guard in the secret center, infiltrating public places to overhear conversations, and making trips to PICH headquarters, "where the files [on people] were stored and they always gave us whatever we asked for."[9]

As Fuenzalida maintained in his statement before the court twenty years later, he was a frequent witness to the torture of prisoners, many of whom died at the hands of the DINA due to the agency's inexperience in applying electric current. For this reason, he said, the DINA incorporated PICH staff into its ranks, because they "were more effective, as a way to put it, with this type of torture."[10]

In May 1974 Fuenzalida was transferred to the DINA's Terranova site, located in the Villa Grimaldi secret center. There, again, he witnessed how prisoners were tortured, including through electric current administered by a group of detectives, whom he took to calling the "Papis," or "Daddies": Risiere Altez, Manuel Díaz, Daniel Cancino, and Hugo Hernández, among others.

In Villa Grimaldi he laid eyes on Luz Arce, Marcia Merino, and María Alicia Uribe—the three by then were enjoying special treatment—and many detainees who ended up dead or disappeared. Among the survivors, he knew Lautaro Videla, brother of Lumi—a young mother and member of the Movement of the Revolutionary Left, who was tortured and assassinated in 1974 and whose body DINA agents tossed into the grounds of the Italian embassy in Santiago.

While at Terranova, Fuenzalida was ordered to transfer the Movement of the Revolutionary Left leader Álvaro Vallejos Villagrán, imprisoned in the Cuatro

Álamos torture center, from Santiago to the town of Parral and from Parral to Colonia Dignidad. Located on the outskirts of Parral, in the South of Chile, Colonia Dignidad was the site of a German sect that opened its doors to the DINA, enabling the agency to torture and "disappear" political prisoners on its grounds. Fuenzalida made the trip with the DINA's agent in Parral, Fernando Gómez. They handed over the prisoner, to this day a disappeared person, to Colonia Dignidad's leader, Paul Schäfer. Vallejos was presumably killed in the colony.

Fuenzalida completed his military service in March 1975 and did not want to continue on in the DINA. Some weeks earlier, he had explained to the agency's head of personnel that his family was in tight financial straits, so he needed to find work to help them out. It wasn't true, but this explanation was enough to authorize his withdrawal from the DINA. Fuenzalida's final step was to show up at the office of one of the DINA's lawyers to sign a statement pledging that he would not provide any account of what he had seen or experienced in the agency. If he did so, they would kill him.[11]

The Agent in Hamburg

In mid-1975, Fuenzalida left Chile for Argentina, distancing himself from the DINA and trying to figure out what to do with his life. He traveled by land to and from Argentina throughout 1976. Finally, in late October of that year he flew from Santiago to Buenos Aires and never came back. From the Argentine capital, Fuenzalida embarked for Europe. He traveled alone, a man adrift.

"I arrived in Holland because that is where the ship reached port, but life propelled me on to Germany," says Fuenzalida.

A person he had gotten to know in Buenos Aires was going to meet him in Amsterdam, but they didn't manage to find each other. A fight broke out in the bar where they planned to connect; the police showed up and Fuenzalida—just off the ship and undocumented—was arrested. His few belongings were in a locker in the train station. He was never able to retrieve them. The police put him on the first train out and expelled him from the country. Fuenzalida got off in Frankfurt, penniless, without any contacts, lacking clothes and personal belongings.

"I slept in the train station," he relates. "I had nothing to live on and stole food. I asked for work in a hotel run by an Argentinian Italian couple who had fled Argentina. I approached the Chilean embassy because I was afraid I would be expelled. I spoke with a colonel and requested a passport in order to return to Chile, although I wasn't planning on doing that. He sent a telex to Santiago and so he found out who I was. The embassy gave me a bit of money."

At work and in the neighborhood, he identified himself as an immigrant sailor, not as a former DINA agent or political exile. He moved on later to Hamburg, when he was able to speak a smattering of German and managed to save some money.

In Hamburg he met a Chilean who had requested political asylum, by claiming—falsely—that he was a DINA deserter.

"He recommended that I do the same. I fashioned a half-true, half-phony story. They gave me a form for aspiring asylum seekers," he says.

One day Fuenzalida, now enjoying stable work with Mercedes-Benz, came across a demonstration by Amnesty International (AI) on a street in Bonn. The demonstrators were handing out leaflets about Colonia Dignidad. He told them that he had been there but with the military. That was how he met Lutheran bishop Helmut Frenz. Bishop Frenz was executive secretary of AI's branch in Germany and one of the founders, in Chile, of the Comité Pro Paz, an ecumenical group that helped those persecuted for political reasons after the military coup. He was expelled from Chile in 1975. Fuenzalida recounted to the bishop how he had dropped off a prisoner at Colonia Dignidad. Soon thereafter he approached Chilean exiles to speak with them about the DINA. They tested him in various ways, and eventually Fuenzalida managed to overcome the barrier of mistrust.

In March 1977, AI and the German magazine *Stern* published reports denouncing the use of Colonia Dignidad as a torture center, thanks to the testimonies of detainees who came out of the place alive, such as Adriana Bórquez, Luis Peebles, and Erick Zott. In return, Private Social Mission, founded by Schäfer and the parent organization in Germany of Colonia Dignidad, filed a complaint against AI and *Stern* for defamation.[12]

In the civil case heard in Bonn in 1979, survivors of Colonia Dignidad testified about what they went through in the colony, and AI presented a star witness: the former DINA soldier Samuel Fuenzalida.

Colonia Dignidad's lawyers in Germany sent an urgent request to Chile's National Center for Information, the successor agency to the DINA: Who, exactly, was Fuenzalida?

As the decade of the 1990s began, and after her trip to Chile to share information with the PICH and the courts, Luz Arce arrived back in Germany. She knew Fuenzalida from her time with the DINA.

"Luz had already spoken with the police. So we set out to write about what we knew," states Fuenzalida.

An Invitation from Santiago

In the first days of May 1993, CACI inspector José Plaza contacted Fuenzalida to determine just how the former conscript should appear before Judge Dobra Lusic. The judge was investigating several abductions and homicides carried out by the DINA, such as the disappearances of Mónica Llanca, Álvaro Vallejos, and Sergio Pérez as well as the assassination of Lumi Videla, all of which occurred in 1974.

Lautaro Videla, a onetime political prisoner himself, was trying to obtain information about the fate of his disappeared brother-in-law, Sergio Pérez, and gain justice both for him and for his own sister, Lumi. As part of this effort, the Chilean exile and Colonia Dignidad survivor Erick Zott mentioned Fuenzalida to him. The two soon entered into conversation.

Lautaro Videla had visited the PICH to provide a formal statement in connection with Osvaldo Romo's return to Chile the year before. He had mentioned to Inspector Plaza that he had been in touch with an ex–DINA soldier who was living in Germany and willing to cooperate with the authorities.

"Due to what was going on here, Samuel Fuenzalida wanted to cooperate with us, furnish information that would be useful to us. We looped Judge Lusic into it. We managed to connect by telephone, and he told us he was prepared to come to Chile," says Plaza.

On May 3, Judge Lusic formally instructed the CACI to locate Fuenzalida and arrange his appearance before the court in the case of Mónica Llanca's disappearance. She needed his statement, as a witness, to help clear up this and other crimes. Lusic had already indicted a handful of DINA agents.

"I wanted to go but asked them for guarantees," explains Fuenzalida. "The guarantee was that they wouldn't record my entrance and that the police were going to pick me up in Buenos Aires."

After speaking on the phone with Fuenzalida, the detectives set in motion a plan for him to reach Chile while safeguarding his privacy and physical well-being. However, because the former soldier enjoyed the status of political refugee in Germany, Inspector Plaza explained to Director Nelson Mery that some "additional efforts" were required: (a) address an "invitation" to him that refers to the purpose of the trip, which he in turn will submit to AI, with a recommendation to the local administrative authorities; (b) obtain a Chilean passport for him to leave Germany; and (c) adopt appropriate security measures during his trip and his stay in the country.[13]

The plan was to have him travel from Hamburg to Buenos Aires and stay one night in the Argentine capital before continuing on to Santiago. He would meet up with the CACI's detectives in Buenos Aires, and they would bring him into Chile under conditions of maximum secrecy.

His immediate contact in the PICH was Inspector Plaza, who was then the CACI's interim chief. After the time he spent in Brazil searching for Osvaldo Romo, Luis Henríquez had returned to the Higher Academy, dividing his hours between the CACI and his course of instruction.

Negotiations over the telephone and by fax and telex went on for weeks between Hamburg and Santiago. To get the case moving faster, Judge Lusic stepped in to assemble the documentation needed to extend a Chilean passport to Fuenzalida. She herself asked the Foreign Relations Ministry to instruct Chile's consul in Hamburg to furnish a passport in the name of Samuel Fuenzalida Devia. On Thursday, May 13, Henríquez asked the Foreign Relations Ministry undersecretary's chief of staff to send the documents, plus the "invitation" signed by Director Mery, via diplomatic pouch.

Inspector Plaza called Fuenzalida and brought him up to date on these efforts, telling him that he could go to the consulate to collect his passport at the beginning of the coming week. In turn, the ex-conscript explained that he would be ready to travel to Chile between May 25 and 28.

In a fax he sent to Plaza, Fuenzalida proposed an agenda for his testimony before the court: he would cover his time in the Calama regiment and the time spent on assignment with the DINA between 1973 and 1975. He wanted to furnish information about the victims with whom he had come into contact; identify DINA agents, including their physical descriptions; specify the sites used by or belonging to the DINA (including their locations and the distinctive features of buildings, detention centers, clinics, and places for lodging and recreation); describe particular DINA undertakings and repressive operations; and expose the network of informants recruited by the DINA from what he (Fuenzalida) termed the "underworld."[14]

Samuel Fuenzalida's wish was to talk about all these matters in Chile. He had already done so before delegates from the Rettig Commission in Hamburg, lawyers from the Vicariate of Solidarity, United Nations bodies, AI, and a Bonn court during both the 1979 Colonia Dignidad civil suit and another such court affair eight years later, also involving Colonia Dignidad. Moreover, he had compiled a long list of DINA agents who served as guards between 1974 and 1975 in different Metropolitan Intelligence Brigade sites and passed it on to Luz Arce in Europe so she could hand it over to the PICH.

The thirty-nine-year-old Fuenzalida needed to return to Santiago to ratify all this information before the police and the courts.

Around this time, the Chilean media disclosed a vital fact: the Foreign Relations Ministry's telephones were being tapped. That revelation caused Inspector Plaza to fear the worst: namely that the highly secret measures being taken to bring Samuel Fuenzalida to Chile might have leaked. The chief of staff for the ministry's undersecretary played down the possibility, but the uncertainty persisted.

As it turned out, what impeded and held up Fuenzalida's arrival were not the tapped telephones but foot dragging on the part of the Chilean consulate in Hamburg. Inexplicably, it couldn't manage to issue a passport in the name of Samuel Fuenzalida, despite the judge's request and the express authorization given by the Foreign Relations Ministry. Nor had it allocated any time to schedule a personal interview with him. It simply wasn't cooperating.

Exasperated over the delay, Fuenzalida took the documentation that the PICH sent him, including the "invitation," and requested permission to leave the country from the local police in Hamburg. They obliged by furnishing him a special German passport. The Chilean passport was never issued to him.

Fuenzalida was set to leave for Chile on Wednesday, June 2. He paid the cost of the trip out of his own pocket. In Santiago, Director Mery approved sending two CACI detectives on assignment to Buenos Aires on that same day so they could meet Fuenzalida on June 3. Inspector José Plaza and detective Abel Lizama were chosen to make the trip.

Fuenzalida proposed the Hotel Colón as their meeting place because he was already familiar with it. It was a good choice, because it had both a front and a rear entrance. The two detectives went out on the town that night with Fuenzalida, dining in a restaurant and then visiting a tango hall. The comradery enabled the two parties to start building trust in each other.

"I had a good impression of the two police officers. If I hadn't, I wouldn't have come [to Santiago]. I trusted them. I believed them, even though I always distrusted the police. I remember that Abel was timid, and very young," says Fuenzalida.

Trapped in Buin

Abel Lizama was the son of working-class parents and one of four brothers. They lived in a small locality, called Polonia, near the city of San Fernando, in central Chile. In 1971, as a result of the country's agrarian reform program, the vineyard where Abel's father worked was divided up, and he lost his job. The family resettled in San Fernando, and the head of the household went to work as a bus driver.

When the military coup took place, Lizama was only seven years old, so it scarcely registered with him. Politics was not a topic of conversation in the house. His thing was soccer. His older brother, however, became a student leader in the 1980s, after winning a President Pinochet scholarship to study civil and electrical engineering in Valparaíso. He wound up being expelled, arrested, and condemned to internal exile.

Abel, on the other hand, began to study technical drawing at the Professional Institute of Santiago. His father found work in a pork sausage factory in the capital, and father and son lived together in the city.

"I would step out of the university and there were rocks being thrown, protests, electric lines cut, blackouts, but I didn't get caught up in it. I was a small-town guy and had an uncle who was a Carabinero. He worked in the canteen in Santiago's First Police District and was a good sort," says Lizama.

After a year in the factory, his father lost the job, and the two went back to San Fernando. Abel returned to the soccer pitch and rose to the level of Colchagua's Second Division. His father, who went to work as a truck driver for the Coca-Cola Company, came home one day holding a brochure announcing that applications were being accepted for the Investigations School.

"Up to that point becoming a detective had never entered my mind. You could have something secure there, my father told me. And I, to please him, considering our skimpy incomes, applied, took the tests, and did well," he relates. "I was young, a soccer player, little engaged with what was actually going on in the country. Under the dictatorship, if the newspaper reported that extremists were killed, I didn't question it. I saw myself solving crimes and serving society."

It was 1986, a year of heightened unrest, when he enrolled in the Investigations School and his brother went into exile in Germany. Lizama graduated as a detective in 1988, when the country held a plebiscite to decide whether the Pinochet regime should have eight more years in power. Like the majority of his fellow citizens, he voted no. Lizama was detailed during his first three years to a judicial district in the municipality of Buin, in the Santiago Metropolitan Region.

"Mr. Henríquez trapped me in Buin," he states, laughing about it.

In 1991 the court in Buin issued an investigative order regarding the discovery of human remains on a slope of the Chada hill. The order was handed to the district's youngest detective, Abel Lizama. The remains were identified as those of Movement of the Revolutionary Left members Humberto Menanteaux and Hernán Carrasco. The two had been arrested by the DINA in 1975. Still undetermined, however, was how they died. Both showed signs of having been tortured.

Lizama gathered all the information available, located the families and interviewed them—a minor miracle, given the lack of trust in the police and his own inexperience and naïveté, he explains. He devoted himself to reading about the broader context, the DINA's different sites, and the sheer cruelty of the tortures inflicted. It was all new to him. Lizama called the CACI office in Santiago, and the staff summoned him to a meeting. He set off by bus to the capital with a folder containing the notes from his investigation. Lizama was all of twenty-two.

"I was very disciplined. I went regularly to the CACI and, with its support, mounted a really strong investigation. Luz Arce was already cooperating with Miranda and Henríquez. They were breaking down Arce's statements, forming a picture of the DINA's operational groups, and I was piecing together my puzzle with the information they furnished me," he explains.

Before he joined Department V as its driver, Luis Núñez performed the same function in the Buin judicial district, and now he tried to persuade Lizama to come on board with the CACI. "The group's chief, Luis Henríquez, asked to have me transferred to his department," says Lizama.

The detective, however, did not want to move to Department V because of the stigma it bore of officers acting as informants on their own colleagues. In mid-1992, when the CACI was seeking reinforcements in anticipation of Osvaldo Romo's arrival, they again prevailed on him to join the team. This time he wasn't given the option of saying no.

Lizama became the CACI's newest member some two months before Romo's return. During this period, they passed on to him an investigative order issued by Judge Mauricio Silva that had already passed through several hands. Silva was investigating the disappeared persons from the La Moneda assault, but he also wanted to go beyond that and account for everything that occurred on September 11, 1973, inside the presidential palace. Lizama interviewed the La Moneda survivors, including his own chief, Luis Henríquez; the former Department V chief, José Sotomayor; and other colleagues in retirement. He was unable, though, to duplicate that with members of the military—getting them to respond to a police officer's inquiries still met with resistance.

"I was the first detective after the transition to democratic government to investigate what took place inside the La Moneda palace," affirms Lizama. "It was super interesting to learn about the life stories. I saw it all on TV when I was a boy, but to come to picture it in situ, finding out how it occurred, where they were, how they moved about. . . . I tried to transport myself back into the moments through which they were living. It was very impactful."

When Osvaldo Romo was brought in, Lizama had to put the La Moneda investigation aside. From temporary add-on, he wound up remaining in Department V for a year and a half, until early 1994, when he was posted to Coyhaique, in the country's far South. In 2000, Lizama returned to working on human rights cases. Partnering with detective Sandro Gaete, he was able to dive back into and eventually wind down the case of La Moneda's disappeared.

Staging of the Black Berets

On the morning of May 28, around sixty elite combat troops, the Chilean Army's "black berets" (*boinas negras*), with their faces painted, surrounded the armed forces building, located on Zenteno Street in front of the presidential palace. They were supposedly there to "protect" both the building and the nearly forty generals who were gathered inside to meet with Pinochet.

That was the pretext.

Like the "readiness and coordination exercise" of December 1990, this second military "tantrum," known as the *boinazo*, set off alarm bells in La Moneda. President Aylwin was in Copenhagen, Denmark, on a visit to the Scandinavian countries. Interior minister Enrique Krauss, now taking on the duty of vice president, had the task of putting out the fire.

The army's show of force reflected its discontent with the government's attempts to reform the Armed Forces Organic Law. The reform aimed at limiting their political power and restoring the government's authority to remove commanders in chief. They were also protesting the presidential pardons for political prisoners. The army also wanted to put the brakes on human rights investigations and objected to what it considered the degrading way it was treated by the media.

The *boinazo*, however, was actually triggered by Pinochet when he saw that his son Augusto was again mired in problems.

Days before, the State Defense Council had succeeded in reopening the Pinocheques case in the Fifth Criminal Court, with Judge Alejandro Solís in charge. This news made the headlines of the May 28 early morning edition of the government newspaper *La Nación*: "Pinochet Check Case Reopened." In addition, the paper noted, eight army generals would be issued summonses to make statements. The former dictator already possessed this information, but the lack of discretion shown by the paper infuriated him.

"The main reason for the army's complaints was always the protection of Pinochet's family," states former minister Krauss. "The two events [the readiness and coordination exercise and the *boinazo*] stemmed from that. When the *boinazo* took place, Gen. Jorge Ballerino called me, specifically because Pinochet was upset that his son's company was being declared bankrupt. That was the ostensible reason. But later, when I met with Pinochet, he arrived with a list of demands that included the treatment of military officials in the courts. The change in the list of complaints was clear."

The generals had considered various ways of pressuring government authorities, but they decided, finally, to limit themselves to declaring a grade 1 quartering of troops in the barracks and maintaining the ominous presence of the well-armed black berets in the street fronting La Moneda.

On Sunday, May 30, Krauss went to Ballerino's house with presidential chief of staff Enrique Correa to try and defuse the crisis. They were going to meet with Pinochet. Notably, defense minister Patricio Rojas was not participating. Although he was technically Pinochet's immediate superior, the ex-dictator was unwilling to deal with him and never accepted the legitimacy of his authority. To the contrary, he treated Rojas with scorn, as though the defense minister were his subordinate.

No agreement was reached, but Pinochet had already prepared the minutes of the conversation. An army official brought them in when the group's conversation finished.

"His list of demands included removing Rojas as defense minister and beefing up military salaries. In addition, he complained about the treatment members of the military received in the courts. I promised to open a dialogue to see how we would get the situation resolved," relates Krauss.

Aylwin tried to maintain an air of normalcy amid a situation that was clearly strained but did not speed up his return to Chile.

A Protected Witness

The dust had not settled yet when Samuel Fuenzalida landed in Buenos Aires. The next day, the CACI's chief, Luis Henríquez, called the Hotel Colón several times to speak with Plaza. Henríquez was worried. The detectives were due to board a flight that day to Santiago, but the atmosphere in Chile was tense; it wasn't safe.

For his part, Fuenzalida telephoned Lautaro Videla's office in Santiago. Videla wasn't there, but the call was taken by Pedro Alejandro Matta, who was already collaborating with the CACI in his own investigations into the DINA and its sites and victims.

"Luis Henríquez warned me, as Pedro had, about what was taking place in Chile. Henríquez assured me that he would get me out of the country if something happened. It didn't overly worry me because I already knew what I needed to do: seek protection in the German or U.S. embassy. I had those two options," says Fuenzalida.

The former DINA conscript did not alter his plans. He readied himself to travel on a commercial flight to Chile that same day with the two police officers.

When they arrived in Santiago on June 4, the state of alert for the army's troops had just been lifted and President Aylwin was still abroad.

The day before, Judge Dobra Lusic had ordered that the witness be afforded protection. The CACI's detectives had to ensure his safety for a period of twenty days. The police and a group of former political prisoners who had helped extend a bridge to the former DINA conscript were waiting for him in the airport. Fuenzalida did not go through either customs or passport control. Instead, the PICH's men collected his suitcases and escorted him "extra-officially" into the country.

On the day of his arrival, Fuenzalida made his first extensive statement before inspector José Plaza in Department V. He handed over photocopies of several documents, including the announcement about his "deserved rest period."

And, as the days went by, he shared everything that he had come to tell.

For the first few nights Fuenzalida slept in the PICH's headquarters building. After that he stayed in different locations, including the house of some relatives who lived in the northern section of Santiago. The detectives dropped him off there at night and picked him up early in the morning.

"We took turns protecting him," notes the former administrative employee, Miguel Reinoso. "As a rule, one or two police officers and one of the administrative staff accompanied Fuenzalida. When we worked a night shift, we stayed with him. He was never alone."

During the three weeks that he remained in Santiago, Fuenzalida did not miss a day in making a formal statement, whether to the detectives or Judge Lusic, who came to the PICH building for this purpose. He also met with Lautaro Videla, whom he knew from earlier times, and spoke with Pedro Matta, Erika Hennings, and other former political prisoners.

He testified regarding different cases, checked over information, and identified—from mug-shot albums—forty-five DINA agents along with political detainees who were either executed or never accounted for. He furnished a list of DINA agents and guards, an organizational chart showing different sites, and the names of employees—their aliases, deployments, and personal characteristics. If he could manage to match detainees to specific sites and buildings, he provided that information, and he also furnished a sketch indicating where Sergio Pérez might be buried on the Rinconada de Maipú land that the DINA had occupied.

Fuenzalida made appearances before Judge Lusic, with great care taken that his presence in Chile not leak out, although its secrecy made little difference at the end of his stay.

On the morning of Friday, June 25, just hours before leaving to fly back to Europe, the former DINA conscript agreed to be interviewed by two media outlets: *La Nación* and National Television. Later, at the airport, he participated in a press conference, accompanied by Lautaro Videla and Socialist congressman Sergio Aguiló. Fuenzalida used the occasion to recount his experience, what he declared before the judge and detectives, and what he knew about human rights crimes.

Then he boarded a KLM flight to Hamburg, with a layover in Buenos Aires, where—for his protection—he was accompanied by Congressman Aguiló.

A few days later, Director Mery sent a report to Interior Minister Krauss, informing him of Fuenzalida's arrival in Chile and the cases under investigation for which he had provided statements. He reported what Fuenzalida had testified to regarding the likely fate of Sergio Pérez, the death of Álvaro Vallejos in Colonial Dignidad, and how Osvaldo Romo had presumably strangled Lumi Videla.

Luis Henríquez told Director Mery that Fuenzalida's statements were "coherent and consistent with" the testimony of other witnesses, noting—at the end of his summary: "In his statements Fuenzalida avoids tying himself into any human rights violations. This is justifiable in that he provides his testimony as a conscript who did no more than perform administrative functions and guard duty. It is important to document that there is no testimony in the records indicating the contrary. It is believed that since he served for almost two years in his capacity as a conscript, it is unlikely that he would have had access to more critical information related to the DINA's operations and the ultimate fate of its victims."[15]

One year later, in April 1994, Samuel Fuenzalida made a second, two-week trip to Chile to provide testimony in the Sergio Pérez case, among other matters. He came face-to-face with Osvaldo Romo, whom he knew well, and Basclay Zapata, alias "Troglo" (from "troglodyte"). According to Fuenzalida, both agents had taken Pérez to the DINA's National Intelligence School, in Rinconada de Maipú, where he would have been killed. Another conscript, also a DINA recruit, had shown Fuenzalida the exact spot where Pérez was buried. He supplied a map indicating its location.[16]

No one learned of Fuenzalida's presence in Chile during this second trip until after his departure on April 29. Months later, several judges sought him out to take statements from him, but he was already back in Germany.

"Later I took a liking to being in Chile and traveled here every year. I rediscovered myself. I kept making trips here, providing testimony in face-to-face encounters. I even accompanied the police to Colonia Dignidad," remarks Fuenzalida.

Following Fuenzalida's first trip to Chile, Sergio Aguiló sent a note to Interior Minister Krauss. He was strongly affected by the government's inaction with respect to Colonia Dignidad. From Fuenzalida's statements to the police, Aguiló indicated, it emerged that the agents responsible for disappearing people, and who therefore knew of their fate, numbered no more than 100, and they were conclusively identified. In addition, he confirmed that Colonia Dignidad served not only as a place of imprisonment and torture but also as a cemetery.

"In light of the above," Aguiló wrote to Krauss, "I believe there are no longer any reasons to put off a decision by the government enabling it to restore national sovereignty over Colonia Dignidad's lands."

Immediately afterward, Aguiló asked the government to take several actions: cancel the residence visas granted to the colony's leaders and expel them from the country, to facilitate their appearance before German courts; recover full national sovereignty over the land occupied by the colony; and launch an exhaustive investigation to locate where on the colony's grounds the disappeared prisoners lay buried.[17]

These were the same initiatives that survivors of the colony, victims' families, and human rights groups had urged for years now, as far back as 1966, when the first member of the colony, a youth named Wolfgang Müller, escaped and told the world about the enslavement, repression, and pedophilia to which the German colonists were subjected.[18] It seemed that some things never changed.

Stillborn

Upon his return from Europe nearly a week after the *boinazo*, President Aylwin began a series of conversations and consultations with top military brass, political leaders, Catholic Church officials, legal experts, and human rights lawyers. In addition, he summoned Pinochet to a meeting in his personal residence at the beginning of July. Aylwin was looking for some means of crafting a definitive solution to the "problem" of human rights and civil-military relations. The discussions held during the president's round of consultations focused on "speeding up judicial proceedings."

Besides securing an end, once and for all, to the Pinocheques affair, the army also wanted permanent closure of cases that had been temporarily dismissed and a new amnesty law, or passage of a law that reinterpreted the existing law and accepted as judicially valid the armed forces' conclusion that disappeared persons were deceased.[19]

Some within the government's own coalition were also anxious to accelerate the treatment of human rights cases in order, they said, to normalize relations with the armed forces and advance the consolidation of democratic governance. One of the persons within this camp was the then president of the Chamber of Deputies, the socialist José Antonio Viera-Gallo.

"It's a real problem for civil-military relations," the congressman offered to the press, "that so many cases exist against officials on active duty, encompassing a much wider field than just the major cases."[20]

Viera-Gallo's idea was that judicial proceedings in cases that arose before 1978, covered by the Amnesty Law, should be investigated by a special set of judges and ruled on within a short time frame. Cases arising after 1978, which he mistakenly described as "not many," would continue going forward.

"The function of the specially appointed judge would be to speedily investigate and then apply amnesty," stated Viera-Gallo.[21]

The president of the Senate, the Christian Democrat Gabriel Valdés, proposed that the president, the commanders in chief, and a representation of ministers and authorities meet weekly or monthly to analyze the situation as it evolved. A good many gambled that both the matter of judicial cases and the friction with the army would be resolved before the government turned over in 1994—two conditions that needed to be met before the end of the democratic transition could be pronounced.

For those on the Right, the Aylwin doctrine, positing that amnesty did not preclude carrying out investigations, further complicated the democratic process. What was needed, they proposed, was to reinterpret the Amnesty Law to bring it in line with its original spirit: amnesty extended a priori, closing cases even when it wasn't known who had to be amnestied—because no investigation of incidents would take place. In addition, some suggested that detainees still unaccounted for be declared, presumptively, as dead—to prevent judges from continuing to categorize an abduction as an ongoing crime.

Victims' families and human rights groups remained vigilant, fearing the adoption of this plan of action into law.

The president's consultations continued during the troubled winter of 1993 and bore fruit at the beginning of August, in the form of a bill that was soon dubbed the Aylwin Law.

The bill, Aylwin told his cabinet on August 12, avoided two extremes: (1) amnesty outright, ipso facto, and (2) the complete elimination of amnesty. As he submitted, human rights legal cases could not be dragged out forever, but neither were persons going to come forward with information if they felt they would pay the price of moral or social condemnation and if they were not incentivized by criminal penalties being withheld or mitigated.[22] The controversial bill entailed appointing fifteen special investigating judges for human rights cases covered by the Amnesty Law, estimated by the government to be fewer than 200; protecting the identity of those who furnished information about the location of the disappeared; and keeping secret all related testimony and factual data. The judges would be granted a two-year period in which to collect information and determine the fates of the disappeared, after which the Amnesty Law was to be applied.

This bill, if passed into law, would go beyond existing legislation that reduced a sentence significantly if the accused provided information. Those who cooperated with the justice system would not receive just reductions in penalties but, rather, outright guarantees of impunity. Once information was provided that established the truth of what happened in a given case, that case would be closed by virtue of the Amnesty Law.

"It is this government's aim," declared Aylwin's spokesman Enrique Correa in a June interview with the newspaper *El Mercurio*, "not to leave human rights issues [pending] for the next administration."[23]

The reaction was immediate and scathing. While the Chamber of Deputies debated the proposed law, members of the Association of Relatives of the Detained and Disappeared began a hunger strike, the first since the time of the dictatorship. Popular protests against impunity were suppressed with heavy force by the Carabineros. Legislators and political leaders in the government's coalition found themselves split over the bill.

For human rights organizations, the Aylwin Law was nothing more than validation (or revalidation) of the Amnesty Law and the consecration of impunity. For the ruling coalition, it meant a trying internal struggle that brought it almost to the point of fracturing. And for the military and its civilian allies on the Right and in Congress, it was never sufficient.

During these weeks of tense discussions about the proposed law, the Second Military Court in Santiago reopened some twenty human rights cases that had been temporarily closed, for the sole purpose of pronouncing them amnestied and closed definitively.[24] It was the court's way of influencing the debate.

Finally, a month later, the president and his advisers backed off from pushing the bill and promised not to include it in the next legislative session. At that point it became a dead letter, though in a certain sense the law was stillborn because it never gained anyone's approval.

The investigations continued as usual, their success hanging on the will and decisions of each judge, the quality of the police work, and the composition of the various chambers of the Supreme Court. And, true to form, the armed forces and the Carabineros offered no help.

Toward the end of 1993, with tensions still high following the failure of the

Aylwin Law, the country was rocked by two more judicial bombshells: In September Judge Milton Juica brought charges against the civilians and members of the Carabineros involved in the Slit-Throats Case. Two months later, Judge Adolfo Bañados handed down a sentence in the first instance against Manuel Contreras and Pedro Espinoza for the assassination of Orlando Letelier.

It was election season, and some in the government wanted to put an end to the "issue" of human rights as soon as possible. This was also the desire of Christian Democratic presidential candidate Eduardo Frei Ruiz-Tagle. Even though tragedy had also landed on his own doorstep—for years he resisted believing that the death of his father, a former president and opponent to Pinochet, was not from natural causes—human rights investigations were never one of his priorities.

On Edge

"After the *boinazo* everyone was on edge," relates Luis Henríquez. "For example, the wife of one of the DINA's top torturers, Marcelo Moren, told René Sandoval the tables will turn and we're going to shoot all of you. That was the mildest [of it]. One pursued investigating under those conditions."

René Sandoval was the CACI's newest detective. He was barely out of the Investigations School when he joined the team in 1993. He knew very little about what had taken place in Chile and was equally in the dark about the crimes that Department V was investigating. As Henríquez saw it, that was an advantage. The CACI was looking for detectives with a clean slate, men who were not tainted by the past and conducted their investigations with maximum care and dedication.

The team Sandoval joined was composed of Henríquez, Plaza, Cabión, and Lizama. What they stressed above all was maintaining confidentiality about the work they were doing.

"We selected them based on the quality of the reports they sent to the CACI," Henríquez explains. "We chose them for their ability to carry out investigations. We sought those who were quick on the mark, were attentive to details and acted appropriately, and took down statements in the right way."

Sandoval was from the town of Molina, in Chile's southern region of Maule, and he enrolled in the Investigations School in 1990. He was the first detective to join the human rights teams whose training in and graduation from the school came after the restoration of democracy and, conversely, the sole CACI detective who, to that point, had not been part of the PICH during the dictatorship. Another who enjoyed that status, Freddy Orellana, would soon come on board.

When he left the Investigations School in 1992, Sandoval was assigned to the

First Police District, in downtown Santiago, from where Henríquez requested him for the CACI.

Perhaps because of his age or emotional detachment from the crimes, it was less trying for Sandoval to deal with types such as Moren. He treated him as "my commander," who had put himself on the line for the country. "This is how Chile repays you," Sandoval would say to him, to gain his confidence. Sandoval even had tea with Moren in his apartment. Moren treated him like an underling. So, taking this tack, Sandoval gradually convinced Moren to go to PICH headquarters to make a statement.

The first thing Sandoval needed to do when he joined the CACI was familiarize himself with everything that the group's work entailed. They passed along to him police reports and other information related to the investigation of Osvaldo Romo and information about how Romo's location was pieced together.

"This is the sort of thing we investigate, so you get the idea of it," they told Sandoval.

It was a grind to assimilate to what he had gotten himself into. The milieu was unfamiliar and, as happened with his fellow recruits, the Investigations School did not prepare him for investigating human rights violations committed by agents of the state.

"I remember having thought, 'Wow! What I've got myself mixed up in,'" notes Sandoval. "I was the youngest and looked up to Pepe [José] Plaza a lot. He was an extraordinary detective, the image of the detective one wanted to be."

Having just come on the team, they packed Sandoval off in search of an ex–DINA agent to deliver a court summons to the man. Sandoval was accompanied by the driver Luis Núñez and inspector José Plaza. They looked for the former agent at several residences and, finally spotting him, tailed him in their car. They stayed behind him until they reached a building by a park.

Sandoval got out of the vehicle and went up to the apartment. Plaza remained below. The door hardly opened when the man yanked Sandoval by the arm, pushed him into the apartment, shut the door, and stuck a pistol in his temple.

"How long are you going to chase after me?" he threatened him.

"I'm not chasing you. I'm only fulfilling a judicial order," Sandoval replied.

The man's wife had to intervene.

"He's only doing his job," she said to her husband.

"Tell the judge that I'm not going to say anything else and I'm not going anywhere," the former agent stated.

When Sandoval came down, got back in the car, and recounted what happened, the detectives took it in stride. By now it was a simple fact of life that the detectives working human rights cases—both in Department V and in the Homicide Brigade—were insulted, threatened, tailed, and harassed.

"When I came into Internal Affairs and investigated cases involving detectives, I never received threats, but when I began human rights cases I and my people received calls spouting foul language that can scarcely be reproduced. They warned us they were going to kill us like dogs and things of that nature. This was constant and didn't stop until 1996, by which time we had gotten ahold of things," notes Luis Henríquez.

The PICH delved into the calls and discovered that almost all of them were made from public telephones in downtown Santiago, adds Henríquez.

Detectives from Department V and from the Homicide Brigade's Fifth Subprecinct were investigating crimes that penetrated to the heart of the DINA, the National Center for Information, and Pinochet's inner circle and revealed their criminal activity abroad. In addition, more than a few of those investigated were high-ranking army officials still in active service.

The Army Intelligence Directorate (DINE) monitored judicial investigations from top to bottom, recording the statements made by agents, coordinating their responses, withholding information, and following detectives to observe what they did, with whom they spoke, and where they went.

None managed to escape being a recurrent target of monitoring, not to mention intimidation and threats. Even some of the witnesses who made statements in certain cases were harassed.

Director Mery made a point of periodically informing the government about all such interventions.

"Mery always had our backs," says Nelson Jofré, who investigated several very high-profile cases. "It was clear to him from the beginning that our investigations treaded on delicate ground and that we were going to be hugely vulnerable. And because we carried on living a normal life, something could very easily happen to us. Perhaps we were naïve, but I never took precautions, for mental health's sake. One knows how to size up the streets; I was aware that they were spotting me. The DINE wanted to know what we were up to each and every day."

Director Mery met with government officials on various occasions to review this matter. "The detectives," he pointed out in a report to Interior Minister Krauss, "learn to live with threats as inherent in investigative police work and they adopt precautionary measures, planning out their own strategies for personal security, with help from institutional resources. It's also clear that they maintain their total determination to go on with the investigations without losing their nerve in these situations."[25]

A Mountain of Work

From its creation in April 1991 to December 1993, the CACI had coordinated with eighty-four judges on the national level, three judges on the court of appeals, one Supreme Court judge, and two military prosecutors. The team investigated 256 cases involving 427 victims of human rights abuses, including cases declared by the Rettig Commission as having lacked "conclusive evidence."

In addition, its detectives investigated another 663 cases, as requested by the CNRR. In October 1993 the government prolonged the life of the CNRR until December 31, 1994, and it was later extended for an additional year. The CACI team managed to discover forty-eight victims who were not listed in the Rettig Report, not even as "inconclusively proven" cases, and they discarded another eight, in which the persons claimed to be among the disappeared were found to be alive. The detectives located and interviewed them.[26]

In a meeting with the CACI's officers, lawyers from the CNRR requested assistance in supporting initial inquiries. The request did not have to do with formal criminal complaints or judicial orders but, instead, with gathering preliminary information, establishing residences, and verifying facts—in short, carrying out extensive investigation into either new cases or those lacking sufficient evidence. The CNRR was also interested in investigating persons who, though they died from bullet wounds, had not been categorized as victims of human rights abuses.

"We had to compile and bring together information, including autopsy reports, determine who had identified the cadaver, where the body had been found, and whether there was a police report or not. If we managed to locate who had retrieved the cadaver from the morgue, we interviewed him or her, informally," recalls Abel Lizama.

It was a mountain of work, and time was short.

The CACI asked for reinforcements to support its efforts, persons to come on temporarily, just for a period of months. Henríquez selected six detectives, all recent graduates of the Investigations School. He wanted men trained under democracy, who hadn't used corrupt practices or been implicated in the military dictatorship. He inquired into which units had the largest contingents of new detectives and recruited the six from these, specifically from three different units in Santiago. All six had graduated in late 1993 and were on their first assignment. Freddy Orellana, from the Peñalolén judicial district, was part of the group.

"We all came into the CACI because Henríquez had marked us out. He perceived our abilities, competencies, and commitment. I don't think we let him down. Most of us were young, and the atmosphere was very satisfying, with really good comradery. We shared a lot. We took trips by car to Arica (just south of the border with Peru), to Chiloé (in the extreme South), spent quite some time outside [the office] together, in close company, cooperating. The group was exceptionally tight, loyal, full of dedication, professionalism, ready for action," Lizama recalls of that time.

Orellana, who was born the same year as the military coup and came of age under democratic government, had been in Peñalolén only a few months when he was brought into Department V. He was assigned to assist the team of José Luis Cabión and René Sandoval and was the only one out of the six detectives brought on as reinforcements who wound up staying in Department V, because he asked to do so. Orellana spent eighteen years working on human rights cases in the PICH.

"The subject fascinated me, and I knew nothing about it. I always viewed it as a call to service. There were victims, mothers, family members who had suffered so much, and it all had to be investigated, the truth established, whatever it might be," says Orellana.

Two police drivers, Emilio Araneda and José Aguilar, were also added to the team, so with Luis Núñez there were now three drivers.

The detectives worked the streets by day and came back at night to enter data into the one available computer. The computer was new to them, and they took turns learning how to use it.

The CNRR soon had more information. Consequently, it began to reactivate investigative orders while also filing complaints over new cases, which added to Department V's already heavy workload.

The heartrending testimony of torture victims, witnesses, and the families of the executed and disappeared began to weigh on the spirits and psyches of the police officers. Listening, day after day, to dreadful accounts of torment and terror and having to lay out in detail the horrors the victims lived through and the cruelty the perpetrators practiced began to take its toll.

To differing degrees, the detectives were left shocked and distressed by what they were steadily coming to know. It was one thing to read about it in a report or in the press and another to hear it described, day after day, from the mouths of those personally affected. Empathizing with the victims was inevitable.

They couldn't see a psychologist, because that would mean telling the person what they had heard, done, and experienced. Taking days off was difficult, given the amount of work and the shortage of staff.

"I was turning this matter over in my head," comments Mery. "I saw that some of them were going around very downcast. They themselves told me so, or I noted their dejected look. Sometimes they asked to go on vacation. It wasn't [something] constant, but there were moments of crisis. The situation became acute after the multiple trips to Argentina in June 1992."

One way of mitigating those crises or slumps was via assignments to go abroad to hunt for witnesses, adds Mery. Leaving Chile, varying the routine, and getting to know another country meant a chance to breathe new air, even though the detectives went on with their investigations just like before. Frequently, however, the sole means of reinforcing their top-notch work and lifting their spirits was talking things out.

Across PICH, however, morale was on the rise. A career director was at the helm, corrupt elements in the force had been significantly weeded out, and material conditions had been improved. The PICH was in full renewal phase, with respect to both its personnel and their training as well as resources, infrastructure, and staff numbers. The PICH had scored noteworthy gains in combating narcotrafficking and disrupting political-military organizations that continued to operate even after the dictatorship. Never in its history had the PICH received such a level of material support and resources from the government.[27]

Gaining Momentum

The teams dedicated to pursuing human rights cases had gained substantial momentum. By the end of 1993, nearly 200 agents of the repression—both civilians and members of the military—had been charged with kidnapping, murder, or causing death through torture. In good measure, this achievement derived from the work of the plainclothes police, acting as an arm of the justice system.

"The government never gave me instructions on how to proceed regarding human rights matters. No government minister or anyone else in the government ever told me that I should move cautiously or slacken off because I could create a problem," affirms Mery.

Part of this stepped-up process involved the CACI team going up against their own colleagues. It was not a very comfortable situation.

For example, Abel Lizama had to go to the apartment of Gen. Ernesto Baeza, former PICH director under the dictatorship, to notify him of a judicial summons. In another instance, Inspector Plaza interviewed the retired police officer Risiere Altez, a onetime DINA torturer in several secret detention centers, who doubtless claimed that he had merely performed administrative work.

On October 6, 1993, Judge Dobra Lusic ordered Department V to summon seventeen detectives, some in retirement, others actively serving. Among those providing testimony, Luz Arce, Osvaldo Romo, and Samuel Fuenzalida had identified detectives who had participated in the DINA, and Judge Lusic wanted to throw the book at them.

"Appearance before the court will have to be complied with under threat of arrest to guarantee appearance should the summons be rejected or obstructed in some other way," the judge ordered.

The CACI asked the personnel office for a list of all PICH detectives who had been assigned to the DINA between 1974 and 1977. They were given seventeen names and addresses; several fell outside the capital. One in the group had passed away, while two others were still in active service. Prefect Daniel Cancino, who fell into the latter category, was chief of intelligence.

Detectives José Plaza, José Luis Cabión, and Abel Lizama divided up the names and went out to look for them.

The only one who posed a problem was fifty-nine-year-old Juan Urbina. Inspector Plaza and his men knocked on Urbina's door in a working-class district.

"He greeted us respectfully, but his uneasiness was evident. He was hoping that we would make some dumb move with him," recalls Plaza.

To assure the proceedings' confidentiality, Judge Lusic decided to have them all meet in the PICH headquarters building. She summoned them to appear on Saturday, October 9, 1993, at ten in the morning.

The detectives shepherded their colleagues into an ample first-floor office in the legal department, arranging them around a large conference table. Once everyone was seated, they called in Judge Lusic.

Plaza introduced the judge to the group. She got right to the point.

"The atmosphere was tense. She let them know what she was doing and that she knew about their participation in the DINA and thus expected their cooperation. If they were not forthcoming, she would go after them another way. They already knew what had happened with Romo, so they were a little frightened," relates Plaza.

Not one of them said a word. The meeting was over in less than fifteen minutes. Judge Lusic interrogated some of the men that same day—among them Eugenio Fieldhouse, one of the few who admitted to having witnessed prisoners being tortured with electric current in Villa Grimaldi. Fieldhouse provided some useful information. It went beyond the piddling statement he had made three years earlier under questioning by his colleagues from Department V. The judge ordered others in the group to return on Monday for interrogation.

In the years that followed, Department V detectives repeatedly interviewed everyone in this group. Today, many of them are serving prison sentences after being convicted of committing crimes against humanity.

The Gift

In February 1993, one year after taking the position, deputy superintendent Miguel Jara was replaced as chief of Department V by superintendent Roberto Rozas. Rozas, however, lasted scarcely seven months in the job. He faced strong resistance from the human rights community. Both lawyers and victims' relatives voiced a lack of confidence in Rozas, because his brother, Maj. Raúl Rozas, was the judge in the Sixth Military Prosecutor's Office. The judge had gained notoriety in 1990, when he shut down the "Passports Case" connected to the assassination of Orlando Letelier, and again in 1993, when he closed the investigation into the abduction of Alfonso Chanfreau.

Roberto Rozas was removed as head of Department V in September 1993. The man who stepped into the role after him was Luis Henríquez. In contrast to Sotomayor, Jara, and Rozas, Henríquez not only took charge of matters intrinsic to Internal Affairs, but he also continued as head of the team dedicated to human rights. Moreover, after the restoration of democracy, he stayed on longer as chief of Department V than any other PICH official: a total of four years and three months.

"Henríquez was utterly demanding, a perfectionist," notes Sandro Gaete, who joined Department V a couple of years later.

In 1993, the Chilean police began to teach classes to their Central American counterparts. The subject matter comprised both the professionalization of police forces and human rights. Between August 30 and September 3, a combination seminar and workshop was organized in Panama City for police from throughout the subregion. It formed part of a training program for the police and military across Latin America and the Caribbean, established by the European Commission and the Inter-American Institute for Human Rights, part of the Organization of American States.

The speakers included the lawyer Andrés Domínguez, a professor in the PICH's Higher Academy and, at this juncture, secretary-general of the CNRR; the chief of the Metropolitan Homicide Brigade, Osvaldo Carmona; the CACI's chief, Luis Henríquez; and the chief of the Second Assaults Precinct, José Bucarel. The following year this group taught three similar classes.

November 26 marked Patricio Aylwin's seventy-fifth birthday. He had but a few more months in office before finishing the four most complex years of the post-dictatorship political transition. Mery sent him a heartfelt card expressing his good wishes:

> Speaking personally, and as a career police official, it has been a high honor and deep source of pride that you confided in the undersigned [sufficiently] to have appointed him to the position of Director General after the Institution came through a difficult situation. That confidence has called for my personal commitment, [just] as it also calls for commitment by all the members of the Investigations Police. I believe, soberly and with modesty, I have done everything possible to respond to repay that confidence. Indeed, we are pushing the institutional project ahead with conviction and energy,

which will need some years to be securely in place, [and] which would not even have gotten off the ground without your aid. For this, not only is the Investigations Police, as an institution, in your debt, but all the citizenry in the near future will have clear reasons to appreciate such support.[28]

Along with the letter, Mery sent Aylwin a small present: a photo of the 1947 session of the PICH's qualifying board holding its meeting in the offices of the institution's general directorate. Appearing in the photo is the president's father, Miguel Aylwin, who at the time served as a Supreme Court judge and member of this board.

At the end of 1993 the PICH's leadership offered some of Department V's officers the opportunity to choose their next place of assignment. A portion of its staff were by now worn down physically and emotionally. José Plaza left for the far North, to Arica, and Abel Lizama went in the opposite direction, to Coyhaique, in the country's extreme South. In addition to Henríquez, that left José Luis Cabión, René Sandoval, and Freddy Orellana as the CACI's team.

So many investigative orders had been spread across the country that it was no longer possible to maintain the regular round of consultations with the CACI with respect to police reports and lines of investigation. Similarly, the weekly meetings held to analyze cases and determine how to proceed with them could no longer be sustained. It was time to move into a new phase.

In February 1994, weeks before Frei's administration picked up the reins of government, the CACI—the Commission for Institutional Analysis and Coordination—ceased to exist as a separate entity. It was absorbed into Department V of Internal Affairs.

"A commission for analysis is fine, but that stage was already surpassed," states Mery. "We are detectives, and now the methods of criminal investigation had to be employed. And the other business was to compile information, form an archive, 'take in' everything observed, overheard, learned, although it might seem useless."

As of 1994, "Department V" could technically be called the unit in charge of pursuing criminals accused of committing crimes against humanity. In reality, however, this effort belonged to a small, nameless team dedicated to human rights cases that operated within Department V. The rest of the department's officers continued to focus on traditional internal affairs matters.

The True "Ronco"

On the morning of Saturday, July 9, 1994, Nelson Mery was invited to attend the Peldehue regiment's military flag-swearing ceremony. President Aylwin, defense minister Patricio Rojas, and other high-ranking army officials were also present.

Mery, seated in the second row, saw Fernando Torres—head of the army's legal department—get up from his seat and move away from the grandstand to take a call on his cell phone. Holding his oversized mobile phone and pacing back and forth, Torres was obviously not pleased with what he heard. Mery had unscrewed and removed the antenna from his own cell phone so it wouldn't ring during the ceremony and could also fit in the inside pocket of his jacket. Moments after the ceremony ended and while he was heading for the cocktail reception, Mery reattached the antenna, turned on the phone, and immediately answered an urgent call from Department V's chief, superintendent Luis Henríquez.

Henríquez told him that, to comply with a judicial order, they had been forced to detain the former DINA agent and now retired colonel Marcelo Moren, because he defied a summons to appear in court. Several police officers had gone to his residence with two squad cars. Henríquez told Mery that everything was under control.

During the reception, army officials appeared to give the PICH's director general the cold shoulder. He spoke again with Henríquez, but Department V's chief insisted that everything was in order. Not so for the army.

That morning, detectives Plaza, Lizama, and Sandoval had arrested Moren in his apartment, causing a scandal to erupt. The three had gone armed with Judge Dobra Lusic's judicial order.

When this affair broke, Plaza and Lizama had already left Department V and were installed in other units. Nonetheless, Judge Lusic had promised that if and when she issued detention orders against DINA officials, she would ask these two to carry out orders on the officials whose cases they had investigated.

"She kept her promise and sent for Plaza and me and we came in on assignment. Moren was the only member of the military detained by the police. Krassnoff was actively serving, so the army brought him before the judge. It was the icing on the cake. We had investigated Moren and now it fell to us to arrest him," says Lizama.

The PICH's agreement with the army stipulated that if an officer were to be issued a summons or detained, the handover or action was to be coordinated with the army's legal department. When retired officers were faced with a summons, not only was the legal department to be notified but the officer in question was to be accompanied to the court by one of its lawyers. Quite often this task was fulfilled by Jorge Balmaceda, the army counsel who had convinced Fanta to give himself up in Paraguay.

Judge Lusic had wanted to summon Moren several days earlier, but the legal department objected—the date she originally proposed was a weekday; the court would have been open to the media and public, and Moren could be met with protests.

The legal department argued that it posed a risk for his safety and was anxious to avoid any publicity. So the judge consented to let them bring in Moren on Saturday. The legal department, however, failed to follow through; the retired colonel did not appear at the agreed-upon time. As a result, Judge Lusic ordered his immediate detention.

Armed with the arrest order, Plaza, Lizama, and Sandoval arrived at an apartment building in the upscale Las Condes district. This was the same building in which Ángela Jeria, one of Moren's victims, lived. Jeria was the mother of Michelle Bachelet, future president of Chile. Both women had been detained in Villa Grimaldi in 1975, where Moren tortured prisoners. Moren was known as "Ronco," for his loud, hoarse voice.

Two other police vehicles, ready to assist, were stationed more than 100 meters from the apartment building. It was a discreet operation; the detectives did not want to provoke a confrontation. They spoke with the doorman, telling him that they had an urgent summons to deliver in person to Moren.

He opened the door, and the detectives introduced themselves.

"He was pretty scared. It was better to give the impression that it was a simple procedure. We told him that we had instructions from Judge Dobra Lusic, that she wanted to speak with him without delay, and that we had an order [from her] to bring him to her office. We didn't tell him that it involved an arrest order so as not to alarm him," relates Plaza.

"OK, I'll go," Moreno said. He had gone to the courts on many previous occasions to make statements.

"No, we've come to take you, because the judge wants to speak with you now. Our vehicle is outside."

"Why wasn't this done through the lawyer?" Moren asked.

"Look, the judge ordered us and we're here."

"I'm not leaving here without speaking with my lawyer," he answered defiantly.

The former DINA agent called one of the army legal department's lawyers and handed the phone to Plaza. The lawyer demanded that he read, word for word, the judicial order they had brought with them. Plaza did just that.

"That's not a summons; it's an arrest order!" the lawyer blurted out.

"Yes. I need to bring him before the court," explained Plaza.

Moreno was furious.

"So you are going to take me away under arrest?" he asked Plaza.

"Yes, but there are two ways to do it. One is that you go by invitation, and the other is that you go under arrest. I prefer that you go by invitation."

"All right, I'm going to get ready."

"Plaza was very calm, very deliberative; I learned a lot from him," notes Lizama. "In that moment my only thought was that I had to comply with a judicial order. Moren had committed terrible crimes and had to be put under arrest. But I didn't stop to think about what it meant. It sunk in years later."

Moren headed to his bedroom, saying that he would change clothes, because he was still in his pajamas. He entered the bedroom alone. The detectives weren't sure how he might react. Would he come out with a weapon?

"That triggered our anxiety," recalls Plaza. "It's a matter of making a decision when one wants to calm things down, lower the temperature, ease up. The actions you take are going to be interpreted, so if a person sees others decompressing, he's also inclined to decompress. But it's a risk that you take. It was just a moment's flash, but for us it was an eternity."

They came back down to the street around midday with Moreno unhandcuffed to avoid annoying him further, but it angered him anyway when he saw there were two other police vehicles. They took him to headquarters in a line of police cars, telling him there were some administrative procedures to clear before bringing him into court. They entered through the rear part of the PICH's building. Once the "administrative procedures" were finished, all that remained was to book him, like any other person under arrest. The detectives brought him to the section in the building where employees verify the identity of detainees, take their mug shot, and fingerprint them.

Moren flew into a rage.

"That's when the real Moren appeared, the 'Ronco,'" says Lizama. "'No!' he shouted in a booming voice that was heard far and wide. It was just as the [political] prisoners described it in their accounts—they who had heard his loud, hoarse voice. He pounded the table. It was really startling."

Moren refused to let them take his fingerprints or complete the booking process, and they left it like that, to avoid causing any more conflict. They could just as easily get his fingerprints from the civil registry, and the mug shot—they figured—could be taken later. The important thing was to get him to calm down, curtail his agitation. It worked. He was subdued when he arrived in court.

The arrest of one of the DINA's top brass had leaked to the press, and when he was brought before Judge Lusic, reporters and photographers were waiting for him in the hallways outside the courtroom. Moren was incensed.

A short while later, Abel Lizama returned to his unit in Coyhaique and José Plaza to his in Arica. The story, however, did not end there.

The DINE complained to Director General Mery, charging that more than twelve heavily armed police and six vehicles took part in Moren's arrest and that when he arrived at the court, they had "laid siege to it and occupied it." The army called attention to the "the familiarity with which the detectives relate to the witnesses for the defense ('all of them ex-MIR terrorists')."

This infuriated Pinochet, who complained to the minister of defense and the Supreme Court, making known to them his displeasure at the actions of Judge Lusic, "for her lack of sound judgment and humanity to [so] treat an officer convalescing from a serious illness."[29]

It was all an exaggeration, except for the illness. The year before, in early October, Moren had been admitted to the military hospital after suffering a cerebral thrombosis. He was hospitalized for at least a month and a half, while several criminal courts were requiring him to answer for different crimes.

Director Mery had to account for the affair to Defense Minister Rojas.

"I described to the minister everything that happened. I told him that the army's claim of the amount of force and [number] of vehicles in that place was impossible because the institution was [languishing] in a Franciscan state of poverty," recalls Mery.

As all parties understood, an agreement already existed in which the army complied with judicial orders—which were passed on to the plainclothes police—that involved the military. Nonetheless, new discussions ensued about coordinating this kind of situation. The police by now had several years under their belt functioning like this, with the mediation of the army's legal department. The judicial orders would be complied with, but how was up for discussion. It was decided to name a coordinator. Accordingly, a few days later a midranking member of the military showed up at Mery's office, to serve as the intermediary, but the PICH's director did not accept him.

Mery decided to call the director of the DINE, Eugenio Covarrubias. By chance, they knew each other personally. Without realizing it, both were having houses built at the same time on the same street, right across from each other, in the Las Condes district. In fact, the army had complained that the PICH—and even Mery himself—was spying on the DINE's director after the security teams for both men came across each other in the street. The truth was that both Mery and Covarrubias had gone to see how the work was progressing. Eventually, the two neighbors-to-be met.

Covarrubias proposed that they have lunch together; he extended the invitation to smooth over the bad feelings. They arranged to meet at Parrilladas Argentinas, a steak house located on the highway.

Mery arrived with several men, who spread out around the restaurant's exterior, while Covarrubias's guards tried to camouflage themselves among the diners. The two shared a laugh over the slack discretion of both security details.

Mery complained that a major (in the army) had been sent to coordinate directly with him—a man not of his rank. He proposed to Covarrubias that two men enjoying their confidence, operatives of similar rank, be named to work out the coordination.

"With regard to Moren, you are the person responsible for that impasse," Mery told him. "You are the chief of intelligence. You would have had to foresee what was going to happen if he didn't show up in court."

"But they made it into a scandal."

"There was no scandal."

The coordinator never panned out. The scheme already in use under Fernando Torres and Enrique Ibarra in the army's legal department was maintained. The PICH's relations with the DINE were never good.

To the Extent Possible

When Eduardo Frei assumed the presidency in March 1994, twenty-three former agents of the dictatorship's security forces were awaiting sentencing; out of this total, eighteen were already in custody, charged with the assassination of Nattino, Guerrero, and Parada. Another five—including DINA chiefs Manuel Contreras and Pedro Espinoza, convicted in the assassination of Letelier—were still free, appealing their sentences. These were virtually the only cases in which justice was effectively rendered during the decade of the nineties, but that was still not at all clear.

"The fact that some of them could go to prison was far from a sure thing," noted a report by the international human rights organization Human Rights Watch in May 1994.[30]

Various additional cases were cleared up and the responsible parties identified. Nonetheless, there were also significant setbacks. One of the crimes of greatest public notoriety, the DINA-engineered September 1974 assassination in Argentina of the former commander in chief of the army Gen. Carlos Prats and his wife Sofía Cuthbert, had never been investigated in Chile, even though the people who planned and carried it out were—excepting Michael Townley—Chileans and lived in Chile. In Argentina, the judicial inquiry into the crime inched ahead slowly.

Despite the tireless efforts of the victims' daughters, the Supreme Court declined to appoint a judge to open the case in Chile. As a result of the information brought out in the investigation of the Letelier case, they requested that the Chamber of Deputies' Human Rights Commission investigate the role played by Chilean state agents in the assassination of their parents in Buenos Aires. Given the accumulation of evidence, the lower house voted in favor of the Supreme Court appointing a judge to investigate the double homicide, but the highest court in the land rejected the vote, arguing that the crime fell outside its jurisdiction.

A case involving another high-profile crime—the 1976 assassination of the Spanish Chilean international employee Carmelo Soria—was reopened in March 1991 and investigated by the plainclothes police. Before a year was out, the police determined that Soria had been assassinated by the DINA in Michael Townley's house, and they singled out several persons who had planned the crime. In May 1992, the court of appeals responded positively to the government's request and appointed Judge Violeta Guzmán to investigate it. Based on Judge Adolfo Baña-dos's investigation into the Letelier case, the confession of one of the authors of the crime, and her own probings, Judge Guzmán identified six members of the military as responsible for Soria's assassination. Two of them were active-duty army officers: Brig. Gen. Jaime Lepe, the army's secretary-general, and Col. Pablo Belmar.[31] Little time passed before the military justice system claimed jurisdiction over the case. Judge Guzmán resisted transferring it, but the Supreme Court took it out of her hands in November 1993.

In the face of this outrageous decision, on which even the secretary-general of the United Nations weighed in, the Spanish government demanded that its Chilean counterpart ask the Supreme Court to appoint one of its judges, as it had done in the Letelier case, because the situation affected relations between the two countries. The Supreme Court reluctantly complied, but the case did not advance. Less than a month later, in December 1993, Judge Marcos Libedinsky applied amnesty and closed the investigation.

The Soria family filed an appeal, and in April 1994 the Supreme Court ordered the case reopened and appointed Judge Eleodoro Ortiz to handle it. The judge indicted two of the persons involved but subsequently closed the case in June 1996 by also applying amnesty.[32]

Another significant judicial reversal in 1993 pertained to investigations that bore upon the relationship between the DINA and Colonia Dignidad. The young judge Lientur Escobar took on an investigation into the disappearance of twenty-one people in Parral. It was the same case as the one José Luis Cabión looked into in 1991 that led to him joining the CACI.

In February 1993, Judge Escobar indicted five people, charging them with kidnapping and belonging to a criminal enterprise. They were the Carabineros and army officials Cabión had interviewed two years earlier, plus the now retired army colonel and then DINA chief in Parral, Fernando Gómez.[33] The judge had them detained and held incommunicado while he brought them face-to-face with relatives of the victims. All of the victims, who lived in the vicinity of Colonia Dignidad, were detained between 1973 and 1974 and taken to the colony, where—presumably—they were executed and "disappeared."

Escobar had also taken on an investigation into the disappearance of Álvaro Vallejos, who was killed in Colonia Dignidad. Fernando Gómez and Osvaldo Romo were already under indictment for this crime.

The judge had not had an easy time of it. His investigations into these crimes no longer concerned only local members of the military and the Carabineros. Now they began to cross a line leading straight into the German enclave. Escobar received constant death threats on his telephone. On one occasion, his opponents left a briefcase with a fake bomb in it outside the court. Other times they slashed the tires on his car or splashed paint on its sides. He was under permanent police protection, but that didn't lessen the harassment.

Less than two weeks after the indictments, the court of appeals in Santiago transferred the case to a military tribunal, which in turn decided to lift the charges against Fernando Gómez and the Carabineros official Pablo Caulier.[34]

The reprisals against the judge, who had dared to go as far as he did, were not long in coming. In March 1993, without offering any explanation, the Supreme Court downgraded Escobar to list 4. This place on the list signified his immediate removal from the bench. It was an exemplary punishment.

The Álvaro Vallejos case also wound up in the military justice system and was closed under amnesty.[35]

According to the human rights organization Christian Churches Foundation for Social Assistance, the year 1993 ended with fourteen cases shut down by the military justice system. In seven of these, the Supreme Court had applied the Amnesty Law.[36]

The fresh currents of air that flowed in early 1993 had once again been polluted.

"Many cases were closed in that period, such as Alfonso Chanfreau's, Lumi Videla's, my sister's [Bárbara Uribe], and so on down the line," states Viviana Uribe. "I realized, then, that justice in Chile had not changed one iota."

The operation of justice was erratic, as Human Rights Watch effectively spelled it out: "Deep disagreements are found in the courts concerning the way in which the [amnesty] law should be interpreted. Numerous cases have been closed and reopened, and then closed again. The courts have reversed sentences that they themselves handed down years before. Cases have been left open whose circumstances appear identical to those in cases that have been closed. Constant conflicts over jurisdiction have arisen between the civil and military courts. To this point, the confidential efforts to determine accountabilities have consumed a huge quantity of judicial resources, to say nothing of the frustration and wear they caused victims' relatives."[37]

President Eduardo Frei made no attempt to reverse this backward move in the quest for justice. The issue got in his way. He wanted the judicial proceedings to end quickly, within a few months, so the political transition could be concluded and his energies directed toward the economy, trade agreements, and state reforms.

Nonetheless, he was unable to avoid his first impasse with the military, in April 1994, just weeks after taking up the office, when Judge Milton Juica ruled in the Slit-Throats Case. The judge advised that the military justice system should indict the director general of the Carabineros, Rodolfo Stange, for obstruction of justice. There was nothing Frei could do other than ask Stange to search his conscience regarding the situation, as the president was powerless (bound by constitutional constraints) to force his resignation. Stange refused to resign and received the backing of the Carabineros' high command. He resigned a year and a half later, when he felt like doing so.

Looking for a way to improve relations with the armed forces, Frei put his friend and close adviser, fellow Christian Democrat Edmundo Pérez, in charge of the Ministry of Defense. Some ten days after assuming his new position, Pérez— known for being tight with the military—was invited by Pinochet to attend a meeting in the armed forces building on Zenteno Street, in front of the presidential palace. His predecessor, Patricio Rojas, had never received such an invitation.

Pérez quickly allayed the military's concerns: "No one has moral superiority for judging the governments of the last 30 years," he declared in May 1994— a year after the *boinazo*.[38]

9

A PRISON FOR TWO

THE TIME HAD COME. Inspector Nelson Jofré stepped into the first chapel he came across and began to pray. He had just left a meeting at Investigations Police (PICH) headquarters, where the topic of discussion was the secret order for the operation to arrest, again, retired general Manuel Contreras.

The scene in June 1995 was very different from that in 1991, when Jofré had been picked to travel with Contreras from Fresia to Santiago so the former Directorate of National Intelligence (DINA) chief could be indicted for the assassination of Orlando Letelier. This time General Contreras was staring at the prospect of jail.

On November 12, 1993, Judge Adolfo Bañados had sentenced the ex–DINA chief to seven years of confinement and his second-in-command, Brig. Gen. Pedro Espinoza, to six years for their role in concocting and instigating the murder of Letelier. In 1995, Chile's Supreme Court upheld the sentences.

The sentences were very light in comparison to the magnitude of the crime but meant punishment nonetheless—the first given to the two top officials of the DINA, the military dictatorship's principal arm of repression.

As always, Contreras claimed he was innocent while continuing to insist that Letelier's assassination was the work of the CIA.

"I won't go to any jail," Contreras declared when he learned of the judge's ruling.

Bañados's decision exceeded 400 pages and summarized more than two years of judicial investigation in Chile as well as the FBI's findings from the 1970s on.

Protecting Himself from the Fugitive

The first thing Bañados did after taking on the Letelier case was to ask U.S. authorities to send copies of testimony and other evidence gathered and submitted through the trail of investigations that started in the United States beginning in 1976. In September 1991, the assistant U.S. attorney for the District of Columbia,

Eric B. Marcy, complied with Judge Bañados's request. He sent the judge seventeen documents that implicated not just Manuel Contreras and Pedro Espinoza in the double homicide but also other high-level Chilean military officials for their participation in the cover-up that followed it.

As of 1989, Marcy was the lead prosecutor pursuing the case against two Cubans who took part in the crime: José Dionisio Suárez and Virgilio Paz. The two had been on the run since their indictments in 1978. Suárez was arrested in 1990 and Paz the following year. Both were living in Florida when apprehended. Each was found guilty and sentenced to twelve years in prison. In addition, Marcy had the job of continuing the investigation into the deaths of Letelier and Ronnie Moffitt and bringing to justice two Chilean fugitives from the law: Contreras and Espinoza.

The evidence that Marcy sent to Judge Bañados included four statements that the U.S. citizen and ex–DINA agent Michael Townley had put in writing in March 1978, before he was expelled from Chile. Townley was a native of Waterloo, Iowa. When he was fourteen, he and his family moved to Chile when his father, a Ford Motor Company executive, was made general manager of the company's new assembly plant in Santiago. Townley developed a strong interest in electronics and "things mechanical." At age eighteen, he married an older woman, the writer Mariana Callejas.

During the period of Allende's government, Townley linked up with the Frente Nacionalista Patria y Libertad (Fatherland and Liberty Nationalist Front), an ultraright paramilitary organization, and offered his services to the CIA. The agency turned him down. Years later, his wife declared in a legal statement that Townley had in fact applied to join the CIA in 1970 but was rejected because of his lack of academic preparation.[1]

Shortly after the military coup, however, the nascent DINA needed someone with his skills and his loyalty. Townley was a key member of both the agency's Mulchén Brigade and its International Department. He participated in missions to scout out, monitor, and eliminate opposition figures outside of Chile. In 1978, despite his unswerving dutifulness to the DINA, Contreras, and Pinochet, the military regime expelled him from Chile, handing him over to the U.S. Department of Justice. The betrayal by his superiors, his DINA comrades, and the country he had served inflicted a wound on Townley that would never heal.

Five years later, after serving half of the ten-year sentence imposed on him by a federal court for helping mastermind and carry out the assassination of Letelier and Moffitt in Washington, D.C., Townley resumed life under a new identity in an undisclosed location. Not long after the reopening of the Letelier case in Chile in 1991, he provided a sworn statement before a federal attorney in the capital as evidence to be introduced in the Chilean courts.

Townley had nothing to lose. He felt resentment toward Contreras and Pinochet for abandoning him to his fate and by now had revealed everything he knew. There was no price to pay for cooperating. He was shielded from any investigation or criminal sanction in cases distinct from the Letelier murder, for which he had now served his time, and he was immune from extradition to answer, anywhere, for other crimes. In fact, when Townley was freed from prison in 1983, Argentina sought his extradition to face justice in that country for the assassination of Carlos Prats and his wife. A U.S. federal judge, however, denied the request. Townley felt safe.

He had composed the four statements, the attorney Marcy pointed out in a sworn statement of his own, "with a view toward protecting himself from the fugitives Manuel Contreras and Pedro Espinoza and to thwart his possible expulsion from Chile."[2]

One of Townley's statements was a nine-page text titled "History of [My] Activities in DINA." It constituted a chronological account of his participation in the agency and his operations outside of Chile and related how he was ordered to set up a chemical laboratory in a house located in the upscale Santiago neighborhood of Lo Curro, with the intention of producing sarin gas.[3] This was the DINA's so-called Project Andrea. The second statement, titled "Confession and Accusation," begins with a warning: "If there was sufficient cause to open this envelope, I accuse the government of Chile of my death. Specifically, as the brains behind it, General Manuel Contreras."[4] The third statement, numbering five pages, is an account of events in the killing of Letelier, and the fourth, titled "Statement of Assumed Identities," enumerates the fictitious names that he employed while serving the DINA.

Townley himself, along with his wife—also a DINA collaborator—gave the documents to Marcy in mid-1990, when the federal attorney was preparing to go to trial against Dionisio Suárez. Eight years earlier, the couple had furnished the federal district attorney's office with other incriminating material: a letter from Townley to Contreras pointing out the mistakes made in the assassination of Letelier and its cover-up, an account book from 1975 to 1976 that detailed the couple's income and expenses from their services to the DINA, and receipts for the construction of the Lo Curro chemical laboratory.

The suite of documents that Marcy sent to Chile also included letters written by Maj. Armando Fernández and the agreement he reached with U.S. authorities when he gave himself up to the FBI in January 1987. Another text contained a lengthy statement by a U.S. State Department employee regarding a ten-hour meeting he had with Fernández in Chile in January 1987.

Judge Bañados requested—and obtained—Súarez's and Paz's statements from the investigations done in the United States, although Suárez, who was imprisoned, refused to offer a new statement as formally requested via a rogatory letter from the judge. As a result, six months were tacked onto his sentence.

Bañados, however, did manage—through a formal request—to obtain statements from several high-level U.S. government employees, although for the most part they didn't contribute much. The respondents included then president George H. W. Bush, who was CIA director in 1976 when the car-bomb assassination occurred;[5] CIA deputy director and army general Vernon Walters, with whom Manuel Contreras had met; and George Landau, U.S. ambassador to Paraguay between 1972 and 1977.[6]

President Aylwin had paved the way for this cooperation by U.S. officials after President Bush's 1990 visit to Chile, and he reinforced the overture during his own trip to the United States in May 1992. He made a point of discussing the Letelier case on both occasions.

A Room in the Marriott Hotel

In Chile, Judge Bañados, as well as Homicide Brigade officers Rafael Castillo and Nelson Jofré, interrogated dozens of witnesses, government authorities who had served during the dictatorship, and DINA agents and chiefs. Among the agents they interviewed was a woman who "let the cat out of the bag" and provided valuable information: Townley's onetime secretary and right hand, Alejandra Damiani.

From the U.S. perspective, the case surrounding Letelier's assassination in Washington, D.C., was wrapped up in less than two years. Townley and Armando Fernández had provided testimony in mid-1992 in response to a formal request by Judge Bañados. Their statements were the key pieces needed to drive home sentences against Contreras and Espinoza in the Letelier case. In addition, Townley's testimony was particularly useful in facilitating the investigation into various other high-profile crimes authored by the DINA outside the borders of Chile. These included the murder of Carlos Prats and Sofía Cuthbert in 1974 in Argentina, the assassination of the Spanish Chilean citizen (and United Nations employee) Carmelo Soria in 1976, and the 1975 attempt on the life of the Christian Democratic leader Bernardo Leighton and his wife, Anita Fresno, in Rome.

Still, Townley needed to be interviewed in person. On Bañados's instruction, three PICH officials traveled to the United States at the end of August 1992: Castillo and Jofré from the Homicide Brigade and deputy superintendent Eduardo Riquelme, assistant chief of Interpol Chile.

They made a stop in Miami, having planned to interview Fernández, who had gone on to build a successful business career in South Florida. His brother served as intermediary. The detectives had set everything up from Santiago. They planned to speak with Fernández in Miami and take a flight afterward to Washington, D.C., to meet with Townley.

Fernández, however, changed his mind and backed out.

"Fernández consented to our interviewing him, but I think he got scared. He never spoke with us; it was always through his brother," relates Jofré.

Castillo, Jofré, and Riquelme were still trying to make a success of it, stomaching the hot, steamy Miami air and trying to convince Fernández to speak with them, when Jofré's wife in Santiago received a disturbing phone call.

The telephone rang at five in the morning. Jofré's wife was still asleep, as were their young children. All she knew was that her husband was outside of Chile, on assignment to interview someone.

"Michael Townley here. I want to speak with your husband," intoned the voice at the other end of the line.

"He's not here, he's on a trip," the woman replied, half-asleep.

The man hung up on her.

Waking up in the morning, she remembered the call and was worried. Jofré's wife called her brother-in-law, who was also a detective, and told him about it. He got in touch with colleagues in Interpol. They in turn sent a message to Jofré in Miami: you need to call home at once.

"I asked Townley about this afterward. I think he did it to verify whether the one who had made the trip was really me. I don't know how he got my home telephone number, but I know that Townley still has contacts in Chile; he knows everything that goes on. He always took care that we didn't have anyone tailing us. He thought they wanted to do away with him because he came down strongly on Manuel Contreras and the DINA's top people. He disclosed almost everything," affirms Jofré.

They departed Miami frustrated but were much luckier in Washington, the site—sixteen years earlier—of Orlando Letelier's assassination. They were met at the airport by FBI agents, who took them to a hotel. On the morning of September 2, agents came by to pick them up and, without revealing where they were headed, drove them to Annapolis, on the shore of Chesapeake Bay, in Maryland. Under strict security measures, the PICH detectives interviewed Townley in a

Marriott Hotel room. Also present and participating were Eric Marcy; Jeff Johnson, Townley's lawyer; and Bruce Tienay, an FBI agent and Marcy's translator.

The sessions in the Marriott extended over two days. With the exchanges taking place in Spanish, they covered the assassinations of Orlando Letelier, Carmelo Soria, and Carlos Prats and the attempt on Bernardo Leighton's life. The Prats assassination had been investigated in Buenos Aires and legal proceedings dealing with the attempt on Leighton had begun in Rome, Italy, in 1992.[7]

Townley tied three Chilean military officials, Pedro Espinoza, Raúl Iturriaga, and Armando Fernández, to the murders of Prats and Cuthbert and supplied previously unknown information about aspects of the DINA. In addition, he addressed the subject of biochemist Francisco Oyarzún, who worked for the DINA and, at the time of the interview, was on the faculty of the University of California.

"Townley wanted to collaborate. He never put up any obstacles. He was eager to get at Manuel Contreras," says Jofré.

It was entirely what they needed. Townley spoke openly, even to the press.

Inspector Jofré met with the former DINA agent on half a dozen occasions in the years that followed. Some of these meetings coincided with the detective's visits to the United States on other PICH business or for different reasons, but he took the opportunity to call Townley. He always had more questions to ask him about the DINA and its operations outside Chile.

The two had devised a system. Townley employed a U.S. telephone number that functioned like a local call and wasn't traceable. Jofré called him at this number and told him where he would be staying. Townley contacted Jofré there and informed him of their meeting place. The detective then changed hotels, and the former DINA agent spent a full day running a series of checks. He took extreme precautions to make sure they weren't being followed or watched.

Townley picked him up, invariably in his own car, and they spent the full day together, eating breakfast and lunch, driving around the city, and conversing. At the end of the day Townley dropped Jofré off at his hotel. Jofré says:

> He felt confident speaking with me because I never betrayed him; I never went before the press in Chile to relate what we talked about. He didn't lie to me, but when he felt pressed by some subject I posed to him, he told me, 'I'm passing [on that one], let's move on and talk about other things.' So, I managed to learn everything about his private life in the United States, all the details, and I know it's just me and his family who are in on that. When his father passed away, he called that same day to tell me; that was the level of trust he had in me.

The Shadow of the DINE

From the outset of their work with Judge Bañados, Inspector Jofré left his house early every morning and stopped by to pick up Deputy Superintendent Castillo. They began the day's work together, whether in the police facility or the Supreme Court. They got together with Bañados in his office to analyze the course of the investigation and receive his guidance and instructions.

"What we didn't know then was that we would receive an order and, the next day, Gen. Fernando Torres and Colonel Ibarra, from the army's legal department, showed up to speak with the judge. They already knew who was being summoned. The situation began to repeat itself. We were the first line, but they immediately found out," says Jofré.

Later it was discovered that Óscar Delgado, the court clerk who typed the investigative orders, was leaking the information that Judge Bañados composed by hand. He was apparently leaned on to do so by the legal department through his brother, an army employee. When Delgado was relieved of this task, Torres's frequent visits to the court came to an end.

Retired military officers resisted accepting a summons funneled through the plainclothes police, and those still on active duty refused for the most part to speak with them. Everything had to be coordinated through the army's legal department. And following that sprang the tug of war over where they would undergo interrogation.

The information the detectives obtained during the interviews with Townley, supplemented by other testimony and findings, opened the floodgates to assigning responsibility beyond the Letelier case, for the assassinations of Prats and Soria and the attempt on Leighton. This development was very troubling to those in Pinochet's inner circle. The statements taken from witnesses and former agents of the security services by Castillo and Jofré zeroed in on numerous high-level army officials, many still on active duty.

After a year had elapsed, the two Homicide Brigade detectives were handling a much bigger workload. Despite the judicial ups and downs and other obstacles that hampered progress in criminal investigations against those who planned and committed the crimes, Rafael Castillo and Nelson Jofré continued with their investigations, both within and outside Chile.

As a result, they were favorite targets, though not the only ones, of harassment by the Army Intelligence Directorate (DINE), which lost no time in devising ways to intimidate them.

Its agents poisoned Castillo's two Alsatian police dogs on his own premises and lobbed flaming objects into his garden. They sent Jofré's wife a newspaper, at her place of work, with a threatening note inside for him. They tapped their home phones and, in Jofré's case, followed him into the building where he lived. Jofré realized, when he left home at 7:40 on the morning of March 27, 1992, that a Suzuki with three men inside was following him. He noted its license plate number, which—it turned out—corresponded to one of the DINE's vehicles. Jofré and his family had moved into their condominium only six months before, and his address was not registered anywhere. Only a few members of the Homicide Brigade knew where he lived.

That same day, the chief of the Metropolitan Homicide Brigade, deputy prefect Osvaldo Carmona, informed director Nelson Mery of this incident. In turn, Mery informed interior minister Enrique Krauss and defense minister Patricio Rojas.

The army also harassed them through legal channels. The opportunity arose on August 17, 1993, when Castillo and Jofré traveled to Argentina to testify before Judge María Servini. They did so as witnesses in the Prats case thanks to the mass of information they had gathered. The noncommissioned army officer and ex–DINA agent Carlos Labarca also happened to be on their flight. At this stage, Labarca was one of the police's key collaborators. Judge Servini had summoned him to make a statement as well. A third party had boarded the same LAN Chile flight: watching them from the shadows was the DINE official Maj. Arturo Silva, the man in charge of the operation that spirited agents out of the country to evade justice.[8]

Days later, a DINE official called Labarca's spouse and berated her over the information her husband was supplying the detectives about the DINA and the assassination of Prats. In addition, he threatened reprisals against "those" police officials: Castillo and Jofré.[9]

The military prosecutor Raúl Rozas revived an old detention order directed against Labarca for a supposed financial crime that had occurred eight years earlier. He ordered Labarca's detention and charged the two detectives with allegedly aiding Labarca in eluding justice when they accompanied him to provide testimony in Argentina. The former DINA agent was arrested, his house raided, and he was subjected to interrogation by the DINE regarding what he told the detectives and how he managed to leave the country and travel to Argentina.

In January 1994, Rozas indicted Castillo and Jofré. The two police officers were periodically required to sign a ledger in the military prosecutor's office until the Supreme Court annulled the sentence six months later. The threats went on for years in relation to different cases. They targeted the police, former agents who collaborated with the justice system, or simply people who furnished information. Director Mery issued instructions on how to avoid possible attacks and urged his employees to take preventive measures for their own security, with the aid of institutional resources. Mery himself made it known that one of the telephone lines in his house was tapped and that for years he was followed and put up with threats, both at home and at the office. The threats included warnings that members of his family would be harmed.

"Over time these episodes intensified when notable progress was made in different criminal investigations," Mery notes.[10]

How to Detain a General

The Supreme Court's decision in the Letelier case, which could lead to prison terms for the DINA's two former top officials, riveted the public. The court therefore took the unprecedented step of allowing the oral arguments delivered on January 25, 1995, to be televised. Approximately 100 people jammed into the overheated court chamber, and hundreds more stood by expectantly outside while the plaintiffs' lawyers, Fabiola Letelier and Juan Bustos, among others, presented their arguments. It was nothing like what was normally seen on television.

The countdown had begun. If the high court rejected the sentences, it would disrupt the political transition, strain relations with the United States, and end by burying the credibility of the judiciary, which was already at rock bottom.

Preparations had to be made. The plainclothes police turned to working out a plan for when the time came.

"Today nothing happens if a member of the military is sentenced and jailed, but in those days it wasn't like that," states former director Mery. "At that stage in the democratic transition it was natural to take a certain amount of care to find out what was going on with the army, Contreras's real political power, how the army might react. We were on alert."

Around a month before the Supreme Court made its decision, Mery met with Judge Bañados in the latter's house. It was early in the morning, and the meeting bore all the signs of being secret. Nonetheless, by the time it was over reporters were congregating outside.

The two conversed at length. Mery laid out the possible scenarios to Bañados once the arrest order was issued. One outcome could be an armed confrontation with Contreras's guards. Versions of one narrative already circulating had the PICH moving hundreds of officers to the country's South, where Contreras was dug in. The police denied it. Mery told Bañados that the layout of the house and the area around it had to be researched along with other particulars, as did the question of whether the arrest should be carried out on a weekday or during the weekend.

"I bounced all of this off the judge," says Mery. "He told me, 'Director, you will be the first to know when the arrest order is issued. And you take it from there.' He issued the order, and we considered how to execute it."

Mery instructed his top staff to devise an operational plan for the arrest of Manuel Contreras. When it was worked out, they brought it to his office. The director was horrified. On the one hand, he pointed out, the document referred to the man sentenced for murder in adulatory terms. And on the other, it proposed a major deployment of forces to lay virtual siege to the ex–DINA chief in his rural estate. The contingent would be split into several security rings, while a group of three or four officers served the arrest order. Their plan assured a confrontation.

Mery showed it to an adviser for the general directorate, a retired army colonel with the surname Gálvez, whose cooperation he had requested in the preparation of the plan. The colonel had been Mery's professor in the Higher Academy and had been in the PICH since the time of the dictatorship. In his advisory capacity, he prepared analyses of the evolving situation in the country for the general directorate, many of them in manuscript form. According to Mery, Gálvez went into retirement because of the military coup and his doubts concerning Pinochet.

When Mery showed him the operational plan to arrest Contreras, Gálvez's reaction was unequivocal: "This is madness! Who came up with this?"

"The top staff. Didn't I ask you to collaborate on this?" Mery asked him.

"My cooperation is here, with you, between the two of us. It can't be done like this. This can provoke an unnecessarily bloody situation. It's better to go with a small group."

The plan was replaced with one considerably more low-key. A much scaled-back contingent would go, which included Inspector Jofré. His former partner and chief on the investigative team, Rafael Castillo, was not part of it, because he was currently on assignment in Peru.

When Mery and DINE chief Eugenio Covarrubias saw each other at meetings of the security council in La Moneda, the PICH director took the opportunity to speak with Covarrubias about the Supreme Court's imminent ruling (on the Letelier case). He also spoke with him more than once by simply crossing the street and talking to him in the general's house. Covarrubias played down the whole situation. Everything would be fine, he assured Mery, because Contreras could no longer count on the army's backing.

The order to carry out the operation, however, was never set in motion.

A Historic Decision

On May 30, 1995, the chief clerk of the Supreme Court, Carlos Meneses, took a seat in a hall full of Chilean and foreign reporters and proceeded to read the decision reached by the Fourth Chamber. It was past six in the evening, and the Supreme Court was crammed with people. Outside, hundreds more waited beyond barriers that the Carabineros had set up the day before around the entire building. They held up posters with messages such as "Contreras and Espinoza to jail" or "Mamo [i.e., Contreras]: seven years of prison and [spend] the rest in hell."[11] A police helicopter flew over the capital's downtown area.

In a unanimous decision, the five high court judges upheld the sentences. Meneses had hardly gotten the words out when a wave of jubilation was heard rippling through the wide hallways of the building. Outside on the street—amid applause, shouts, embraces, and tears—people began singing the national anthem. The streets overflowed, and the thousands of people who had packed the area around the courts began spontaneously marching down the city's main avenue, Alameda, toward the east. Confrontations broke out with the Carabineros, and that night barricades went up in several working-class neighborhoods. A dozen people were injured and forty-four arrested. News of the decision and its aftermath traveled around the globe.

Orlando Letelier's son, Juan Pablo Letelier, who was then serving in the Chamber of Deputies, praised the Supreme Court for having simply fulfilled its duty and purpose. He felt, he said, a "profound and sincere gratitude in the decision by the Supreme Court, which has had the courage to administer justice."[12]

That cold and gray autumn day was historic, but the follow-through, how to manage getting the former DINA director to jail, was still an unknown.

Entrenched on his estate in Fresia, Contreras, recently turned sixty-five, stated that he would not abide by the court's decision. The Channel 13 reporter Pablo Honorato conducted a live interview with him from Santiago that same night.

True to form, he railed against the parties in government: "I want to highlight the irregularities and abnormalities of these political proceedings and denounce how the same Communists, socialists, and all that Marxist crowd that betrayed the fatherland continue cogoverning in this country and act brazenly, at bottom looking to destroy the armed forces and public security," Contreras exclaimed in front of the camera.

"I'm not going to go to any jail while there isn't real justice," he asserted.[13]

The following day, Contreras held a lengthy press conference from his estate,

El Viejo Roble. He avowed that the guards who accompanied him were active-duty military and that the court's decision had left the army "wounded."[14]

On the other hand, in a public letter, Brig. Gen. Pedro Espinoza said that he accepted the ruling but not the charges or the "humiliation and cowardice" of subjecting himself to "mortifying and degrading conditions."[15] Espinoza's days were numbered. Once he was sentenced, he would have to be let go from the army, with no hope of staving off the dismissal.

That same day in the capital, President Eduardo Frei analyzed the situation, in all its complexity, with his cabinet. They discussed the steps to follow to ensure that the court's sentence was fulfilled. The army, meanwhile, convened a special meeting of thirty generals in the Military Club, situated in the Lo Curro neighborhood. Defense minister Edmundo Pérez and undersecretary of war Jorge Burgos also participated in the meeting. Some of the generals championed a pardon for Contreras; others argued that he should serve out the sentence in his house in the South. Pinochet called an end to the meeting without endorsing either position. As he made his way out, however, Pérez offered a guarantee that the army would comply with the court's decision, adding that he had no doubts on that score.

During a Channel 13 interview two days later, Pinochet confirmed the defense minister's prediction. The problem was personal to Contreras, he said; neither he nor the army entered into it.

General Pinochet let Contreras and Espinoza take the fall. It was the necessary sacrifice to consolidate and retain the exceedingly comfortable terms of the post-dictatorial transition.

It wasn't clear what Contreras would do. Would he flee? Or mount resistance from his estate? Would he get admitted to the military hospital to impede receiving notification of his sentence? That the former DINA director might meekly hand himself over was seen as the least plausible scenario.

Contreras stuck it out in El Viejo Roble with his wife, Nélida Gutiérrez, his children, and an indeterminate number of guards. He was visited by farmers in the region, former mayors from the Pinochet era, and the onetime DINA agent Ingrid Olderock, who arrived in a red car with a Chilean flag tied to its grill.

"Inside the estate," the newspaper La Nación wrote, citing police sources, "are an undefined number of military officers who arrived there a short while before the ruling of the Fourth Chamber was known."[16]

Meanwhile, both Contreras and Espinoza played their final cards, filing every type of appeal before the Supreme Court. They managed to get their sentences reduced by a year and three months, by subtracting the time they spent detained in the military hospital in 1978 pending resolution of the United States' request for their extradition. But the rest of the appeals by which Contreras tried to have his sentence reconsidered or its completion delayed were rejected. The way was cleared for Judge Bañados to order the arrest and surrender of the two convicted men so they could begin serving their sentences.

A multitude of reporters, cameramen, and photographers positioned themselves at the entrance to the estate, withstanding extreme cold, drenching rain, and high wind. At night they frequently slept in their vehicles and warmed themselves by lighting bonfires. Channel 13's crew was the only one authorized to set up their equipment and operate inside the grounds.

From afar, the entire country nervously awaited an uncertain outcome.

Twice in Hiding

Manuel Contreras's first attempt to elude his imminent arrest entailed an operation authorized by the army's vice commander in chief, Gen. Guillermo Garín, and carried out by members of the army's IV Division. At dawn on Sunday, June 11, Contreras and his wife, his four children, his guards, and army soldiers took a secondary road from the estate, heading for the Twelfth Sangra Infantry Regiment in Puerto Montt. Thirty minutes earlier, the lights had been cut off across the entire surrounding zone to facilitate his escape.

The pretext given for the operation was that Contreras had to seek refuge in the regiment after a supposed armed confrontation with dozens of police officers who entered the estate to arrest him. The story was completely false: he invented the exchange of gunfire, and his son publicized it in irate statements to the media in which he called the PICH's detectives "whores" and "wretches."

The surprise move foundered that same afternoon after the army complied with the government's order to give up the regiment's "guest." Contreras, beaten at his own game, returned that night to his estate. Two days later, however—with the help of the army and navy and, this time, Minister Pérez's consent—he again maneuvered to dodge the order.

Late on the night of June 12, the jet belonging to the army command landed at the nearby aerodrome in Osorno, with the chief of the army's advisory committee to coordinate Contreras's departure. In the hours that followed, several jeeps from the Sangra Regiment arrived at the estate. They later guarded the vehicles that ferreted the Contreras family away in different directions. In the early morning hours of June 13, the former DINA chief was driven to the Ninth Arauco Regiment, in Osorno, where he boarded a helicopter that flew him some

430 kilometers north, to the Talcahuano Naval Hospital. The army subsequently explained that Contreras had suddenly suffered a health crisis while on the road to Santiago to turn himself in. This story, too, was false.

Judge Bañados summoned the clerk on the case, Hermes Ahumada, and Inspector Jofré to his office. Jofré brought detective Mario Zelada with him, the latest to join the investigation. The judge handed Jofré two sealed envelopes to be given to Director Mery. One contained Bañados's decision mandating Contreras's detention, placing him in the hands of Chile's national prison service. The other was directed to the chief of the army's telecommunications command, asking him to take similar action with respect to Brigadier General Espinoza.

That afternoon Mery met with the two deputy directors of the PICH, the chiefs of intelligence and of the metropolitan zone, and others to discuss how Contreras's arrest would be carried out. Jofré was there but did no more than listen to the discussion.

"There was going to be a police cordon, and I remember that the chief of intelligence majorly upped the ante: he wanted a contingent of around eighty detectives in the area to surround the Fresia estate. I thought it was going to be suicidal, because Contreras was not going to be alone; he was going to have a regiment of absolute loyalists [at his side]," says Jofré.

The following day, June 15, the deputy director for operations, Simón Tapia, handed the inspector the plan of action.

"I was to go with Judge Bañados's order, accompanied by the Puerto Montt prefect and an employee from the Intelligence Department, sporting a hidden microphone so everything that was said could be heard," says Jofré.

That moment propelled him to seek God's help in the chapel on Santo Domingo Street.

He prayed for his family.

The first two cellblocks of a special new prison for the military were to be ready within twenty-four hours.

A Special Prison

As a result of the 1993 *boinazo* and the sentence in the first instance handed down by Judge Bañados in the Letelier case, Aylwin's government began to sketch out ideas for a special place to detain members of the military, separate from ordinary prisoners. The army itself had proposed such a facility, although at the same time this posed a dilemma: to request a special prison implied accepting sentences pronounced on comrades, beginning with Manuel Contreras.

The first proposal came from the army in 1993: its Guayacán recreational club located in the Cajón del Maipo, a beautiful valley and tourist area situated at the foot of the Andes Mountain range. This suggestion was promptly dismissed, because it offered few security guarantees and too closely resembled a vacation spot. The second idea came from the director of the national prison service, Claudio Martínez, a member of the Socialist Party. He proposed using the abandoned prison of Quillota, 125 kilometers northwest of the capital.[17] This suggestion was also rejected, again for security reasons and because the army did not like it.

The government weighed its options all through 1994. There was no time to spare. A third alternative was a site in Colina, thirty-four kilometers to the north of the capital, on property that had been in the hands of the military since 1988.

The municipality of Colina and its mayor, Manuel Rojas, immediately objected. It was already home to two prisons, Colina I and Colina II. Moreover, the development plan promised by former president Aylwin, to mitigate the impact caused by the installation of the second prison, had so far come to naught. The previous government had committed to constructing a school and a health clinic in the community and to paving some roads and undertaking other projects, none of which was done. Colina's municipal council passed a resolution against authorizing the construction of the new prison.

Nonetheless, the government decided to go around the municipal council and move ahead with the plan by executive order. In December 1994, Ricardo Lagos, the then minister of public works and the country's next president, was holding on to the order to begin construction. It only required his signature, but he declined to sign it and, instead, submitted his resignation to the cabinet. Lagos was not about to shoulder, purely on his own, the political responsibility of authorizing a special prison for Manuel Contreras. President Frei refused to accept his resignation and agreed, as an alternative, to send a bill to Congress to accomplish the measure. In this way the responsibility for implementing a troublesome and unpopular decision would be shared by multiple parties—the government, Congress, and political parties.

In January 1995, the government announced its decision to construct a special facility in Colina, under the jurisdiction of the national prison service, for members of the armed forces and the Carabineros as well as "other persons in the public sphere who, by virtue of their activities, could be subject to special risk if sharing their confinement with common criminals."[18]

If passed into law the bill would, among other things, empower the national prison service to construct penitentiaries. The bill also included a key reform to the Code of Military Justice: not only would convicted members of the military serve out their sentences in national prison service facilities common to them, but those military under indictment would also be incarcerated, preventively, in this way. To this point, members of the police and military charged in human rights cases were detained in facilities maintained by their own institution.

Despite the government's insistence that these offenders would not be granted special privileges, the idea of constructing and fitting out a separate prison for the military was strongly resisted by the Left, members of the governing coalition, and human rights associations and lawyers. Fabiola Letelier, an attorney and sister of the assassinated foreign minister, argued that this initiative wasn't justified, since the Colina II prison already had separate units for "special" prisoners, so the conditions already existed to take in the convicted military.

In addition, the price tag—not inconsiderable—for putting up a new prison carried a cost for all the country's citizens via taxes and the expenditure of public funds.

"There are other priorities to which to direct the resources of the nation," stated lawyer Nelson Caucoto, of the human rights organization Christian Churches Foundation for Social Assistance. "This is a very tangible demonstration of the pressures [exerted] by the military on the government."[19]

The proposed law was approved in less than three weeks. Due to the opposition of both legislators on the right and the designated senators, an intermediate solution was negotiated to remain fully in effect until at least the end of 1997. The agreement, or compromise, as finally approved stipulated that if someone who received a firm sentence was, at the same time, under indictment for other crimes, that person could remain in a military facility.

The government also conceded with respect to who would have charge of watching over the incarcerated. The prison guards were to be mixed, with employees of the national prison service maintaining the perimeter watch, while military personnel would control the security ring closest to the detainees.

"This regime of exception only makes sense in the current context called 'transition toward democracy.' That a regime of exception ends up being a regime of privileges is the responsibility of the executive branch," stated the former director of the national prison service, Claudio Martínez, in an opinion column many years later.[20]

The time was pressing after the completion of oral arguments before the Supreme Court in January 1995, but the residents of Colina remained firm in their opposition to the new prison. A different site on which to construct it needed to be found without further delay. Consequently, the prison service offered some land on its "Agricultural Colony," located in the Punta Peuco area of Til Til, a rural district some fifty kilometers to the north of Santiago. The prison service operated a farm there for the rehabilitation and training of low-risk inmates.

Work began on the new prison facility during the second week of March 1995 and went on full-bore around the clock. The goal was that by the end of June at least one section of the new Punta Peuco prison would be completed to hold the first of those convicted.

The total cost projected to construct the prison was around 1 billion pesos, equivalent to 2.5 billion pesos in today's currency (or US$3 million).

The Patient

The plan had changed. With Contreras in the Talcahuano Naval Hospital, the responsibility for coordinating his handover now belonged to the chief of the PICH's Seventh Zone, prefect Luis Sepúlveda. In Espinoza's case, it fell to the chief of the metropolitan zone, prefect inspector José Sotomayor, formerly head of Department V and one of the veteran "detectives of La Moneda."

On the morning of June 16, Sotomayor notified the chief of the telecommunications command, where Espinoza was staying, of the arrest warrant against the former DINA agent, but he declined to receive it and instead rerouted the judicial order to Espinoza's superior officer, the chief of the army's Santiago garrison, Brig. Gen. Carlos Krumm. Judge Bañados was forced to issue a new order. Three days later, the detectives tried again to serve Espinoza the order, this time through Krumm.

Espinoza put up a fight for a short while, but the order came from above. Compelled to give up when the army sped up his discharge from the institution, Espinoza accepted his fate, and on June 20 he was transferred to Punta Peuco. He was its first inmate. Less than three months later, he requested a presidential pardon. The request was turned down the following year by President Frei.

In the meanwhile, guarded by two navy vehicles, Prefect Sepúlveda and Inspector Jofré showed up in person at the Talcahuano base. Inside the installation, the two police officials presented the arrest order for Contreras to the naval hospital's director, while outside, the gathered reporters' anticipation continued to grow. After an hour, however, Sepúlveda and Jofré left the base empty-handed, due to the patient's supposedly delicate state of health—the details of which were still unknown.

Later in the day the naval hospital released a statement to the public indicating that Manuel Contreras had entered the facility "purely for medical reasons" and was being evaluated for a "metabolic and cardiovascular compromise, before deciding on a possible surgical procedure, from complications stemming from an earlier surgery."[21]

In response, Bañados ordered medical examinations to determine whether

Contreras was really ill and sent Inspector Jofré back to the naval base. He flew there on a PICH aircraft. When he reached Talcahuano, he found that all the hotels in the vicinity of the base were filled to capacity, jammed with media teams from up and down the country. Jofré knew there were quarters inside the base where officers lived, so his next step was to speak with the admiral in charge.

"I told him that it was complicated for me because I was here solo and if I went to a hotel it was going to be full of reporters, and I wanted to avoid all of that. And I proposed to him, 'Admiral, is there a possibility of my putting up here?' I stayed with them and, in fact, lunched and dined with naval officers. We avoided the subject of Contreras," states Jofré.

Thus began a soap opera whose political denouement resulted, four months later, in what the journalist Rafael Otano describes as "the most humiliating tug-of-war that any government of the Coalition ever suffered."[22]

Closing the Book, Again

For the Right, it was time to consign human rights cases to the grave, time for the judiciary, once and for all, to act in a manner faithful to the spirit of the 1978 Amnesty Law. The police thriller that Manuel Contreras led during these months offered the ideal context in which to resume the attack. Apply amnesty and close down cases and, in addition, seek pardons from the government for the hundreds of military and police under criminal investigation—these were the expectations of the Right and the armed forces.

The tension stirred up by the Letelier case and the Contreras and Espinoza convictions "arose from the fact," said Jovino Novoa—the then president of the ultraright Independent Democratic Union party—"that, contrary to what the government claims, there is a greater problem that affects the Armed Forces as a whole, beyond a specific legal case that has already led to convictions, which the government must address."[23]

What is more, the then senator and twice former president Sebastián Piñera proposed a bill with two complementary elements: strict application of the Amnesty Law and a general amnesty applied to all the remaining crimes of the dictatorship that occurred between 1978 and 1990.[24]

President Frei, like Aylwin before him, wanted to finalize the transition. To transfer power from the military to the political sphere and to resolve the "issue" of human rights once and for all entailed pushing through certain vital reforms. Aylwin, with his homonymous law, had failed in 1993. Still, the government persisted in believing the fallacy that the "reconciliation" of Chilean society could be forcibly achieved via laws and measures negotiated between the political elite and the armed forces.

In this round, the three bills Frei announced in August 1995 on the national television channel aimed to establish criteria to determine the truth in human rights cases, restore authority to the presidency when it comes to the removal of military leaders, eliminate the position of designated senator, and restructure the composition and functioning of the Constitutional Court and National Security Council. In short, the Frei administration sought to undermine the presence and power of the military in decision-making, in return for which a certain degree of impunity would be guaranteed.

The proposal remained bottled up and had to be negotiated with some of the leaders of the rightist party Renovación Nacional, because the Independent Democratic Union totally closed ranks behind the military. In November an agreement, known as the Figueroa-Otero agreement, was reached on the question of human rights.[25] Among other things, the new proposal increased the number of special judges considering human rights cases, protected and granted varying degrees of impunity to those providing information about the fate of disappeared detainees, and established a set period for judicial investigations, with amnesty included.

For victims' families and human rights associations, sacrificing justice in exchange for a bit of questionable truth was unacceptable. And for their part, the armed forces would not cede a fraction of their quota of power within the post-dictatorial institutional setup or acknowledge any responsibility for their crimes.

The Figueroa-Otero bill foundered months later, in April 1996. It could not overcome opposition from the Independent Democratic Union, the most conservative wing of Renovación Nacional, or the designated senators. It was also opposed by the coalition's most progressive legislators, who did not want to pay the political price of endorsing impunity. It was back to square one.

The Road to Til Til

Months were spent disputing the results of contradictory medical reports issued by naval hospital specialists, the national prison service, and the national Legal Medical Service with respect to Contreras's true state of health and whether he was in a condition to be transferred to prison.

"I was called on two or three times to make a trip to Talcahuano to deal with the medical reports issue, but the situation was beginning to stall," recalls Nelson Jofré.

In any event, Contreras's lawyer, the air force colonel Julio Tapia, filed a battery of legal appeals—nearly a dozen, including a request that Contreras be allowed to serve his sentence in the confines of his home—drawing out for weeks any definitive resolution about the fate of the convicted former DINA chief.

Demonstrations in favor of and against Contreras took place during these months, both in front of the armed forces building in Santiago and outside the walls of the new prison in Til Til. On Saturday, July 22, by order of their superiors, several hundred active-duty army and noncommissioned officers and their families turned up at the entrance to the Punta Peuco prison. It was the lunch hour, so they came with something to eat. The event became known as the "Punta Peuco picnic." One by one, small groups of people went inside to visit Pedro Espinoza—the sole inmate—while outside the rest of the crowd munched on their food and sang military marches and the national anthem. No one was in uniform, but they carried weapons.

The gathering was more than an expression of solidarity with Espinoza. It was also a clear manifestation of the discontent within the "military family," due not only to the incarceration of one of its own but to the inauguration of a new chapter in the Pinocheques case. The State Defense Council had asked that the former dictator's son and three retired army officers be subject to indictment.

Judge Jorge Colvin, who replaced Alejandro Solís in 1993 when Solís disqualified himself, rejected the request. The predictable next step was a State Defense Council appeal of the judge's decision, but the moment could not have been more inopportune. Too much had come into play and was at stake during these weeks of high tension surrounding the Contreras affair. President Frei expressly asked the State Defense Council's interim president, Davor Harasic, not to appeal the decision. He grounded his request on "reasons of State": it could endanger the maintenance of the rule of law. By nine votes to three, the State Defense Council decided to forego an appeal. At the end of July 1995, the Pinocheques case was closed and passed into history.

After analyzing the different medical reports, the Supreme Court ruled that Contreras could be transferred to prison as of October 23 or sooner if his doctors discharged him. Ultimately, Inspector Jofré did not participate in Contreras's handover to the national prison service, nor did it fall to the PICH to bring him into custody. How and when the transfer would take place, and how he would be guarded in Punta Peuco, was a matter to be negotiated between the government and the army. Pinochet cut loose his confidante, his most faithful subordinate—even to the point of leaving the country in the middle of the process, unconcerned and out from under having to respond to questions or offer any public explanation.

"It was a grinding process, difficult, because public opinion thought us incapable of imposing our will," said ex-president Eduardo Frei years later in an interview with the Museum of Memory. "They were tense times, but the president's determination was evident that the sentence had to be served; that was the order we gave and that's how the high command, including Pinochet, understood it. . . . The interchange was clear and categorical: There is a ruling on justice here and it must be complied with. If a special prison has to be built, [then] it will have to be built, but he has to be imprisoned."[26]

The army oversaw the operation, in which a high-level official of the national prison service also took part. At sunset on Friday, October 20, a military helicopter transferred Contreras from the Talcahuano Naval Base to the Gen. Justo Arteaga military fort, situated in Peldehue, in the municipality of Colina. That was the site where, in September 1973, some twenty detainees from La Moneda Palace were executed. Contreras dined and fraternized with his comrades in the fort that night. At dawn the next morning he climbed into a police vehicle that brought him to Til Til, escorted by a caravan of six other vehicles.

When Manuel Contreras at last set foot in the Punta Peuco prison, Pedro Espinoza was the sole inmate serving time inside it. The relationship between the two men was extremely tense. Within a year, the new prison built specially for the military counted some thirteen additional inmates. The list of prisoners incarcerated in Punta Peuco during this period included two Carabineros convicted for murdering Nelson Carrasco (1984) and Carlos Godoy (1985);[27] army captain Pedro Fernández, for the death of the young photographer Rodrigo Rojas De Negri in 1986;[28] and eight persons involved in the Slit-Throats Case. Miguel "Fanta" Estay remained confined for some time longer in Colina II.

Contreras regained his freedom at the beginning of 2001 but in January 2005 was reimprisoned to serve a twelve-year sentence for the 1975 disappearance of the Movement of the Revolutionary Left militant Miguel Ángel Sandoval.

On this latest occasion, in a scene that could be out of a television series, Contreras resisted accepting his detention order when a contingent of some fifteen detectives entered his Santiago condominium to carry it out. He threatened to fire his gun. The confrontation then descended into a wild scene of struggling, shouting, and the hysterics of his family.

He ended up being taken by force, guarded by the just-appointed head of the PICH's newly created Investigative Brigade for Special Affairs and Human Rights, Sandro Gaete, and by his colleagues Abel Lizama and Rafael Castillo. Castillo had just become the head of the National Command against Organized Crime, of which the brigade was a subunit.

History repeated itself, and the government anticipated certain events. Contreras would go to prison one more time, so it was necessary to find a suitable place in which to house him. In 2004, President Ricardo Lagos—who as public works minister a decade earlier refused to sign the construction order for a special prison for the military—now acted on his own. He ordered that a different prison, the Centro de Cumplimiento Penitenciario Cordillera, be fitted out to hold military inmates. This facility was located on land belonging to the army's telecommunications command, in Peñalolén, a municipality at the eastern end of the capital, at the foothills of the Andes Mountains. The DINA's former top leaders were held in this pleasant penitentiary, with its gardens and cabins, until September 2013, when President Sebastián Piñera ordered it closed and its inmates transferred to Punta Peuco.

This second sentence handed down against Contreras marked the beginning of the end for the dictatorship's strong man, Pinochet's right arm in the regime's bloody train of political persecution. He was never to leave prison again. Manuel Contreras died in August 2015 while serving more than 100 sentences. They added up to a total of 526 years in prison.

In mid-2018 Punta Peuco held 117 prisoners sentenced for crimes against humanity. Another forty-two were confined in the Colina I prison, and thirteen more were incarcerated in jails in other cities around the country.

10

IN SEARCH OF
PERMANENT UNCLE

JOSÉ LUIS CABIÓN AND RENÉ SANDOVAL were the last detectives to see Paul Schäfer in Colonia Dignidad. It was around lunchtime on March 30, 1994. The leader of the German sect lay in bed in the hospital that the colony maintained on its grounds. He was using an oxygen mask. Seventy-three years old, Schäfer was very ill, perhaps in his final days of life, according to Dr. Hartmut Hopp, the hospital's director and Schäfer's right-hand man.

That day, facing the sick man's bed, Hopp alone spoke to them. Even so, the colony's leader signed the judicial notice in his own hand. His state of health was not so perilous. In fact, he still had sixteen years ahead of him: two hiding out inside his own stronghold, nine as a fugitive from justice, and the last five as an inmate in Santiago's high-security prison.

There were three barriers that prevented entry into the impenetrable community. Surprisingly, the two police officers and their driver were allowed to pass through them to deliver the judge's subpoena. The local court in Bulnes, about 432 kilometers south of the capital, had ordered Department V to ascertain Schäfer's whereabouts and, if they found him, hand him the subpoena to appear before the court at noon on April 5. The court was acting on the official request of the government of Germany.

By now, Colonia Dignidad—also known as Villa Baviera—had lost its legal status as a "charitable and educational association." Its leaders were under close scrutiny for a variety of crimes and infractions from kidnapping to tax fraud. It faced judicial and administrative investigations spun off by several government departments as well as by families of the disappeared. In addition, the attorney general's office in Bonn, Germany, was, since 1985, pursuing an investigation into Schäfer and other Colonia Dignidad leaders in connection with crimes and misdeeds alleged by three Germans who had fled the colony.[1]

"As we were going to the car, I look behind me and see the old goat standing at the window, laughing at us," Sandoval recalls. "I'd never gone to the colony [and] had no idea what it was. But Cabión had been stationed in Parral and already knew the saga. He told me about it [while we were] on the road."

The World Upside Down

Colonia Dignidad was founded in 1961 by the self-proclaimed evangelical preacher Paul Schäfer. Accompanied by his followers, he fled that year from Germany, where he was accused of sexually abusing minors. He had started the Private Social Mission (Private Soziale Mission) in his native country. The organization worked with socially at-risk minors, whom Schäfer raped. Wanted for embezzlement of funds and with an arrest order pending for the abuses, Chile's government issued him a temporary residence visa, thanks to the intervention of Chilean diplomats in Europe.

The colony's first tract of land, El Lavadero estate, was purchased by two of its leaders. Situated forty kilometers to the east of Parral, in southern Chile, the estate was to house a self-sufficient agricultural community and offer health, educational, and social welfare services to needy people. The community secured its legal status as the Dignidad Charitable and Educational Association in October 1961 and from that point on enjoyed tax and customs benefits. In time, its leaders vastly expanded Colonia's lands, which stretched almost to Chile's mountainous border with Argentina.

Distinct from Colonia Dignidad's leaders, the colonists lived trapped, laboring like slaves, without wages or work contracts. Parents were separated from their children, deprived of the ability to live as a family, and boys were separated from girls. The colonists lived collectively, without any personal possessions. Schäfer exercised total control over their lives, their minds, and their bodies. Periodically, they had to come before their leader to make a "confession." The children called him "Permanent Uncle."

Colonia Dignidad's hospital, opened in 1968, provided free medical services to impoverished Chileans living in the region. Like children, however, who came to the colony for a "vacation" and were prevented from leaving, some of the babies and children born or attended to in the hospital weren't turned over to their families. Instead—with the complicity of local civil registry employees—they were illegally adopted by the colonists. Women were subjected to forced sterilization, and hospital staff administered psychotropic drugs, applied electric shock, and dealt out other forms of punishment to those who stepped out of bounds, engaged in sexual behavior, or acted on sexual impulses perfectly appropriate for their age.

Until 1991, both the hospital and the boarding school received state subsidies. The latter opened in 1985 to serve Chilean boys in the area. Since colonists were not allowed to marry or procreate, Colonia's population was quickly aging. The boarding school provided Schäfer a steady pool of children he could abuse. As in Germany, in southern Chile Schäfer preyed on boys, preferably preteens.

Save for members of the Colonia leadership—whose sons were not spared from Schäfer's sexual assault—the colonists were beaten, tortured, and drugged if they tried to escape, express discontent, disobey orders or the strict rules of collective life, or resist Schäfer's sexual abuse. Few colony members spoke Spanish; money was unknown to them; they had no access to any communications media or sources of information. It was drummed into them that the world outside was a hellscape of evil and sinfulness. The children had no way of seeking help, no one they could turn to for assistance, affection, or protection.

Colonia Dignidad's land was hemmed in by hills and by the Perquilauquén River, and the colonists were forbidden from going beyond its perimeter. Their activities and movements were controlled through a sophisticated monitoring system that included wire fencing equipped with heat and movement sensors, recording machines and hidden microphones, closed-circuit video surveillance, and a complex network of secondary paths threading the forests that connected with the principal roads—all barred with metal gates and padlocks. Some of these back roads had hydraulic traps designed to block vehicular traffic, and one of them crossed the Perquilauquén River, extending to an adjacent, fifty-hectare piece of land that also belonged to the colony.

Armed guards and dogs helped stop any unauthorized departures, while also warning about the presence of strangers.

This battery of internal security was supplemented by an intricate network of tunnels, bunkers, and other underground constructions used as avenues of escape and communication; towers and lookouts for monitoring; and a state-of-the-art communications system composed of two command posts, digital cell phones, portable radios, and mobile telecommunications units installed in the majority of the colony's vehicles.[2]

Starting in 1996, a succession of police raids on Colonia Dignidad enabled them to discover and peel back the full scope of this security complex.

The slave-like conditions, the forced entrapment, and the sexual abuse had been reported as early as 1966, when—on his third attempt—twenty-one-year-old Wolfgang Müller managed to flee the colony. Later, Wilhelmine Lindemann also escaped its clutches. Müller denounced, among numerous other things, Schäfer's iron grip over the community, how he raped boys, and how—in 1965— a seventeen-year-old girl died after being repeatedly whipped.

The public shock at the gravity of Müller's denunciations and his escape led to the appointment of a special judge to investigate what took place inside the apparently peaceful agricultural community. In the face of that threat, Schäfer faked his disappearance or possible suicide. He left a letter written in German, stating that he was going away because he felt he was being persecuted. A month later, Parral's criminal court indicted Schäfer for "the corruption of minors."

For its part, the Congress's Chamber of Deputies created a commission to investigate the situation in Colonia Dignidad. It concluded that the Chilean state had no control over its German residents, that its directors had acquired land illegally with the aim of conducting profitable mining ventures, and that the Ministry of Education was not in a position to oversee the Villa Baviera German School, located inside the colony (for the community's children), or even provide assurance that the children were completing the basic course of education. This investigative commission was the first of three set up by the legislature's lower chamber over a span of three decades.[3]

Ultimately, Parral's criminal court ordered Wilhelmine Lindemann to return to Colonia Dignidad, even though she was getting ready to leave the country, and Schäfer brought a complaint against Wolfgang Müller for false allegations and slander. The young man was sentenced to five years and a day in prison for having reported the abuses.[4] Aided by the German embassy and a Swiss family, Müller managed to flee Chile and avoid incarceration.

The world had turned upside down.

During the period of the Popular Unity government (1970–73), the fervently anti-Communist Schäfer offered his properties and logistical capabilities to those who conspired against socialist President Allende, and after he was toppled Schäfer offered Colonia's grounds to the military to set up a clandestine detention and torture center for political prisoners. Directorate of National Intelligence director Manuel Contreras sent detainees to the colony, where they were shut away in a barn and tortured in a cellar used for storing potatoes. Schäfer helped Chilean agents perfect their torture techniques and participated in torture sessions. Searches continue even today for the remains of disappeared persons who were executed and buried across the extensive fields and hills of the colony.[5]

Thus, it was no surprise that two months after the 1973 military coup, the court in Parral shut down the investigation of Paul Schäfer that had been initiated after Müller's flight. The reason it gave was that the crimes were covered by the statute of limitations. During the dictatorship, the colony acquired mineral rights for the extraction of titanium, operated lucrative businesses, constructed a small hydroelectric power station, manufactured and trafficked grenades and machine guns, and built up an arsenal of war weaponry.

In the mid-1980s, Colonia Dignidad's directors opened a restaurant some ninety kilometers south of Parral with a games area for children. They also constructed an airfield and a rock-crushing plant on the surrounding land.

Over many years, the testimonies of witnesses, escaped colonists, and political prisoners who survived their ordeals filled in the picture of Colonia Dignidad's crimes and ways of operating.

All of that was known and still ongoing when the military dictatorship ended in March 1990.

Cold Cuts and Pies

That year, the Justice Ministry supplied the governor of Linares province, the lawyer and writer Manuel Francisco Mesa, with a detailed report on the social and legal status of Colonia Dignidad. This initiative called in turn for carrying out on-site inspections and interviewing the colonists, both in Parral as well as in the Bulnes restaurant.

Mesa, however, was not permitted to speak freely with any of the more than 300 residents of the community or get near its buildings, the boys' boarding school, or the colonists' common living quarters. He was likewise prevented from observing the children in their school, whose teachers had neither educational licenses nor formal work contracts. The colony's hospital was not in compliance with the country's vaccination program. On the other hand, Mesa's delegation noted the high number (usually around eight) of drugs listed in the medical prescriptions it issued.

Mesa delivered his report at the end of 1990, concluding that Colonia Dignidad did not comply with its standing as a "charitable society" and that it infringed on Chile's laws. Its decades-long criminal record, reflected in multiple judicial, police, and legislative reports, testimonies from victims, and inquiries by various government agencies, provided ample grounds for closing Colonia Dignidad and arresting and/or expelling its leaders from the country. Nonetheless, President Patricio Aylwin did not go that far. In 1991, he withdrew its legal status as a charitable association, resulting in the colony's loss of its tax and customs benefits. In a public statement, the government pointed out: "The earnings that the Society realizes from its agricultural, logging, mining, industrial, and commercial ventures are all profitable. . . . Nor are these profits applied to the two exclusive social activities they carry out, the Hospital and the elementary school, which largely operate through state subsidies. . . . Colonia Dignidad's assets consist at this time of more than 15,000 hectares of real estate; industrial, commercial, and mining complexes; and an abundance of buildings. . . . Lately, all of these assets have been transferred to the for-profit companies controlled by a restricted group of the colony's leaders."[6]

Over three decades, the enclave became a state within a state. Its leaders cultivated relationships with politicians, businessmen, government authorities, public employees, legislators, the military and police, and persons living in communities dotting the adjacent regions of Maule and Bío-Bío. By organizing recreational outings and distributing not just favors and money but also cold cuts, cheese, and pies, they crafted the image of a clean-cut, hard-working community, one that came to the aid of destitute Chileans, even if its ways were a trifle old-fashioned. They asked to be left in peace, and the favors flowed in both directions. Friends of the colony and watch committees were created that sprang to the defense of the colony, its hospital, and boarding school—sometimes to the point of physical violence.

In 1994, the colony had to turn over administrative control of the Villa Baviera school to the Ministry of Education and terminate the hospital services it offered to local Chileans.

A couple of days later, a group of legislators—led by then ultraright senator Hernán Larraín—organized an event in support of Colonia Dignidad. They formed the Dignidad Advisory Committee, composed of well-known public figures. The following year, the Supreme Court ordered the reopening of the colony's hospital, which continued offering outpatient services until its definitive closure in 2005.

A Boy

Keenly aware of the networks of influence and protection enjoyed by the colony's leaders, Jacqueline Pacheco—a twenty-nine-year-old woman from San Carlos, a city near Colonia Dignidad—decided to travel all the way to Santiago to file a complaint against Schäfer for raping her son. As an active member in the Young People's Permanent Watch, which supported the colony, she understood that its leaders had important friends because she had seen them with her own eyes. And she also knew that employees in Parral's police force and judicial system received free care in its hospital.

She did not trust that the police or local courts would actually investigate Schäfer for having sexually assaulted her twelve-year-old son, CPP, or that they would even believe her.[7] She herself could scarcely believe it. Rumors had always circulated about Schäfer's sexual aberrations, but she defended him. It was just slander, Jacqueline Pacheco thought, until the day she read the letter that her son sent her from the boarding school.

The violation took place at the beginning of June 1996, two months into CPP's time at the school. As was his custom, Schäfer selected his victim and took him to his bedroom in the guesthouse. He shut the door and locked it, ordered the boy to take off his clothes, and to scare him, placed a handgun on a table. But unlike his other young victims, CPP denounced him. He sent a letter, secretly, through another child to his grandmother, telling her what happened and pleading with her to get him out of there.

It was not an easy thing for his family. Both his mother and grandmother were loyal defenders of the colony. His grandmother was president of the Villa Baviera Hospital Friends Group. She abandoned the group as soon as she learned of the assaults suffered by her grandson. His mother, meanwhile, asked for help from the evangelical pastor Adrián Bravo. Bravo, a longtime friend of the colony, presided over several of the committees that supported it. His friendly relations with Colonia Dignidad abruptly ended, however, when he found out about the rape of CPP. On June 11, 1996, Pastor Bravo accompanied Jacqueline to the doors of Colonia Dignidad to take back her son. They stood there for five hours, demanding that they turn him over to her.

Pacheco took her son to a local doctor, and he confirmed the sexual assault. Then she took CPP with her to the capital, where she reported the abuses at the office of the Chilean Human Rights Commission. The commission contacted the chief of Department V, Luis Henríquez, and Henríquez in turn told detective Lautaro Arias to take down her testimony. Department V's chief assigned the task to Arias because Arias came from the region where the crime took place and knew it in and out.

Something Special

The detectives asked to meet privately with the Parral criminal court judge who had jurisdiction over Colonia Dignidad. The judge in this instance was a relatively young man, Jorge Norambuena. He listened carefully to what the detectives had to say, received the complaint, and issued the first investigative order to Department V. Those were the immediate circumstances under which Judge Norambuena opened an investigation, for sexual abuse, into Paul Schäfer.

This was not the first criminal investigation related to Colonia Dignidad nor would it be the last, but it was the one that ultimately led to the conviction against Schäfer and his inner circle as well as to the partial dismantling of Villa Baviera.

Given the nature of the offenses, the investigation would normally be taken on by the Sexual Crimes and Minors Brigade. But this case was different and operated on another level. It did not deal simply with catching a lone sexual predator but, rather, with confronting a well-armed, tight-knit criminal organization that commanded considerable influence and enjoyed wide-ranging protection at the highest levels of the state and society.

Judge Norambuena already had a track record working with the Investigations Police (PICH) team of detectives dedicated to pursuing human rights cases. The investigations into the dictatorship's victims in Parral had resumed. José Luis Cabión was involved again, this time with the young detectives René Sandoval and Freddy Orellana. The three were busy recording witnesses' statements.

Department V's chief assembled an opening team that brought together officers from his own department who knew the region and others who were experienced in handling sexual crimes. All of them had to have an unimpeachable work record.

Henríquez called Department V deputy superintendent Juan Álvarez to his office. With his own family roots in Concepción, also in southern Chile, Álvarez had now spent two years in the Internal Affairs Department in Santiago.

"I have something special for you," Henríquez announced to him one winter morning in 1996.

"Oh, what is it?"

"It's an investigative order [issued] against Paul Schäfer for sexual abuse."

Álvarez knew something about the matter. His father, a naval employee, would bring home newspapers and magazines, and he remembered reading in the 1960s news reports about Wolfgang Müller's escape and what went on in Colonia Dignidad.

The first thing Henríquez asked Álvarez to do before sending him off to the South was to speak with Máximo Pacheco. The Christian Democratic lawyer, with long political experience, was one of the founders of the Chilean Human Rights Commission. He had also represented Amnesty International and the German magazine *Stern* in the legal action brought against them by Colonia Dignidad.

Pacheco spoke with him at length about the sect and furnished him with a copy of the book *Colonia Dignidad*, written by the German journalist Gero Gembella.

"Look, Deputy Superintendent, read this book so you realize what you are going to run into. It's going to serve you well. I salute all of you because you are courageous. But you are not going to come away with anything," Álvarez recalls Pacheco telling him.

Based on the first statements from CPP, it was clear that there could be more victims among the school's children, and they had to be found. Henríquez decided to bring in inspector María Soledad Villanueva, from the San Fernando precinct.

"Somebody with just the right profile had to be found, someone who had the courage and ability to be able to investigate this case. I turned to different detectives, but nobody matched her profile," Henríquez explains.

Villanueva was a veteran of fourteen years in the investigation of sexual crimes. She was experienced and had a fine reputation not only as a detective but for her treatment of minor-age victims of sexual assault. Inspector Villanueva first interviewed CPP's mother and then questioned him. He described what happened to him during his last week in Colonia Dignidad, when Schäfer took him to his bedroom. He spoke about what he personally lived through but not about what the colony was in and of itself, and she needed to know that. Villanueva then spoke with a relative who had lived in Germany. She got hold of Gemballa's book on Colonia Dignidad—but in this case the German edition—and requested a favor.

"I sat down with her over various afternoons to read the book. She translated it for me. I began to grasp who Paul Schäfer was, how he came to Chile, and what he had done. I started to work from scratch, without having any preconceived idea," says Villanueva.

A Police Van and a Typewriter

Juan Álvarez, Lautaro Arias, and María Soledad Villanueva traveled to the site in search of more children who had been sexually assaulted by Paul Schäfer. They needed to find people who could attest to Schäfer's habit of raping boys or who might themselves have been his victims. They could have relied solely on CPP's complaint but instead chose to work more slowly and strategically, building a case that tied Schäfer to a pattern of criminal behavior.

"We had to conduct a solid investigation that could not be brought down," says Henríquez.

The detectives put up with conditions that were far from optimal. Their travel allowance was meager; they drove around in a gray Kia van, then tramped for hours through the region's different rural areas and towns: Parral, Catillo, Chillán, San Fabián de Alico, San Carlos. They went into small shops to talk to local residents and knocked quietly on the doors of families of possible victims, preferably at dusk or at night, when they wouldn't be as readily noticed. They typed up the statements on an old Olympia typewriter, using carbon paper. Not everyone was inclined to register a complaint against "Permanent Uncle."

"Some parents refused to let us interview their children, and the reason was explicit: 'I know what happened with my son, but neither the police nor the government are going to give me work. If you interview my son the Germans will not give me work,' a farmworker told us. There are victims who never came to light because their parents refused [to report the abuses] out of fear. It was very sad," says Álvarez.

The three targeted the homes of boys who by now had left Colonia Dignidad's boarding school and could therefore have suffered sexual assaults or witnessed them. CPP's mother and grandmother were key to identifying them and facilitating contacts, but they paid a heavy price: the colonists unleashed a potent campaign to disparage, harass, and threaten them and other families who gave statements to the police.

In July 1996, one of Schäfer's most loyal followers from the area, a housewife named Olalia Vera, appeared at Jacqueline Pacheco's home with a colonist Pacheco knew only as Klo. The two visitors wanted to know what she was going around saying about Colonia Dignidad and the "doctor." Her testimony, they reproached her, was hurting the hospital. Klo warned Pacheco to be very careful about what she was doing. Klo was Ricardo Alvear, a Chilean who as a child was admitted to the colony's hospital after an accident. Not only was he never returned to his family, but the kidnapped child ended up an unwavering Schäfer loyalist.

After menacing CPP's mother, Vera and Alvear proceeded to visit the boy's grandparents' house, delivering the same message and threats.

On one occasion the two banged on the door of Jacqueline's house at 3:00 A.M. Alarmed, CPP's mother looked out through the window. They had left a coffin in the street, in front of her house.

Measures had to be adopted to protect everyone in the Pacheco family, as was the case later for all the other victims who had the courage to file complaints about the abuse they endured. Additional police officers were moved into the region to protect the children who were reporting the abuses and safeguard their appearance before the court. As part of these efforts and the investigation, two more women came onto the team. One was Margarita Fernández, a "battle-tested and courageous detective who had expert knowledge about the issue of sexual crimes," as Villanueva described her. The two had gotten to know each other while serving in the Sexual Assaults Brigade in the 1980s. The other new member of the team was Celia Bacur, who took charge of protecting the boys and their families.

The detectives spent all of winter 1996 traversing the Maule region— covering its small towns and countryside, bearing up over months of intense traveling. Periodically, they escaped to Santiago to brief Prefect Henríquez and hold work-related meetings. Their driver, Luis Núñez, held up stoically under the numberless days and hours he spent behind the steering wheel. Villanueva laughingly relates:

> In one month we could cover 2,000 kilometers looking for children in different towns, bringing them to Santiago first to confirm their injuries, then next to the special service that attended to victims of sexual assault, and after that turning around to take them back to their homes. Following that, the process geared up again, our traveling around the South looking for more victims and reassuring the mothers, who had just begun to recover some trust in the police. For the most part, we lived in the hotel in Chillán. We got back at one in the morning and were back on our feet at 6:30 A.M. Sometimes we went without eating or slept poorly. It wasn't an easy or normal investigation. I was thirty-seven and had a fifteen-year-old daughter. It was a life that another detective would perhaps not have put up with from Henríquez.

This critical stage in the investigation bore fruit thanks to the coordinative efforts of key parties, including a crack team of detectives on the ground, families that never bowed down, a committed lawyer who went above and beyond the call of duty, and a judge who never doubted the children's words.

"Paul Schäfer manipulated everything except Judge Norambuena," states Henríquez.

They were "the anonymous heroes" of the lengthy criminal prosecution of Colonia Dignidad. Of special note was the lawyer Hernán Fernández, who came on the scene that same year, 1996. Inspector Villanueva had gotten to know him when both were beginning their careers and worked collaboratively: she on sexual crimes and he with the National Minors' Service (Sename).

When she received CPP's complaint, Villanueva immediately thought of Fernández and recommended him to Jacqueline Pacheco. The boy's family and the police themselves knew that looking for a lawyer in the region was useless and even risky.

CPP's mother called Fernández from San Carlos. She barely told him anything: something had happened to her son, and she was looking for a lawyer who wasn't afraid. Fernández did not understand why that had to be a requirement, but he proposed meeting her the next day. He took a bus that same Friday night to San Carlos. They got together on a cold June morning at Jacqueline's parents' house in the countryside.

The lawyer offered his legal services without expecting anything in return. For years, and right up to the present, Fernández has paid out of his own pocket for countless trips to the region to assist the families of sexually abused children, working closely with the police.

"He never imagined that act of generosity on his part would change his life. He quickly understood that not only was he facing clients who hadn't the slightest financial ability to pay his fees, but he would have to confront an entire team of professionals who took up the defense of the accused," notes Henríquez.[8]

The State Defense Council was party to the legal action against Schäfer for sexual assault. The Chilean government, however, never collaborated—either financially or otherwise—on legal assistance for the children abused by the "state" that, for so many years, was allowed to operate "inside the state." They had only Hernán Fernández.

A Bottle with Urine

The detectives knew that the colonists and their local friends were monitoring their movements. Although they used a special—not the universal—radio frequency, they still detected that their signals were being intercepted. They had to alter their routines and, as a precaution, met on the side of the highway to talk, and when they needed to update Henríquez on their activities and accomplishments they did so via public telephone.

One night, after a day full of meetings and other work, they were gathered at a Copec gas station along the highway. Deputy Superintendent Álvarez was on a public phone with Henríquez while the detectives filled up the tank and stretched their legs. All of a sudden they spotted a pinpoint of red light coming from a van parked to one side of the gas station. They were being filmed and photographed.

The detectives came up to the van to ask for ID. The driver was one of Schäfer's blindly loyal followers, Wolfgang Zeitner, and seated next to him was Olalia Vera. There was a second vehicle, a small truck, situated about twenty meters away. It had one occupant—a Chilean who belonged to the colonists' support group.

They refused to identify themselves or acknowledge the judicial order or police badges. On the contrary, the detectives were met with shouts and blows.

"Punches were being thrown back and forth," recalls Villanueva. "Olalia Vera scratched our driver, Luis Núñez, and tore his skin. Lautaro came out with injuries and I with a neck sprain and contusions on my right knee. I was in a cast for a month but kept working just the same. Later on, I had to have an operation on my knee, and even now it bothers me a good deal."

When they checked the car of the Chilean who was by himself, the detectives found a large plastic soda bottle. It was half-full of urine.

"This indicated that he had been on our tail for some time," says Álvarez.

The detectives inspected the vehicles and seized rolls of film and microcassettes, thus discovering—with the latter—the recordings made of Vera's and Alvear's intimidating conversations with CPP's family.

They confirmed the extent of their injuries in the public health service clinic, made Judge Norambuena aware of the attack, and submitted a complaint before the San Carlos court. Nonetheless, as with virtually everything related to Colonia Dignidad, nothing came of it.

"The investigation has been meddled in and interfered with" by Zeitner, Vera, and others, stated Deputy Superintendent Álvarez in a police report.

> It's assumed that they receive instructions from third parties to track police vehicles, [and] it's believed with good reason that they have intercepted communications [transmitted] through the radio equipment of these vehicles; that they have visited many of the people who had already been interviewed by the team in different sectors of San Carlos, in order to find out the tone and tenor of the actions taken and prevent these people from backing up their statements in court, while in addition creating with their intimidating interventions an atmosphere of doubt and mistrust among those who constitute part of this process.[9]

The tracking became constant and the harassment more aggressive. The police took different roads and altered their routines, but they were pursued as before. What is more, the colonists and their followers did not even bother to conceal themselves.

"Wanted: Paul Schäfer Schneider"

These incidents were taking place out in the field, across the Maule region. Meanwhile, Colonia Dignidad's beefed-up coterie of defense lawyers flooded the courts with legal actions and appeals on various fronts. The colony maintained legal teams in Santiago, Parral, and Concepción. Beginning in 1990 they presented one legal appeal after another to keep the German sect from being broken up. They sought, unsuccessfully, to freeze the nullification of their legal status as a charitable organization. They also launched multiple appeals against the audits by Chile's Internal Revenue Service, half a dozen legal claims over the fines leveled by the Labor Department, and a host of others against the Customs Court of Santiago and the Ministries of Health and Education.

This line of attack was amplified by a battery of writs of protection filed over the actions of the PICH, characterized by the defense attorneys as unbridled harassment, "privations, disturbances and threats" inflicted on and against witnesses, the abuse of power, and the slandering of Schäfer. Judge Norambuena, however, did not bow to intimidation.

In past investigations Colonia Dignidad's leaders almost immediately got hold of a copy of the judicial dossier and witnesses' statements, but it did not prove so easy this time. To break this pattern and prevent leaks, Judge Norambuena decided to hand the case over to Department V and keep the dossier sealed. The colonists, unaccustomed to such treatment, were initially thrown off guard, disconcerted. Furthermore, the region's police officers and public employees who were friendly with the colony now found themselves on the sidelines of the investigation. To them, Department V was a mystery, and it quickly became their main enemy.

After three months, the detectives had managed to take statements from some twenty sexually victimized Chilean boys from poor families living on the outskirts of Colonia Dignidad. In addition, they collected corroborating testimony about Schäfer's culpability in the rape and sexual abuse of minors. Of the total cluster, however, only half persisted with the judicial process.

The original investigative team, formed by Juan Álvarez, María Soledad Villanueva, Lautaro Arias, Margarita Fernández, and Celia Bacur, was boosted by the collaboration of Department V detectives René Sandoval and Freddy Orellana, who dealt with human rights cases, and Juan Vargas from Internal Affairs, whom Henríquez added to the team because he was from the Chillán area.

The team faced a basic obstacle: they could not interview the German children in the colony who had also suffered sexual abuse, nor could they take a statement from the accused offender himself. When it came to Schäfer, the gates of the colony were barred.

They sought out the colony's lawyer, César Valero, to ask his assistance in setting up a meeting with his client. That was not feasible, Valero told them. In August 1996, Judge Norambuena issued the first of three detention orders against Schäfer, but—as always—the pederast couldn't be located.

"When we went to carry out the procedure there were always colonists in wait. The element of surprise never existed because they were always on top of our movements. And true human shields were installed at the first barrier—children, women, farmworkers, and a Chilean spokesman, often Hernán Escobar.[10] Not any Germans," recalls Álvarez.

They pursued the same aim in outlying areas of Parral and San Carlos, positioning themselves at fixed points in different places where Schäfer might make a move outside the colony, and they looked for him at the restaurant in Bulnes.

Coming up empty-handed, the detectives concluded that it wasn't possible to fulfill the detention order by employing ordinary police procedures.

Schäfer and the top leaders of Colonia Dignidad, they added, had "no intention of obeying what the court ordered and, to counteract these decisions, had since the start of the investigation launched an intensive campaign to discredit Judge . . . Jorge Norambuena, as well as the detectives of this department, arguing that the judicial process would be a political investigation [designed] to close the hospital and harm the local population."[11]

In addition, the colonists and their friends had undertaken a vigorous campaign against the victims and their families, assuring the media that the complaints of abuse were false and amounted to nothing more than a political stunt. Paralleling that, they threatened and intimidated those testifying in court.

Consequently, Álvarez proposed a new strategy to Judge Norambuena. To bring about Schäfer's detention, he maintained, a new judicial order was needed, and to guarantee the mission's success, two measures had to be adopted: radio and telephone communications in the colony had to be neutralized, and the judge's new order had to authorize the team to detain anyone who obstructed their procedures.

Furthermore, Álvarez added, Schäfer—once detained—would have to be immediately transferred outside the estate by helicopter. If not, violence could break out on the part of the colonists. It would be difficult to control because they possessed firearms and other means of resistance. Later, in fact, the number of legally registered handguns and rifles discovered by the detectives ran to almost forty, without accounting for unregistered weapons.

"In a brief lapse of time, the colony's residents switch from [being] passive to aggressive and vice versa, in unison reaching the point of uttering guttural sounds, by which they alert one another [that it's time] to pivot to a different course of action," Álvarez noted.[12]

In September 1996, the detectives once again approached the colony and tried to serve the detention order, only to discover that the colonists had installed a wooden gate, fastened with a chain and padlock, on the bridge over the Perquilauquén River. It wasn't there two days earlier. They asked a farmworker to open it, and a bus immediately appeared from inside the colony. It parked on the bridge, and some sixty men, women, and children—all farmworkers—got out. In perfect synchrony, they lined up across the width of the bridge, forming a human barricade in front of the police vehicles. No Colonia leader showed up, so the detectives decided to retreat to avoid an incident.

The PICH officers began to put up posters across the region. The heading read, "Wanted: Paul Schäfer Schneider." The poster included his personal details and noted that he was wanted for sexual assault. If anybody had information about him, they should call one of Department V's two telephone numbers for Internal Affairs in Santiago.

The posters, which were widely disseminated, contained a photo of Schäfer facing the front, wearing a half smile and a dark overcoat. The detectives had obtained it from the Parral Traffic Department with the help of a colleague in that city. From that same source they also obtained a file of exams performed on Schäfer when he got his driver's license. The vision test indicated that he had 75 percent vision in his right eye, even though that eye was a prosthesis, said Álvarez. It was another of the favors granted by public employees.

The Return

On November 2, 1996, Judge Norambuena sent an order to the head of Department V, directing the department to enter and raid Colonia Dignidad's properties in Parral, Bulnes, and Santiago. The order authorized officials to force locks and break in through nonguarded, regularly used entrances and—if necessary—have detectives go undercover.

The judge also asked them to photograph and map the spatial layout of these places, gather information about the boarding school, determine who attended it and who collaborated with it, and question the minor-age children they found. They could be accompanied by interpreters and law enforcement technical experts, the judge added.

The plainclothes police and Department V leadership set about planning the operation. There would be multiple, simultaneous raids carried out on the Colonia Dignidad estate near Catillo, the restaurant in Bulnes, and the large house that the colony owned, located on Campos de Deportes Street, in one of Santiago's middle-class residential neighborhoods. The operation had to be very carefully planned to prevent leaks.

In the meantime, Prefect Henríquez reexamined the final details surrounding the arrival in Chile—under strict secrecy—of the German citizen Wolfgang Kneese, the young colonist who escaped in 1966, when his surname was Müller. Now, exactly three decades after his departure from Colonia Dignidad, he was returning to the country with his wife to offer testimony before the court in Parral. He was eager to do so but only with the promise that he and his wife could count on police protection during their stay. He arrived on November 5 and spent a week in Chile.

The sentence handed down against him in the 1960s for slandering Colonia Dignidad remained in effect—but applied to the man named Wolfgang Müller. With his new surname, Kneese, he passed through the usual International Police and passport checks in the Santiago airport without any problems. Luis

Henríquez and other police officials were waiting for him outside. He was taken to a residence the German consul had made available. Early the next morning, Henríquez came by to pick him up and drive him to Parral to testify before Judge Norambuena. Four people made the trip: two detectives, Kneese, and the German consul. No one knew he was in Chile, or so they thought.

Despite the extreme measures taken by the police to ensure that Kneese's arrival and trip down to Parral should go unnoticed, the colonists nonetheless found out about it. Awaiting the final coordination of their arrival at the court, the police stopped at a gas station near Parral to get some coffee. In that brief period of time a car drove up at high speed, braked, and parked on the other side of the highway. A man got out of the car, and Kneese immediately identified him.

"It's Hartmut Hopp," he said.

"He wanted to confront Hopp [Schäfer's right-hand man and director of the Colonia hospital], but we held him back," relates Henríquez.

Hopp crossed the road and looked at Kneese out of the corner of his eye. Then he went into the gas station's bathroom, and Henríquez followed him inside.

"Hopp was at the urinal pretending to relieve himself but was banging his head against the wall," says Henríquez. "It was odd. I sidled up next to him, and he looked at me. It was as if I had seen the devil."

The doctor quickly left the bathroom and crossed the highway. His wife, Dorotea, was waiting for him in the car.

"How did he know?" the consul, flummoxed, asked.

The question hung in the air, unanswered. Department V's chief had notified only the court, and Judge Norambuena, says Henríquez, was "tight-lipped."

Dark-Skinned, Short, and Poor

The November 1996 raid required additional manpower, so more detectives were requested from around the region and from different specialized units in Santiago and other cities. Police officers were also added to the mission from the Immigration Department and from Department V, which numbered on the order of twenty staff, including those working in Internal Affairs or on human rights cases, plus administrative employees and drivers. Everyone in Department V was assigned to the operation. Among them was one of its newest members, Sandro Gaete.

The young detective was brand new to Internal Affairs, having joined the unit in October. He came from the Robbery Brigade but had notable experience dealing with sexual crimes, particularly serial rapists. On these cases, he was called upon to work with Villanueva. Gaete joined Department V on her recommendation and that of her first tutor, Hugo Rebolledo, one of the original members of the Analysis and Institutional Coordination Commission.

Gaeta was of Abel Lizama's generation. He had enrolled in the Investigations School in 1986, after studying literature for a year at the University of Chile. He abandoned those studies to help his family financially. They lived in Villa Sur, a neighborhood near the militant Santiago settlement of La Victoria. His mother brought him up virtually by herself.

In the early months of 1996, while serving in the Robbery Brigade, he was contacted by Rebolledo, who was back in Department V but assigned to internal affairs matters. Department V's chief, Luis Henríquez, wanted to create a small unit to investigate detectives' ties to narcotrafficking. Rebolledo recommended that Gaete join. This group, however, never actually became functional. But Gaete and other detectives were already in Department V. So Henríquez assigned them all to Internal Affairs, except for Gaete, to whom he proposed an assignment in the human rights area, which needed extra hands.

"When I started working on human rights I was well versed in all that they signified. I have an uncle who was a political prisoner. My grandmother, a footwear factory worker, was a socialist and union leader. My mother had always been a leftist, and we lived in a working-class neighborhood. So, I didn't just discover human rights when I joined Department V in 1996," he states.

One of his first cases that year was the disappearance of the Communist leader José Luis Baeza. Baeza was detained in 1974 and tortured in the Air War Academy. Gaete was working the case when they sent him south, just in time to participate in the huge operation to get inside Colonia Dignidad.

D-Day

The night before, the majority of Department V police put up in Talca, but a few spent the night in Molina, at the home of detective René Sandoval's family.

Sandoval was unable to take part in the operation because he was getting married the day of the raid. Some of his colleagues came by Molina later to celebrate with the couple.

María Soledad Villanueva decided to dye her hair, since some of the colonists and their Chilean allies had no trouble placing her. In the string of legal actions presented by the colony's lawyers, reference to a "blond" detective always came up, and it was she.

"I changed the color of my hair to black and cut it really short. A fellow officer also had her appearance altered, but she wound up looking like me, and they wanted to hit her," recalls Villanueva.

The police massed at dawn on Saturday, November 30, in the Talca prefecture. Luis Henríquez delivered instructions and parceled out tasks and objectives to those present. The raids began at seven in the morning. The police arrived at each of the three sites—the estate in Parral, the restaurant in Bulnes, and the house in Santiago—with two judicial orders: one to detain Schäfer and the other to locate and bring out a child, ASV, from the boarding school, whom the colonists refused to hand over to his family.

Henríquez headed up three sets of forces that entered the Parral estate: the Department V teams and the specialized units from Santiago and Talca. In all, they comprised eighty police officers in twenty-two police vehicles, plus two motorcycles. It was not an extravagant number, given the enormous size of the estate's property.

Problems began as soon as they reached Parral. The police vehicles were making their way along the dusty route leading to Colonia Dignidad when they encountered a Mercedes-Benz bus filled with colonists coming toward them. The bus was being driven at high speed down the middle of the road, and it wasn't by chance. All the police vehicles managed to swerve around the bus, except for one, which was forced into a ditch. Several officers helped drag it out.

In subsequent raids, the police discovered why the colonists always knew in advance of their approach. It wasn't just because of the contacts they had with local authorities and police but also because of a lookout post they manned at the crest of a hill. From that vantage point they had an open view of the Perquilauquén bridge and miles of roads leading to the estate. Spotting the dust raised by the vehicles invariably gave them ample time to hide Schäfer and prepare for the arrival of outsiders.

Now, at the entrance to the estate, a German colonist from Schäfer's inner circle began to film the police from close range. Police officers quickly moved him away from Henríquez and stripped him of his video camera. Everything happened amid the shouts and protests of the watch committee, a group of Chileans who took turns keeping permanent guard over the enclave.

"Afterward, their lawyers arrived. They didn't want to let us in," recalls Detective Gaete. "I didn't get it. I came from working in the Robbery Brigade, and here we had to practically ask permission to enter."

One of the German leaders, Hans Jürgen Blanck, came out and confronted the police; he was furious.

"This is private property, and you are committing an abuse!" he upbraided them.

Henríquez ordered some of the officers to verify the identity of everyone who was blocking their passage and gave Blanck a peremptory order: "Open the gate!"

Ultimately, the colonists conceded that they had to give way to the police.

"I brought along specialists from the crime lab and capable detectives from different units, because we knew that we were going to come up against people who were armed. We had already been informed that they had weapons by pastor Adrián Bravo, who supplied really valuable information about Colonia Dignidad," says Henríquez.

Up to this point, the police officials who had investigated the sexual abuse complaints lacked direct knowledge of the site where they occurred; all they had to go on were the statements and descriptions of the location inside the guesthouse as provided by the children.

A group of police, led by Henríquez, reached the guesthouse. The colony called it the Freihaus. Schäfer's bedroom was somewhere in it. They had changed things around but not enough. The children had described the tile at the entrance to the house, and because that hadn't been tampered with, the detectives knew they were in the right place.

They reached the bedroom, but nobody had the keys to open it. The colonists said they had no idea who might have them, and besides, they didn't understand the language. The police always faced the same barrage of excuses.

"Sir, we can't get in here because the windows and doors are reinforced. We would have to use explosives to get in," one of the specialists pointed out.

"The colonists hounded us; they had orders to create problems for us, intimidate us. They were like robots. I realized that tempers were fraying on both sides. There was pushing and shoving, and the firearms they stored under the roof of the main office were now in sight. So, I ordered a retreat," states Henríquez.

Leaving the guesthouse, they ran into a large group of colonists outside who struck a defiant posture and began to shout in German. They were young, athletic types; some were carrying tools. Their shouting, however, was in the form of strange sounds, not words.

"We couldn't predict what might happen if we encountered Schäfer, but we figured it would be pretty challenging because lots of the colonists, especially the young men, were wearing long raincoats and concealing, as was evident, something inside them. We assumed they could be rifles, though we never saw them. These colonists formed themselves into a shield and emitted guttural noises. It was wild, out of control," recalls Álvarez.

The police inspected and photographed the layout of the colony's buildings, the storehouses full of grain, and the landing strip, while the colonists got in their way at every step. They even tried, at the hospital, to lock inspector Claudio Pardo in a walk-in freezer. It was impossible to cover the full extent of the property.

Henríquez had proceeded with caution, which did not sit well with everyone. Afterward, some blamed him for not having managed to detain Schäfer that day because he hadn't wanted to break down the door to his bedroom. It was highly unlikely, however, that the fugitive was there. Colonia Dignidad's security system let its inhabitants know about approaching vehicles at least thirty minutes before they arrived at the main gate. That was more than enough time for Schäfer to hide.

At some point the police took a lunch break to eat some of the food they had brought with them. After the experience one of the officers had earlier, Henríquez had forbidden them from taking any food or drink from the colonists.

"We had all heard about the poisoning of a Department V colleague who had gone into the restaurant in Bulnes to leave a summons for Schäfer. They let him in and offered him some juice, but on the way out his stomach began to hurt, and he ended up in the hospital," says Freddy Orellana.

Hours later the detectives withdrew from Colonia Dignidad, peppered by the shouts, insults, and blows of its supporters gathered outside. The former Independent Democratic Union senator Hernán Larraín characterized the operation as "high-handed" and "repressive in nature, doing violence to the life and actions of its inhabitants."[13]

They couldn't come face-to-face with Schäfer this time, but at long last they had gained access to the place where he raped and abused boys and were able to confirm the complaints. They all lined up.

A Surreal Invitation

Some fifty officers, from both Santiago and the surrounding region, entered the restaurant in Bulnes under the command of officer Pedro Valdivia from Department V. The entrance gate was locked. It was seven in the morning, and no one was around other than some colonists and workers who slept in the restaurant's rooms and offices. The police buzzed the intercom, but nobody answered, so they cut through a barbed-wire fence and got in that way.

For the next three hours the officers split into six groups, each inspecting a different part of the restaurant or its exterior: the road leading up to the restaurant, the area surrounding it, the road to the rock-crushing plant, the restaurant's interior rooms, the aerodrome, and the landing strip. They cut away and breached wire and padlocks and checked bedrooms, storerooms, and offices.

The Homicide Brigade's regional detective, Sergio Claramunt, had the job of watching the gates that kept people out of the restaurant's grounds.

"We got in, and the looks shot at us were not very friendly," he recalls. "We didn't exactly get a warm reception. Afterward they [grudgingly] accepted that they had to show us the different areas. They didn't speak much Spanish."

A native of the region, Claramunt was relatively new to Concepción's Homicide Brigade, having previously been assigned to different units in Santiago and Tomé. Now he was part of the contingent of officers, plucked from all the region's brigades, participating in the Bulnes raid. Two decades later (2016–17), Claramunt became the national head of the PICH's unit dealing with human rights crimes.

Meanwhile, on the inside, they asked for Schäfer, but nobody had the slightest idea about him, so they said, or they simply ignored the officers. Gerhard Laube, who introduced himself as the restaurant's manager, said it had been months since he'd set eyes on Schäfer and he didn't know where he was.

A few of the colonists let go of some dogs, which attacked a group of detectives. Two of their comrades started filming the goings-on, but the police seized their video cameras.

They came across a huge quantity of closed-circuit communications equipment that monitored all movement inside and outside the restaurant and an office, with several monitors, from where all the staff's movements were captured.

A shipping container had been adapted into a bedroom for employees living on the grounds. It was also equipped with monitors to keep track of workers' movements in the rock-crushing plant.

Meanwhile, some 265 miles to the north in the capital, fourteen or so officers from specialized Santiago police units, commanded by deputy superintendent Alex Sanhueza, showed up at the colony's house. Since the entry gate was not manned, they jumped over the venerable house's outer wall. At that point, one of the sect's leaders, Albert Schreiber, appeared and let them in. They stepped into a large dining room, where they read out the judicial order. Following that formality, they photographed and made a record of everything: not just the living spaces, offices, dining rooms, and bedrooms but also the chimneys, roofs, antennas, the furnace and heating system located in the basement, security and communications equipment, storerooms, the electrical system, a Mercedes-Benz truck, a Mitsubishi van, and a platform that provided access to a bunker in the interior patio.

"What surprised me most was the sheer size of the house. From outside it seemed like an ordinary house, but inside it contained things you wouldn't have imagined. It had several basement levels, served by [no less than] an elevator," notes detective Freddy Orellana, who took part in another raid on the house the following year.

At the back of one of the two rooms in the basement, the detectives found a cord in the ceiling that activated a device that opened an interior wall. The wall had a metal box built into it. In one of the room's other walls there was a control panel with three buttons. When the officers pressed the buttons, they heard an explosive sound on the patio. They had accidentally detonated four explosive noise charges located at different points in the outer wall. When they left, they saw what remained of the devices and, leading from them, an electrical cable that went up and got lost in the tangle of a climbing plant.

Schreiber told them that he no idea the bunker or the explosive charges were there. But before the police left, he cordially invited Deputy Superintendent Sanhueza to visit Villa Baviera's restaurant in Bulnes and sample its products.[14]

After the simultaneous raids in Parral, Bulnes, and Santiago, the writs of protection filed by the colony multiplied in number, but none of them achieved their purpose. They were all worded the same, as were the names of the supposed witnesses. They claimed intimidation, high-pressure tactics, threats, rough treatment, insults, and police violations of the freedom and security of the Germans and their Chilean friends.

"They introduced an avalanche of writs of protection. It was their way of seeking to neutralize the investigations. With each appeal they accused us of violating their rights, that we had physically struck the elderly, women, and children. It was horrible, they accused us of the most serious crimes, but they could never prove anything," states Henríquez.

The raids did not turn up the child ASV, because he was farther south that day, in Puerto Montt, with Olalia Vera and her husband, Hugo Hidalgo. Six days later, however, the couple brought him to the court in San Carlos. After making a statement, Vera promptly bundled the child into a taxi, pressed some money into his hands, and told the taxi driver to head to the San Miguel road. The child needed to wait for her there. Meanwhile, Olalia Vera posed as an anguished mother in front of reporters who were waiting outside the court.

ASV was found by the Carabineros and returned to his family. By order of the court of Parral, the Department V detectives finally managed on that same night of December 5 to take the boy and his parents to Santiago so he could undergo physical and psychological examinations and then receive whatever special assistance he might need.

"I Know You"

On January 14, 1997, as a result of the multiple complaints and lawsuits involving Colonia Dignidad, the government requested that the Supreme Court step in and appoint a senior judge. The task fell to Hernán González, who sat on the Talca Appeals Court. González took on all the cases related to the German enclave as of March 1997.

There were more than fourteen ongoing legal proceedings tied to the colony in different courts in Santiago and southern Chile. They encompassed not only sexual abuse but also participation in a criminal organization, the abduction of minors, causing damage to public property, illegal exercise of a profession, not handing over minors, attacks against authority, partial destruction of a government vehicle, identity theft, obstruction of justice, medical negligence, inducing minors to abandon their home, and covering up sexual abuse. In addition, there were twenty-five cases in process over tax crimes. And still, the government did not move to dismantle Colonia Dignidad.

At the top of this list, of course, Schäfer's detention was still pending.

Judge González went to the colony shortly after assuming the case. This wasn't just any inspection visit. He went there with several children and their mothers to examine firsthand the site where things had occurred. In addition to González, several others entered the estate that afternoon: the local judge, Jorge Norambuena; CPP and his mother; and three other mothers whose sons—between eight and thirteen years old—were in the boarding school. They wanted their children returned to them, but all they encountered was a wall of silence.

Judge Norambuena authorized the lawyer Hernán Fernández to accompany them. Fernández had scarcely slept the previous night. Aware that Schäfer was capable of anything and that the colonists had weapons, he was tormented by the possibility that the sect's leader might emulate David Koresh in Waco[15] or Jim Jones in Guyana[16] and cause a massacre of his own people.

Once the visitors were inside, the colonists videoed what was happening, hindered access to the sites they wanted to see, insulted the mothers, flaunted the judge's instructions, and assaulted the detectives. They managed to get into Schäfer's bedroom but were forced to quickly withdraw in the face of insistent harassment by the colonists.

"The situation was getting completely out of hand, because they edged violently toward the judge, and we had to get him out of there. The colonists were really incensed about the investigation," relates Juan Álvarez.

Some days later, two of the children were finally handed back to their families but not the third, fourteen-year-old Rodrigo Salvo. In his case, their cruelty was such that they held on to him for almost two years to prevent him from testifying. He was one of Schäfer's pet victims. Prying him loose from the colony's grasp cost considerable effort and time.

Five arrest orders were issued for Schäfer in 1997, and Judge González requested one after another action and inspection inside the estate. The detectives traveled either from Santiago or from other units around the country to carry these out, after which the judge issued new orders.

Midyear, in June, the colony's leaders staged a maneuver to distract the police, causing the police to launch a fruitless search in Argentina. One of the men close to Schäfer, Max Rudolph, the pilot of Concepción's Air Flying Club, checked into a hotel in Bariloche, Argentina, under the name and with the identify card of the colony's fugitive head.

Since an international order for his capture was in effect, the Argentinian police went to the hotel to arrest him, and the man who pretended to pass for Schäfer tried to flee through a window.

The police, frequently combining forces from the PICH and the Carabineros, carried out a dozen raids all through the year in search of the pederast. For the most part, the purpose was simply to look into a specific matter, but two of the raids—in June and November 1997—were of much greater magnitude.

Six months into his investigation, Judge González had indicted fifteen people: eight German leaders and seven Chileans, including Olalia Vera, for obstruction of justice, abduction of minors, persuasion of children to abandon their homes, and refusal to hand back minors. Those indicted also included Dr. Hopp, for covering up the sexual assaults and obstructing the judicial investigation. The judge ordered him held in custody for several weeks in the Parral jail.

Protect the Children

The years 1996 and 1997 were intense and draining. The setbacks and grow-ing pressure from the courts on Colonia Dignidad's Achilles' heel—the sexual abuses by its top leader—provoked an equally intense campaign of harassment and obstruction of justice on the part of the colony's leadership and local sup-port committees. The colonists needed to prevent information from leaking and ensure that the children stopped reporting the abuses. And above all, they had to protect Schäfer.

At the same time, the colonists and their loyal Chilean friends never ceased harassing and threatening the victims and their families, including the family of the boy who had spirited CPP's note out of the boarding school. The idea was to frighten and intimidate them from coming forward and testifying.

They made a practice of driving by at night in their oversize pickups, shining their headlights at the houses, illuminating the interiors. One of the mothers complained that members of the Villa Baviera Hospital's friends committee came to her house to threaten and insult her. They went so far as to warn her that they would contract someone to harm her. Another woman friendly with the colonists, Elma Gutiérrez, constantly intimidated and threatened one of her neighbors, Verónica Fuentes. Fuentes continued desperately to try and get back her son, Rodrigo Salvo, who was still being held by the colonists.

Another mother, Rosa Verdugo, had to send her son to live with his grandmother to keep him safe. Members of the colony's friends committees approached Verdugo's employers to convince them to stop using her laundry services.

And Jacqueline Pacheco, the first mother to file a complaint about the rape of her son, continued to be provoked and harassed by the colony's supporters. Their chosen method was to drive by her house and photograph and film her at all hours.

Pastor Adrián Bravo was also the constant target of scare tactics. In the eyes of the colony, he stood out as one of its worst traitors. Throughout the night and at dawn cars drove around his neighborhood and parked nearby. Pamphlets were tossed out of vehicles with a crudely written message: Bravo had better keep a watchful eye on his wife, because she was cheating on him with men from "V," a reference to the PICH's Department V. Bravo also required police protection.

All these and similar actions, noted detective Sandro Gaete in a report to Judge González, "are taking place as part of an organized campaign to instill fear and cast aspersions . . . with the purpose of creating an atmosphere of insecurity and helplessness that leads them to quit submitting their complaints."[17]

In Santiago, the lawyer Hernán Fernández's apartment was robbed twice in 1996. The first time, they rummaged through everything, pulled out boxes, and scattered his papers over the floor but only took his laptop and a television, leaving behind anything else of value. The intruders managed to get in without breaking any of the door's three locks. The second robbery occurred when Fernández was in Parral and his cleaning lady was inside. Hearing the front door open, she came out to see what was happening. Two men, again entering without damaging the locks, abruptly ran off.

The following year in the capital, the lawyer had colonists following him. He passed one in the street near his apartment.

"They were permanently watching me," states Fernández.

Sometime later, a former colonist told Fernández about a sinister plan, hatched by Schäfer in March 1997, that he had been ordered to lead. Fernández relates:

> Schäfer cleverly convinced them that they needed to save the community from its "ruinous enemies" and showed them photos of me, Judge Norambuena, and Luis Henríquez. I seemed to be the most vulnerable target, and he ordered them to put sarin gas in my car one day at dawn. They followed

me all day, from the moment I left the hotel. They never came across my car, since they were ignorant of the fact that I didn't have one, so they got back at night, unsuccessful [in their mission], to receive a dressing down from Schäfer. A remorseful colonist who later went to Germany told me this, and along with telling me what he had done, thanked me, with tears in his eyes, that he had been able to gain his freedom and have a family.

Years later, the lawyer found out from another former colonist that the pederast had been very upset by the failure and issued instructions that a future attack should be carried out against both him and Pastor Bravo, with whom he went around on occasion visiting victims.

"This time his instruction was short and sweet: they should chop us up and bury us, without further ado," states Fernández.

The efforts to release the underage youths, hand them over to their families, put them through medical exams, begin reparative therapy, and ease them toward telling their painful and deeply personal stories to the police, social workers, psychologists, and judges required a huge logistical effort, the deployment of numerous resources, and great human staying power.

To further this work, Judge González issued more investigative orders to ascertain the whereabouts of missing children from the boarding school as well as the whereabouts and movements of the persons responsible for hiding them. González also tried, through his orders, to return the children to their families.

For his part, Judge Norambuena continued extending or drawing up new measures to protect the youths, their families, and witnesses. The Supreme Court had charged him with investigating and assessing the risk factor in Colonia Dignidad for both boys and girls under eighteen years of age. By the end of November 1997, fifteen underage youths inside the enclave were categorized as being in physical or psychological danger, unable to appear before the courts.

As for the kidnapped Rodrigo Salvo, the colonists dragged him far and wide across Chile. Wherever they went, they first sent an advance party to verify that the police or people in the area would not react adversely. Then days later the group holding the youth showed up.

Since there was an all-points bulletin out on him, the detectives received clues from colleagues in widely different places about his possible location. Local police often carried out checks, and occasionally detectives Sandro Gaete, María Soledad Villanueva, and Fabián Pacheco—from the Talca prefecture—traveled to some of these spots with their driver, Luis Núñez. Eventually, they covered large areas of southern Chile looking for the youth.

At last, in 1999 when the situation had become untenable, one of the colony's lawyers, Cirilo Guzmán, handed Rodrigo over to a juvenile court.

A Sensational Escape

It had been more than thirty years, dating to Wolfgang Müller's flight in 1966, since Colonia Dignidad had witnessed an escape as sensational as that pulled off by Tobías Müller in mid-1997.

It was the night of July 26, and the colonists were celebrating the founding of their community in Chile. The main event was taking place at the entrance to the estate. Twenty-four-year-old Tobías had decided to flee. He had been brought to the sect from Germany by his grandmother in 1983, when he was ten. She'd promised his parents that the child would be protected and receive an education in Chile. The reality was starkly different. Tobías went through his adolescence being raped repeatedly by Schäfer.

When the PICH began its periodic raids on the estate, the young man played a double role. On the one hand he joined in the shouting against the police, but on the other, when Luis Henríquez passed by him, he whispered, "Please, help me."

"I told him in passing that I could help him, but only if he got out of there," relates Henríquez.

Tobías began to plan his flight with an eighteen-year-old Chilean friend, Salo Luna, a member of the Young People's Permanent Watch, one of the colonists' support groups. Luna, who didn't live in the estate but stayed there on weekends and over vacations, delivered a letter from Tobías to Judge González. Tobías explained in the letter that he wanted out of Colonia Dignidad. The judge summoned the young man to come before the court, but Schäfer would not allow that. Salo then looked for a helping hand from Pastor Bravo, who passed on the information to Department V and asked for their cooperation getting Tobías out of the enclave.

The police, however, feared it might be a trap set by the colonists, and they didn't trust Salo Luna. If their misgivings proved correct, they could be accused of kidnapping or illegal detention.

"We didn't know if it was a trap. Tobías was close to Schäfer. We were extraordinarily exacting. Any mistake made with respect to Colonia Dignidad meant losing control of the investigation. With the number of lawyers the colony employed, and its extensive resources, we took a great deal of care," explains Henríquez.

Late at night on July 26, both young men set their flight in motion. A support network also sprang into action. It was led by Pastor Bravo and Hernán Fernández and joined later by the former colonist Heinz Kühn and his son Peter as well as by German diplomats.[18] Wolfgang Kneese offered to take them in when they reached Germany.

Free of the estate, Tobías and Salo stayed in the Santiago residence of the German embassy's first secretary, with police protection provided by detectives from Department V.

Inspector Hugo Rebolledo and detective Lautaro Arias questioned Tobías Müller in the PICH's main building. The sessions and statements were lengthy and videotaped. By this point, Rebolledo had replaced Juan Álvarez as head of the team dedicated to investigating Colonia Dignidad.

There, in PICH headquarters, Tobías told them that the colony's leaders always knew ahead of time when a raid was going to occur. Several days before, he told them, someone from the Carabineros or one of the intelligence services placed a call to notify them of the police's plans. After that, a meeting was called to plan how to confront the raid. They discussed putting up a "passive defense," which entailed putting groups together in a fixed spot, with everyone then throwing themselves onto the ground, shouting, refusing to get up, in order to stop the police from advancing any farther. Schäfer, he said, delivered these instructions at the meeting. Tobías also told the detectives about the cameras concealed in the trees and at the estate's entrance.

"First, they prepared places from where one could film and take photos that were hidden from view, to have material [for] later, to take down details on each one of you, where you live and your name and what rank you have, all those things. And afterward they put them in an album, something like that, and they have a card for everyone," Müller assured the detectives in his broken Spanish.

"What would happen if they found Schäfer?" Rebolledo asked him.

"That would be something else again. They are ready to die to defend themselves, every one of them."

"What are the instructions they have about that?"

"They've talked it over but not come to any decision on it. What they're going to do is they are going to come up [against the police] in an armed confrontation."

"They are not going to let us bring Schäfer out?"

"No, under no circumstances. They're not going to let it happen."[19]

They had personal weapons and weapons of war—rifles, explosives, and grenades—and furthermore, they manufactured their own weapons, he added.

Schäfer hid during the raids in a spot near the landing strip, where there was an entrance to a concrete tunnel, Müller explained. He hid in different locations and constantly changed the place where he slept, but he was always on the estate and went around armed, said Müller. Only three men knew where Schäfer was during a raid, and one of them was always by his side on those occasions.

The plainclothes police flew Tobías Müller and Salo Luna to Talca in one of the PICH's light aircraft, so they could make a lengthy statement before Judge

Hernán González in the court of appeals. They left the next day for Frankfurt, accompanied by the German consul from Santiago, Sabine Collins.

A Science Fiction Movie

Almost one year after the first large-scale raid of Colonia Dignidad, the police staged a second raid of massive proportions in November 1997. Some 200 PICH and Carabineros officers entered the colony, accompanied by Judge González, in search of Schäfer. They failed to find him, but—over the operation's seven hours—they uncovered a complex network of tunnels, along with what one detective described as the elements of a "science fiction movie."

The first thing they did that morning right after entering the grounds was cut the telephone lines and sever the wire fencing around the aerodrome. A Carabineros helicopter and numerous officers occupied part of the landing strip to prevent the colonists' small planes from taking off, as had happened previously. Two managed to get in the air, however, despite the repeated police orders to abort takeoff.

"We knew that anything could happen," states Villanueva. "For example, we found that if we kicked a rock and it didn't budge, it was because the 'rock' was a movement sensor. Nobody told us how or where to look for anything, nobody cooperated with us; the Chileans who had been there were clueless, and I believe the Germans themselves didn't know all that there was."

It was like pulling at a thread without knowing what it would finally lead to. For Juan Álvarez, it was jolting to have on-the-ground confirmation that what he had read in Gemballa's book so closely matched what he encountered.

"The book said that one of the security measures was that they placed microphones and sensors in the trees. We climbed up a small hill and began to feel around in the trees. I came into contact with a branch that in fact was Styrofoam painted over and inside had a sensor and microphone. The book also referred to ground sensors, set at various places around the perimeter fencing that made an escape impossible," Álvarez said.

In terms of technology, Colonia and the PICH were worlds apart. The Germans in Colonia Dignidad possessed a sophisticated electronic monitoring network and cutting-edge gadgetry. The Chileans could barely rely on some walkie-talkies that, in any case, the colonists had jammed.

"What the media and Chilean society never understood was that we made our way into a place that was a veritable fortress, with a security apparatus that didn't exist in Chile and was brought from Germany. We went in one day and the next day the trees that were in one place appeared somewhere else, because they had been moved mechanically. They had every type of technology. We subsequently found out that the weapons and explosives that were discovered afterward had been hidden at the bottom of a lagoon," states Luis Henríquez.

The police were received in the usual way: with resistance, shouting, pushing and shoving, aggression, and denials. While the officers were checking different areas, the colony's leaders used a group of children to get in the way of their work. Detective Sandro Gaete described the tactic as follows: "The colonists rounded up a group of some fifty youngsters who marched in formation toward the police officers and began to hurl insults, as two colonists supervised their actions. This stunt was coordinated to perfection with the entrance of reporters . . . who proceeded to capture images of what was happening."[20]

Months later, the detectives were able to interview two of these children, Chilean brothers from the Young People's Permanent Watch. One of them was seventeen-year-old ES. He began to frequent the colony on weekends and during vacations, when he was younger. He eventually became one of Schäfer's favorites, his personal servant. When ES was twelve, Schäfer began repeatedly abusing him. In the first months of 1998, now free of the German enclave, ES filed a complaint against Schäfer and was part of a group of youths who sought justice. He explained what happened the day of the raid: "During the raid we heard a shout from 'Hamster' [Hans Jürgen Riesland], who was egging on the kids to make a fuss about the police's action in search of an innocent person who wasn't there, [by] making us sing in Spanish a song known by the youth as 'Hoy Amigo' and obstructing the police's actions with our bodies, at the same time they were calling on the media near us to witness that not even on All Soul's Day were they left in peace."[21]

His younger brother, eleven-year-old MS, said the goal was that "the media realize that we were happy there." Later, he added, they took the children to a spot near the school and congratulated them on their spirited performance.

ES added, anecdotally, that Colonia Dignidad's leaders called Department V the "Mongrel Department," Judge Norambuena "Pig Snout," and the press *perrodisten*, a combination of the words for dog and journalist.

Disaster

By this time, Paul Schäfer and his security team were already far from Colonia Dignidad, fleeing from the long—to this point uncorruptible—reach of the justice system. Tobías Müller's escape was a heavy blow. He could furnish vital information about hideouts and the operational methods and capabilities of Schäfer and the colony's leaders.

"His escape set off urgent meetings, and representatives of the colonists found themselves obliged to face Schäfer's rage and ask him to conceal himself somewhere else, because they were positive that the escapee would confirm that the leader was in Villa Baviera and would disclose the places where he hid himself during the raids," states Luis Henríquez.[22]

The time had come to once and for all get Paul Schäfer out of Chile. One of the colony's principal leaders, Hans Jürgen Riesland, planned the operation. The enclave's former security chief Erwin Fege asserts that in August 1997, one month after Müller slipped away, he drove the vehicle in which Schäfer fled the country. He left with his right-hand man, Peter Schmidt, and the youth Mathias Gerlach. Gerlach was born in 1971 in Colonia Dignidad's hospital as Carlos González and remained thereafter in the colony. On that cold winter night, Fege left them on the other side of the Perquilauquén River, in the Trabuncura sector. Two cars, each with a Chilean driver, were parked there, waiting for them. Waiting there, too, for his leader, was Riesland.[23]

Colonia Dignidad's pilot, Wolfgang Zeitner, had flown to Argentina the previous month, on July 31, taking with him Paul Schäfer's illegally adopted daughter, Rebeca. She was brought to the colony's hospital as an infant and never given back to her mother. Zeitner and Rebeca set things up in anticipation of the fugitive's arrival. Schäfer and his inner circle settled down on a piece of rural land in Chivilcoy, some 160 kilometers west of Buenos Aires.

Other versions have Schäfer leaving Chile at the beginning of 1998, not in August 1997, as Fege tells it. The whole affair would be clarified years later, but Schäfer's departure represented the definitive blow in the debacle that befell the German community. At the end of 1997, the number of complaints filed and presented in the courts against Schäfer for the abuse of minors totaled nine, and Judge González ordered an investigation of the entry into and departure from the country of 286 colonists, including Schäfer's adopted daughter.

Welcome to Talca

Luis Henríquez set himself up in Talca—some ninety kilometers north of Parral—as 1998 got under way. The naming of the PICH's new high command at the end of 1997 brought a shuffling of positions. Superintendent Pedro Valdivia remained in Department V's leadership, and Henríquez was appointed head of the Talca prefecture. He would no longer have direct control over the entirety of human rights investigations but would stay on top of what happened in Colonia Dignidad. He took the driver Luis Núñez with him.

"By now, Colonia Dignidad was not just a problem of Schäfer's pederasty; it was a human rights problem. And Henríquez was in Department V, so he was the ideal man to send down there. Human rights groups trusted him," explains former PICH director Nelson Mery.

One of the first things Henríquez did, as the newly installed chief of the Talca prefecture, was to assure that Wolfgang Kneese—who in 1966 was the first to escape the colony—arrived safely in Parral on February 25, 1998, to offer his testimony to the court. For the second time—but on this occasion with a huge media presence—Kneese arrived heavily guarded by PICH officials, while a large contingent of Carabineros watched the exterior perimeter in case he was harassed or provoked demonstrations. Kneese testified for six hours. On leaving, he publicly urged the colonists to be "courageous" and to abandon the enclave and approach the court because "times have changed."[24]

For Prefect Henríquez, however, they weren't that different.

"I discovered that the network of informants and protection that Paul Schäfer had in Parral did not end there but extended to San Carlos, Chillán, and all around that area and the Bío-Bío region as well. I was hemmed in, with my hands tied. I moved around and they followed me. That was when I brought on Sandro Gaete," says Henríquez.

The year before, in November, Gaete had replaced Hugo Rebolledo as coordinator of the investigation into Colonia Dignidad in Department V. He continued in that role for years to come.

Gaete arrived in Talca in March 1998 to a warm welcome from the colonists. Opening the door to his house early one morning, he found a dead black cat in front of him, at the entrance.

"The front yard was around fifteen meters deep, so those guys did the work of killing the cat, coming into the garden and leaving it on the doorstep. Evidently, it was a way to intimidate me," relates Gaete.

Years later, one of Colonia Dignidad's escapees, Franz Baar, recounted that the colonists had forced him to kill a cat and dump it at the house of a top-level police official in Talca.[25] The house he described was Sandro Gaete's.

Continuous Surveillance

Colonia Dignidad was treated to another massive and, this time, surprise raid during the early morning hours of March 24, 1998. It marked the first of forty days of a "continuous watch" by day and night of the two police forces—plainclothes and the Carabineros—in an all-out effort to find Schäfer. The original thirty-day occupation order was extended by ten days. This raid was the biggest mounted thus far with the aim of capturing the fugitive leader, even though there were indications that Schäfer had already fled the enclave.

The operation was directed by the top leaders of the Carabineros stationed in the region, not the PICH, and a large percentage of the officers who participated in it were from the area or had lived there for a long time. These factors, as the children's defense lawyer, Hernán Fernández, pointed out, offered no guarantees that the operation would succeed.

At the conclusion of the first thirty days, Fernández submitted an official request to Judge González to put the PICH in charge of the operation, because it was entirely possible that some relationship existed between the colonists and the area's Carabineros. They weren't to be trusted, he said.

"A connection exists, historically, between the Carabineros and Colonia Dignidad," the lawyer maintained. Besides, "80 percent of the intelligence and investigatory work in Villa Baviera has been carried out by the Investigations Police, which provides assurance of incorruptibility and the absence of ties to the ex–Colonia Dignidad."[26]

But the judge did not change his mind.

The Carabineros positioned a helicopter on the landing strip in the colony to prevent aircraft from taking off. Similarly, PICH officers stationed themselves in the vicinity of the enclave so they could see which vehicles drove in and out.

"A man who lived on the other side of the Perquilauquén River and was harassed by the colonists kindly offered us space on his property, and from there we had an observation point," relates Henríquez.

A couple of days later, the police made two important discoveries. They found a system of cameras installed to surveil movements inside the estate and on its access roads within a two-kilometer radius and a tunnel under a white-painted gate near the colony's main entrance. From the outside it looked like a ventilation duct, but inside, the opening widened to a meter and a half and was lined with brick. It housed all kinds of cables. The man then serving as the colony's spokesman, Chilean Hernán Escobar, disavowed any knowledge of the tunnel. That, too, was the colonists' refrain whenever anything else was discovered during the forty-day raid.

During this period of "continuous surveillance," the officers from Department V did not spend nights on the estate. Instead, they got together every night in the Chillán hotel, where Henríquez gave out instructions, sorted out the teams, and explained the next day's goals. Then it was off to sleep and up by dawn.

"We went on covering the estate parcel by parcel, because we already knew its sections, and the layout of the entire area had already been mapped. Consequently, we could head for a particular spot, see what we found and what use it had for us in the investigation," explains Villanueva.

They spent the whole day in Colonia Dignidad. They ate what they brought with them, never deviating from Henríquez's strict instructions not to accept anything that came from the hands of the colonists.

The young women and girls were kept locked up in different areas. The leaders told them that it was for their protection, since the detectives could bother or mistreat them. As always, the colonists resisted the inspections. Communicating among themselves by two-way radio in German, they obstructed sites, denied access, filmed, took photographs, jammed the police's own radio communications, and patrolled back and forth all day long.

"They knew perfectly well who we were, so conversation [with them] wasn't easy and they were never friendly. At the beginning they were very hostile, but eventually some would shoot us a secret smile," says Villanueva.

Over several weeks, they found a network of tunnels, an electronic surveillance system, armored shacks, rooms set up for telemonitoring, hydraulic traps, some 500 movement sensors placed in gates, walls, trees, and camouflaged rocks, and a one-meter-high black plastic drum containing documents, videos, and photographs of and about the colony.[27]

The estate was so extensive that at times they even got lost.

On April 17, Judge González ordered the detention of six members of the colony's German leadership and one of the Chilean leaders living on the estate and indicted them as accessories to a crime. The occupation was reinforced that same day with around 300 police officers—plainclothes and uniformed—registration of all the colony's residents, and confiscation of all the weapons that might be found in their possession.

Scaling Technological Heights

Likewise, that same day, up-to-date ground-penetrating equipment capable of detecting anomalies, voids, and structures down to five meters below the surface was put to use for the first time. The equipment scanned the subsurface by means of electromagnetic waves. A reflected signal, triggered when objects or vacant spaces were encountered, projected an image onto a screen. The image varied according to the speed and intensity of the signal.

The police were finally able to match the Germans technologically, thanks to the collaboration offered by the Santiago engineering company, Geored. Its cofounder and general manager, Ángel Tamayo, had returned from exile in Germany. His was the only company in Chile in this period to have equipment of this type.

Tamayo's equipment was new; he had purchased it that same year. He and his staff were out in the field one day giving demos of its effectiveness when another Geored partner put Tamayo in contact with Carabineros in the Maule region. The police, with the Colonia Dignidad operation fully under way, wanted to confirm the existence of tunnels and their features. To do so, they needed Geored's services.

The company initially sent two technical staff with the georadar equipment: a geophysicist from Scotland, Ian MacInnes, and the engineer Agustín Jaque. The Carabineros brought them directly to the guesthouse on Colonia's grounds, where they scanned the subsurface and located a kind of underground chamber along the length of a floor railing that separated the dining and living rooms.

In the wake of this discovery, the Carabineros decided to bring down Tamayo from Santiago the next day.

"The police knew that I spoke German, so they asked me to try to listen, whenever the situation called for it, to what the colonists were saying among themselves," states Tamayo.

But in that twenty-four-hour lapse, the signal—and therefore the image—had changed. What yesterday was observed as an entrance to a tunnel below the floor now appeared filled.

"The only explanation is that during the night they went into this—what resembled a tunnel—and filled it. They should have opened it immediately that first day before colonists had a chance to plug it," says Tamayo.

The colonists refused to cooperate by way of data or maps. They supplied false information or withheld it and obstructed access to different places, "turning the opening of every door into a true military operation," as noted in the technical report Tamayo furnished the Carabineros' police post in Catillo.[28]

Two days later, in an alfalfa field, they came across two bunkers a meter and a half deep. Both bunkers were impressively large, some fifteen meters long and twenty meters wide, and were connected by a network of tunnels. The police brought in backhoes to scoop up the earth until they reached the cement floor.

Tamayo, MacInnes, Jaque, and a group of Carabineros did the rounds of the main buildings and their adjacent land. In the reception house, the team detected the entrance to a tunnel under the floor and a large number and variety of cables that could be used for transmitting power, voice, data, and video signals. There were also switches to activate alarms. Some of the cables ran from the attic and disappeared into the depths of the subsurface. Outside the house they detected a structure that was three levels below ground and buttressed with supports underneath.

They examined the building that housed the kitchen, which Tamayo describes as a "labyrinth," where they found double walls, concealed to the eye at first glance. They also checked the grain storage room, known as "the barn," which was used in the 1970s to confine political prisoners. They detected an underground entrance there. Tamayo returned to Colonia Dignidad the following year with the georadar equipment to examine the space it led to, this time with Department V detectives, Judge Juan Guzmán, specialists from the crime lab, National Medical Service employees, and former political prisoners who identified the barn as the place where they had been held and tortured.[29]

A week later, they discovered some underground structures in the aerodrome hanger. They were so far down below the surface that the georadar was incapable of capturing their full dimensions. This place coincided with the site where Tobías Müller said Schäfer hid during the raids. They also discovered cables around the aerodrome; a portion were used as power lines and others to transmit videos. Some were not far from the surface and could be traced as they wound along various stretches, but they lost sight of others that soon disappeared belowground. Excavating these would be difficult because the shafts that contained the cabling were packed with stones.

Tamayo decided to make a trip back to Santiago to purchase a costly piece of equipment designed expressly to trace cables and determine their direction and depth. The person who sold it to him, a Frenchman by the name of Philippe Manieu, ended up traveling to the colony to collaborate on the work.

The next day, returning to the aerodrome, Tamayo was tracking a collection of cables, when they suddenly sank into the ground, deep down, where even the high-tech equipment could not follow them.

A short time before the extended occupation period ran out, the detectives came across an abandoned lookout post at the top of a hill. It was camouflaged in green, and its windows were covered with metal sheeting. The site gave the colonists a view of all the access points leading to Colonia Dignidad, and inside the lookout they found a telescope, binoculars, and telegraphic equipment.

While an array of discoveries had been made, the operation ended without succeeding in its primary objective—finding Paul Schäfer. Still, Luis Henríquez did not consider it a failure.

"For me it was a step forward in the investigative process, not a setback. We accomplished what had never been done before and we have to double-down on our efforts to bring about Schäfer's arrest. . . . It's obvious that another kind of technology has to be employed, because they are an organization with a military

structure and intelligence capabilities, can tap deep sources of funding and pos-
sess a remarkable range of high-tech equipment. We are talking about sky-high
amounts [of resources] to neutralize the work of the police," Henríquez said in
a press interview.[30]

Too Late

Perhaps no organization in Chile has managed to enjoy so much impunity, for
so many crimes, over so much time as Colonia Dignidad. Despite the mountain
of evidence accumulated since the first abused youth fled in 1966, neither the
Chilean nor the German state had taken decisive action against the pederast, nor
had they moved to dismantle his sect. Now it seemed to be too late.

"It was the courageous Chilean children and their families who began to put
an end to Colonia Dignidad," states the lawyer Hernán Fernández. "It wasn't
[through] Chilean state authority or power or state actions taken by Germany.
The Chilean boy[31] who opened the way for the investigation into Colonia Dignidad in 1996 finds himself in the march of history with the German boy[32] who
refused to accept his loss of freedom."[33]

In 2005 Paul Schäfer was located in Argentina and extradited to Chile.[34] Upon
arrival in the country, he was initially confined to a PICH unit in Santiago. Detective María Soledad Villanueva had gone into retirement that year but felt the
need to see Schäfer, to confirm with her own eyes that the man responsible for
destroying so many lives had at last been captured.

"I was disgusted, repelled by him. My satisfaction is that no child was ever
again raped by him thanks to our investigation, even though we didn't manage
to arrest him. Without a doubt it's the most important thing that I've done. It
was on a scale that still stirs my emotions. But I feel that a debt still exists on the
part of the state to make reparations to the children and their families for the life
they had," says Villanueva.

One of the minors who suffered "Permanent Uncle's" abuses, Rodrigo Salvo,
whom the colonists kept kidnapped for almost two years, died of cancer in 2007
at the age of twenty-four.

Another abused child, Danilo Cisternas, died two years earlier, while working
in the fields. A bolt of lightning struck him in the middle of an electrical storm.
He was twenty-three years old.

EPILOGUE

THE INCURSION INTO COLONIA DIGNIDAD was a climax of sorts for the Investigations Police team dedicated to working human rights cases. It was the most heavily resourced operation to that point. It tested the professionalism, determination, and tenacity of a small law enforcement unit confronted with serious limitations and obstacles on multiple fronts. It did not manage to capture Paul Schäfer, but Department V was consolidated as the specialized unit for human rights in the plainclothes police, even though the department's institutional mission continued to be internal affairs.

The teams formed within the Homicide Brigade to work with the judges appointed to investigate the human rights cases of greatest public notoriety gradually dissolved as the cases came to an end, whether because they were settled or because they languished in a judicial limbo—immobilized, amnestied, temporarily closed, or cast into the black hole of the military justice system. At the end of the 1990s, these teams found themselves effectively dismantled. Their officers were sent to other units or deployed on other missions. From that point through 2005, subsequent investigations into these same or other human rights cases were exclusively under the jurisdiction of Department V.

Prefect Luis Henríquez may have been reassigned 250 kilometers to the south, as head of the Talca prefecture, but he didn't part ways with investigating the dictatorship's crimes. On the contrary, along with Sandro Gaete and other detectives, he continued directing the pursuit of Schäfer and Colonia Dignidad's top leaders to see that they answered for the kidnapping, torture, and disappearance of political detainees, as well as for the sexual abuse of minors and their many other crimes.

Henríquez's transfer at the start of 1998 coincided with the opening of a new investigative angle. By the end of that year, it marked a distinct before and after with respect to the treatment of human rights cases.

On January 12, 1998, the then general secretary of the Chilean Communist Party, Gladys Marín, and the lawyer Eduardo Contreras filed the first criminal complaint against Pinochet for the 1976 abduction and disappearance of the party's leaders. The case was known as Calle Conferencia, in reference to the street where the victims were taken captive. By drawing lots, the appeals court assigned Judge Juan Guzmán to investigate the case.

Nobody had ever filed a judicial action aimed squarely at Pinochet. It was a moral imperative but considered by many to be a purely symbolic gesture, completely futile: the case would transfer over to the military justice system or be quickly closed through amnesty or the statute of limitations, as had happened up till then.

This unprecedented court action emboldened other victims' families and their lawyers to introduce new criminal complaints. By the end of 1998 there were more than a dozen. At first, Judge Guzmán handled all of them. Within a few years, he was overseeing nearly 100 human rights cases. Two or three police officials were permanently assigned as protection detail for the judge while he conducted investigations.

Laying Hands on the Untouchable

On October 16, 1998, Judge Guzmán was in the country's North with Department V police officials, taking part in excavations aimed at locating the remains of disappeared detainees. Meanwhile, on the other side of the Atlantic, the then lifetime senator Augusto Pinochet was arrested inside a London clinic.

The former dictator had relinquished command of the army in March of that year, becoming a senator for life, in accord with a provision established in the authoritarian constitution imposed by his regime in 1980. He was arrested on the order of Spanish judge Baltazar Garzón, who was investigating the crimes committed against Spanish citizens in Chile. After 503 days during which Pinochet remained under arrest in London while Spain's request for his extradition was contested, the British government decided to set him free for humanitarian reasons.

In Chile, meanwhile, hundreds of complaints filed against him were stacking up.

Pinochet's arrest in London sparked a radical change in the terms agreed upon for the transition back to democracy. It was a political test, and President Eduardo Frei's government understood it in that light, as could be read into the November 26, 1998, letter that Frei sent to British home secretary Jack Straw. The letter was dispatched just one day after the House of Lords ruled that Pinochet did not, as former chief of state, enjoy immunity from prosecution for crimes against humanity such as torture.

"The criminal charge that underlies the extradition request can be interpreted as [rendering] a political judgment on Chile's transition to democracy" that would "seriously disrupt the process of democratic transition and national reconciliation," in the words of the Chilean government.[1]

At the midpoint of the second transitional government, President Frei found himself at a crossroads over events already realized that eluded his control.

Managing to bring Pinochet back to Chile—as the right-wing opposition and the military demanded—with the promise of putting him on trial, would permit the government to reverse the serious deterioration in its image abroad, where no one understood why the democratic government was making such a great effort to bring the general home instead of allowing him to be tried in Europe.

In addition, this decision would demonstrate the government's consistency with respect to observing the universal principles of human rights. Just weeks before Pinochet's arrest, the government had signed the Statute of Rome, which created the International Criminal Court to try those responsible for genocide, war crimes, or crimes against humanity.[2]

At the same time, however, this course of action would entail a partial break with the explicit and implicit agreements that the government's coalition of parties reached with the military and the Right at the end of the dictatorship. It implied, in other words, removing the veil of impunity shielding the former dictator.

At this same time, too, the judiciary was undergoing its own transformations. A judicial reform approved during Frei's government set the obligatory retirement age for judges at seventy-five, increased the number of judges on the Supreme Court, and opened the highest court in the land to lawyers who hadn't pursued a judicial career. The package of reforms, which forced several Pinochet appointees to retire and was crowned by the appointment of eleven new members in 1998, signified a renewal of the Supreme Court.

This generational turnover and replenishment opened the way for the elevation of a new breed of judges more aligned with the evolution of international criminal law. Previously, the Supreme Court had ruled in favor of international human rights conventions and treaties over the country's own laws (i.e., the statute of limitations and the Amnesty Law) on only two occasions. It wasn't until September 9, 1998, that it "broke with its sustained tradition of applying the Amnesty Law."[3]

In the decisions they reached going forward, both the Supreme Court and the appeals courts began to recognize the primacy of international human rights treaties over national law in viewing human rights violations as crimes against humanity—overriding amnesty and the statute of limitations.[4] Nonetheless, questions continue to be raised to this day about how slow the authorities are to ramp up investigations and how light the sentences are for persons convicted of these crimes.

As the twenty-first century began, judicial investigations into human rights cases took on a new dynamic. When Augusto Pinochet again stepped onto Chilean soil in March 2000, his all-powerful aura had evaporated, and the fear that attended it had receded substantially. Pinochet's arrest and confinement in England had smashed the psychological barrier of his inviolability and empowered not only victims' families and their lawyers but a good part of Chilean society, which saw that justice could now apply to the former dictator.

The nine years Department V spent quietly accumulating information and experience, mapping the structure of the dictatorship's apparatus of repression, identifying its agents, and coming to understand its modus operandi fed into the new series of investigations. The same process occurred with its archive, doggedly built up by Department V's administrative staff.

"We had grown in the institution as investigators and were keenly aware that we had the backing of the courts and the government. We came through convinced of what we were doing and how to make progress and reach the point of pounding the table with the military. Having command of the issue we were investigating helped a lot. There wasn't much in the way of technology, so you yourself were transformed into a computer," as Abel Lizama puts it.

Within three years, the number of criminal complaints filed against Pinochet exceeded 330. The judges in charge of investigating them also ballooned in number, as did the police officers assigned to the cases. At the end of 2004, the new director of the Investigations Police, Arturo Herrera, created the Investigative Brigade for Special Affairs and Human Rights and named Sandro Gaete to head it. The group of detectives then busy with human rights cases was merged into this new specialized brigade, and as of January 1, 2005, Department V devoted itself solely to "internal affairs." The new brigade made its debut that same month when, yet again, it arrested Manuel Contreras.

Two years later, at the end of 2007, Director Herrera created a national-level human rights police body, the Jefatura Nacional de Delitos contra los Derechos Humanos. He named José Luis Cabión as its first chief. The Investigations Police's current Investigative Brigade for Crimes against Human Rights, led initially by Abel Lizama, came under its administrative authority.

Of all those who were on Department V's human rights investigative team in the 1990s, only two were still on active duty in 2021: deputy prefect Freddy Orellana and prefect inspector Lautaro Arias, who is now part of the institution's high command.

A Necessary Truth

For several detectives who participated in the human rights investigations in the 1990s, the experience—for different reasons—left a bitter taste. Some continued on an upward career path, but others saw their careers truncated or found themselves openly penalized, particularly during Herrera's directorship. He had been close to the Investigations Police's directors under the dictatorship.

Some of the plainclothes police active in the 1990s, such as Luis Henríquez, Sandro Gaete, and Rafael Castillo, attained prominence as public figures. Others labored in virtual anonymity: the names José Plaza, José Miranda, or Robinson Muñoz, to cite three examples, were rarely reported in the press.

Those were trying years. The detectives worked exhausting rounds with meager resources and faced constant harassment by the military as well as mistrust within and outside the institution while fulfilling a mission they never dreamed of and for which not one of them had been prepared.

"We all bear the scars," notes Luis Henríquez. "Healing from the pain takes a toll. A person reaps a lot of suffering with this job."

Some experienced anxiety, stress, and depression and felt emotionally drained. It was the result, as retired detective José Miranda spells out, of "knowing the darkest side of a human being when you grant him power, and the other side, the most terrible side, that of the victims and their families who are forced to wander about in that darkness."

Yet, whatever the burdens, these officers remember those years with pride and satisfaction. They feel they helped establish and deliver a necessary truth to the country, despite all the obstacles and the frustration in realizing that conditions are still not such as to achieve full, effective, and timely justice.

"That there was fear, yes—of course," confirms José Plaza. "There was fear because of what one was doing, and we were aware that it could all boomerang on us. It could be distressing as well. But it had to be done."

NOTES

Chapter 1

1. The abbreviation for the Investigations Police in this period was PICH, which will be used in this book. The abbreviation was changed to PDI in 2008.

2. In 1985, Chile's professional medical association suspended Carlos Pérez from its professional society because of his participation, several years earlier, in the extended torture of a woman who had been arrested.

3. The investigation conducted by Judge Adolfo Bañados focused solely on the death of Orlando Letelier. In 2012, however, the appellate court in Santiago ordered that the case be reopened in order to try those responsible for Ronnie Moffitt's death. In June 2016 Judge Mario Carroza prosecuted, in absentia, former DINA operatives Michael Townley and Armando Fernández, both then residing in the United States.

4. Fernández was handed over to the U.S. Department of Justice in January 1987; he reached an agreement with the department in exchange for his cooperation and spent eight months in prison. Since then, Fernández has lived in Florida under his true identity. In 1999 Zita Cabello, the sister of one of the victims of the Caravan of Death and a U.S. resident, took Fernández to court in Miami for the death of her brother, Winston Cabello, and in 2003 Fernández was found guilty of torture and assassination. In 2016 the Supreme Court of Chile approved a request that Michael Townley and Fernández be extradited to answer for the death of Ronnie Moffitt and in July 2017 approved another extradition request for Fernández, to face charges for the 1974 kidnapping and murder in Pisagua of a man who had been detained and arrested for political activities.

5. International League for Human Rights, *The Long Road to Justice: A Report on the Letelier-Moffitt Case* (New York: International League for Human Rights, 1991), 21.

6. International League for Human Rights, 17.

7. It has been proven in court that in October 1973 Joaquín Molina, who was at that time deployed in the Coyhaique regiment, participated in the kidnapping and disappearance of three people.

8. "Contreras dice sentir respaldo del Ejército," *La Nación* (Santiago), September 12, 1991.

9. In July 2012, Chile's Supreme Court sentenced Atiliano Jara to five years in prison and fined him for committing monetary fraud in the military hospital between 1991 and 1994 while he was its director.

10. The Chilean Supreme Court confirmed the indictments and their committal for trial two months later.

11. Rafael Otano, *Nueva crónica de la transición* (Santiago: LOM Ediciones, 2006), 99.

12. The military was represented or wielded influence in the structure and operations of the state through so-called authoritarian enclaves, as set down in the 1980 constitution; among these were the National Security Council, appointed senators, and a constitutional tribunal. These enclaves were entirely dismantled fifteen years after the return to a democratic system, under the 2005 constitutional reform signed into law by President Ricardo Lagos.

13. Provisional copy of analysis prepared before a luncheon meeting held by President Patricio Aylwin with the army's top-line generals corps, June 18, 1990, Archivo de la Presidencia de Patricio Aylwin, Universidad Alberto Hurtado, Santiago (hereafter cited as APPA).

14. The advisory committee acted almost as though it were a shadow military cabinet. Composed of more than seventy-five military officials, the committee took on a wide spectrum of institutional tasks with respect to the "country's development." It justified its existence on the basis of Pinochet's participation in the National Security Council. Despite the fact that the government considered it illegal, the advisory committee served as a useful bridge in facilitating discussions and negotiations between the government and the army. General Ballerino was the principal voice at the table representing Pinochet.

15. Ministerio Secretaría General de la Presidencia, "Informe de análisis," December 21, 1990, APPA.

16. Otano, *Nueva crónica*, 186.

17. During this period, the coalition comprised fourteen political parties, the principal ones being the Christian Democratic Party, the Socialist Party, the Party for Democracy, and the Radical Social Democratic Party.

18. Steve Stern, *Reckoning with Pinochet: The Memory Question in Democratic Chile, 1989–2006* (Durham, N.C.: Duke University Press, 2010), 21.

19. Patricio Aylwin, interview by Marcia Scantlebury, 2009, Audiovisual Documentation Center, Museum of Memory and Human Rights, Santiago.

20. Ministerio Secretaría General de la Presidencia, "Informe de análisis," January 4, 1993, 5, APPA.

21. Nathaniel C. Nash, "Pinochet Assails Chilean Rights Report," *New York Times*, March 28, 1991.

22. Sergio Bitar and Abraham Lowenthal, eds., *Transiciones democráticas: Enseñanzas de líderes políticos* (Barcelona: Galaxia Gutemberg, 2016), 104.

23. Thought up and propounded by Gonzalo Vial and other anonymous authors in the *Libro blanco del cambio de gobierno en Chile*, "Plan Z" entailed a plot in which "terrorist commandos" would physically eliminate the top leadership of the armed forces and the Carabineros as well as opposition union and political leaders during the 1973 Independence Day festivities. According to this book, underwritten by the CIA, the Cuban government would be behind this plan, and to implement it tons of Cuban and Czech armaments had been brought into the country, which had also been infiltrated by 13,000 "foreign guerrillas." See *Libro blanco del cambio de gobierno en Chile*, 21–23.

24. Secretaría General de la Presidencia, "Informe de análisis," October 5, 1990, APPA.

25. Secretaría General de la Presidencia.

26. Secretaría General de la Presidencia, "Informe de análisis," June 8, 1990, APPA.

27. As of October 2021, the Legal Medical Service has managed to identify twenty-three of them.

28. As of October 2021, the Legal Medical Service has managed to identify thirteen of them.

29. Bitar and Lowenthal, *Transiciones democráticas*, 102.

30. "Ejército presenta denuncia contra jefe de Investigaciones," *El Mercurio* (Santiago), June 25, 1990.

31. Secretaría General de la Presidencia, "Informe de análisis," July 6, 1990, APPA.

32. Secretaría General de la Presidencia, "Informe de análisis," June 15, 1990, APPA.

33. Secretaría General de la Presidencia.

34. Provisional copy of analysis prepared before a luncheon meeting held by President Patricio Aylwin with the army's top-line generals corps, June 18, 1990, APPA.

35. Secretaría General de la Presidencia, "Informe de análisis," July 6, 1990, APPA.

36. The exhumation was ordered by Judge Andrés Contreras, who served on the Twenty-Second Criminal Court of Santiago, following a lawsuit brought by the Vicariate of Solidarity alleging illegal internment.

37. Starting in 1993, the remains of many of these victims were identified by the Legal Medical Service and turned over to relatives. Years later, however, it was discovered that many of the identifications were wrong, such that the whole process had to be thoroughly reexamined. The Legal Medical Service is still immersed in this work.

38. Jaime Lepe remained in this post until 1998, when President Eduardo Frei vetoed his promotion because of his ties to the DINA. In August 2015 he was prosecuted for the Soria crime.

39. In 2007 Hugo Salas was sentenced to life in prison for the CNI's 1987 assassination of twelve members of the Manuel Rodríguez Patriotic Front as part of the agency's Operation Albania; he directed the CNI between 1986 and 1988.

40. Miguel Krassnoff has been convicted of multiple crimes and sentenced to a total of more than 460 years in prison.

41. "Actos y declaraciones del ejército y del Sr. Comandante en Jefe del ejército," January 14, 1991, APPA.

42. Notes taken by the author from "Fuerzas armadas," folder 5936, APPA.

43. "Tareas especiales Ministerio de Defensa 1992," n.d., APPA.

44. Ascanio Cavallo, *La historia occulta de la transición: Memoria de una época, 1990–1998* (Santiago: Editorial Grijalbo, 1999), 30.

45. Pascale Bonnefoy, "Cómo los archivos en microfilme de la dictadura de Pinochet se hicieron humo," *New York Times*, October 30, 2017.

46. Cavallo, *La historia occulta*, 138.

47. Hernán Ramírez committed suicide in August 2015 after being sentenced to twenty years in prison for belonging to a criminal organization and for the death of the DINA chemist Eugenio Berríos.

Chapter 2

1. Juan Seoane, *Los viejos robles mueren de pie: Relato autobiográfico de un policía leal* (Santiago: Universidad Bolivariana, 2009), 101.

2. Emilio Cheyre was the father of former army commander in chief Juan Emilio Cheyre Espinosa.

3. Luis Henríquez, *Los detectives de La Moneda* (Santiago: Editorial Occidente, 2014), 45.

4. Seoane, *Los viejos robles*, 101.

5. Seoane, 82.

6. Seoane, 86.

7. Henríquez, *Los detectives*, 100.

8. Henríquez, 126.

9. Juan Seoane went into exile in Argentina in December 1973 and later lived in Cuba and Mexico. In 1980 he relocated to Nicaragua, where he was engaged as an adviser to the nascent Sandinista police force. Seoane returned to Chile in 1982. He passed away in Santiago in June 2017.

10. Detective Quintín Romero was also dismissed some weeks after the coup.

11. Henríquez, *Los detectives*, 138.

12. David Garrido remained in the PICH until 1979.

13. In December 1978, as part of Operación Retiro de Televisores, their remains were exhumed. Some were discovered years later in Patio 29 of the Santiago General Cemetery, while others would have been pitched into the ocean. In October 2016 Judge Mario Carroza prosecuted twenty-three retired army officers in connection with these crimes.

14. Ascanio Cavallo, "Toro, o la manera en que muere la transición," *La Tercera* (Santiago), September 20, 2014.

15. Jorge Andrés Richards, "General (r) Horacio Toro: Por una democracia sin tutelaje de las armas," *APSI*, October 24–30, 1988, 17.

16. Mónica González, "General Horacio Toro: Carta de subalternos busca dañar a general Zincke," *Análisis*, April 24–30, 1989, 22.

17. Richards, "General (r) Horacio Toro," 19.

18. In 2005 a modification of the Organic Law came into force, establishing that the appointment of the top leadership would continue to be the exclusive privilege of the president of the republic, and its members would be selected and appointed by the president from among the police officials having the greatest seniority, those at the rank of prefect general or prefect inspector.

19. Retired colonel Jaime Krauss was aide-de-camp to the Chamber of Deputies until 2004, when he had to resign after being prosecuted for the murder of seven political prisoners in Pisagua in 1974.

20. Luis Toro and Horacio Toro were not related.

21. Gonzalo Asenjo participated in a CNI brigade and became the regional head of the agency in Copiapó, in northern Chile, between 1988 and 1990. He opted to retire in 1995 and in 2006 was prosecuted for being an accessory to the 1987 disappearance of

five members of the Manuel Rodríguez Patriotic Front. He committed suicide before receiving notification of his indictment.

22. Ministerio Secretaría General de la Presidencia, "Aporte fiscal en Investigaciones, informe de análisis," October 31, 1991, 6, Archivo de la Presidencia de Patricio Aylwin, Universidad Alberto Hurtado, Santiago (hereafter cited as APPA).

23. Gabinete del Director General de la Policía de Investigaciones, "Bases para una política policial," October 16, 1990, 3, APPA.

24. "Discurso de aniversario del director general Horacio Toro," *Revista institucional*, no. 73 (April–June 1990): 14.

25. "Discurso de despedida del director general Nelson Mery en 2003," cited in *Detective*, no. 167 (May 2016): 72.

26. "Discurso de aniversario," 13–17.

27. *Revista institucional*, no. 75 (October–December 1990), editorial page; *Revista institucional*, no. 72 (January–March 1990), 153.

28. *Revista institucional*, no. 72 (January–March 1990): 153.

29. Gabinete del Director General de la Policía de Investigaciones, "Bases para una política policial," October 16, 1990, 5, APPA.

30. Aylwin to Andreotti, September 13, 1991, APPA. The materials Italy donated arrived at the beginning of 1993.

31. Currently, those enrolled in the Academia Superior de Estudios Policiales who aspire to the career of detective must take courses on ethics and human rights, and since 2009 the Education Division has had a Department of Ethics and Human Rights.

32. Andrés Domínguez Vial, "Cuando la alianza entre los derechos humanos y la policía produce justiciar y seguridad," in *Activistas e intelectuales de sociedad civil en la función pública en América Latina*, ed. Carlos Basombrío (Santiago: FLACSO, 2005), 201.

33. Domínguez Vial, 201.

34. Domínguez Vial, 204.

35. In 1993, under the directorship of Nelson Mery, this arm of internal control was strengthened with the creation of Department VII, overseeing the control of police operations. This was further adjusted in 1997 through General Order No. 1496, which established procedures for collecting and chemically analyzing urine samples to detect drug use by personnel.

36. Gabinete del Director General de la Policía de Investigaciones, "Bases para una política policial," October 16, 1990, 6, APPA.

37. Head of Department V to general directorate, confidential memorandum, "Remite antecedentes y peticiona recursos humanos y materiales que indica," n.d., 1995.

38. The groups spotlighted were the Manuel Rodríguez Patriotic Front, the Lautaro Rebel and Popular Forces, and—to a much lesser extent—the Movement of the Revolutionary Left.

39. Roberto Hernández and Jule Salazar, *De la policía secreta a la policía científica* (Santiago, 2006), 124.

40. That is, 1994 to 2011.

41. *Revista institucional*, no. 76 (January–March 1991), 41.

42. Horacio Toro, "No hubo apremios ilegítimos," *La Nación* (Santiago), July 30, 1991.

43. Toro.

44. Human Rights Watch/Americas, *Un asunto no resuelto: Los derechos humanos en Chile al iniciarse la presidencia de Frei* (New York, May 1994), 14.

45. Report of the Special Rapporteur Nigel S. Rodley to the United Nations Human Rights Commission, Doc. E/CN.4, 1994, 31.

46. Department V, PICH general directorate, confidential note no. 357, July 22, 1994.

47. Human Rights Watch/Americas, *Un asunto no resuelto*, 60–61; "Fuerte reacción de presidencia de Brasil por caso de sicóloga detenida," *La Nación*, August 10, 1993; "Contradicciones sobre fecha de detención de la sicóloga," *La Nación*, August 11, 1993.

48. "Gobierno desmintió torturas a brasileña," *La Nación*, August 8, 1993.

49. Department of Bilateral Policy of Chile's Ministry of Foreign Relations, *Visita oficial a Chile del Excmo. Presidente de la República Federativa de Brasil, Señor Itamar Franco*, 1993, 100.

50. In March 1994, the Supreme Court withdrew the charges against Tania Cordeiro. Once again a free person, she was able to return to Brazil. In 1998, Solís sentenced eight detectives to a prison term of 540 days but released them from having to serve the time.

51. Mónica González, "Si se comprueban torturas, yo renuncio," *La Nación*, August 15, 1993.

52. Committee against Torture, *Examen de los informes presentados por los estados partes de conformidad con el Artículo 19 de la Convención, Chile*, UN Doc. CAT/C/20/ Add.3, 1994.

53. "195 denuncias por violaciones a DD.HH. entre 1995–1996," *La Nación*, January 31, 1997.

54. Former PICH director Nelson Mery declined to reveal this person's identity.

55. "Relación de personal PICH servicio activo que desempeño funciones en organismos de seguridad," sección análisis de derechos humanos de la Jefatura Nacional de Delitos Contra los DD.HH., January 30, 2008.

Chapter 3

1. María Eugenia Camus, *La Cutufa: Su historia secreta* (Santiago: Editorial Planeta, 2001), 174.

2. Secretaría General de la Presidencia, "Informe de coyuntura no. 57," November 1990, Archivo de la Presidencia de Patricio Aylwin, Universidad Alberto Hurtado, Santiago (hereafter cited as APPA).

3. Secretaría General de la Presidencia, 5.

4. Dr. Elías Escaff directed the Institute of Criminology between 1991 and 2003.

5. Secretaría General de la Presidencia, "Informe de análisis," January 25, 1991, 2, APPA.

6. Patricio Aylwin, interview by Marcia Scantlebury, 2009, Audiovisual Documentation Center, Museum of Memory and Human Rights, Santiago.

7. Among the National Security Council's powers were the following: "Make known, to the President of the Republic, the National Congress, or the Constitutional Court, its opinion regarding a certain event, act, or subject which, in its judgment, seriously

infringed on the foundations of institutional order or could compromise national security." It also had the authority to appoint three senators and two ministers of the Constitutional Court. The constitutional reform of 1989 made the comptroller general of the republic a sitting member of the National Security Council.

8. National Security Council, memorandum 8, March 27, 1991. I am grateful to journalist Catalina Gaete for sharing with me these minutes of the National Security Council meeting.

9. "Informe de la Corte Suprema al presidente Patricio Aylwin," May 13, 1991.

10. Oficio reservado 176, "Estudio y análisis del Informe de la Comisión Nacional de Verdad y Reconciliación," Jefatura Jurídica de la Dirección General de la Policía de Investigaciones, April 5, 1991.

11. Roberto Libedinsky, minuta 5, "Normas especiales aplicables en la función policial en procedimientos relacionados con integrantes o ex integrantes de las Fuerzas Armadas y de Orden," Jefatura Jurídica de la Policía de Investigaciones de Chile, March 27, 1991.

12. Sentence handed down in the court of first instance in the case of Tucapel Jiménez by the special investigating judge Sergio Muñoz Gajardo, August 5, 2002, 340.

13. Army prosecutor general Fernando Torres Silva was convicted in 2010, along with eleven Chilean military officers and three Uruguayan officers, for the murder of former DINA chemist and civilian Eugenio Berríos in Uruguay. Summoned to court for the Letelier case, Berríos was taken out of Chile by army intelligence in 1991 as part of Operation Casualty Control, but due to his emotional instability and attempts to flee his protectors, he became their captive. Chilean and Uruguayan agents eventually killed him and buried him secretly the following year. His remains were found in 1995 on a Uruguayan beach. Torres has been imprisoned since 2015, serving a ten-year sentence.

14. PICH general directorate, General Order No. 26.1, April 8, 1991.

15. PICH general directorate, General Order No. 4, April 9, 1991.

16. José Sotomayor declined to be interviewed for this book.

17. "Acta sobre exposición y debates sobre Informe de Comisión de Verdad y Reconciliación," PICH general directorate, n.d.

18. "Carta de servicio no. 1 del director general de la Policía de Investigaciones," April 15, 1991.

19. "Carta de servicio no. 2 del director general de la Policía de Investigaciones," May 15, 1991.

20. Loreto Meza points out that between the delivery of the Rettig Report in February 1991 and the creation of the CNRR a year later, the commission's archives remained in La Moneda Palace. They subsequently remained under the care and control of the CNRR. Years later, ex-president Aylwin's Democracy and Development Foundation copied all of the documentation produced by the Rettig Commission, digitized it, and placed it in the National Archive.

21. PICH general directorate, General Order No. 6, March 12, 1992.

22. PICH general directorate to Twenty-Second Criminal Court, unnumbered letter concerning events leading up to the murder in September 1973 of Martín Saravia González, n.d.; PICH general directorate to Twenty-First Criminal Court, letter no. 59,

concerning events leading up to the murders in October 1973 of Luis Alberto Fuentes Soriano and José Abraham Adasme Mora, September 30, 1991; and others.

23. Sixty-two of the cases were handled in the Santiago Metropolitan Region. The remaining thirty-three were handled across the other nine regions (which are not named) in the cities of Pozo Almonte, Copiapó, Vicuña, San Felipe, Petorca, Parral, San Javier, Cauquenes, Talca, Yungay, Bulnes, Los Ángeles, Tomé, Chillán, Panguipulli, Temuco, Curacautín, Pitrufquén, Lautaro, Puerto Montt, Castro, and Aysén. Head of CACI to PICH general directorate, attachment to *oficio* no. 9, June 11, 1991.

24. Head of CACI to PICH general directorate.

25. Head of CACI to PICH general directorate.

26. Head of CACI to PICH general directorate, *oficio* no. 17, July 22, 1991.

27. Head of CACI to PICH general directorate.

28. Head of CACI to PICH general directorate.

29. Head of CACI to PICH chief legal staff, private *oficio* no. 18, July 16, 1991.

30. Head of CACI to PICH general directorate, *oficio* no. 36, August 21, 1991.

31. Upon leaving the Investigations School for their first tour of duty, the detectives were assigned to a higher-level official, who acted as their tutor.

Chapter 4

1. The crime of torture was not defined as such in the Chilean penal code until 2016; before then it was termed *apremios ilegítimos*, or, roughly and much less pointedly, "unlawful treatment."

2. Luz Arce, *El infierno* (Santiago: Editorial Planeta, 1993), 77–78. Arce's book, translated by Stacy Alba Skar, was published in English by the University of Wisconsin Press in 1994 as *The Inferno: A Story of Terror and Survival in Chile*.

3. Miranda to First Criminal Court, police report no. 99, July 1, 1991, 12–13.

4. Patricio Silva Garín was prosecuted in 2009 for his involvement in the 1982 murder of former Chilean president Eduardo Frei Montalva.

5. Arce, *El infierno*, 349.

6. Miranda to First Criminal Court, police report no. 99, July 1, 1991, 33.

7. Extrajudicial testimony of Juan Fernando Bustamante Figueroa to Department V of the PICH, March 13, 1991.

8. Extrajudicial testimony of Eugenio Fieldhouse Chávez to Department V of the PICH, March 20, 1991.

9. Extrajudicial testimony of Nibaldo Jiménez Santibáñez to Department V of the PICH, March 25, 1991.

10. In 2013, experts from the National Legal Medical Service carried out excavations on a rural estate owned by Lailhacar in Curacaví. In subsequent testimony before the law, Lailhacar affirmed that the bodies of at least six "disappeared" persons had been dumped there.

11. On July 15, 1981, two Movement of the Revolutionary Left militants tried to kill Olderock as she left her house.

12. That is, the former head of the Carabineros, César Mendoza, who served on the military junta as the first representative from his institution.

13. Extrajudicial testimony of Ingrid Olderock Bernhard to Department V of the PICH, April 18, 1991.

14. Extrajudicial testimony of Ingrid Olderock Bernhard.

15. Nancy Guzmán, *Ingrid Olderock: La mujer de los perros* (Santiago: Ceibo Ediciones, 2014), 39.

16. Arce, *El infierno*, 356–57.

17. Paula Chahin, "Luz Arce declaró cinco horas ante los tribunales chilenos," *La Nación* (Santiago), February 15, 1992.

18. Arce, *El infierno*, 369.

19. Statement by Andrés Valenzuela Morales to the National Commission on Truth and Reconciliation in Paris, November 10, 1990.

20. Mónica González and Héctor Contreras, *Los secretos del Comando Conjunto* (Santiago: Ediciones del Ornitorrinco, 1989), 279.

21. Judge Carlos Cerda Fernández was punished for this bold move, getting downgraded to list 3, which left him one step from being expelled from the judiciary.

22. Hugo Rebolledo declined to be interviewed for this book.

23. José Miranda Alderete returned to Department V a couple of years later. On this tour, however, he was assigned to internal affairs, not human rights. He remained in this unit until the beginning of 1996, when he enrolled in the Higher Academy.

Chapter 5

1. Documents attached to the Report of the Special Commission on Intelligence Services, Chilean Chamber of Deputies, December 1992, 63.

2. "Los párrafos marcados del documento," *La Nación* (Santiago), March 19, 1992.

3. Ascanio Cavallo, *La historia oculta de la transición: Memoria de una época, 1990–1998* (Santiago: Editorial Grijalbo, 1999), 139.

4. Amelia Miranda and Aida Hanania, "UDI pide renuncia de Toro," *La Nación*, March 19, 1992, 4.

5. Miranda and Hanania.

6. Aylwin to Toro, March 20, 1992, Archivo de la Presidencia de Patricio Aylwin, Universidad Alberto Hurtado, Santiago.

7. Patricio Parraguez, "Semblanza del ex-Director General Horacio Toro: Rindió promesa, como uno de los nuestros," *Detective*, no. 163 (November 2014): 52.

8. "Palabras pronunciadas por el Director General de la Policía de Investigaciones de Chile con motivo de la celebración del 59° aniversario," *Detective*, no. 77 (June 1993): 31.

9. Reinaldo Berrios and Gabriel Freire, "Entre aplausos se fue Toro," *La Nación*, March 21, 1992, 3.

10. The government later named him as Chile's consul in Seville, Spain.

11. "Toro había alertado al gobierno," *La Nación*, September 24, 1992.

12. The army's request to participate in the campaign against subversion, which it had been making since 1990, was categorically rejected by the government.

13. "Caso de seguimiento de Investigaciones: Argumentos posibles para rebatir ataques UDI," n.d., APPA.

14. Nelly Yáñez, "Agrupación pidió a Cumplido no nombrar a Mery," *El Mercurio* (Santiago), July 18, 2003.

15. Jorge Zincke rose to become deputy commander in chief of the army at the end of the military dictatorship.

16. Roberto Portilla, "Confesiones de Mery," *Crónica Digital* (online), September 25, 2006.

17. The grandmother and godmother of María Isabel Beltrán's daughter gave her up for adoption when she was three years old. She was adopted by a right-wing couple who did not tell her about her past. She came to know her true origin by accident when she was twenty-five. The writer Mónica Echeverría tells her story in her book *Difícil envoltorio* (Santiago: Editorial Sudamericana, 2000).

18. PICH Special Affairs and Human Rights Investigative Brigade to appeals court judge Alejandro Solís, police report no. 541, April 28, 2005. Julio was undersecretary of foreign relations during the dictatorship. Subsequently, until 2005, he was on the faculty of the National Academy of Political and Strategic Studies (Anepe), which operated under the Ministry of Defense.

19. Portilla, "Confesiones de Mery."

20. PICH Department V to Second Criminal Court of Linares, police report no. 102, March 27, 1996.

21. PICH Department V to Second Criminal Court of Linares.

22. "Interrogador o entrevistador," *La Nación*, July 17, 2003; "Procesan a cinco militares y dos detectives por secuestros en Linares," *El Mostrador* (Santiago), April 19, 2006.

23. In 2006 Judge Alejandro Solís indicted five officials of the artillery school in Linares and two detectives for the disappearance of nine people: Arturo Riveros Blanco, Jaime Torres Salazar, Jorge Yáñez Olave, José Saavedra Betancourt, Gabriel Campos Morales, María Isabel Beltrán Sánchez, Anselmo Cansino Aravena, Héctor Contreras Cabrera, and Alejandro Mella Flores. Those indicted were Gabriel del Río, Claudio Lecaros, Antonio Aguilar, Carlos Morales, Juan Morales, and detectives Héctor Torres and Nelson Volta Rosas. In 2011 the Supreme Court absolved Gabriel del Río and sentenced Juan Morales, Claudio Lecaros, Antonio Aguilar, and Félix Cabezas to five years of conditional freedom and Humberto Julio to three years without jail time. None of them was ever imprisoned.

24. PICH general directorate, General Order No. 1042, January 2, 1992.

25. Amelia Miranda, "Nelson Mery, ratificado al frente de Investigaciones," *La Nación*, June 5, 1992.

Chapter 6

1. Fabián Llanca, "Honorato y su entrevista en un avión: 'Romo era fanfarrón y hablaba mucho,'" *Las Últimas Noticias* (Santiago), July 5, 2007.

2. "Sentencia revela cómo la DINA amenazó a los jueces," *La Nación* (Santiago), May 15, 2007.

3. Raquel González Chandía, court testimony, January 14, 1993.

4. "Osvaldo Romo Mena, cambió de rostro," *Las Últimas Noticias*, April 5, 1980.

5. Pamela Jiles, "Se busca al Guatón Romo," *Análisis*, January 7–13, 1986, 16.

6. Romeo Tuma was director general of the Department of Social and Political Order of São Paulo between 1977 and 1982. The department was recognized as an arm of repression during the Brazilian dictatorship (1964–85) and was responsible for the capture, torture, and disappearance of its opponents, something that Tuma always denied. The book *Habeas corpus, que se presente el cuerpo*, published in 2011 by the Special Office for Human Rights of Brazil's presidential administration, makes clear that Tuma participated in concealing the bodies of executed political prisoners and falsifying information about the fate of the disappeared. He was named director general of Brazil's federal police in 1985, a position he occupied until 1992. Tuma died in 2010; he was a senator representing the Workers' Party of São Paulo at the time.

7. Head of CACI to PICH director general, memorandum no. 31, July 1, 1992.

8. PICH director general to Romeu Tuma, June 21, 1992.

9. CACI to PICH head office, confidential memorandum no. 93, July 20, 1992.

10. CACI to PICH head office.

11. Osvaldo Romo, interview by Luis Henríquez, offices of the Department of Federal Police in São Paulo, July 31, 1992.

12. PICH director general to interior minister, memorandum, July 30, 1992.

13. Undersecretary of foreign relations to Chilean embassy in Brazil, secret telex, July 31, 1992.

14. Henríquez to PICH director general, memorandum no. 1, August 5, 1992.

15. Henríquez to PICH director general.

16. José Ale, "Romo permanece en 'casa de custodia,'" *La Tercera* (Santiago), August 9, 1992.

17. "Cómo cayó el 'Guatón Romo,'" *La Nación*, August 9, 1992.

18. Henríquez to PICH director general, memorandum no. 4, August 10, 1992.

19. "Romo involucró a altos jefes de la DINA," *La Época* (Santiago), October 3, 1992.

20. "Ex agente: Voy a hacer temblar a varios," *La Tercera*, October 10, 1992.

21. Henríquez to PICH director general, memorandum no. 10, August 16, 1992.

22. Jaime Castillo, "Sola Sierra viajó para presionar entrega de Romo," *La Nación*, August 17, 1992.

23. Margarita Fernández, Viviana Uribe, Teresa Lastra, and Patricia Flores, *Mujeres en el* MIR: *Des-armando la memoria* (Santiago: Pehuén Editores, 2017), 146.

24. After a few years the case was closed and then reopened ten years later. In March 2018 the Eighth Chamber of the court of appeals in Santiago sentenced four DINA agents. Several others who were guilty had already died.

25. Presentation by Green Party delegate Carlos Galeao Camacho before the president of the Regional Electoral Tribunal, September 24, 1992.

26. Olga de los Santos, "Romo está muy abatido, está llorando mucho," *La Nación*, October 13, 1992.

27. "Caso Romo: Un regreso demorado e inevitable," *La Época*, October 16, 1992.

28. "Impacta en Brasil fallo de la C. Suprema favorable a Romo," *El Mercurio* (Santiago), October 15, 1992.

29. Memorandum without sender or recipient, October 16, 1992. One understands from the tone of its contents that it was written by Luis Henríquez and sent to his boss in Santiago.

30. Chile's ambassador in Brazil to minister of foreign relations, secret memorandum no. 08/92, November 20, 1992.

31. "Fin al suspenso: Llegó Romo," *La Nación*, November 17, 1992.

32. PICH general directorate, "Directiva de Seguridad Orión para la custodia del detenido Osvaldo Romo Mena," October 28, 1992.

33. Fernández et al., *Mujeres en el MIR*, 150.

34. Henríquez to PICH director general, confidential memorandum no. 1, November 26, 1992.

35. The Chanfreau case was reopened in December 2003. The definitive sentences waited another twelve years, until April 2015, by which time Romo had already passed away.

36. Claudio Pizarro, "El sepulturero del Guatón Romo: Cómo iban a sepultar al diablo con las monjitas?," *Clinic* (Santiago), September 9, 2013.

Chapter 7

1. José Robinson Muñoz passed away in 2011.

2. Out of this group, José Barrera, Luis Garay, and Osmán Arellano are deceased.

3. Mirna Concha, "BH investiga crímenes 1973–1990," *La Nación* (Santiago), February 19, 1992.

4. Roberto Amaro, "'El Fanta' cuenta su verdad," *La Nación*, August 24, 1997.

5. Francisca Skoknic, "Miguel Estay, El Fanta: Las razones de un verdugo," *Ciper* (online), November 2, 2007.

6. Amaro, "'El Fanta.'"

7. Skoknic, "Miguel Estay, El Fanta."

8. Ascanio Cavallo, *La historia oculta de la transición: Memoria de una época, 1990–1999* (Santiago: Editorial Grijalbo, 1999), 246.

9. Nelson Caucoto and Héctor Salazar, *Un verde manto de impunidad* (Santiago: Ediciones Academia, 1994), 75.

10. José Fuentes, judicial statement, May 27, 1992.

11. Carabineros director general to minister of the interior, confidential memorandum no. 97, April 6, 1992.

12. Reinaldo Berríos, "Osvaldo Carmona, jefe de la BH: 'La policía civil resucitó,'" *La Nación*, June 7, 1992. Osvaldo Carmona retired in early 1995.

13. Chile's ambassador in Paraguay to director of bilateral policy in the Chilean Ministry of Foreign Relations, secret memorandum no. 01/92, September 22, 1992.

14. Minister counselor of the embassy of Chile to director of bilateral policy in the

Chilean Ministry of Foreign Relations, confidential memorandum no. 15/92, April 24, 1992.

15. Moreno was not successful. Senegal's candidate, Jacques Diouf, was elected director general of the Food and Agricultural Organization.

16. "Juica informa sobre 'filtración' a la corte," *La Nación*, July 8, 1992.

17. Chile's ambassador in Paraguay to undersecretary of foreign relations in Chile, telex no. 107, June 7, 1992.

18. "El degollador chileno ya no está en el país; fue expulsado por 'indeseable,'" *Última Hora* (Asunción), July 7, 1992.

19. "En Paraguay dicen que 'es un fantasma,'" *La Nación*, July 9, 1992.

20. Chile's ambassador in Paraguay to undersecretary of foreign relations in Chile, telex no. 109, July 7, 1992.

21. Department of Americas–Bilateral Policy of the Chilean Ministry of Foreign Relations, confidential memorandum, July 8, 1992.

22. "Ministro del Interior paraguayo: 'El Fanta es protegido desde Chile,'" *La Nación*, July 13, 1992.

23. "'El Fanta' se dirige a frontera con Brasil," *La Nación*, July 10, 1992.

24. Paraguay's vice minister of foreign relations to ambassador of Chile in Asunción, diplomatic note no. 943/92, September 24, 1992.

25. Chile's ambassador in Paraguay to director of bilateral policy in the Foreign Relations Ministry of Chile, confidential memorandum no. 74/92, September 30, 1992.

26. Nancy Guzmán, *El Fanta: Historia de una traición* (Santiago: Ceibo Ediciones, 2016), 367–68.

27. Chilean minister of foreign relations to Chilean ambassador in Paraguay, December 18, 1992.

28. Chilean embassy in Paraguay to Chilean foreign relations undersecretary, confidential telex no. 214, December 19, 1992.

29. Chilean embassy in Paraguay to Foreign Policy Department of Chile's Foreign Relations Ministry, confidential memorandum no. 87/92, November 6, 1992.

30. Chilean embassy in Paraguay to Foreign Policy Department of Chile's Foreign Relations Ministry, confidential telex no. 151, September 21, 1992.

31. Chilean embassy in Paraguay to chief of staff of undersecretary of Chile's Foreign Relations Ministry, secret and urgent telex no. 223, December 24, 1992.

32. In September 1992, Homicide Brigade officers Rafael Castillo and Nelson Jofré traveled to the United States to interrogate onetime Directorate of National Intelligence agent Michael Townley. This development is covered in chapter 9.

Chapter 8

1. Human Rights Watch/Americas, *Un asunto no resuelto: Los derechos humanos en Chile al iniciarse la presidencia de Frei* (New York: Human Rights Watch, 1994), 6.

2. CACI chief to office of PICH director, confidential memorandum no. 123, March 10, 1993.

3. Steve Stern, *Reckoning with Pinochet: The Memory Question in Democratic Chile, 1989–2006* (Durham, N.C.: Duke University Press, 2010), 119.

4. In referring to the Geneva Conventions and arguing that war crimes proscribed the statute of limitations and the granting of amnesty, the judges had to legitimize the fiction of Legal Decree No. 5, imposed by the military junta on September 12, 1973, which asserted that the state of siege put into force on the previous day because of internal disruption had necessarily to be understood as a "state or time of war."

5. Stern, *Reckoning with Pinochet*, 119.

6. Ministerio Secretaría de la Presidencia, "Informe de análisis," January 4, 1993, 8, Archivo de la Presidencia de Patricio Aylwin, Universidad Alberto Hurtado, Santiago (hereafter cited as APPA).

7. Ministerio Secretaría de la Presidencia, 8.

8. I am grateful to Arak Herrera Godoy for this reference to the property in Rinconada de Maipú.

9. Samuel Fuenzalida Devia, extrajudicial statement to PICH Department V, June 4, 1993, 5.

10. Fuenzalida Devia, 6.

11. Samuel Fuenzalida Devia, statement to delegates of the Truth and Reconciliation Commission, Hamburg, Germany, November 6, 1990.

12. The court in Bonn prohibited AI and *Stern* from continuing to disseminate the information. The prohibition remained in force until 1997, when the case was closed. This is considered one of the longest-lasting civil suits in German history.

13. CACI acting director to PICH director general, confidential memorandum no. 88, May 7, 1993.

14. E. [Enrique] Fuenzalida to Plaza, "Agenda," fax no. 6724074, May 17, 1993.

15. Head of CACI to PICH director general, confidential memorandum no. 151, July 5, 1993.

16. The spot was excavated in late 1994 but did not yield positive results.

17. Aguiló to Krauss, June 30, 1993, Audiovisual Documentation Center, Museum of Memory and Human Rights, Santiago.

18. Müller later changed his surname to Kneese.

19. Stern, *Reckoning with Pinochet*, 123.

20. Mily Miranda, "Gobierno busca agilizar procesos contra militares," *La Nación* (Santiago), June 13, 1993.

21. "La búsqueda de una formula alternativa al 'punto final,'" *La Nación*, June 14, 1993.

22. Notes from the regular meeting of the cabinet, August 12, 1993, APPA.

23. Raquel Correa, "Los 'ejercicios' del gobierno," *El Mercurio* (Santiago), June 6, 1993.

24. Elizabeth Lira and Brian Loveman, *El espejismo de la reconciliación política: Chile 1900–2002* (Santiago: LOM Ediciones, 2002), 121.

25. PICH director general to minister of the interior, memorandum no. 111, September 14, 1993, 3.

26. The CNRR's report, delivered in August 1996 to President Eduardo Frei, recorded

3,197 victims. Of these, 1,102 fell into the category of disappeared persons. A subsequent report from the Advisory Commission for the Qualification of the Disappeared, Executed, and Victims of Torture and Political Imprisonment, created in February 2010, added another thirty victims of execution or forced disappearance as well as 9,795 victims of torture.

27. "Palabras pronunciadas por el director general de la Policía de Investigaciones de Chile con motivo de la celebración del 59° aniversario," *Detective*, no. 77 (June 1993): 30–31. Between 1990 and mid-1993 the funds contributed to the institution increased by 44.4 percent, with 771 persons added to its staff. The PICH now boasted a Cessna aircraft, new labs and telecommunications equipment, more weaponry, and 917 new police vehicles (220 of which were donated by the Italian government). In addition, eighteen new precinct buildings were under construction across the country.

28. PICH director general to Aylwin, November 26, 1993, APPA.

29. "Acciones contra PICH durante gestión director general Nelson Mery Figueroa (1992–2003)," preliminary memorandum, August 6, 2003, 4.

30. Human Rights Watch/Americas, *Un asunto no resuelto*, 8.

31. In 1997, President Frei vetoed a promotion for Jaime Lepe based on this case.

32. In February 1997 the Soria family filed a complaint before the Organization of American State's Inter-American Commission on Human Rights against the Chilean state on grounds of denial of justice. In 2003, the Chilean government promised to comply with the commission's recommendation and the agreement reached with the Soria family. This included compensation; a public declaration that Chile, through the actions of state agents, accepted responsibility for the crime; the creation of a memorial for Soria (installed in 2007 in the Santiago office of the Economic Commission for Latin America, where Soria worked); and assurance that the Chilean government would request that the judiciary reopen the criminal investigation. The case was reopened in 2013, and in August 2015—nearly forty years after Soria's murder—the first fifteen DINA agents were indicted. Six army officers were convicted of the murder in 2019, including former DINE head Eugenio Covarrubias.

33. The Carabineros and army officials were Hugo Cardemil, Pablo Caulier, Luis Hidalgo, and Diógenes Toledo. Despite confessing to having murdered the cobbler Adán Vergara, Toledo was not indicted for this crime because the Parral court found that he was protected by the statute of limitations.

34. As a new decade got under way in 2000 and with Judge Juan Guzmán and then Judge Alejandro Solís in charge, substantive progress was made toward advancing the case and initially realizing some measure of justice. In 2007, however, the Supreme Court reduced the sentences that Solís had handed down and let the guilty parties go free.

35. The case was reopened years later and, in 2015, six DINA agents and one of Colonia Dignidad's leaders were convicted and sentenced to prison.

36. Human Rights Watch/Americas, *Un asunto no resuelto*, 10.

37. Human Rights Watch/Americas, 29.

38. Stern, *Reckoning with Pinochet*, 150.

Chapter 9

1. Mariana Callejas Honores, statement in case file 1–91 concerning the murder of Orlando Letelier, December 2, 1991.

2. Eric B. Marcy, sworn statement before the First Judge of the Federal District Court of the District of Columbia (United States), September 1991.

3. Townley covers other, less well-known operations in this document, such as the 1977 abduction of the businessman Vittorio Yaconi and how the DINA made off with $39,000 of his assets.

4. Eric B. Marcy, sworn statement before the First Judge of the Federal District Court of the District of Columbia (United States), September 1991.

5. Due to his inauguration, Bush did not personally respond. State Department legal adviser Alan Kreczko answered in his place.

6. Landau's testimony had to do with granting visas to Michael Townley and Armando Fernández Larios in July 1976 so they could travel to and enter the United States.

7. Giovanni Salvi, the Italian judge in charge of the proceedings regarding the attempted murder of Leighton, interrogated Townley in December 1992 in the United States. Townley confessed that he had organized the attack on the orders of Manuel Contreras.

8. Deputy superintendent Luis Garay and inspector Héctor Moraga to Judge Sergio Valenzuela, police report no. 32, case file 1643 on the deaths of Tucapel Jiménez and Juan Alegría, December 22, 1995, 13.

9. PICH director general to minister of the interior, memorandum no. 111, September 14, 1993, 3.

10. "Acciones contra PICH durante gestión Director General Nelson Mery Figueroa (1992–2003)," preliminary memorandum, August 6, 2003.

11. "Una jornada de emociones," *La Nación* (Santiago), May 31, 1995.

12. Alicia Aravena, "Con emoción la familia de Letelier conoció fallo," *La Nación*, May 31, 1995.

13. "No voy a ir a ninguna cárcel," *La Nación*, May 31, 1995.

14. Jorge Escalante, "Me protegen los escoltas," *La Nación*, June 1, 1995.

15. "Espinoza espera notificación en recinto militar," *La Nación*, June 1, 1995.

16. Francisco Artaza, "Toda su familia acompaña a Contreras en el 'Viejo Roble,'" *La Nación*, June 8, 1995.

17. Ascanio Cavallo, *La historia oculta de la transición: Memoria de una época 1990–1998* (Santiago: Editorial Grijalbo, 1998), 265.

18. Ministry of the Interior, press release, January 5, 1995, published in *La Nación*, June 13, 1995.

19. "Abogados de DD.HH. rechazaron la idea," *La Nación*, January 7, 1995.

20. Claudio Martínez Cerda, "Penales Cordillera y Punta Peuco," *La Tercera* (Santiago), September 26, 2013.

21. María Eliana Vega and Quintín Oyarzo, "Policía no pudo detener a Contreras," *La Nación*, June 17, 1995.

22. Rafael Otano, *Nueva crónica de la transición* (Santiago: LOM Ediciones, 2006), 443.

23. Claudia Valle, "Derecha pide interpretación de Ley de Amnistía," *La Nación*, June 13, 1995.

24. Elizabeth Lira and Brian Loveman, *El espejismo de la reconciliación política: Chile 1990–2002* (Santiago: LOM Ediciones, 2002), 146.

25. Named for interior minister Carlos Figueroa and Miguel Otero, a senator representing Renovación Nacional.

26. Eduardo Frei Ruiz-Tagle, interview by Marcia Scantlebury, 2009, Audiovisual Documentation Center, Museum of Memory and Human Rights, Santiago.

27. Fernando Valdés Cid was sentenced to six years for the death of Carrasco, and Héctor Díaz Anderson was sentenced to three years and one day for the murder of Godoy.

28. Fernández was sentenced to 600 days for his responsibility in burning alive Rodrigo Rojas De Negri and Carmen Gloria Quintana, who survived. Fernández was released from prison after serving only one year.

Chapter 10

1. Hugo Baar and Georg and Lotti Packmor escaped from Colonia Dignidad in 1984 and 1985, respectively.

2. Investigative report on Colonia Dignidad prepared by deputy superintendent Sandro Gaete, Department V of the Investigations Police, December 10, 2004.

3. The lower chamber's three investigative commissions were established in 1968, 1995, and 1997. In 1990, the chamber's Human Rights Commission visited Colonia Dignidad.

4. Fifty years later, in August 2017, the Supreme Court annulled the sentence.

5. Subsequent judicial investigations confirmed that many detainees were assassinated at Colonia Dignidad and buried in secret graves. In 1978, on Schäfer's orders, three colonists disinterred the bodies, put them in sacks, and burned them. The ashes were tossed into the Perquilauquén River.

6. Joint public statement by the interior and justice ministers, February 1, 1991.

7. To safeguard his privacy only the initials of his name are being used.

8. Luis Henríquez, "Colonia Dignidad: La investigación criminalística," in *Colonia Dignidad: Verdad, justicia, y memoria*, ed. Evelyn Hevia and Jan Stehle (Santiago: Ocho Libros Editores, 2016), 127–28.

9. PICH Department V to Criminal Court of Parral, police report no. 250, August 20, 1996.

10. Hernán Escobar was one of Colonia Dignidad's most visible spokesmen at the end of the 1990s. His father brought him as a child to the enclave in the mid-1970s, and his mother was never able to get him back.

11. PICH Department V to Civil Court of Parral, police report no. 144, August 14, 1996.

12. PICH Department V to Civil Court of Parral.

13. "Polémica por operativo en ex Colonia Dignidad," *La Tercera* (Santiago), December 4, 1996.

14. Sanhueza to Supreme Court, report, December 24, 1996.

15. Leader of the Branch Davidian sect in Waco, Texas. Federal agents laid siege to its compound for more than fifty days in 1993, at the end of which a fire broke out that killed seventy-six people.

16. Leader of the Peoples Temple who orchestrated the mass suicide of more than 900 of his followers in Jonestown, Guyana, in 1978.

17. PICH Department V to special investigating judge of Civil Court of Parral, police report no. 1, from January 5, 1998.

18. Heinz Kühn fled Colonia Dignidad in 1968 and settled down in Los Ángeles, a city farther south, from where he lent support to a series of escapes.

19. Tobías Müller, interview transcript, August 1, 1997, in PICH Department V to Civil Court of Parral, police report no. 3/3, August 13, 1997.

20. PICH Department V to special investigating judge of Civil Court of Parral, police report no. 69, February 23, 1998.

21. PICH Department V to special investigating judge of Civil Court of Parral.

22. Henríquez, "Colonia Dignidad," 128.

23. Erwin Fege, statement to the police, May 13, 2005.

24. "Maratónica declaración de Müller," *La Tercera*, February 26, 1998. Wolfgang Kneese has continued to this day to assist the courts and the police on the matter of Colonia Dignidad.

25. Franz Baar was born as Francisco Morales into a large, impoverished family in Catillo, a rural hamlet near Colonia. His mother brought him to Colonia Dignidad in 1965, when he was ten. He ended up being kidnapped and illegally adopted by one of the colony's founders, Hugo Baar, who abandoned the sect in 1984. In 2003, Franz Baar escaped the colony with his wife, Ingrid, and his in-laws. His younger brother, Efraín, had fled the year before. Efraín, brought to the colony's hospital at age two months, was also kept in the enclave and illegally adopted by the colonist Johanna Vedder. In 2002, both men—now adults—discovered they were flesh-and-blood brothers.

26. Pedro Vega, "Duro cuestionamiento a labor de Carabineros," *La Nación* (Santiago), April 24, 1998.

27. During successive 2005 raids in Parral and Bulnes, the police discovered underground bunkers containing rifles, small arms, rocket launchers, explosives, antipersonnel mines, grenades, chemical components, and munitions, as well as 40,000 cards with information on victims of the repression and public figures. In Bulnes, they found nearly 3,000 kilos of weaponry and vaporizers to create smoke screens.

28. Ángel Tamayo, "Informe perital Villa Baviera: Utilización de equipos georadar y rastreador de cables," May 29, 1998, 1.

29. Over four days in January 1999, they searched the guesthouse and its surrounding area, the east side of the landing strip, the brick factory and area around it, the pork factory, and the barley storehouse. In this last place they found anomalies in its supports, the subsurface, and the filler material behind the walls. They also dug up the

ground in two places where, based on the confidential testimony of a pair of witnesses, bodies might have been buried illegally. They got down to a depth of two meters, before running into untouched soil, without finding any vestiges of human remains.

30. Manuel Villar, "Hay que usar otra tecnología," *La Nación*, May 4, 1998.

31. CPP.

32. Wolfgang Müller, today Wolfgang Kneese.

33. Hernán Fernández, "Justicia, impunidad y Colonia Dignidad," in Hevia and Stehle, *Colonia Dignidad*, 93.

34. In November 2004 Judge Hernán González handed down the first sentences against twelve members of the enclave's leadership as accessories and accomplices to the sexual abuse of twenty-six minors. Hartmut Hopp fled to Germany in 2011, before the Supreme Court could ratify his sentence. In 2019, a German court closed the case against Hopp on the grounds of insufficient evidence. Hopp continues to live in Germany, as do other Colonia fugitives.

Epilogue

1. "Representación con relación a las 'autorizaciones para proceder' a la extradición de Pinochet." Government of Chile to Jack Straw, November 26, 1998, in Jaime Lagos, *El "caso Pinochet" ante las cortes británicas* (Santiago: Editorial Jurídica de Chile, 1999), 255, 261.

2. Chile signed the Statute of Rome on September 11, 1998, but right-wing legislators in Congress blocked its ratification for almost eleven years.

3. Miriam Henríquez, "Jerarquía de los tratados de derechos humanos: Análisis jurisprudencial desde el método de caso," *Revista de estudios constitucionales* 6, no. 2 (2008): 87–91, 96.

4. This tendency intensified after 2006 with the finding of the Inter-American Court of Human Rights in the Almonacid case, which ordered Chile to annul and abolish the Amnesty Law. Although this law remains on the books today, it is no longer applied.

Lightning Source UK Ltd.
Milton Keynes UK
UKHW042254181122
412472UK00002B/7

9 781469 670157